CONTENTS

Certified Accounting Technician

ADVANCED LEVEL

Paper 6 (UK)

Drafting Financial Statements

STUDY TEXT

PUBLISHING

British Library Cataloguing-in-Publication Data

A catalogue record for this book is available from the British Library.

Published by:

Kaplan Publishing UK
Unit 2 The Business Centre
Molly Millars Lane
Wokingham
RG41 2QZ

ISBN   978-1-84710-652-0

Printed and bound in Great Britain

Acknowledgments

We are grateful to the Association of Chartered Certified Accountants for permission to reproduce past examination questions. The answers have been prepared by Kaplan Publishing.

INTRODUCTION

This is the new edition of the CAT study text for Paper 6 (UK), *Drafting Financial Statements,* approved by the ACCA and fully updated and revised according to the examiner's comments.

Tailored to fully cover the Syllabus, this book has been written specifically for CAT students. A clear and comprehensive style, numerous examples and highlighted key terms help you to acquire the information easily. Plenty of activities and self test questions enable you to practise what you have learnt.

At the end of most of the chapters you will find practice questions. These are examination-style questions and will give you a very good idea of the way you will be tested.

A full review by the current examiner has ensured that this book fully reflects what could be tested in the exam.

SYLLABUS AND STUDY GUIDE

Position of the paper in the overall syllabus

A thorough knowledge of Paper 1, *Recording Financial Transactions*, and Paper 3, *Maintaining Financial Records*, is required for Paper 6.

Syllabus

1 **General framework   Chapters 1–3, 6, 8 and 9**

(a) General purpose of financial statements, users and their needs

(b) Financial statements

   (i)   profit and loss account

   (ii) balance sheet

   (iii) interaction of the profit and loss account and balance sheet

(c) Elements of financial statements and their interaction

   (i)   assets

   (ii) liabilities

   (iii) ownership interest

   (iv) gains

   (v) losses

   (vi) contributions from owners

   (vii) distributions to owners

(d) Conceptual framework

   (i)   Statement of Principles

   (ii) accounting concepts, principles and policies

(e) Regulatory framework

   (i)   standard-setting process

   (ii) relevant accounting standards

   (iii) legal framework and obligations of directors

   (iv) statutory format of accounts and disclosure requirements

(f) Notes to the financial statements

Only the following notes to the financial statements will be examinable:

   (i)   statement of movements in reserves

   (ii) fixed assets

   (iv) disclosure of exceptional items

   (v) events after the balance sheet date

   (iv) contingent liabilities and contingent assets

   (vi) research and development expenditure

(g) Business organisation

   (i)   structure

   (ii) procedures and policies

2 **Preparing financial statements**

Chapters 4–9, 15–18

(a) Preparation of partnership and limited company financial statements from a trial balance, including adjustments where appropriate for:

   (i)   accruals and prepayments

   (ii) corporation tax

   (iii) dividends

   (iv) depreciation

   (v) irrecoverable debts and allowances for debtors

   (vi) closing stock

   (vii) issue of share capital

   (viii) revaluation of assets

   (ix) provisions

   (x) admission and retirement of partners

   (xi) dissolution of a partnership

(b) Taxation

   (i)   presentation of corporation tax

(c) Fixed assets

   (i)   distinction between capital and revenue expenditure

   (ii) accounting for the acquisition and disposal of assets

   (iii) depreciation – definition, reasons for and methods, including straight line, reducing balance and sum of digits

   (iv) research and development

   (vi) elementary treatment of goodwill

(d) Current assets

   (i)   stock

   (ii) debtors, including accounting irrecoverable debts and allowances for debtors

   (iii) cash

KAPLAN PUBLISHING

(e) Current liabilities and accruals

(f) Shareholders' equity

(g) Events after the balance sheet date

(h) Contingencies

(i) Reporting financial performance, including the statement of total recognised gains and losses

3   Cash flow statements   Chapter 10

(a) Preparation of a single company cash flow statement

(b) Notes to the cash flow statement

(c) Interpretation of a cash flow statement

4   Interpretation of financial statements

Chapter 11

(a) Ratio analysis

   (i)   profitability ratios

   (ii) liquidity ratios

   (iii) working capital efficiency ratios

   (iv) investor performance ratios

   (v)   financial risk ratios

(b) Identification of unusual issues or trends

(c) Presentation of reports targeted at the user and drawing appropriate conclusions

5   Consolidated accounts   Chapters 12–14

(a) Groups of companies – preparation of basic consolidated financial statements for a simple group

   (i)   consolidated balance sheet

   (ii) consolidated profit and loss account

(b) Overview of distinction between a subsidiary and an associate

Excluded topics

The following topics are specifically excluded from Paper 6:

- detailed or computational questions on deferred tax or discounting of provisions

- group cash flow statements

- joint ventures

- long-term contracts

- foreign currency, segmental reporting, impairment of assets, retirement benefits, derivatives and capital instruments.

Key areas of the syllabus

The two main skills required for Paper 6, *Drafting Financial Statements,* are:

- the ability to prepare basic financial statements and the underlying accounting records on which they are based

- an understanding of the principles on which accounting is based.

The key topic areas are as follows:

- preparation of financial statements for partnerships and limited companies

- basic group accounts – consolidated balance sheet and profit and loss account for a simple group

- elements of financial statements and the interaction between the elements

- accounting conventions and concepts

- interpretation of financial statements

- cash flow statements.

Study sessions

1   Framework of financial reporting

Chapters 1, 2

(a) Explain the need for, and objectives of, financial statements

(b) Identify the users of financial statements and their particular interests in the statements

(c) Discuss how the accounting systems of an organisation are affected by its organisational structure, its administrative systems and procedures and the nature of its business transactions

(d) Describe and explain the following elements of the financial statements and their interaction:

   (i)   assets

   (ii)   liabilities

   (iii) ownership interest

   (iv)   gains

   (v)   losses

   (vi)   contributions from owners

   (vii) distributions to owners

(e) Recognition of elements for inclusion in financial statements

2   Conceptual framework   Chapter 1

(a) Discuss the nature and purpose of a conceptual framework

(b) Explain the potential benefits and drawbacks of an agreed conceptual framework

(c) Explain the role and general issues covered by the Statement of Principles

(d) Identify and explain the qualitative characteristics of financial information

(e) Define, discuss and apply accounting concepts, principles and policies

(f) Discuss the shortcomings of historical cost accounting and how they might be overcome

3   The UK regulatory framework   Chapter 1,2

(a) Explain the legal framework and obligations of directors

(b) Explain the standard-setting process and the role of the:

    (i) Financial Reporting Council

    (ii) Accounting Standards Board

    (iii) Urgent Issues Task Force

    (iv) Financial Reporting Review Panel

(c) Explain the advantages and disadvantages of accounting standards

4 & 5 Fixed assets   Chapter 6

(a) Distinguish between capital and revenue expenditure

(b) Explain, calculate and demonstrate the inclusion of the profit or loss on disposal of fixed assets in the profit and loss account

(c) Account for the revaluation of fixed assets

(d) Account for gains and losses on the disposal of revalued assets

(e) Account for depreciation – definition, reasons and methods, including straight line, reducing balance and sum of digits

(f) Account for changes in the useful economic life or residual value of assets

(g) Explain and demonstrate how fixed asset balances and movements are disclosed in the financial statements

6, 7 & 8 Partnership accounts
Chapters 15–18

(a) Identify the key features of a partnership

(b) Outline the advantages and disadvantages of operating as a partnership, compared with operating as a sole trader or limited company. Explain the accounting differences between partnerships and sole traders:

    (i) capital accounts

    (ii) current accounts

    (iii) division of profits

(c) Outline the conventional methods of dividing profit and maintaining equity between partners

(d) Draft an appropriation account for a partnership

(e) Distinguish between partners' capital and current accounts

(f) Record the partners' share of profits and losses and their drawings in the ledger accounts

(g) Record introductions and withdrawals of capital in the ledger accounts

(h) Draft the trading and profit and loss account, appropriation account and the balance sheet for a partnership incorporating period end adjustments including:

    (i) accruals and prepayments

    (ii) depreciation

    (iii) irrecoverable debts and allowances for debtors

    (iv) closing stock

(i) Explain why a revaluation is required after an admission, a change in the profit-sharing ratio or a retirement

(j) Revalue the partnership and calculate goodwill

(k) Make appropriate entries in the ledger accounts

(l) Draft the partnership financial statements after a change in the partnership

(m) Draft the partnership financial statements after a merger of two sole traders

(n) Account for the dissolution of a partnership

(o) Prepare final accounts from incomplete records

9,10 & 11 Limited company financial statements
Chapter 3–9, 18

(a) Prepare the financial statements for a limited company including adjustments for items including:

    (i) corporation tax

    (ii) dividends

    (iii) depreciation

    (iv) irrecoverable debts and allowances for debtors

    (v) closing stock

    (vi) share capital

    (vii) accruals and prepayments

    (viii) revaluation of assets

    (ix) provisions

(b) Prepare a statement of total recognised gains and losses

(c) Prepare the following notes to the financial statements:

    (i) statement of movements in reserves

    (ii) fixed assets

    (iii) exceptional items

    (iv) events after the balance sheet date

    (v) contingent liabilities and contingent assets

    (vi) research and development expenditure

(d) Distinguish between extraordinary and exceptional items, including their accounting treatment and disclosure requirements

(e) Derive missing figures from incomplete records

12 Statutory format of accounts and disclosure requirements   Chapters 3–9

(a) State the requirements of the Companies Act regarding the duty to prepare annual accounts

(b) Prepare the financial statements of limited companies in accordance with the prescribed formats and relevant accounting standards

(c) Discuss relevant accounting standards and be able to apply them

13 Taxation   **Chapter 5**

(a) Define current tax

(b) Account for current tax on the profits of companies (a detailed knowledge of deferred tax is not required)

(c) Draft appropriate disclosure in the published statements

14 Goodwill and intangible assets

Chapter 6, 13

(a) Define and calculate goodwill

(b) Distinguish between purchased and internally generated goodwill

(c) Explain and apply the accounting treatment for both types of goodwill

(d) Explain and apply the requirements of Accounting Standards for Research and Development

15 & 16 Share and loan capital   **Chapter 2, 5**

(a) Distinguish between issued and authorised share capital and between called up and paid up share capital

(b) Distinguish between ordinary and preference shares

(c) Account for a share issue

(d) Explain the share premium account

(e) Define and account for a bonus issue

(f) Define and account for a rights issue

(g) Outline the advantages and disadvantages of a rights issue and a bonus issue

(h) Distinguish between the market value and nominal value of a share

(i) Explain why companies will be concerned with the value of their shares

(j) Define and account for debentures

(k) Explain the advantages and disadvantages of raising finance by issuing debentures rather than issuing ordinary or preference shares

17 &18 Events after balance date, contingent liabilities and contingent assets   **Chapter 8**

(a) Define an event after the balance sheet date

(b) Distinguish between adjusting and non-adjusting events

(c) Account for each category of event in the financial statements

(d) Define a provision, contingent liability and contingent asset

(e) Understand and apply the general recognition principle

(f) Account for provisions, contingent liabilities and contingent assets

19, 20 & 21 Cash flow statements   **Chapter 10**

(a) Explain the need for a cash flow statement

(b) Prepare a cash flow statement including relevant notes for a single company in accordance with accounting standards

(c) Appraise the usefulness of, and interpret the information in a cash flow statement

22, 23, 24 & 25 Consolidated accounts

Chapters 12–14

(a) Describe and be able to identify the general characteristics of a parent company, investment, subsidiary and associated undertaking

(b) Describe the concept of a group and the objective of consolidated financial statements

(c) Describe the circumstances and reasoning for subsidiaries to be excluded from consolidated financial statements

(d) Prepare a consolidated profit and loss account and balance sheet for a simple group including adjustments for pre and post acquisition profits, minority interests and consolidated goodwill

(e) Explain why intra-group transactions should be eliminated on consolidation

(f) Account for the effects (in the profit and loss account and balance sheet) of intra-group trading and other transactions including:

   (i) unrealised profits in stock and fixed assets

   (ii) intra-group loans and interest and other intra-group charges

26, 27, 28, & 29 Interpretation of financial statements

Chapter 11

(a) Calculate the main ratios used to appraise and interpret financial statements:

   (i) profitability ratios

   (ii) liquidity ratios

   (iii) working capital efficiency ratios

   (iv) investor performance ratios

   (v) financial risk ratios

(b) Analyse and interpret the ratios to give an assessment of a company's performance in comparison with:

   (i) a company's previous period's financial statements

   (ii) another similar company for the same period

   (iii) industry average ratios

(c) Identify and discuss the limitations of ratio analysis

(d) Prepare a financial analysis report of a company in a suitable format

30, 31 & 32 Revision

THE EXAMINATION

Format of the examination

The examination is a three-hour written paper. The paper consists of four compulsory questions:

	Number of marks
Question 1	30 to 40
Question 2	25 to 30
Question 3	15 to 20
Question 4	15 to 20
Total	100

Examination tips

- Spend the first few minutes of the examination reading the paper and where you have a choice of questions, **decide which ones you will do**.

- Unless you know exactly how to answer the question, spend some time **planning your answer**. Stick to the question and tailor your answer to what you are asked.

- **Fully explain all your points** but be concise. Set out all workings clearly and neatly, and state briefly what you are doing. Don't write out the question.

- If you do not understand what a question is asking, **state your assumptions**. Even if you do not answer precisely in the way the examiner hoped, you should be given some credit, if your assumptions are reasonable.

- **If you get stuck** with a question, leave space in your answer book and return to it later.

Answering the questions

Essay questions: Make a quick plan in your answer book and under each main point list all the relevant facts you can think of. Then write out your answer developing each point fully. Your essay should have a clear structure; it should contain a brief introduction, a main section and a conclusion. Be concise. It is better to write a little about a lot of different points than a great deal about one or two points.

Computations: It is essential to include all your workings in your answers. Many computational questions require the use of a standard format: company profit and loss account, balance sheet and cash flow statement for example. Be sure you know these formats thoroughly before the examination and use the layouts that you see in the answers given in this book and in model answers. If you are asked to comment or make recommendations on a computation, you must do so. There are important marks to be gained here. Even if your computation contains mistakes, you may still gain marks if your reasoning is correct.

Reports, memos and other documents: Some questions ask you to present your answer in the form of a report or a memo or other document. Use the correct format – there could be easy marks to gain here.

STUDY SKILLS AND REVISION GUIDANCE

Preparing to study

Set your objectives

Before starting to study decide what you want to achieve – the type of pass you wish to obtain.

This will decide the level of commitment and time you need to dedicate to your studies.

Devise a study plan

Determine when you will study.

Split these times into study sessions.

Put the sessions onto a study plan making sure you cover the course, course assignments and revision.

Stick to your plan!

Effective study techniques

Use the **SQR3** method

Survey the chapter – look at the headings and read the introduction, summary and objectives. Get an overview of what the text deals with.

Question – during the survey, ask yourself the questions that you hope the chapter will answer for you.

Read through the chapter thoroughly, answering the questions and meeting the objectives. Attempt the exercises and activities, and work through all the examples.

Recall – at the end of the chapter, try to recall the main ideas of the chapter without referring to the text. Do this a few minutes after the reading stage.

Review – check that your recall notes are correct.

Use the **MURDER** method

Mood – set the right mood.

Understand – issues covered and make note of any uncertain bits.

Recall – stop and put what you have learned into your own words.

Digest – go back and reconsider the information.

Expand – read relevant articles and newspapers.

Review – go over the material you covered to consolidate the knowledge.

While studying…

Summarise the key points of the chapter.

Make linear notes – a list of headings, divided up with subheadings listing the key points. Use different colours to highlight key points and keep topic areas together.

Try mind-maps – put the main heading in the centre of the paper and encircle it. Then draw short lines radiating from this to the main sub-headings, which again have circles around them. Continue the process from the sub-headings to sub-sub-headings, etc.

Revision

The best approach to revision is to **revise the course as you work through it**.

Also try to leave **four to six weeks before the exam for final revision**.

Make sure you **cover the whole syllabus**.

Pay special attention to **those areas where your knowledge is weak**.

If you are stuck on a topic find somebody (a tutor) to explain it to you.

Read around the subject – read good newspapers and professional journals, especially ACCA's *Student Accountant* – this can give you an advantage in the exam.

Read through the text and your notes again. Maybe put key revision points onto index cards to look at when you have a few minutes to spare.

Practise exam standard questions under timed conditions. Attempt all the different styles of questions you may be asked to answer in your exam.

Review any assignments you have completed and look at where you lost marks – put more work into those areas where you were weak.

Ensure you **know the structure of the exam** – how many questions and of what type they are.

KAPLAN PUBLISHING

Chapter 1

THE REGULATORY FRAMEWORK

This chapter discusses the conceptual framework that underpins modern financial reporting. These concepts help to explain the detailed accounting standards that you will study later on in this text. The sources of accounting practice and the standard setting process is also described. This chapter covers syllabus areas 1(a), 1(b), 1(c), 1(d) and 1(e).

CONTENTS

1   Users of financial statements

2   The regulatory system

3   A conceptual framework

4   Statement of Principles

5   The potential benefits and drawbacks of an agreed conceptual framework

6   FRS 18 *Accounting Policies*

7   Historical cost accounting and its shortcomings

LEARNING OUTCOMES

At the end of this chapter you should be able to:

*   explain the need for, and objectives of, financial statements

*   identify the users of financial statements and their particular interests in the statements

*   describe and explain the following elements of the financial statements and their interaction: assets, liabilities, ownership interest, gains, losses, contributions from owners and distributions to owners

*   identify the three stages of recognising elements for inclusion in financial statements

*   discuss the nature and purpose of a conceptual framework

- explain the potential benefits and drawbacks of an agreed conceptual framework

- explain the role and general issues covered by the Statement of Principles

- identify and explain the qualitative characteristics of financial information

- discuss and apply accounting concepts and policies

- discuss the shortcomings of historical cost accounting and how they might be overcome

- explain the standard setting process and the role of the Financial Reporting Council, Accounting Standards Board, Urgent Issues Task Force and Financial Reporting Review Panel.

1 USERS OF FINANCIAL STATEMENTS

1.1 THE PURPOSE OF ACCOUNTING

The purpose of accounting is to provide information to users of financial statements. Legally, company financial statements are drawn up for the benefit of the shareholders, so that they can assess the performance of their Board of Directors. However, in practice many other groups will use these financial statements, and these groups will all have different needs. These groups, and their needs, are described below.

1.2 MANAGEMENT

Management will be interested in an analysis of revenues and expenses which will provide information that is useful when plans are formulated and decisions made. Once the budget for a business is complete, the accountant can produce figures for what actually happens as the budget period unfolds, so that they can be compared with the budget. Management will also need to know the cost consequences of a particular course of action to aid their decision making.

1.3 SHAREHOLDERS AND POTENTIAL SHAREHOLDERS

This group includes the investing public at large and the stockbrokers and commentators who advise them. The shareholders should be informed of the manner in which management has used their funds which have been invested in the business. This is a matter of reporting on past events. However, both shareholders and potential shareholders are also interested in the future performance of the business and use past figures as a guide to the future if they have to vote on proposals or decide whether to sell their shares.

Financial analysts advising investors such as insurance companies, pension funds, unit trusts and investment trusts are among the most sophisticated users of accounting information, and the company contemplating a takeover bid is yet another type of potential shareholder.

1.4   EMPLOYEES AND THEIR TRADE UNION REPRESENTATIVES

These use accounting information to assess the potential performance of the business. This information is relevant to the employee, who wishes to discover whether the company can offer him safe employment and promotion through growth over a period of years, and also to the trade unionist, who uses past profits and potential profits in his calculations and claims for higher wages or better conditions. The viability of different divisions of a company is of interest to this group.

1.5   LENDERS

This group includes some who have financed the business over a long period by lending money which is to be repaid at the end of a number of years, as well as short-term creditors such as a bank which allows a company to overdraw its bank account for a number of months, and suppliers of raw materials, which permit a company to buy goods from them and pay in, say, four to twelve weeks' time.

Lenders are interested in the security of their loan, so they will look at an accounting statement to ensure that the company will be able to repay on the due date and meet the interest requirements before that date. The amount of cash available and the value of assets which form a security for the debt are of importance to this group. Credit rating agencies are interested in accounts for similar reasons.

1.6   GOVERNMENT AGENCIES

These use accounting information, either when collecting statistical information to reveal trends within the economy as a whole or, in the case of the Inland Revenue, to assess the profit on which the company's tax liability is to be computed.

1.7   THE BUSINESS CONTACT GROUP

Customers of a business may use accounting data to assess the viability of a company if a long-term contract is soon to be placed. Competitors will also use the accounts for purposes of comparison.

1.8   THE PUBLIC

From time to time other groups not included above may have an interest in the company e.g. members of a local community where the company operates, environmental pressure groups, and so on.

1.9   CONCLUSION

Financial statements serve a wide variety of user groups, who have different interests and also different levels of financial sophistication. This makes it particularly difficult to produce accounts which are intelligible to the layman but comprehensive for the expert.

The next section looks at how standards have been developed to try to meet these diverse needs.

2 THE REGULATORY SYSTEM

2.1 INTRODUCTION

The regulatory framework of accounting is made up of a number of legislative and quasi-legislative influences. This section provides an overview of these influences which can be listed as:

(a) Company Law

(b) Accounting Standards issued by the Accounting Standards Board (ASB)

(c) EU Directives

(d) The Stock Exchange.

All four of these sources combine to form what is known as UK GAAP, Generally Accepted Accounting Practice.

The first three are briefly considered below.

2.2 COMPANY LAW

The regulatory framework of accounting is affected by company law in a number of areas.

(a) Financial statements of companies must show a 'true and fair view'.

(b) Accounting standards issued by the ASB have quasi-legal authority.

(c) Prescribed formats for the profit and loss account and balance sheet are required.

(d) Detailed disclosures of information are required.

(e) A company is limited in the amount of profits it can distribute to its shareholders.

(f) Changes in share capital are regulated by law.

Items (c) to (f) are covered in the chapters on limited company accounts to the extent that knowledge is required at this level of accounting. Items (a) and (b) are dealt with below.

2.3 THE TRUE AND FAIR VIEW

Since 1948, statutory financial statements have been required to show a 'true and fair view'. However, there is no universal definition of a 'true and fair view'. A simple, unofficial, definition could be as follows:

- 'True' means that the accounts are arithmetically correct and in compliance with all relevant regulations.

- 'Fair' means that the accounts are unbiased and not misleading.

The meaning of the phrase changes over time. In 1948 there was a great deal of leeway as to how a set of accounts should be drawn up. With the introduction of accounting standards the choices available for preparing a set of accounts have been restricted, and so there will be a much stricter interpretation of a 'true and fair view' today than there was 50 years ago.

2.4 ACCOUNTING STANDARDS

The Companies Act is mainly designed to deal with the problem of inadequate information. Accounting standards set out to tackle a different problem: that of the diversity of treatment of certain items in published accounts.

Definition   **Accounting standards** are authoritative statements of how particular types of transactions and other events should be reflected in financial statements.

There are many areas of accounting where there is more than one generally accepted method of dealing with particular transactions. Because types of businesses often vary so much as between one another, what is suitable as an accounting policy for one business may be unsuitable for another. It is, however, important for a given business to follow its accounting policies from one year to the next, so that valid comparisons of performance may be made.

The following are examples of the areas where variations in accounting practices are recognised:

(a) depreciation of fixed assets

(b) research and development expenditure

(c) hire purchase or instalment transactions

(d) stock and work-in-progress.

2.5 THE ROLES OF THE FRC, ASB, UITF AND REVIEW PANEL

The Financial Reporting Council (FRC)

The FRC comprises around 25 members drawn from the users and preparers of accounts and auditors. It was originally set up to oversee the accounting standard setting process and the quality of published financial information. In July 2003 it was announced that the FRC would also take on the responsibility for supervising the audit profession, audit practice and corporate governance. This paper is only concerned with its financial reporting responsibilities.

The FRC guides the standard setting process and ensures that the ASB's work is properly funded.

The FRC has two operating bodies responsible for accounting standards and financial reporting. These are the Accounting Standards Board (ASB) and the Financial Reporting Review Panel (FRRP).

The standard setting bodies are shown below:

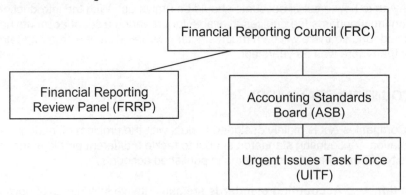

The Accounting Standards Board (ASB)

The ASB has 10 members, including a full-time chairman and a full-time technical director. The aims of the ASB are to establish and improve standards of financial accounting and reporting for the benefit of users, preparers and auditors of financial information.

The ASB works to achieve its aims by:

- developing principles to guide it in establishing standards and to provide a framework within which others can exercise judgement in resolving accounting issues. The ASB's *Statement of Principles for Financial Reporting* is covered later in this chapter

- issuing new accounting standards, or amending existing ones, in response to evolving business practices, new economic developments and deficiencies being identified in current practice

- addressing urgent issues promptly

- working with the International Accounting Standards Board (IASB), with national standards-setters and relevant European Union Institutions to encourage high quality in the IASB's standards and their adoption in the EU.

The ASB issues Financial Reporting Standards (FRSs). A few Statements of Standard Accounting Practice (SSAPs) are still in force; these were issued by the Accounting Standards Committee (ASC) which was the predecessor of the ASB.

The Financial Reporting Review Panel (FRRP)

The Review Panel has about 15 members. It examines apparent departures from the accounting requirements of the Companies Act and relevant accounting standards.

The Review Panel investigates specific matters about a company's financial statements when these are reported. It also actively monitors company financial statements, concentrating on industry sectors where the risk of defective financial statements is believed to be high.

The Review Panel has the power to seek a court order requiring companies to re-draft their financial statements. In practice, it normally attempts to persuade directors to revise defective accounts voluntarily. To date no court orders have been sought.

The Urgent Issues Task Force (UITF)

The UITF is a committee of the ASB. Its function is to address areas where an accounting standard or a Companies Act provision exists, but where unsatisfactory or conflicting interpretations have developed or seem likely to develop. The normal standard setting process is not normally practicable in these cases because of their urgency.

Once an issue has been identified, the UITF operates by seeking general agreement about the accounting treatment to be adopted. It issues UITF Abstracts which set out its pronouncements. UITF Abstracts have the same authority as accounting standards. They must be followed if financial statements are to give a true and fair view.

The standard setting process

Once a topic has been identified, ASB staff carry out research. The members of the ASB debate the issues and then normally proceed as follows:

- A Discussion Paper is issued and interested parties are invited to comment. A Discussion Paper explores the issues involved, discusses possible accounting treatments and sets out the ASB's preliminary conclusions.

- A Financial Reporting Exposure Draft (FRED) is then issued. A FRED is the proposed accounting standard in draft form. FREDs are widely circulated and all interested parties are invited to comment.

- The ASB then considers the comments received. The new FRS is then issued.

2.6 EU DIRECTIVES

It is the aim of the EU that its member states will eventually become parts of a single economic entity. To achieve this goal businesses must operate under the same legal and accounting requirements. As a result two EU Directives have been incorporated into UK Law (and into the law of the other member states). These are:

- the Fourth Directive governing formats and disclosure requirements

- the Seventh Directive relates to group accounts, and is included in the Companies Act.

2.7 2005 AND INTERNATIONAL ACCOUNTING STANDARDS

The European Union has required all publicly quoted companies to apply International Accounting Standards (now known as International Financial Reporting Standards) since January 2005.

2.8 ADVANTAGES AND DISADVANTAGES OF ACCOUNTING STANDARDS

There are obvious advantages of accounting standards. Without them, an entity would be free to adopt any accounting treatment that it chose.

- Accounting standards result in consistency of accounting treatment; this means that (in theory) it is possible to compare the financial statements of different entities in a meaningful way.

- Accounting standards also mean that similar transactions are treated in the same way over time, making it possible to evaluate an entity's performance over time.

- Accounting standards make it more difficult (although not impossible) for entities to adopt accounting treatments that deliberately mislead users of the financial statements.

- The increasing use of international accounting standards means that it is now becoming easier to compare the financial statements of entities that operate in different countries.

- Accounting standards generally improve the quality of the information provided to users of financial statements; (in theory) they ensure that the information in financial statements is relevant to the needs of users and reliable.

However, there are also some disadvantages:

- It can be argued that the selection of accounting policies is a matter of judgement and should be left to individual entities. Different organisations operate under different conditions; an accounting policy that is appropriate for some entities may not be appropriate for others and may actually reduce the usefulness of the financial statements.

- Some preparers will view accounting standards as a set of rules to be circumvented and so standards do not necessarily prevent 'creative accounting'. (However, note that UK accounting standards are based on principles, rather than a set of rules; this makes abuse less likely.)

- Some accounting standards may change the commercial decisions made by entities. An entity could avoid actions that would benefit it in the long term if a standard required a treatment that would (for example) reduce profits in the short term.

- Many recent accounting standards have been drawn up primarily to meet the information needs of large institutional investors in public companies. For many smaller companies, the cost of complying (in time and effort, as well as money) may outweigh the benefits to users and preparers.

- Where accounting standards require complex treatments and extensive disclosures, it can be argued that these make the financial statements harder to understand and therefore less useful.

Most of the disadvantages apply to particular situations, rather than to accounting standards in themselves. Most preparers and users of financial statements accept that the advantages of accounting standards far outweigh the disadvantages.

2.9 CONCLUSION

In the UK the regulatory framework for accounting is made up of the legal framework set out in the Companies Act and the requirements of the accountancy profession set out in SSAPs and FRSs. In the future international standards will be the most important influence on UK accounting.

3 A CONCEPTUAL FRAMEWORK

The UK conceptual framework is known as the *Statement of Principles*. The basic objective of the conceptual framework is to provide a logical and sensible guide for preparing accounting standards and applying them. In effect it will be the constitution within which accountants work, while the standards themselves will be the detailed laws enacted to apply these constitutional principles.

4 STATEMENT OF PRINCIPLES

4.1 INTRODUCTION

In December 1999 the ASB published its Statement of Principles for Financial Reporting. This sets out the principles that the ASB believes should underlie the preparation and presentation of general purpose financial statements. It aims to provide a coherent framework to assist the ASB in the development and review of accounting standards.

There are eight chapters in the Statement of Principles:

1   The objective of financial statements

2   The reporting entity

3   The qualitative characteristics of financial information

4   The elements of financial statements

5   Recognition in financial statements

6   Measurement in financial statements

7   Presentation of financial information

8   Accounting for interests in other entities

4.2 PURPOSE AND STATUS OF STATEMENT

The purpose of the Statement of Principles is to:

(a)   Assist the ASB in the development and review of accounting standards.

(b)   Provide a basis for reducing the number of accounting treatments allowed.

(c)   Assist accountants in applying accounting standards and in dealing with topics that do not form the subject of an accounting standard.

(d)   Assist auditors in deciding whether financial statements conform with accounting standards.

(e)   Assist users in interpreting financial statements.

(f)   Explain the ASB's approach to the formulation of accounting standards.

The Statement of Principles will not become an accounting standard. Nothing in the Statement overrides a specific accounting standard.

4.3 CHAPTER 1 – THE OBJECTIVE OF FINANCIAL STATEMENTS

The objective of financial statements is to provide information about the reporting entity's financial performance and financial position that is useful to a wide range of users for assessing the stewardship of the entity's management and for making economic decisions.

4.4 CHAPTER 2 – THE REPORTING ENTITY

If there is legitimate demand for an entity to produce financial statements, then they should. An entity is any cohesive economic unit under single control. For our purposes this means that individual limited companies must produce financial statements, and that also groups of companies under common control must produce group financial statements.

4.5 CHAPTER 3 – THE QUALITATIVE CHARACTERISTICS OF FINANCIAL INFORMATION

Information provided by financial statements needs to be **relevant** and **reliable**. If there is a choice of approach then the one chosen is the one that maximises the relevance of the information.

The information provided by the financial statements also needs to be **comparable** and **understandable**.

Information is **relevant** if it has the ability to influence the economic decisions of users and is provided in time to influence those decisions.

Information is **reliable** if:

(a) it can be depended upon by users to represent faithfully what it either purports to represent or could reasonably be expected to represent, and therefore reflects the substance of the transactions and other events that have taken place

(b) it is free from deliberate or systematic bias and material error and is complete; and

(c) in its preparation under conditions of uncertainty, a degree of caution has been applied in exercising the necessary judgements.

Information is **comparable** if it enables users to discern and evaluate similarities in, and differences between, the nature and effects of transactions and other events over time and across different reporting entities.

Information is **understandable** if its significance can be appreciated by users that have a reasonable knowledge of business and economic activities and accounting and a willingness to study with reasonable diligence the information provided.

The Statement also considers materiality. Only information that is **material** needs to be given in the financial statements.

Information is **material** if its misstatement or omission might reasonably be expected to influence the economic decisions of users.

The relationship between these characteristics is shown in the diagram below.

The qualitative characteristics of financial information

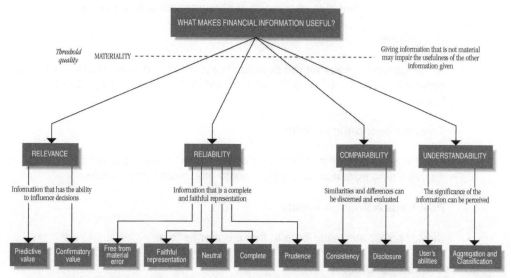

The overriding requirement for financial statements is that they should give a true and fair view of the financial position, performance and financial adaptability of an entity.

4.6 CHAPTER 4 – THE ELEMENTS OF FINANCIAL STATEMENTS

(a) **Assets**

Definition   **Assets** are rights or other access to future economic benefits controlled by an entity as a result of past transactions or events.

Rights or other access to future economic benefits

At its simplest this means that the asset will eventually generate cash. For example:

- A machine will make goods.

- These goods will be sold, generating cash or creating debtors.

- Trade debtors will pay up in cash.

The machine, the goods and the trade debtors all help to generate cash, and so they are all assets.

Controlled by an entity

An entity does not have to own an asset in order to get the economic benefits from it. For example, a leased asset will generate the same economic benefits as an identical asset that is owned by the business.

Past transactions or events

The transaction or event must be 'past' before an asset can arise. For example:

- Trade debtors only arise as a result of past sales.

- Stocks are normally valued at their historic cost (past), not at their hoped for sales price (future).

(b) **Liabilities**

Definition   **Liabilities** are the obligations of an entity to transfer economic benefits as a result of past transactions or events.

Obligations

An obligation implies that the outflow of resources is **unavoidable**. Planned expenditure (such as future repairs) are avoidable, and so they do not create liabilities.

Transfer economic benefits

This could be a transfer of cash, or other property, the provision of a service, or the refraining from activities which would otherwise be profitable.

Past transactions or events

Similar points are made here to those under assets.

(c) **Ownership interest**

Definition   **Ownership interest** is the residual amount found by deducting all of the entity's liabilities from all of the entity's assets.

The above describes the residual nature of ownership interest. Owners' wealth can be increased whether or not a distribution is made. The sharing may be in different proportions.

Ownership interest is usually analysed in financial statements to distinguish that arising from owners' contributions from that resulting from other events. The latter is split into different reserves which may have different applications or legal status.

(d) **Gains and losses**

These are counted as two of the seven elements.

Definition   **Gains** are increases in ownership interest not resulting from contributions from owners.

Definition   **Losses** are decreases in ownership interest not resulting from distributions to owners.

(e) **Contributions from owners**

Definition   **Contributions from owners** are increases in ownership interest resulting from transfers from owners in their capacity as owners.

These will usually be in cash but they could be in other forms of property, by accepting equity in satisfaction of liabilities or by performing services.

The consideration is the granting of rights in the ownership interest.

(f)   **Distributions to owners**

Definition   **Distributions to owners** are decreases in ownership interest resulting from transfers made to owners in their capacity as owners.

Distributions include dividends and purchase of own shares but not bonus issues since ownership interest remains constant.

4.7   CHAPTER 5 – RECOGNITION IN FINANCIAL STATEMENTS

Definition   **Recognition** involves depiction of the item in words and by a monetary amount and the inclusion of that amount in the financial statement totals.

Only items which meet the definition of an element of the financial statements should be recognised. The definitions are set out in Chapter 4 of the Statement as explained above.

4.8   CHAPTER 6 – MEASUREMENT IN FINANCIAL STATEMENTS

Definition   **Measurement** is concerned with the monetary amount of the depiction of an element in the financial statements.

(a)   A measurement basis – either historic cost or current value – needs to be selected for each category of assets or liabilities. The basis selected should be the one that best meets the objective of financial statements.

(b)   An asset or liability being measured using the historical cost basis is recognised initially at transaction cost. An asset or liability being measured using the current value basis is recognised initially at its current value at the time it was acquired or assumed.

(c)   Subsequent remeasurement will occur if it is necessary to ensure that:

(i)   assets measured at historical cost are carried at the lower of cost and recoverable amount; and

(ii)   assets and liabilities measured on the current value basis are carried at up-to-date current values.

(d)   Such remeasurements will be recognised only if:

(i)   there is sufficient evidence that the monetary amount of the asset or liability has changed; and

(ii)   the new amount of the asset or liability can be measured with sufficient reliability.

4.9   CHAPTER 7 – PRESENTATION OF FINANCIAL INFORMATION

This part of the Statement of Principles explores the way in which information should be presented in financial statements in order to meet the objective described in Chapter 1. The presentation decision is taken in the context of a structured set of financial statements comprising **primary statements** and **supporting notes**.

(a) **The primary statements**

Profit and loss account	(financial performance)
Statement of total recognised gains and losses	(financial performance)
Balance sheet	(financial position)
Cash flow statement	

(b) **Notes to financial statements**

The notes to financial statements should amplify and explain the primary statements giving more detailed information on items and in certain instances provide an alternative view of a particular transaction or event from that included in those primary statements. The notes and primary statements form an integrated whole.

(c) **Accompanying information**

Accompanying information is information which is positioned outside the primary statements and notes. This may include voluntary or evolutionary disclosures and information that, perhaps because it is too subjective, is not suitable for inclusion in the primary financial statements and the notes.

Accompanying information may include:

(i) a business review as required by the Companies Act 2006

(ii) information prepared from a different perspective from that adopted in the financial statements

(iii) statistical information

(iv) highlights and summary indicators.

4.10 CHAPTER 8 – ACCOUNTING FOR INTERESTS IN OTHER ENTITIES

Financial statements need to reflect the effect on the reporting entity's financial performance and position of its interests in other entities.

Consolidated financial statements are the financial statements of a group of companies – the reporting entity plus the other entities that it controls.

5 THE POTENTIAL BENEFITS AND DRAWBACKS OF AN AGREED CONCEPTUAL FRAMEWORK

Potential benefits

The potential benefits of a conceptual framework are related to the purposes stated by the ASB for the Statement of Principles. In summary, the benefits are:

- a framework for setting accounting standards

- a basis for resolving disputes

- fundamental principles do not have to be repeated in accounting standards

- there should be a reduction in pressure from vested interests who wish to pursue a particular policy out of self-interest rather than satisfying the general needs of users.

Potential drawbacks

Drawbacks to a conceptual framework include:

- due to their general nature the principles may not, in practice, reduce the options available

- there may be further disagreement as to the contents of the framework in addition to disagreement over the contents of standards.

Conclusion

There is widespread support for a conceptual framework, but aspects of the Statement of Principles have proved to be controversial, particularly the emphasis on the use of current values.

6 FRS 18 *ACCOUNTING POLICIES*

6.1 INTRODUCTION

FRS 18 restates the Statement of Principles. It also describes the difference between accounting policies and accounting estimates, and outlines two accounting concepts; going concern and accruals. These accounting concepts are the basis of all other accounting standards. The Companies Act mentions five accounting principles; these are going concern and accruals (as in FRS 18) plus three more: prudence, consistency and separate valuation. These are also discussed in this section.

6.2 POLICIES

Entities should select the most appropriate accounting policies and apply them consistently. **Accounting policies** are the principles applied by an entity to report transactions, assets, and liabilities in the financial statements. Accounting policies should be based upon all relevant SSAPs and FRSs. If there are no relevant standards then the Statement of Principles should provide some guidance.

The accounting policies chosen by an entity should be disclosed in the financial statements. Any changes should be highlighted, and their effect on profits and net assets disclosed.

6.3 ESTIMATES

Estimation techniques are used to measure monetary amounts. For example, depreciation of assets (spreading out the cost of acquiring an asset over its estimated useful life) is an accounting policy, but the choice between depreciating over five years or 15 years is an estimate.

6.4 GOING CONCERN CONCEPT

The going concern concept assumes that a business (or entity) will **continue in operational existence for the foreseeable future**.

This means that the financial statements are drawn up on the assumption that there is no **intention or necessity to liquidate or curtail significantly the scale of operation**.

Circumstances where the going concern assumption would not be justified would include:

(i)   where there is a specific intention to liquidate the business in the near future

(ii)   where there is a strong possibility that shortage of finance will force the business into liquidation. This may be revealed by preparing a cash flow forecast for the next 12 months where a month-by-month comparison of expected cash inflows and outflows indicates financing requirements that are unlikely to be satisfied by the bank or by outside lenders

(iii)   where there is a strong possibility that shortage of finance will result in the sale of a significant part of the business.

In the above circumstances the going concern assumption would not be valid, and the financial statements would be prepared on a basis which takes the likely consequences into account.

In most cases, however, financial statements will be prepared on a going concern basis and the directors will be able to justify the idea that such a basis is valid. The directors and auditors of a company both have a responsibility to ensure that the company is indeed a going concern if the going concern basis is adopted.

6.5   ACCRUALS (OR MATCHING) CONCEPT

The accruals or matching concept states that costs and revenues should be matched one with the other and dealt with in the accounting period to which they relate.

The starting position should be to use the concept to determine the accounting period in which revenue (i.e. sales) is recognised.

Revenue is usually recognised when it is realised. The realisation of revenue is usually taken to occur on the date of sale rather than on the date when the cash relating to the sale is received.

The efforts of expenditure in the past have led to the revenues accruing now. It is thus logical to match the costs or expenses of earning revenue with the revenue reported in any particular period. The operating profit determined in this way is supposed to indicate how efficiently the resources of the business have been utilised.

Although the accruals or matching principle is conceptually simple, it does run into practical difficulties.

For example, expenditure on fixed assets will provide benefits extending over several accounting periods. When a fixed asset is acquired it is necessary to estimate its useful life. The **service potential** of a fixed asset will diminish over its useful life, and this reduction is a cost or expense to be matched against the revenue of each period and is called **depreciation**.

6.6   PRUDENCE CONCEPT

Prudence states that revenues and profits are not reported and recognised in the financial statements unless realised. Revenues and profits are not deemed realised until the likelihood of conversion to cash is high. In most cases this means the date of sale. By way of contrast, immediate provision is made for anticipated losses, even if such losses are not yet realised.

An example of the prudence concept is the situation in which a liability has been estimated to be between £500 and £600. Some accountants will make provision for the highest estimate on the grounds of prudence. Modern accounting thought though would make provision for the most likely value, high or low.

6.7 CONSISTENCY CONCEPT

A business should be consistent in its accounting treatment of similar items, both **within** a particular accounting period and **between** one accounting period and the next.

For example, in the case of depreciation of fixed assets, there is more than one accepted accounting treatment. One business may use one method, another business may use another. As far as the consistency concept is concerned, once a business has selected a method, it should use this method consistently for all assets in that class and for all accounting periods. Only in this way can users of financial statements draw meaningful conclusions from reported results. If a business were to change any of its accounting policies (e.g. the basis of depreciation) it must have a good reason for doing so and in addition, the financial effect of such a change should be quantified and, if material, reported to the shareholders.

6.8 SEPARATE VALUATION

Each item in the financial statements should be valued separately. In particular, assets should not be netted off against liabilities, and profits should not be netted off against losses.

6.9 HISTORICAL COST CONVENTION

The historical cost accounting system is a system of accounting in which all values are based on the historical costs incurred. This is the basis of accounting prescribed by the Companies Act (although the Act does allow Alternative Accounting Rules that enable certain assets to be revalued and stated at their revalued amounts).

6.10 MATERIALITY

This is the principle that financial statements should separately disclose items which are significant enough to affect evaluation or decisions.

The significance of an item stems from its importance in the overall context of the financial statements.

This convention ensures that only significant items are included in the financial statements in order to improve their clarity. The materiality test i.e. what is and is not significant, will differ from organisation to organisation.

Materiality may be considered in the context of the financial statements as a whole or individual items within them. It may also be considered in relative or absolute terms depending upon the item concerned.

6.11 DUALITY

The duality concept underpins double entry and the balance sheet. For each entry in the accounting records, there is an equal and opposite entry.

6.12 SUBSTANCE OVER FORM

Financial statements should reflect the economic substance of a transaction, rather than its legal form, where these are different.

A good example of this convention is that of assets acquired on hire purchase terms or under certain types of lease agreement. Despite the fact that such assets are not owned by the user until the final instalment has been paid, a fixed asset is recorded in the accounts at the start of the agreement. This is because the user has the benefit of the fixed asset, as if he or she owned it. The hire purchase agreement (or the lease) is simply a way of financing the purchase.

ACTIVITY 1

State the accounting concept(s) being applied in each of these situations:

(1)   Plant and machinery has a net book value of £24m, but it would only fetch £15m if it were to be sold.

(2)   The plant and machinery is being depreciated over five years.

(3)   Stock is valued at £23m, even though it will probably sell for £35m.

(4)   John Ltd has just bought the trade and assets of a Sally, rival unincorporated business. John has changed Sally's accounting policies, bringing them into line with the rest of the business.

For a suggested answer, see the 'Answers' section at the end of the book.

7   HISTORICAL COST ACCOUNTING AND ITS SHORTCOMINGS

7.1   INTRODUCTION

Under historical cost accounting, assets are measured at their original cost throughout their lives, regardless of any changes in their market value.

This is the normal method of accounting. It has many advantages, but it also has serious disadvantages.

7.2   ADVANTAGES OF HISTORICAL COST ACCOUNTING

The advantages of historical cost accounting include:

- records are based on objectively verifiable amounts (actual cost of assets, etc.)

- it is simple and cheap

- the profit concept is well understood

- within limits, historical cost figures provide a basis for comparison with the results of other companies for the same period or similar periods, with the results of the same company for previous periods and with budgets

- lack of competition – no acceptable alternative has been developed.

7.3 DISADVANTAGES OF HISTORICAL COST ACCOUNTING

The disadvantages of historical cost accounting include:

- It overstates profits when prices are rising through inflation. Several factors contribute to this. For example, if assets are maintained at their original cost, depreciation is based on that cost. As inflation pushes prices up, the true value to the business of the use of the asset becomes progressively more than the depreciation charge. This disadvantage can be overcome by revaluing fixed assets. Depreciation is then based on the revalued amount.

- It maintains financial capital but does not maintain physical capital. If a business makes a profit it must necessarily have more net assets. If the whole of that profit is distributed as dividend by a company, or withdrawn from the business by a sole trader, the business has the same capital at the end of the year as it had at the beginning. In other words, it has maintained its financial capital. However, it will not have maintained its physical capital if prices have risen through inflation during the year, because the financial capital will not buy the same stock and other assets to enable the business to continue operating at the same level.

- The balance sheet does not show the value of the business. A balance sheet summarises the assets and liabilities of the business, but there are several reasons why it does not represent the true value of the business. One reason for this could be that the use of historical cost accounting means that assets are included at cost less depreciation based on that cost rather than at current value. (Another reason is, of course, that not all the assets are included in the balance sheet – for example, internally generated goodwill will not appear.)

- It provides a poor basis for assessing performance. The profit is overstated, as explained above, while assets are understated. The result is that return on capital employed is doubly distorted and exaggerated.

- It does not recognise the loss suffered through holding monetary assets while prices are rising. A business holding cash or debtors through a period of inflation suffers a loss as its purchasing power declines.

7.4 ALTERNATIVES TO HISTORICAL COST ACCOUNTING

There are two main alternatives to historical cost accounting.

Current purchasing power accounting

Current purchasing power accounting (CPP) involves adjusting the historical cost accounts using a general price index (the Retail Price Index) so that all items are expressed in £s of year-end purchasing power.

The method has been rejected, most notably because many accountants felt it misleading to adjust specific assets such as stock and fixed assets by means of a general price index which was far more relevant to the spending power of a family than that of a trader.

Current cost accounting

Current cost accounting (CCA) involves taking account of specific price changes as they affect a particular business and will result in a separate set of financial statements, distinct from the historical cost financial statements.

Although accountants generally believe CCA is superior to CPP, the profession has as yet to agree on any single method of accounting for inflation (or indeed, some people would even argue, on the need to do so).

7.5 CONCLUSION

It is largely accepted that historical cost accounts have very severe limitations, but so far the accounting profession has not devised any acceptable alternative. At present there is no requirement to prepare either CPP accounts or CCA accounts.

In practice many organisations overcome the limitations of historical cost accounts by revaluing certain fixed assets (normally land and buildings) and including these valuations in the financial statements. This is sometimes known as 'modified historic cost accounting' and is allowed by the Companies Act and by FRS 15 *Tangible fixed assets*, provided that the revaluations are kept up to date.

KEY TERMS

User groups – people who use published financial information.

Entity – any organisation that is required to publish financial statements.

Accounting policies – the specific accounting standards or the accounting principles adopted by an entity. These should be the most appropriate policies for that entity.

Accounting standards – authoritative statements of how transactions and events are reported in published financial statements. In the UK, these standards are published by the Accounting Standards Board. Accounting standards should comply with the general rules set out in a conceptual framework.

Conceptual framework – acts like an accounting constitution. It set out the objectives of financial reporting, defines the content of financial statements, and outlines the qualities that financial information must possess in order to be useful and reliable.

Statement of Principles – the conceptual framework published by the Accounting Standards Board.

Accounting concepts – FRS 18 defines two accounting concepts, accruals and going concern. These form the basis of all other accounting standards. Accounting concepts are fundamental principles or assumptions that underpin the preparation of financial statements.

Accounting principles – these include going concern, consistency, prudence, accruals and separate valuation. Financial statements should be prepared in accordance with these principles.

Assets – rights or other access to future economic benefits controlled by an entity as a result of past transactions or events.

Liabilities – the obligations of an entity to transfer economic benefits as a result of past transactions or events.

Ownership interest – the residual amount found by deducting all of the entity's liabilities from all of the entity's assets.

SELF TEST QUESTIONS

		Paragraph
1	Who are the main users of financial statements?	1
2	What are the main requirements of management from financial information?	1.2
3	What would be potential shareholders' interests in the financial statements?	1.3
4	What is the name of the accounting standards issued by the Accounting Standards Board?	2.5
5	What is a conceptual framework?	3
6	What is meant by the relevance of information?	4.5
7	What is meant by information being reliable?	4.5
8	Describe the factors in financial statements which make information relevant.	4.5
9	Describe the factors in financial statements which make information reliable.	4.5

10 How does the Statement of Principles define:

- assets

- liabilities

- ownership interest?   4.6

11	Name the two accounting concepts and the five accounting principles.	6.1
12	Does FRS 18 require disclosure of accounting concepts?	6.2
13	What is the going concern concept?	6.4
14	What is another name for the accruals concept?	6.5

EXAM-STYLE QUESTION

DEFINITIONS

Define the following accounting concepts and give, for each, one an example of its application:

(a) accruals   **(5 marks)**

(b) consistency (see note below)   **(5 marks)**

(c) prudence.   **(5 marks)**

Note: Your answer to (b) should include a brief explanation of the circumstances in which the consistency concept should *not* be applied.

(Total: 15 marks)

For a suggested answer, see the 'Answers' section at the end of the book.

Chapter 2

LIMITED COMPANIES

This chapter describes the legal and financial structure of limited companies. It covers syllabus areas 1(a), 1(e) and 1(g).

CONTENTS

1   Types of limited company

2   The legal records of a limited company

3   Company finance

4   Stewardship

5   Accounting systems and business organisations

LEARNING OUTCOMES

At the end of this chapter you should be able to:

- explain the need for, and objectives of, financial statements

- discuss how the accounting systems of an organisation are affected by its roles, organisational structure, its administrative systems and procedures and the nature of its business transactions

- explain the legal framework and obligations of directors

- distinguish between issued and authorised share capital and between called up and paid up share capital

- distinguish between ordinary and preference shares

- distinguish between the market value and nominal value of a share

- explain why companies will be concerned with the value of their shares

- define and account for debentures.

---

1 TYPES OF LIMITED COMPANY

1.1 INTRODUCTION

In the UK the predominant form of business enterprise is the limited company. Most companies are limited by shares, meaning that in the event of the failure of a company, the amount the shareholders can lose is restricted to the amount paid for their shares.

It is important to appreciate that not all limited companies are large – they vary in size from the very small to the huge quoted company which operates worldwide.

1.2 KEY FEATURES OF A LIMITED COMPANY

Shares and shareholders

The ownership of the company is split into **shares**. There are ordinary shares and preference shares, but for now we are only interested in the **ordinary shares** (also known as **equity shares**). Each ordinary share is entitled to a share of the net assets of the company (if and when it is wound up) and to a share of any dividends paid.

Shares are owned by shareholders. A limited company is jointly owned by its **ordinary shareholders**. The ordinary shareholders themselves are referred to as the **members** of the company. The total investment by the ordinary shareholders in the company is sometimes called **equity**.

For legal purposes shares have a **nominal value**. This can be for any amount, but is usually £1. There is no link between the nominal value of a share and its issue price or market value.

Separate legal identity and limited liability

The company has a **separate legal identity** from its shareholders. This is very different from a partnership or a sole trader, where in the eyes of the law the owners and the business are one and the same.

If the company runs into financial difficulties, then the shareholders can lose their entire investment. However, they cannot be forced to make any further contributions to the business. This is a consequence of the concepts of separate legal identity and limited liability, and contrasts with the position of partners who must make good all business losses from their own personal wealth. (The one exception to this rule is when shares are issued partly paid. In these cases the shareholders can be asked to contribute the balance owing on their shares up to their nominal value. However, this situation is unusual.)

Directors and stewardship

The members elect a **Board of Directors** to manage the company. In the election each ordinary share has one vote, so the more shares that a member owns, then the more votes that they will have. This will be important when we come to look at Group Accounts.

The Board of Directors run the company on behalf of the shareholders, not themselves. This is known as **stewardship**.

Legal formalities

Because of the large number of investors involved in a limited company, and because of the problems that limited liability might pose for customers and suppliers, limited companies are more tightly regulated than sole traders or partnerships. Most of these regulations are contained in the **Companies Act 2006**.

One of the main features of this Act is the requirement for the Directors to present an **Annual Report** to their shareholders. This report contains the Statutory Accounts (financial statements). Paper 6 is concerned with how those statutory accounts should be prepared.

Note: The **Companies Act 2006** is coming into force in stages during 2007 and 2008 to replace the 1985 and 1989 Acts. The Companies Act 2006 is examinable from the June 2008 sitting onwards. It should however be noted that as yet there is no replacement legislation for the schedules in the Companies Act 1985(89) which detail the format of accounts. It is eventually intended that this will be contained within secondary legislation to accompany the main Companies Act 2006, There are unlikely to be major changes from the existing requirements of the CA85(89), and therefore it is those which are detailed in this text.

1.3 FINANCIAL DIFFERENCES BETWEEN SOLE TRADERS AND COMPANIES

The main financial differences between companies and sole traders are in the following respects:

(a)   the form of the capital accounts

(b)   the form of loans to the company

(c)   the way in which profits are withdrawn by the proprietors

(d)   the form in which retained funds are presented.

The differences may be summarised as follows:

Item	Sole trader	Company
(a) Capital introduced by proprietors	Capital account	Issued share capital
(b) Loans from third parties	Loan account	Debentures
(c) Profits withdrawn by proprietors	Drawings	Dividends
(d) Profits retained in the business	Capital account	Reserves

These differences will all be considered later in this chapter.

1.4 THE ADVANTAGES AND DISADVANTAGES OF OPERATION AS A LIMITED COMPANY RATHER THAN AS A SOLE TRADER

The advantages of operation as a limited company rather than as a sole trader are as follows:

(a)   The liability of the shareholders is limited to the capital already introduced by them. This is useful if the business venture is relatively risky, but is not such an advantage if the business is low risk. For example, a venture requiring a lot of capital investment and employing a lot of staff should be undertaken via a limited company. However, a low risk venture (such as buying residential property for letting out) does not need the benefits of limited liability.

(b)   There is a formal separation of the business from the owners of the business, which may be helpful to the running of the business. For example, if several members of a family are the shareholders in a company but only two of the family are directors, it is clear to all concerned who is running the company.

(c)   Ownership of the business can be shared between people more easily than other forms of business organisation e.g. a partnership.

(d)   Shares in the business can be transferred relatively easily.

(e)   There may be tax advantages.

The disadvantages of operation as a limited company rather than as a sole trader are as follows:

(a)   The costs of formation of the company. Documentation needs to be prepared to form the company, although these costs are only about £100 for a company with 'normal' type of memorandum and articles of association.

(b)   The annual running costs of the company. Annual returns need to be completed and sent to the Registrar of Companies. The audit fee is a further additional cost though companies obviously derive a benefit from having their accounts audited, not least from the greater reliability they acquire as a result of the audit.

(c)   Directors of a company are subject to greater legislative duties than others running an unincorporated business.

(d)   It is difficult/expensive to return capital surplus to the business's requirements to the shareholders.

(e)   Shares in the business can be transferred relatively easily.

(f)   There may be tax disadvantages.

1.5   PRIVATE COMPANIES AND PUBLIC COMPANIES

Whether a particular company is a private company or a public company is a matter of law.

Definition   A **public** company is a company which must have a minimum allotted share capital of £50,000, of which at least one quarter and the whole of any premium are paid up. A public company has the letters plc after its name, which stand for 'public limited company'.

Definition   A **private** company is a company that is not a public company. A private company has the letters Ltd after its name.

1.6   QUOTED AND UNQUOTED COMPANIES

Legally, only public limited companies are allowed to sell their shares to the general pubic, but not all of them chose to do so. If a company wishes to sell its shares to the general public then it must satisfy the strict criteria of the **Stock Exchange** as well as any legal requirements. Once these criteria have been met, the company is said to be quoted on the Stock Exchange. This gives rise to the term **quoted or listed company**.

This means that the public can only buy shares in a quoted public limited company.

ACTIVITY 1

Charlie Farley is a trained piano tuner and restorer, currently working for a music school in London. He is considering leaving the school and setting up in business. He has identified two possible ventures, noted below.

Piano restorer

- This will require the purchase of tools costing £1,000.

- He will also need a workshop which will cost £200 per month to rent on a short term lease.

- Most restoration jobs will require five to ten days work.

Piano manufacturer

- This will require the purchase of tools and machinery costing £25,000.

- A purpose built factory will also be needed. He has identified one unit that would cost £1,000 per month on a three-year lease.

- He will need to hire four skilled members of staff.

- Each construction job will take about one month.

Required:

Advise Charlie on a suitable legal structure for each venture.

For a suggested answer, see the 'Answers' section at the end of the book.

2 THE LEGAL RECORDS OF A LIMITED COMPANY

2.1 REGISTERED OFFICE

A company must always have a registered office and give notice of its situation because:

- any writ or other legal process is validly served on the company by delivery to its registered office, and

- certain statutory books and other documents of the company open to inspection (by members or in some cases by third parties) are held at the registered office or other specified place. Most books should be available for public inspection for at least two hours per day during business hours.

2.2 STATUTORY BOOKS

The statutory books a company must keep are registers of:

(a) **Members**

Contents – details of shareholders showing name, address, date of ownership of shares, number and type of shares held.

On a total disposal of a person's shareholding the entry would be closed off by inserting the date he ceased to be a member.

(b) **Directors and Secretary**

Contents – personal details (including name and address, nationality, business occupation (if any), date of birth).

(c) **Debenture holders**

Contents – details of debenture holders showing name, address and amount of holding.

2.3 STATUTORY ACCOUNTSERROR! BOOKMARK NOT DEFINED.

At least once in every calendar year the directors must lay before the members of the company in general meeting a profit and loss account and balance sheet (the statutory accounts). These must be filed with the Registrar of Companies within seven months from the end of the accounting period (for a public company) and ten months from the end of the accounting period (for a private company).

Under the Companies Act 2006 the statutory accounts must be filed with the Registrar of Companies within six months from the end of the accounting period (for a public company) and nine months from the end of the accounting period (for a private company). A private company will no longer have to hold an Annual General Meeting, but must still send a copy of the statutory accounts to every member (shareholder) of the company and every debenture holder. (Debentures are covered later in this chapter.)

The requirement to prepare financial statements for the shareholders arises from the directors' stewardship function. This is discussed further in Section 4.

2.4 ANNUAL RETURN

Once a year a company is required to deliver to the Registrar of Companies the annual return. This return includes:

- the address of the registered office
- the type of company and its business activities
- particulars of the directors
- a summary of the company's share capital
- a list of members showing individual shareholdings and changes which have occurred during the year.

3 COMPANY FINANCE

3.1 INTRODUCTION

The way in which the assets of a company (fixed assets, stock, debtors and cash) are financed will vary from one company to another. Part of the finance may be provided by the owners or proprietors of the company (referred to as shareholders), while part may be provided by outsiders including trade creditors, banks and other lenders of funds.

Companies will also normally be partly financed by their own accumulated profits known as reserves.

3.2 THE NATURE AND PURPOSE OF SHARE CAPITAL AND RESERVES

Definition **Share capital** represents the capital invested in the company by its shareholders by the purchase of shares.

Definition **Reserves** represent the balance of net assets belonging to the shareholders. These may include part of past issues of share capital (known as share premium), retained trading profits and revaluation gains on the revaluation of fixed assets.

The total of share capital and reserves represents the book value of the net assets of the company.

3.3 DISTINCTION BETWEEN NOMINAL VALUE AND MARKET VALUE OF SHARE CAPITAL

Definition The **nominal value** of a share is its face value e.g. £1 ordinary shares or 50p ordinary share.

Each share has a stated nominal (or par) value. This has little practical significance except as a base line price below which further shares may not generally be issued. The nominal value is also used as a means of calculating dividends to shareholders.

Definition The **market value** of a share is the price at which that share could be bought or sold.

The market value of a share is not fixed at any particular date. The market value is related to the market value of the business of the company. For example, if a business is worth £100,000 and there are 1,000 £1 shares in issue in the company, the market value of each share is £100 whereas the nominal value is £1.

If the company is listed on a stock exchange then a price will be quoted for the shares based upon recent transactions between purchasers and sellers of shares. This is also referred to as the market value of a share, but this may not be the same value that would apply if the entire business was sold and thus all the shares were sold as one transaction.

3.4 WHY COMPANIES ARE CONCERNED WITH THE VALUE OF THEIR SHARES

Companies are concerned with the value the stock market places on the shares for two main reasons:

(a) Shareholders will look at a steadily rising price of the shares as evidence of sound management of the company by the directors. It would indicate additional profits being made every year.

(b) If the company wishes to raise further finance through the issue of shares, the current market price will be used as a basis for issuing more shares. The higher the price, the less number of shares will need to be issued and the less dilution there will be of the existing shareholders' effective interest in the company.

It is important to appreciate that the market value of a share quoted on the Stock Exchange has no direct relationship to the nominal value.

3.5   SHARE CAPITAL

The share capital of a company may be divided into various classes. The company's internal regulations (the Articles of Association) define the respective rights attached to the various shares e.g. as regards dividend entitlement or voting at company meetings. The various classes of share capital are dealt with below. In practice it is usually only larger companies which have different classes of share capital.

3.6   ORDINARY SHARES

Definition   **Ordinary shares** are the normal shares issued by a company. The normal rights of ordinary shareholders are to vote at company meetings and to receive dividends from profits.

Ordinary shares are often referred to as equity shares. A special class of ordinary share is the redeemable ordinary share where the terms of issue specify that it is repayable by the company.

3.7   PREFERENCE SHARES

Definition   **Preference shares** are shares carrying a fixed rate of dividend, the holders of which have a prior claim to any company profits available for distribution.

The rights and advantages of the shares will be specified in the articles of association.

Special categories of preference shares include:

(i)   Participating preference shares – where shareholders are entitled to participate together to a specified extent in distributable profits and surpluses on liquidation. Again, the rights of the shareholders are set out in the articles.

(ii)   Redeemable preference shares – the terms of issue specify that they are repayable by the company.

Redeemable Preference Shares are more like debt than equity.

3.8   ORDINARY AND PREFERENCE SHARES COMPARED

Aspect	Ordinary shares	Preference shares
Voting power	Carry a vote.	Do not carry a vote.
Distribution of profits (dividends)	A dividend which may vary from one year to the next after the preference shareholders have received their dividend.	A fixed dividend (fixed percentage of nominal value) in priority to ordinary dividend.
Liquidation of the company	Entitled to surplus assets on liquidation after liabilities and preference shares have been repaid.	Priority of repayment over ordinary shares but not usually entitled to surplus assets on liquidation.

3.9 DEBENTURES OR LOAN STOCK

Definition A **debenture** is a written acknowledgement of a loan to a company, given under the company's seal, which carries a fixed rate of interest.

A debenture may relate to a loan from one person. Debenture stock, on the other hand, rather like shares, may be held by a large number of individuals. The conditions and regulations are set out in a debenture trust deed.

Debentures are not part of a company's share capital – they are third party liabilities. Debenture interest is therefore a charge against profit and must be paid whether or not the company makes a profit.

Debentures are shown as liabilities in the balance sheet, just like any other loan.

4   STEWARDSHIP

4.1   THE ANNUAL REPORT

The shareholders own the company, but they do not necessarily run the company. Instead, the shareholders appoint a Board of Directors to manage the company on their behalf. This relationship is known as **stewardship**.

The directors have day-to-day control over the assets and operations of the shareholders' company. The shareholders will want to assure themselves that their company is being run profitably and honestly. Therefore the directors must prepare an account of their performance during the year and a summary of the assets and liabilities of the company at the end of the year. From this, the shareholders can see whether their company is making a profit or a loss, and whether their investment in the company is getting bigger or smaller. These form part of the annual financial statements.

Because the directors have control of the company money, there are always concerns about the amount of money that the directors are paying themselves. Therefore, the directors have to disclose the amount of pay and other benefits that they have received during the year. The other benefits might include pension contributions, perks such as motor cars, or shares issued for free or at a below market price. The amount of pay and benefits received by directors is referred to as **Directors' Remuneration** or **Directors' Emoluments**.

4.2   USING THE FINANCIAL STATEMENTS

Having read the directors' report, the shareholders must then decide the following:

- whether or not to re-elect the Board of Directors

- how much the directors should be paid

- how much dividend should be paid

- whether or not to approve the financial statements.

4.3   RE-ELECTING THE DIRECTORS AND APPROVING THEIR REMUNERATION

If the directors have performed a good job then the shareholders will want to re-elect them, and to reward them with good pay. This will encourage them to do even better in the future. If they have performed badly, then the shareholders may vote-off one or more of the directors, or they may cut their pay. There have been concerns recently that when lazy or incompetent directors have been voted off, they have taken multi-million pound pay-offs with them. It is up to the shareholders to monitor these situations, because it is their money that is being paid out. An unusual situation arose in May 2003, when shareholders in GlaxoSmithKline voted down a proposal that would have given a £22m pay off to one director if he was dismissed.

4.4 DIVIDENDS

Shareholders need a return on their investment. Their return comes in the form of the dividend. Dividends on shares are similar to interest on savings.

The **preference dividend** is normally fixed, and must be paid each and every year.

The **ordinary dividend** is variable. Each year the Directors will review the amount of profit that the company has made, and the amount of cash available. On the basis of this, the directors will propose a dividend. The shareholders must then approve this dividend. They may decide that they want more, or they may decide that the proposed dividend is more than the company can afford. Either way, it is the shareholders who make the final decision.

4.5 APPROVING THE FINANCIAL STATEMENTS

The members (shareholders) must approve the financial statements. This means that they accept that the financial statements are an accurate record of their company's position and performance. To do this they need help from the auditors.

4.6 THE AUDITORS AND THE AUDIT REPORT

You may have noticed that the shareholders assess their directors' performance on the basis of financial statements prepared by the directors themselves. It will obviously be in the directors' interests to be as optimistic as possible in order to boost the company's profits, and consequently boost their own pay. This is where auditors come in.

The shareholders appoint registered auditors to audit the financial statements prepared by the directors. Normally the auditors will report that the financial statements give a **true and fair view** of the financial position and performance of the company. This means that the accounts are not misleading; it does not mean that they are 100% correct. The auditors will also audit certain disclosures, such as Directors' Remuneration. These clean audit reports are known as unqualified opinions.

If the auditors think that the financial statements do not show a true and fair view, then they will issue a qualified opinion. This should state what, in the auditor's opinion, the profit for the year really should be.

In practice, the directors have a lot of influence over the auditors. In particular the directors can award other work to their auditors, such as management consultancy. Therefore, the financial statements must disclose:

- the audit fee for the year; plus

- fees paid by the company to the audit firm for any other work done during the year.

The shareholders will become suspicious if the auditors are receiving as much from their non-audit work as from their audit work. This is because the auditors will be unwilling to criticise the directors for fear of losing valuable work.

5 ACCOUNTING SYSTEMS AND BUSINESS ORGANISATIONS

5.1 INTRODUCTION – THE COMPANIES ACT

The Companies Act states that companies must maintain adequate accounting records.

These records must be sufficient to:

- show and explain the company's transactions

- show with reasonable accuracy, at any time, the financial position of the company

- enable the directors to ensure that any accounts required to be prepared comply with all the relevant requirements of the Companies Act and accounting standards.

This means that a company's accounting records must be able to:

- identify to whom goods and services have been sold (except for retail businesses)

- identify from whom goods and services were bought

- record all cash receipts and payments

- enable annual financial statements to be prepared.

The Act does not tell businesses how to achieve these requirements.

A small company (in terms of volume of transactions) would probably only need a cash book, remittance advices and files of paid and unpaid invoices. There would be no need for a computerised accounts package or even a nominal ledger. As long as these records were kept there would be sufficient information to enable their accountants to prepare the annual financial statements.

Larger companies will obviously need much more formal accounting systems, not just to comply with the law but also to ensure that they have the information to enable them to monitor and control what is going on in their business.

5.2 OTHER LEGAL REQUIREMENTS

For many small businesses, the need for modern accounting systems arises when they hit the VAT threshold and have to start keeping detailed and auditable records of sales and purchases, receipts and payments.

Likewise, once employees are taken on then there is a legal obligation to maintain records of PAYE and National Insurance contributions.

5.3 ORGANISATIONAL STRUCTURES

Businesses can be highly centralised or decentralised. A centralised business will have one large accounts department with very rigid and formal accounting procedures. A decentralised business will have smaller systems at its various locations that then submit returns on a weekly or monthly basis to the head office. This is more flexible than a centralised system, but it does increase the risk of errors and fraud.

The choice of a centralised or decentralised organisational structure will depend upon the nature of the business. A manufacturing business will tend to be centralised, whereas a professional organisation will be decentralised. Indeed, many national chains of accountants or estate agents are often in fact collections of virtually independent offices and businesses.

Overseas operations also tend to be fairly independent of the head office. They will usually have completely separate accounting systems to take into account their different legal and business environments.

5.4 CONFIDENTIALITY

Accountants in all organisations have access to commercially sensitive and personal information. It is essential that this information is kept secure and is not disclosed to unauthorised people. All professional accountants, and that includes CAT students, must treat all information that they receive in the strictest confidence.

All businesses will have commercially sensitive information such as the profitability of their products, the terms that they get from their suppliers and so on. They form a key part of the knowledge and experience that makes them successful. If the information is disclosed it could damage relations with business contacts, or give rivals an opportunity to compete.

Disclosure of payroll information can also be damaging. Not only can it be embarrassing for those concerned and give rise to disputes, but it is also a breach of the company's duty of confidentiality towards its employees.

If you work for a publicly quoted company (a plc whose shares are traded on the stock exchange) then you will have access to what is known as price sensitive information. This is information that might affect the price of the company's shares on the stock exchange. For example, if you knew that your company had just won a hugely profitable new contract, then you could buy some shares in the hope that they would go up in value when the news was publicly announced. Using price sensitive information, or passing it on to others, is known as insider dealing. It is a criminal offence.

KEY TERMS

Limited company – also known as a *limited liability company*. A company jointly owned by shareholders. The shareholders enjoy limited liability.

Limited liability – the shareholders of a limited company are not personally liable for any losses incurred by the company.

Share capital – the money contributed to a company by its owners, the shareholders. Share capital does not have to be repaid.

Directors – the people appointed by the shareholders to manage a company.

Stewardship – the idea that directors are managing a company for the benefit of the shareholders rather than for themselves.

Ordinary shares – the basic sort of share capital. Ordinary shares will claim a share of the profits and net assets of a company, after all other claims have been met. Ordinary shareholders elect the Board of Directors.

Preference shares – all preference shares are different, but typically these shares will receive a fixed dividend and a fixed share of the net assets of the company. Preference shareholders do not normally have any voting rights.

Auditors – an independent group of professional accountants, appointed by the shareholders, who ensure that the annual accounts prepared by the directors show a true and fair view.

SELF TEST QUESTIONS

		Paragraph
1	Who are the managers of a company?	1.2
2	Who are the owners of a company?	1.2
3	What are the key factors that distinguish a company from a sole trader?	1.3
4	What is the difference between a private and a public company?	1.5
5	What is the relationship between the nominal value and the market value of a company's shares?	3.3
6	What are preference shares?	3.7
7	What are debentures?	3.9
8	What is meant by the term 'stewardship'?	4.1
9	What sort of accounting records are required by the Companies Act?	5.1
10	What offence will you have committed if you use or pass on price sensitive information?	5.4

EXAM-STYLE QUESTION

LIMITED COMPANIES COMPARISONS

A client of your firm has been trading successfully as a sole trader in the UK for a number of years. However, her business has grown so much that she now thinks it is time to consider converting the business into a limited company.

You are to meet your client tomorrow to discuss her plans.

Required:

Prepare some brief notes for the meeting that explain:

(a) the main advantages and disadvantages of operating as a limited company rather than as a sole trader **(8 marks)**

(b) the main types of share capital and their characteristics. **(7 marks)**

(Total: 15 marks)

For a suggested answer, see the 'Answers' section at the end of the book.

Chapter 3

THE FORMAT OF PUBLISHED FINANCIAL STATEMENTS

This chapter looks at the format and content of published financial statements. This chapter is mainly here for reference; you are unlikely to be asked to sketch out the Companies Act Formats by themselves. Instead, you should refer back to them when preparing financial statements. Note that the examiner has said that it would be unusual for the exam not to include the preparation of a profit and loss account and/or balance sheet.This chapter covers syllabus area 1(e).

CONTENTS

1   The balance sheet

2   Notes to the balance sheet – fixed assets

3   Notes to the balance sheet – current assets

4   Notes to the balance sheet – creditors

5   Notes to the balance sheet – capital and reserves

6   The profit and loss account – formats

7   Small and medium-sized companies

LEARNING OUTCOMES

This chapter provides reference material for the preparation of company financial statements. The actual preparation of these statements is looked at in the next chapter. At the end of this chapter you should be familiar with:

•   the format and content of the profit and loss account and balance sheet

•   the notes to the accounts.

1 THE BALANCE SHEET

1.1 THE FORMAT

The Companies Act 1985(1989) provides two allowable formats for the balance sheet. It is expected that new legislation to accompany the Companies Act 2006 will maintain this. The most popular, Format 1 (the vertical balance sheet) is illustrated below.

The example is annotated by notes (which would not, of course, appear in a set of published accounts) setting out the most important disclosure and accounting requirements of the Companies Act. These notes refer to the appropriate paragraphs where each of these items is explained further.

Example plc
Balance sheet at 31 December 20X4

	Notes	20X4 £000	20X3 £000
Fixed assets			
Intangible assets	(2.2)	153	101
Tangible assets	(2.3)	1,986	1,753
Investments		29	33
		2,168	1,887
Current assets			
Stocks	(3.2)	1,637	1,598
Debtors	(3.3)	2,079	1,635
Investments	(3.4)	126	39
Cash at bank and in hand		75	41
		3,917	3,313
Creditors: amounts falling due within one year	(4.2)	3,010	2,980
Net current assets		907	333
Total assets less current liabilities		3,075	2,220
Creditors: amounts falling due after more than one year	(4.3)	910	495
Provisions for liabilities	(4.4)	27	13
		937	508
		2,138	1,712
Capital and reserves			
Called up share capital	(5.1)	1,500	1,500
Share premium account		23	23
Revaluation reserve	(5.2)	25	25
Other reserves	(5.2)	117	67
Profit and loss account	(5.2)	473	97
		2,138	1,712

The accounts were approved by the directors on 3 March 20X5.

Colyn Example

Director

1.2 APPROVAL AND SIGNING OF ACCOUNTS

A company's individual (and consolidated) accounts must be approved by the board of directors and the company's individual balance sheet must be signed on behalf of the board by a director. The copy of the balance sheet which is sent to the Registrar of Companies must also be signed by a director.

In addition, the directors' report must be approved by the board of directors and signed on behalf of the board by a director or the company secretary.

1.3 ACCOUNTING POLICIES

The notes to the accounts must state the accounting policies adopted by the company for all material items in the financial statements, for example, depreciation of fixed assets and valuation of stocks.

2 NOTES TO THE BALANCE SHEET – FIXED ASSETS

2.1 CLASSIFICATION OF FIXED ASSETS

Assets are classified as fixed assets if they are intended for use on a continuing basis in the company's activities.

Fixed assets are subdivided as follows:

Intangible fixed assets: These are assets that have no physical form, such as patents and goodwill.

Tangible assets: These assets have physical form, such as buildings.

Investments: This relates to long-term investments in other companies. It includes shares and loans made to other companies.

2.2 INTANGIBLE ASSETS

The notes to the accounts will detail the total of intangible assets in the balance sheet. The following intangible assets are on your syllabus.

	20X4 £000	20X3 £000
Development costs	73	31
Concessions, patents, licences and trade marks	26	13
Goodwill	54	57
	153	101

2.3 TANGIBLE FIXED ASSETS

The tangible fixed asset note analyses the total net book value shown in the balance sheet by category, and by cost and cumulative depreciation.

The movements for the year (by category, cost and depreciation) are disclosed as follows:

- opening balance

- additions/charges for the year

- effect of revaluations

- disposals

- closing balance.

Tangible fixed assets are covered in detail in a later chapter.

An example of a fixed asset note is shown below:

	Land and buildings	Plant and machinery	Fixtures, fittings, tools and equipment	Payments on account and assets in course of construction	Total
	£000	£000	£000	£000	£000
Cost or valuation:					
At 1 January 20X4	871	998	207	27	2,103
Additions	74	809	25	13	921
Disposals	–	(23)	(5)	–	(28)
At 31 December 20X4	945	1,784	227	40	2,996
Accumulated depreciation:					
At 1 January 20X4	33	292	25	–	350
Provision for year	11	622	27	8	668
Disposals	–	(4)	(4)	–	(8)
At 31 December 20X4	44	910	48	8	1,010
Net book amount: at 31 December 20X4	901	874	179	32	1,986
at 31 December 20X3	838	706	182	27	1,753

2.4 FIXED ASSET INVESTMENTS

These are investments that the company intends to keep for more than twelve months from the balance sheet date. They will normally be stated as costs and charged against profit in the profit and loss account. However, investments can also be treated as an expenditure creating a fixed asset.

3 NOTES TO THE BALANCE SHEET – CURRENT ASSETS

3.1 CLASSIFICATION OF CURRENT ASSETS

Current assets are assets that are expected to be converted into cash within twelve months. For example, stocks will be sold and converted into cash or debtors. Debtors in turn will settle their debts in cash. If it becomes apparent that the amount of cash that will be received will be less than the book value of the asset, then the asset should be written down to its recoverable amount. This is the basis for valuing stocks at the lower of cost and net realisable value, and for making allowances for doubtful receivables.

3.2 STOCKS

Stocks are stated at the lower of cost and net realisable value. They will be analysed as follows:

	20X4	20X3
	£000	£000
Raw materials and consumables	437	505
Work in progress	306	281
Finished goods and goods for resale	894	812
	1,637	1,598

Long-term contracts are also part of stocks, but they are specifically excluded from the CAT Syllabus.

3.3 DEBTORS

The carrying value of debtors will be reduced by an allowance for irrecoverable debts. Debtors will be analysed as follows:

	20X4	20X3
	£000	£000
Trade debtors	1,327	1,191
Other debtors	408	250
Prepayments and accrued income	344	194
	2,079	1,635

The total amount of debtors that will not be settled within one year are disclosed separately.

3.4 CURRENT ASSET INVESTMENTS

These are investments that the company intends to sell within the next 12 months from the balance sheet date. They will normally be stated at the lower of cost and market value.

4 NOTES TO THE BALANCE SHEET – CREDITORS

4.1 CLASSIFICATION

On the face of the balance sheet, creditors are analysed between amounts due within one year and amounts due after one year. The notes to the accounts should also note any amounts that are not due for more than five years.

4.2 CREDITORS: AMOUNTS FALLING DUE WITHIN ONE YEAR

In a sole trader's balance sheet, this section would be described as current liabilities. A typical creditor's note will include the following items:

	20X4	20X3
	£000	£000
Debenture loans	200	–
Bank loans and overdrafts	20	20
Trade creditors	1,281	1,007
Taxation and social security	35	11
Proposed dividends	30	–
Other creditors	62	613
Accruals and deferred income	1,382	1,329
	3,010	2,980

Technically, overdrafts are due on demand and so they are shown as being due within one year. Only the current portion of debentures and loans will be shown here. Instalments due after one year will be classified separately (see below).

4.3 CREDITORS: AMOUNTS FALLING DUE AFTER MORE THAN ONE YEAR

Typically, this will only include debentures and loans. An example is noted below:

	20X4	20X3
	£000	£000
Debenture loans	510	300
Other loans	400	195
	910	495

The interest rates and repayment dates of these loans should also be disclosed.

4.4 PROVISIONS FOR LIABILITIES

	20X4	20X3
	£000	£000
Deferred taxation	24	10
Other provisions	3	3
	27	13

Provisions are made for liabilities of uncertain timing or amount.

5 NOTES TO THE BALANCE SHEET – CAPITAL AND RESERVES

5.1 CALLED UP SHARE CAPITAL

	20X4	20X3
	£000	£000
Allotted and fully paid:		
Ordinary shares of £1 each	1,200	1,200
6% preference shares of 50p each	300	300
	1,500	1,500

Any movement in the share capital of the company should be disclosed. The authorised share capital should also be disclosed.

5.2 RESERVES

The movements on reserves should be disclosed.

	Profit and loss account	Other reserves	Revaluation reserve
	£000	£000	£000
At 1 January 20X4	97	67	25
Transfer between reserves	(50)	50	–
– Retained profit for the year	426	–	–
At 31 December 20X4	473	117	25

6 THE PROFIT AND LOSS ACCOUNT – FORMATS

6.1 THE FORMATS

As with the balance sheet there is a choice of profit and loss account formats.

Format 1 is known as the 'operational' statement. It is the most common, and the example in 6.2 below uses this format. The alternative, Format 2, is known as the 'type of expenditure' statement. A list of the usual headings for Format 2 is noted in 6.6 below.

6.2 THE PROFIT AND LOSS ACCOUNT – AN EXAMPLE OF PRESENTATION

Example plc
Profit and loss account for the year ended 31 December 20X4

	Notes	20X4 £000	20X3 £000
Turnover (sales)	(6.3)	4,910	3,505
Cost of sales		(2,475)	(1,210)
Gross profit		2,435	2,295
Distribution costs		(716)	(946)
Administrative expenses		(756)	(1,198)
Other operating income		13	7
Interest receivable and similar income		19	11
Interest payable and similar charges		(85)	(57)
Profit on ordinary activities before taxation	(6.4)	910	112
Tax on profit on ordinary activities	(6.5)	386	22
Profit for the financial year		524	90

6.3 TURNOVER (SALES)

Turnover should be analysed by geographic location and business category. However, the detailed disclosures required by SSAP 25 *Segmental Reporting* are not on the CAT Syllabus.

6.4 PROFIT ON ORDINARY ACTIVITIES BEFORE TAXATION

Various items charged in reaching this figure must be disclosed. A typical example would include the following:

	20X4 £000	20X3 £000
Profit before taxation is stated after charging		
Depreciation and amortisation	701	450
Staff costs	2,022	2,290
Auditors' remuneration	28	22
Directors' remuneration	307	142
Exceptional items: Stock write off	123	–

6.5 TAX ON PROFIT ON ORDINARY ACTIVITIES

	20X4 £000	20X3 £000
Taxation on the profit for the year:		
UK corporation tax at 31%	356	39
Under (over) provision in previous year	12	(27)
Deferred tax	18	10
	386	22

6.6   TYPICAL HEADINGS FOR FORMAT 2

1   Turnover

2   Change in stocks of finished goods and in work in progress

3   Own work capitalised

4   Other operating income

5   Raw materials and consumables

6   Staff costs:

7   Depreciation

8   Other operating charges

9   Income from fixed asset investments

10   Other interest receivable and similar income

11   Amounts written off investments

12   Interest payable and similar charges

13   Tax on profit or loss on ordinary activities

14   Profit or loss on ordinary activities after taxation

15   Profit or loss for the financial year

7   SMALL AND MEDIUM-SIZED COMPANIES

7.1   INTRODUCTION

The Companies Act allows small or medium companies to file 'abbreviated' accounts with the Registrar of Companies. They are, however, still required to send full accounts to their members.

7.2   CRITERIA

A company qualifies as small or medium if, for the financial year in question and the immediately preceding financial year, it is within the limits of at least two of the following three criteria:

Size criteria	Small	Medium
Balance sheet total (i.e., total assets)	£2,800,000	£11,400,000
Turnover*	£5,600,000	£22,800,000
Average number of employees	50	250

* adjust pro rata where period more or less than 12 months.

Public companies, banks and insurance companies cannot file abbreviated accounts.

7.3 EXEMPTIONS AND ABBREVIATIONS PERMITTED FOR SMALL COMPANIES

(a)   A directors' report is not required.

(b)   A profit and loss account is not required.

(c)   An 'abbreviated balance sheet' is allowed.

(d)   Only a limited number of the notes to the accounts.

7.4 EXEMPTIONS AND ABBREVIATIONS PERMITTED FOR MEDIUM-SIZED COMPANIES

(a)   A full directors' report is required.

(b)   An abbreviated profit and loss account is allowed which begins with the item 'gross profit or loss'.

(c)   A full balance sheet is required.

(d)   A full set of notes is required, apart from details of turnover.

7.5 FINANCIAL REPORTING STANDARD FOR SMALLER ENTITIES (FRSSE)

The ASB has issued a revised Financial Reporting Standard for Smaller Entities (FRSSE).

The FRSSE is a comprehensive standard containing the measurement and disclosure requirements most relevant to smaller entities. It contains the requirements in existing accounting standards and UITF Abstracts that are relevant to smaller entities, in simplified form. It also includes the relevant requirements of the Companies Act.

The FRSSE applies to:

(a)   companies incorporated under companies legislation and entitled to the exemptions available for small companies when filing accounts with the Registrar of Companies; or

(b)   entities that would have come into category (a) above had they been companies incorporated under companies' legislation.

Adoption of the FRSSE is optional. An entity that chooses to adopt the FRSSE is exempt from all other accounting standards and UITF Abstracts.

SELF TEST QUESTIONS

Paragraph

1   What disclosure is required for tangible fixed assets?   2.3

2   What are the general rules for valuing current assets?   3.1

3   What are the typical categories for *creditors: amounts falling due within one year?*   4.2

4   What are the main modifications to financial statements that are allowed for small companies?   7.3

Chapter 4

FROM TRIAL BALANCE TO PUBLISHED ACCOUNTS

This chapter looks at the preparation of published financial statements in the Companies Act format. Most of the techniques in this chapter are the same as for sole traders, and so they should be familiar to you from Paper 3. The exercises concentrate on the format of the statements and the presentation of capital, dividends, and taxation. Later chapters will look at individual elements of the financial statements in more detail. This chapter covers syllabus area 2(a).

CONTENTS

1   Key differences between a sole trader's accounts and limited company accounts

2   Worked example: Simple plc

3   Other adjustments and apportioning expenses

4   Limited company accounts for internal use

LEARNING OUTCOMES

At the end of this chapter you should be able to:

- prepare the financial statements for a limited company from a trial balance, including adjustments for items including:

    (i)   corporation tax

    (ii)   dividends

    (iii) closing stock

    (iv) share capital

    (v)   accruals and prepayments

- prepare the financial statements of limited companies in accordance with the prescribed formats and relevant accounting standards.

1 KEY DIFFERENCES BETWEEN SOLE TRADER'S ACCOUNTS AND LIMITED COMPANY ACCOUNTS

Before we prepare our first set of limited company accounts we need to identify the key differences between sole trader's accounts and published financial statements of limited companies. This is obviously not a complete list; the rest of the text will fill in some more of the detail.

1.1 CAPITAL AND RESERVES

In limited company accounts the capital introduced by the shareholders is classified separately in the balance sheet. It is split between nominal value and share premium. The nominal value is defined by law. The premium is any extra money received by the company when the shares were first issued.

The reserves are the retained profits of the company. They consist of the brought forward reserves, plus the net profit for the year, less dividends. This movement on reserves is often noted at the end of the profit and loss account, although it can also be shown in a note.

1.2 DIVIDENDS

Dividends for limited companies are the equivalent of drawings for a sole trader. They are debited to the profit and loss reserve, but are not shown on the face of the profit and loss account. The total dividend for the year consists of an interim dividend (which will normally be recorded in the trial balance) and a final dividend, which may need to be adjusted for.

1.3 TAXATION

Tax does not appear in a sole trader's profit and loss account. However, limited companies pay corporation tax, and this will be charged to the profit and loss account. The tax will not be paid until nine months after the year-end, and so the charge for the year will be a liability at the year-end. The closing liability is an estimate, and any over or under estimate is reversed out through the following year's profit and loss account.

1.4 COST OF SALES

Only the net cost of sales will be shown in the profit and loss account. The detailed working is not disclosed.

1.5 DISTRIBUTION COSTS: ADMINISTRATIVE EXPENSES

All other operating expenses are grouped together under one of these two headings. In the following example this has already been done for you, but future examples will require you to allocate expenses to these headings.

1.6 FIXED ASSETS

Fixed assets are analysed out in a note to the accounts. Only the total net book value appears in the balance sheet.

1.7 NOTES AND WORKINGS

Notes are printed and published as part of the financial statements. Their contents are often specified by law or by an accounting standard.

Workings are confidential. They will not be published.

2 WORKED EXAMPLE: SIMPLE PLC

This example takes a simplified trial balance and prepares a profit and loss account and balance sheet in limited company format. The Trial Balance has already been adjusted for most routine items such as accruals, prepayments, bad debts and depreciation. However, the following items will need to be adjusted for:

- closing stock

- taxation

- dividends.

2.1 SITUATION

Simple plc has been trading for a number of years manufacturing domestic appliances. Its trial balance for the year-ending 31 August 20X4 is noted below, along with some additional information.

Additional information

(1)   Closing stock has been counted and valued at £978,000.

(2)   The tax charge for the year has been estimated at £879,000.

(3)   A final dividend of 75 pence per share was prepared.

(4)   All other routine adjustments have been made (e.g. depreciation, irrecoverable debts).

Required:

Prepare Simple plc's Profit and Loss Account and Balance Sheet for the year-ended 31 August 20X4.

Simple plc
Trial balance as at 31 August 20X4

	Dr £000	Cr £000
Sales		14,345
Opening stock	1,456	
Purchases	4,239	
Manufacturing wages	2,386	
Other manufacturing costs	646	
Selling and distribution costs	1,895	
Administration costs	998	
Interest payable	400	
Interim dividend paid	900	
Long-term investments	900	
Fixed assets at cost	6,579	
Depreciation		2,756
Trade debtors	1,923	
Prepayments	489	
Staff loans	12	
Bank and cash balances	267	
Bank overdraft		450
Trade creditors		534
Accruals		123
Debenture redeemable in 20Y8		3,000
Two million ordinary shares of 25 pence each		500
Share premium		250
Retained profits: 1 September 20X3		1,132
	23,090	23,090

Guidance

General guidance

(a)   The **headings** in the Companies Act format must be kept to.

For example, only the net amount for cost of sales is shown on the face of the P&L, whereas a sole-trader's profit and loss account shows the full calculation. For a company, the detailed workings are confidential and are never published.

Also, only the total amount for creditors will be shown on the face of the balance sheet. The individual components are shown in a note to the accounts. The same is true for fixed assets and debtors.

(b)   **Notes** and **workings**.

Notes form part of the financial statements. They are printed and published for all to see. Notes should tie in exactly with the relevant line in the balance sheet or profit and loss account. For example the net book value for fixed assets from the fixed asset note equals the value for fixed assets shown on the face of the balance sheet.

Workings are confidential, and they are not published. They do not form part of the financial statements.

Detailed guidance

(a)   The **cost of sales** should be calculated as a working. Cost of sales will include all manufacturing costs, not just purchases. A pro forma has been provided to guide you. Don't forget to adjust for the closing stock. The journal entry will be:

Debit	Balance sheet	Stock
Credit	Profit and loss account	Cost of sales

(b) **Taxation**. Companies have to pay Corporation Tax on their profits. At the year-end the accountant will estimate the amount of tax which will be payable and provide for it in the financial statements. This is a charge against profits and a liability at the year-end. The journal entry will be as follows:

Debit	Profit and loss account	Tax expense
Credit	Balance sheet	Creditors: Corporation tax

It is payable nine months after the year-end.

(Tax does not appear in the accounts of sole traders and partnerships. This is because the owners of unincorporated businesses pay their tax personally. The tax charge is calculated on the basis of how much the individual has earned from all sources, rather than on how much profit one particular business made. The tax is also a personal liability of the proprietor rather than a liability of the business.)

(c) **Dividends**. The owners of the business – the shareholders – own all of the post-tax profits. However, they will not want to take out all of the company's profits otherwise there would be no cash left for re-investment and growth. The amount of cash that they take out is known as the dividend. It is a distribution of profits, and it is similar to drawings in a sole trader. Dividends must be shared out equally amongst all of the equity shares in issue, and so they are calculated on the basis of pence per share.

Typically there will be two dividends in any one accounting period. An interim dividend will be proposed and paid half way through the year. The trial balance will have accounted for this. A final dividend will be proposed at the year-end but not paid until after the year-end.

Dividends payable are not normally included in the financial statements. This is because they are not usually declared (confirmed) until after the year-end and so are not liabilities of the company at the year-end. Dividends proposed at the year end, but not yet declared are disclosed in a note to the financial statements (Note 1 in this example).

The exception to this rule is where a dividend is actually declared at or before the year-end. In this case, the dividend **is** a liability of the company and is accrued as a post-trial balance adjustment (as in this example).

The journal entry will be:

Debit	Profit and loss account reserve Dividends paid and payable.
Credit	Balance sheet	Creditors: Dividends payable.

Only accrue for a dividend if the question clearly states that it was declared before the year-end.

(d) The profits left in the business are known as the retained profits and they form part of the reserves of the company. The retained profits for this year are added to those brought forward from last year to form the carry-down reserves. These carry-down reserves form the profit and loss account or reserve shown in the balance sheet. (The brought forward reserves are taken from the trial balance.)

(e) **Investments** can either be long-term or short-term. Long-term investments are treated as fixed assets, whereas short-term investments are current assets.

(f) **Tangible fixed assets**. Only the total net book value is shown on the face of the balance sheet. The notes will detail the categories of asset by their cost, depreciation and net book value.

(g) The total amount of **debtors** will be shown on the face of the balance sheet. The notes will disclose the details.

(h) **Cash** in hand is an asset. **Overdrafts** are liabilities. They must not be netted-off.

(i) The total amount of **creditors** will be shown on the face of the balance sheet. The notes will disclose the details. Remember to split out long-term liabilities from those due within 12 months.

Simple plc: Profit and loss account: Year ended 31 August 20X4

		£000
(a)	Turnover	
	Cost of sales	
	Gross profit	
	Distribution costs	
	Administrative expenses	
	Operating profit	
	Interest received/paid and similar items	
	Profit on ordinary activities before taxation	
(b)	Taxation	
	Profit for the financial year	

Simple plc: Balance sheet as at 31 August 20X4

			£000	£000
	Fixed assets			
(e)	Investments			
(f)	Tangible fixed assets	*Note 2*		
	Current assets			
	Stocks			
(g)	Debtors	*Note 3*		
	Investments			
(h)	Cash			
(i)	**Creditors:** Amounts due within one year	*Note 4*		
	Net current assets			
	Total assets less current liabilities			
(i)	**Creditors:** Amounts falling due after more than one year			
	Net assets			
	Capital and reserves			
	Called up share capital			
	Share premium			
(d)	Profit and loss reserve			
	Total shareholders' funds			

Notes to the accounts

Note 1   Dividends

£000

Interim dividend paid of   45   pence per share
Final dividend proposed of   [   ]   pence per share

(Remember that there are two million shares in issue.)

Note 2   Tangible fixed assets

£000

Cost or valuation
Depreciation
Net book value

(Note: This is a very simplified version of the full note required by law.)

Note 3   Debtors

£000

Trade debtors
Prepayments
Other debtors

Note 4   Creditors: amounts falling due within one year

£000

Bank overdrafts
Trade creditors
Accruals
Corporation Tax
Dividends

(W1) Cost of sales

£000

Opening stock
Purchases
Manufacturing wages
Other manufacturing costs
Less closing stock

(W2) Profit and loss reserve

£000

B/f
Profit for the financial year
Dividends paid
C/f

2.2 SOLUTION TO SIMPLE PLC

Simple plc: Profit and loss account: Year ended 31 August 20X4

	£000
Turnover	14,345
Cost of sales (W1)	(7,749)
Gross profit	6,596
Distribution costs	(1,895)
Administrative expenses	(998)
Operating profit	3,703
Interest received/paid and similar items	(400)
Profit on ordinary activities before taxation	3,303
Taxation	(879)
Profit for the financial year	2,424

Simple plc: Balance sheet as at 31 August 20X4

		£000	£000
Fixed assets			
Tangible fixed assets	**Note 2**		3,823
Investments			900
			4,723
Current assets			
Stocks		978	
Debtors	**Note 3**	2,424	
Cash		267	
		3,669	
Creditors: Amounts due within one year	**Note 4**	1,986	
Net current assets			1,683
Total assets less current liabilities			6,406
Creditors: Amounts falling due after more than one year			(3,000)
Net assets			3,406
Capital and reserves			
Called up share capital			500
Share premium			250
Profit and loss reserve (W2)			2,656
Total shareholders' funds			3,406

Notes to the accounts

Note 1   Dividends

	£000
Interim dividend paid of 45 pence per share	900
Final dividend proposed of 75 pence per share	1,500
	2,400

Note 2   Tangible fixed assets

	£000
Cost or valuation	6,579
Depreciation	(2,756)
Net book value	3,823

Note 3   Debtors

	£000
Trade debtors	1,923
Prepayments	489
Other debtors	12
	2,424

Note 4   Creditors: amounts falling due within one year

	£000
Bank overdrafts	450
Trade creditors	534
Accruals	123
Corporation tax	879
	1,986

(W1) Cost of sales

	£000
Opening stock	1,456
Purchases	4,239
Manufacturing wages	2,386
Other manufacturing costs	646
Less closing stock	(978)
	7,749

(W2) Profit and loss reserve

	£000
B/f	1,132
Profit for the financial year	2,424
Dividends paid	(900)
C/f	2,656

ACTIVITY 1

Straight plc has been trading for a number of years manufacturing steel girders. Its trial balance for the year ending 31 March 20X6 is shown below, along with some additional information.

Straight plc
Trial balance as at 31 March 20X6

	Dr £000	Cr £000
Sales		28,297
Opening stock	3,206	
Purchases	8,162	
Manufacturing wages	7,333	
Other manufacturing costs	974	
Distribution costs	2,020	
Administrative expenses	635	
Investment income		246
Interest paid on the bank overdraft	50	
Interim dividend	800	
Long-term investments	2,885	
Fixed assets at cost	15,753	
Depreciation		4,396
Trade debtors	2,967	
Prepayments	132	
Staff loans	23	
Bank and cash balances	110	
Bank overdraft		1,978
Trade creditors		756
Over-provision for taxation as at March 20X5		56
Accruals		423
10% Debenture redeemable in 20Y5		3,000
Four million ordinary shares of 50 pence each		2,000
Share premium		300
Retained profits: 1 April 20X5		3,598
	45,050	45,050

Additional information

(1) Closing stock has been counted and valued at £1,263,000.

(2) The tax charge for the year has been estimated at £1,924,000.

(3) A final dividend of 60 pence per share has been proposed. This dividend was not declared until 15 April 20X6.

(4) No interest has been paid or charged on the debenture. The debenture was raised on 1 April 20X5. This will have to be accrued for.

(5) All other routine adjustments have been made (e.g. depreciation, irrecoverable debts).

Required:

Prepare Straight plc's profit and loss account and balance sheet for the year-ended 31 March 20X6. You should answer in £000s.

For a suggested answer, see the 'Answers' section at the end of the book.

3 OTHER ADJUSTMENTS AND APPORTIONING EXPENSES

3.1 OTHER ADJUSTMENTS

The previous examples only adjusted for closing stock and accrued tax and dividends. In real life, and in questions, you may need to adjust for accruals, prepayments, doubtful debts, and depreciation. These adjustments are made in the normal way, as for a sole trader.

3.2 APPORTIONING EXPENSES

The company profit and loss account classifies and reports expenses under three headings:

- cost of sales
- distribution costs
- administrative expenses.

In the previous examples the expenses had already been allocated to these headings. In real life, and in examinations, you may be asked to perform this task yourself. This is done in two stages:

(1) Specific costs are allocated to the appropriate heading e.g. purchases are charged to cost of sales, advertising to distribution costs.

(2) General costs are apportioned e.g. rent could be apportioned to the three heading on the basis of the amount of floor space taken up by the factory (cost of sales), distribution depot and marketing office (distribution), and the general office (administration). Any reasonable basis of apportionment is acceptable. An exam question should make the basis of apportionment obvious.

Example

Solo Ltd's trial balance shows the following expenses:

	Notes	£000
Opening stock	1	132
Purchases		867
Factory wages		465
Depreciation of machinery		213
Depreciation of delivery vehicles		150
Depreciation of office equipment	2	87
Rent and rates	3	207
Office salaries	4	360
Advertising		138
Debenture interest		55

Notes

(1) Closing stock is £174,000.

(2) 2/3 of the office equipment by net book value is used by the sales and marketing department. The rest is used for general administration.

(3)   Rent and rates will be apportioned in accordance with floor space as follows:

Factory	6,000 square metres
Delivery facilities and marketing office	2,000 square metres
General administration	1,000 square metres

(4)   65% of the office salaries relate to delivery, sales and marketing staff.

Required:

Allocate and apportion these expenses between *cost of sales*, *distribution costs*, and *administrative expenses* from the Format 1 Profit and Loss Account.

Solution

The easiest approach is to set out a table with a line for each expense and a column for each classification. Then go through the expenses allocating and apportioning them as appropriate.

	Total from TB £000		Cost of sales £000	Distribution £000	Admin. £000
Opening stock	132	Allocated	132		
Purchases	867	Allocated	867		
Factory wages	465	Allocated	465		
Depreciation:					
Machinery	213	Allocated	213		
delivery vehicles	150	Allocated		150	
office equipment	87	0 : 2 : 1		58	29
Rent and rates	207	6 : 2 : 1	138	46	23
Office salaries	360	0 : 65 : 35		234	126
Advertising	138	Allocated		138	
Closing stock		Allocated	(174)		
			1,641	**626**	**178**

Note

*   Closing stock is not normally shown in the trial balance.

*   Interest is a finance cost and will be disclosed separately.

4   LIMITED COMPANY ACCOUNTS FOR INTERNAL USE

In this chapter and the previous chapter, we have looked at the preparation of company financial statements for external use (often called published financial statements). As we have seen, these must be set out in a particular format and specific items must be disclosed.

Limited company accounts may also be prepared for internal use by management. These need not comply with the exact requirements of the Companies Act. In practice, accounts for internal use are normally more detailed than those for external use:

*   The profit and loss account shows amounts for purchases, opening stock and closing stock rather than one figure for cost of sales.

*   It also lists the expense accounts individually, rather than summarising them as distribution costs and administrative expenses.

EXAM-STYLE QUESTION 1

FLOYD LTD

You are presented with the following summarised trial balance of Floyd Ltd in respect of the year ended 31 March 20X5:

	£	£
Ordinary share capital (25p shares)		100,000
Plant and machinery:		
Cost	307,400	
Depreciation (1 Apr 20X4)		84,600
Debtors	52,030	
Creditors		38,274
Stock	61,070	
Profit and loss b/d		45,910
Cash at bank	41,118	
Cash in hand	126	
Share premium account		20,000
Sales		998,600
Dividend paid	2,500	
Provision for doubtful debts		1,860
9% debenture stock 20X9		75,000
Cost of sales	800,000	
Administrative costs	100,000	
	1,364,244	1,364,244

The following final adjustments are required:

(1)   The allowance for doubtful debts is to be adjusted to 5% of the debtors figure. The charge is to be included in administrative costs.

(2)   Corporation tax on the current year profits is estimated at £31,200.

(3)   Depreciation at 10% of cost is to be provided. The charge is to be included in cost of sales.

(4)   Interest for the year ended 31 March 20X5 was paid on 1 April 20X5. No accrual has been made.

You are required to prepare a profit and loss account for the year ended 31 March 20X5, and a balance sheet as at that date, insofar as information permits.

(20 marks)

EXAM-STYLE QUESTION 2

MOORFOOT

Moorfoot Limited operates a chain of wholesale grocery outlets. Its trial balance at 30 June 20X1 was as follows:

	£000	£000
Sales revenue		13,600
Purchases	8,100	
Stock 1 July 20X0	1,530	
Distribution costs	1,460	
Administrative expenses	1,590	
Interest on debentures	50	
Dividends paid: Final for year ended 30 June 20X7	480	
Interim for year ended 30 June 20X8	360	
Freehold land at cost	1,510	
Buildings		
– Cost	8,300	
– Accumulated depreciation at 30 June 20X0		1,020
Warehouse and office equipment		
– Cost	1,800	
– Accumulated depreciation at 30 June 20X0		290
Motor vehicles		
– Cost	1,680	
– Accumulated depreciation at 30 June 20X0		620
Trade debtors	810	
Allowance for doubtful debts		18
Cash at bank	140	
Trade creditors		820
10% debentures (issued five years ago and to be redeemed 20Y1)		1,000
Called up share capital – Ordinary shares of 25p each		1,200
Share premium account		2,470
Profit and loss account 30 June 20X0		6,772
	27,810	27,810

The following additional information is available:

(1) Closing stock was £1,660,000.

(2) Trade debts totalling £6,000 are to be written off and the allowance for doubtful debts increased to £30,000. It is the company's practice to include the charge for irrecoverable and doubtful debts in administrative expenses in the profit and loss account.

(3) Accruals and prepayments:

	Prepayments	Accruals
	£000	£000
Distribution costs	60	120
Administrative expenses	70	190
Interest on debentures		50

(4) In early July 20X1 the company received invoices for credit purchases totalling £18,000 for goods delivered before 30 June. These invoices have not been included in the purchases ledger at 30 June 20X1.

It was also found that credit sales invoices totalling £7,000 for goods delivered to customers before 30 June 20X1 had mistakenly been dated in July 20X1 and thus excluded from sales for the year and from debtors at the year end.

The goods received had been included in the year end stock figure given at (1) above, and the goods sold had been excluded from it. No adjustment to the stock figure is therefore required.

(5)   Depreciation should be provided as follows:

Land	Nil
Buildings	2% per year on cost
Warehouse and office equipment	15% per year on cost
Motor vehicles	25% per year on cost

All depreciation is to be divided equally between distribution costs and administrative expenses.

Required:

Prepare the company's profit and loss account for the year ended 30 June 20X1, and balance sheet as at that date, complying as far as possible with the requirements of the Companies Act. Ignore taxation. Notes to the financial statements are not required.

(30 marks)

For suggested answers, see the 'Answers' section at the end of the book.

Chapter 5

SHARE CAPITAL, DIVIDENDS AND TAXATION

This chapter takes a closer look at share capital, taxation and dividends, including how to adjust for these items from the trial balance. This chapter covers syllabus areas 2(a), 2(b) and 2(f).

CONTENTS

1   Ordinary shares

2   Ordinary dividends

3   Preference shares and dividends

4   Accounting for reserves

5   Debentures and other loans

6   Taxation

LEARNING OUTCOMES

At the end of this chapter you should be able to:

*   define and account for current tax

*   draft appropriate disclosure of current taxation in the published statements

*   distinguish between issued and authorised share capital and between called up and paid up share capital

*   distinguish between ordinary and preference shares

*   account for a share issue

*   explain the share premium account

*   define and account for a bonus issue and a rights issue

*   outline the advantages and disadvantages of a rights issue and a bonus issue

*   distinguish between the market value and nominal value of a share

- explain why companies will be concerned with the value of their shares

- define and account for debentures

- explain the advantages and disadvantages of raising finance by issuing debentures rather than issuing ordinary or preference shares.

1 ORDINARY SHARES

1.1 ORDINARY SHARES AND EQUITY

Every limited company must have ordinary shares in issue. These shares are known as the **equity** of the business. These shares represent the ownership interest in the business. Each ordinary share normally has one vote, and these votes appoint the Board of Directors. The shares themselves will be owned by **shareholders**. The ordinary shareholders as a body are known as the **members** of the company.

They are the last claimants to be repaid when a company is dissolved. They will receive all of the residual assets of the company after all of the liabilities have been settled. This means that they will receive all of the profits made by the company. It also means that if the company's assets exceed its liabilities then they will receive nothing. However, it must be remembered that the shareholders will not normally be required to make good any losses.

This section looks at how to record the initial issue of ordinary shares by a company. Once shares have been issued the shareholders may buy and sell their shares as they please. These later sales will not affect the books of the company. (In the same way that selling your car on the second hand market has no effect on the dealer that you bought your car from.)

1.2 AUTHORISED AND ISSUED SHARE CAPITAL; CALLED UP AND PAID UP SHARE CAPITAL

The **authorised share capital** is the maximum number of shares that a company may issue. This prevents the directors from issuing extra shares to themselves or their friends.

The Companies Act 1985 required every company to have an authorised share capital. The Companies Act 2006 has abolished authorised share capital for new companies. Existing companies will continue to have a maximum number of shares that can be issued.

The **issued share capital** is the actual number of shares in issue at any point in time. It is the issued share capital which appears on a company's balance sheet.

Usually, all of the shares in issue will have been paid for in full. However, when shares are first issued they are often paid for in instalments. This gives rise to the difference between called up and paid up share capital.

The **called up** share capital is the total nominal value payable by the share holder.

Paid up share capital is the amount of nominal value paid at the current date.

In Paper 6 all shares will be issued and paid for in full at the same time. There will be no partly paid shares.

1.3 ISSUE OF SHARES AT NOMINAL VALUE

When shares are issued at their nominal value they are said to have been issued at par. The double entry for issuing shares at their nominal value is:

		Debit	Credit
Debit	Cash	X	
Credit	Share Capital Account		X

with the issue proceeds.

Example

A company issues 200,000 50p ordinary shares at par. Write up the ledger accounts.

Solution

Cash book

	£		£
Ordinary share capital	100,000		

Ordinary share capital account

	£		£
		Cash	100,000

1.4 ISSUE OF SHARES AT A PREMIUM

Companies often issue their shares for more than their nominal value. The difference between the proceeds of issue and the nominal value is called the **share premium**, and it is credited to a separate account.

The double entry for issuing shares at a premium is:

		Debit	Credit
Debit	Cash	X	
Credit	Share Capital Account		X
Credit	Share Premium Account		X

Although shares can be issued at a premium, the Companies Act prohibits the issue of shares at a discount – in other words at a value less than their nominal value.

Example

Axe Ltd has just been incorporated. Its initial share issue was for 200,000 ordinary shares of 50 pence each at an issue price of 75p.

Required:

(a)   Write up the ledger accounts.

(b)   Show how these shares will be presented in the balance sheet.

Solution

Cash book

	£		£
Ordinary share capital	100,000		
Share premium	50,000		

Ordinary share capital account

	£		£
		Cash	100,000

Share premium account

	£		£
		Cash	50,000

Axe Ltd – Balance sheet extracts

		£
Net assets	(Cash)	150,000
Capital and reserves		
Called up share capital	200,000 Ordinary Shares of 50 pence each	100,000
Share premium account		50,000
P&L reserve		–
		150,000

ACTIVITY 1

Bradawl Ltd has been trading profitably for many years. Its balance sheet immediately before the share issue in this activity is noted below. Bradawl Ltd has just issued a further 500,000 ordinary shares of 25 pence each. The issue price for each share was 60 pence.

Bradawl Ltd – Balance sheet extracts

		£
Net assets (cash)		456,789
Capital and reserves		
Called up share capital	900,000 ordinary shares of 25 pence each	225,000
Share premium account		75,000
P&L reserve		156,789
		456,789

Required:

(a) Write up the ledger accounts.

(b) Show how these shares will be presented in the balance sheet.

Guidance

(1) The existing share capital and premium will be the brought forward balances in the T accounts.

(2) The net assets in the balance sheet will be increased by the cash proceeds.

(3) The balance sheet will show the carry down values for the share capital and share premium.

For a suggested answer, see the 'Answers' section at the end of the book.

1.5 USES OF THE SHARE PREMIUM ACCOUNT

The share premium account is a non-distributable reserve. It cannot be used to pay a dividend. The share premium account can be used to cover the cost of new share issues, and can also be turned into share capital via a bonus issue.

1.6 ISSUES AT FULL MARKET PRICE AND RIGHTS ISSUES

The simplest form of share issue is when new shares are issued at their full market price. The share issue is open to anyone who can afford the asking price. This type of share issue is most common when a company's shares are first issued.

It is normal practice for any subsequent issue of shares to be a *rights issue*. In a rights issue existing shareholders have the right to purchase enough shares to maintain their original percentage shareholding. The issuing company offers new shares to existing shareholders at slightly below the market price. This encourages the existing shareholders to take up their rights entitlement and promotes shareholder loyalty.

Example of a rights issue

Wright plc has 800,000 £1 ordinary shares in issue. They were originally issued at a premium of 40 pence each. The current market price of these shares is £3.50.

Wright plc has announced a *1 for 4* rights issue at £3 per share.

Tasks

(1)   Prepare the ledger accounts to record this transaction.

(2)   Prepare the share capital and share premium section of the balance sheet before and after the rights issue.

(3)   Mr Bright owned 32,000 shares in Wright plc before the rights issue. How many shares will he own after the issue? What will his share of the voting right in Wright plc be before and after the rights issue? Assume that he takes up his full entitlement of shares.

Solution

(1)   Prepare the ledger accounts to record this transaction.

Ordinary shares

		Opening balance		800,000
		New issue	(a)	200,000
Closing balance	1,000,000			
	1,000,000			1,000,000

Share premium

		Opening balance	(b)	320,000
		New issue	(c)	400,000
Closing balance	720,000			
	720,000			720,000

Cash

Proceeds of new issue		
Capital	200,000	
Premium	400,000	

(a)   One new share will be issued for every four shares already in issue. There are 800,000 shares in issue and so 200,000 shares will be issued, bringing the total share capital to £1m.

(b)   800,000 shares @ 40 pence = £320,000.

(c)   The new shares are issued at £3 each, which is a premium of £2 per share. 200,000 shares at £2 per share gives a premium on issue of £400,000. The new balance on the share premium account is £720,000.

(2) Capital and reserves	*Before*	*After*
	£	*£*
£1 ordinary shares	800,000	1,000,000
Share premium	320,000	720,000
	1,120,000	1,720,000

(3)   Mr Bright's shares and voting rights.

Before the rights issue Mr Bright owned 32,000 shares out of a total of 800,000 shares. This gave him 4% of the voting rights of the business.

The 1 for 4 rights issue gives him another 8,000 shares and increases his share holding to 40,000. He now owns 40,000 shares out of 1,000,000 shares, which is 4%. Mr Bright's voting rights have been preserved.

1.7   BONUS ISSUES

Bonus issues are also known as *capitalisation issues* and *scrip issues.*

In a bonus issue a part of the company's existing reserves are reclassified as share capital. New shares will be issued fully paid, and these will be distributed to the existing shareholders in proportion to their existing shareholdings.

There are a number of uses for a bonus issue.

(1)   Increasing the number of shares in issue will make it easier to divide the shares between a larger number of shareholders. This is useful when a company wants to bring in new shareholders.

(2)   Increasing the value of the company's share capital will strengthen the balance sheet. This is useful if a company has grown rapidly, and the share capital is out of proportion to the net assets of the business.

(3)   The market price of each share will fall. This makes the shares more affordable, and encourages more people to buy shares. This is the most common reason for publicly quoted plc's to make a bonus issue.

Example of a bonus issue

Bowness Ltd is a successful private company owned and managed by its three founding shareholders. The founders wish to distribute shares to their children and to their employees, but at present there are only 50 shares in issue. They also wish to bring their share capital more into line with the net assets of the business. The balance sheet of Bowness Ltd immediately before the bonus issue is as follows:

	£
Ordinary shares of £1 each	50
Revaluation reserve	380,000
Revenue reserves	570,000
Shareholders' funds and net assets	950,050

The terms of the bonus issue are that 10,000 new £1 ordinary shares will be issued fully paid in respect of each share already in issue. The bonus issue will be financed firstly from the revaluation reserve and then from revenue reserves.

Required:

(a) Prepare the ledger accounts to record this transaction.

(b) Prepare the capital and reserves section of the balance sheet after the rights issue.

Solution

(1) Ledger accounts

Ordinary shares

			Opening balance		50
			New issue	(a)	500,000
Closing balance		500,050			
		500,050			500,050

Revaluation reserve

			Opening balance	380,000
Capitalisation	(b)	380,000		
		380,000		380,000

Revenue reserves

		Opening balance	570,000
Capitalisation	120,000		
Closing balance	450,000		
	570,000		570,000

(a) 500,000 new shares will be issued. This is 10,000 new shares for each of the 50 existing shares.

(b) The first £380,000 will be paid-up from the revaluation reserve, and the balance of £120,000 will be paid-up by reducing the balance on the revenue reserves.

(2)   The balance sheet immediately after the bonus issue will be as follows:

		£
Ordinary shares of £1 each	50 + 500,000	500,050
Revaluation reserve	380,000 – 380,000	–
Revenue reserves	570,000 – 120,000	450,000
Shareholders' funds and net assets		950,050

The net assets of the business are unchanged.

It will now be easier for the founders to redistribute some of the 500,050 shares in issue than it was to share out the original 50 shares.

ACTIVITY 2

(a)   A plc has 200,000 50 pence ordinary shares in issue and makes a bonus issue of 50,000 50 pence ordinary shares. Its only available reserve is the profit and loss account balance of £230,000.

(b)   B plc has 200,000 50 pence ordinary shares in issue and makes a rights issue of 50,000 50 pence shares at a price of 80 pence each and the issue is fully taken up.

Write up the ledger accounts for each transaction.

For a suggested answer, see the 'Answers' section at the end of the book.

1.8   ADVANTAGES AND DISADVANTAGES OF ISSUES AT FULL MARKET PRICE, RIGHTS ISSUES AND BONUS ISSUES

An issue at full market price, open to all investors, will raise the most money. However, it may result in rival businesses building up an influential or controlling interest in the company. This may be a disadvantage to the existing shareholders in the long run. The costs of a new issue at full market price can be high, making these issues fairly risky.

A rights issue may not raise as much money as a full market price issue, but the process is cheaper and the existing shareholders are normally keen to purchase shares in a rights issue. (The shareholders will either keep the new shares to preserve their voting rights or sell them straight away at a profit.)

A bonus issue does not raise any cash at all. The main purpose of a bonus issue is to increase the marketability of the shares.

1.9   MARKET VALUE

The shares of a quoted public limited company (plc) may be traded on the stock exchange. These shares will be bought and sold at their market price, which will fluctuate daily. The company whose shares are being bought and sold will not be affected by these transactions. The company only receives any cash from its shares when they are initially issued, not when they are traded between investors.

However, the directors of public companies cannot ignore their company's share price. The following problems may be caused by a low share price:

- A low share price may anger share holders. The shareholders may then refuse to re-elect their board of directors, or they may sell their shares to a rival company. Either way, the directors may lose their jobs.

- Some directors receive part of their remuneration in shares. If the price of their shares falls, then the value of their pay also falls (and vice versa).

- Public companies use new share issues to raise finance. The higher their share price then the more money they can raise from the same number of shares.

2 ORDINARY DIVIDENDS

The ordinary dividend is paid on the ordinary shares. The amount of ordinary (or equity) dividend paid will depend upon two things:

- sufficient distributable profits to cover the dividend; and
- sufficient cash to pay the dividends.

Distributable profits are defined by law. Basically, they are the cumulative retained profits (less any losses and previous dividends). Because these profits are based on the cumulative position, a company can make a loss in one year and still pay a dividend (provided that the company has been profitable in the past).

The dividend will be proposed by the Board of Directors, but it must then be approved by the shareholders after they have read the annual report. Shareholder approval is normally a formality.

The dividend can be described as an amount per share or as a total amount (which would then have to be shared out between the shares in issue).

Typically, a large company pays two dividends; an interim dividend during the year and a final dividend which would be proposed at the year end and then paid a few months later.

Equity (ordinary) dividends are normally reported in the financial statements when they are paid. The total dividend for the year, including the proposed final dividend, is disclosed in the notes to the financial statements.

Example

Noted below is the summary trial balance of Chisel Ltd for the year-ending 30 June 20X7.

	£	£
Turnover		3,293,000
Operating expenses	1,737,000	
Interim dividend	300,000	
Sundry fixed assets	1,104,000	
Sundry current assets	835,000	
Sundry current liabilities		243,000
150,000 Ordinary Shares of 50 pence each		75,000
Share premium		175,000
P&L Reserve		190,000
	3,976,000	3,976,000

Notes

(1)   The corporation tax charge for the year has been estimated at £545,000.

(2)   An interim dividend of £2 per share was paid. The Directors have proposed a final dividend of £3 per share.

Required:

Prepare extracts from Chisel Ltd's profit and loss account and balance sheet for the year-ending 30 June 20X7 incorporating the corporation tax and final dividend.

Chisel Ltd: Profit and loss account

	£
Turnover	3,293,000
Operating expenses	(1,737,000)
Profit before tax	1,556,000
Taxation	(545,000)
Profit for the year	1,011,000

Chisel Ltd: Balance sheet

	£	£
Fixed assets		1,104,000
Current assets	835,000	
Creditors due within one year **Note 2**	(788,000)	
Net current assets		47,000
Net Assets		
		1,151,000
150,000 ordinary shares of 50 pence each		75,000
Share premium		175,000
P&L Reserve (190,000 + 1,011,000 – 300,000)		901,000
		1,151,000

Note 1   Dividends

				£
Interim paid	150,000 shares @	£2	per share	300,000
Final proposed	150,000 shares @	£3	per share	450,000
				750,000

Note 2   Creditors due within one year

	£
Sundry current liabilities	243,000
Provision for corporation tax	545,000
	788,000

3 PREFERENCE SHARES AND DIVIDENDS

3.1 CHARACTERISTICS

Although every company must have ordinary shares, preference shares are an optional extra. Indeed, companies having preference shares are in the minority. Also, although the rights of ordinary shares are defined by law and apply to all ordinary shares, the rights of preference shares are varied, and are set out in their own issue documents. However, there are some typical characteristics of preference shares. These are set out below.

Votes

Preference shares do not normally participate in the election of the Board of Directors.

Dividends

Preference shares usually have a **fixed dividend**. This is often expressed as a percentage of the nominal value of the shares.

The preference dividend can only be paid if there are distributable profits. In any year the preference dividend must be **paid before the ordinary shareholders** receive their dividend.

Cumulative preference shares take this a stage further. Sometimes there will not be enough profits or cash to pay any dividends at all. In future years the arrears of cumulative preference dividend must be settled before any dividend is paid to the ordinary shareholders.

Repayment of capital

When a company is wound up, the preference shareholders are **paid off before the ordinary shareholders.** (The ordinary shareholders receive whatever is left over.) However, although the preference shareholders are paid before the ordinary shareholders, they are still paid off after every other creditor.

Redeemable preference shares have the right to be repaid, just like a loan or debenture. (Accounting for redemption is not on the syllabus.)

Convertible preference shares may be converted into ordinary shares, normally on generous terms. (Accounting for conversion is not on the syllabus.)

Example

A *12% £1 redeemable preference share (20Y9)* will receive a dividend of 12 pence per annum until it is redeemed in 20Y9.

3.2 PRESENTATION IN THE BALANCE SHEET

Typically, preference shares have the same characteristics as liabilities. For example, they have a fixed rate of interest and a fixed date of repayment. Therefore they are classified as liabilities in the balance sheet.

Example

The following balances have been summarised from Layout Ltd's trial balance:

	£	£
Sundry fixed assets	764,000	
Sundry net current assets	536,000	
15% Debentures redeemable in 20Y5		450,000
12% Preferences share redeemable in 20Y2		300,000
Ordinary shares		100,000
Share premium		175,000
Reserves		275,000
	1,300,000	1,300,000

Solution

Layout Ltd: Balance sheet

	£
Sundry fixed assets	764,000
Sundry net current assets	536,000
	1,300,000
15% Debentures redeemable in 20Y5	(450,000)
12% Preference shares redeemable in 20Y2	**(300,000)**
Net assets	550,000
Capital and reserves	
Ordinary shares	100,000
Share premium	175,000
Reserves	275,000
	550,000

3.3 PRESENTATION OF THE DIVIDEND

The preference dividend is treated as a finance cost and is reported in the profit and loss account as part of interest payable.

4 ACCOUNTING FOR RESERVES

4.1 REVENUE RESERVES

The most common reserve is the revenue reserve. (This is also called retained profits, accumulated profits, P&L Account or P&L reserve.) These are the distributable reserves of the company out of which dividends will be paid. They represent the increase in shareholders' wealth generated through trade.

These days, most companies will just have one, single revenue reserve. However, in the past it was quite common for companies to set up different categories of revenue reserve. These would be created by transfers from retained profits.

Although these reserves look distinct on the face of the balance sheet, there are no funds allocated specifically to the different reserves. The only effect they have is to encourage the directors to retain funds within the business rather than pay them out in dividends.

4.2 CAPITAL RESERVES

In certain circumstances the law requires a capital reserve to be set up. The three most common are:

(a) share premium account (already covered in this chapter)

(b) capital redemption reserve (not within the syllabus)

(c) revaluation reserve (covered in a later chapter).

These reserves are sometimes referred to as **statutory reserves** or **non-distributable reserves**. The latter name relates to the fact that these reserves cannot be used to pay a dividend.

4.3 MOVEMENT ON RESERVES

Transfers to and from reserves can be shown at the foot of the profit and loss account. However, it is easier to understand what is going on if the movements on reserves are tabulated in a note.

Example

The summary trial balance of Mallet Ltd for the year-ending 31 December 20X6 is noted below:

	£	£
Net assets	1,175,000	
Profit after tax		567,000
Dividends paid	167,000	
Ordinary shares of £1 each		100,000
Share premium account		50,000
General reserve		350,000
Retained profits		275,000
	1,342,000	1,342,000

Notes

This trial balance does not show the issue of 200,000 ordinary shares at a premium of 75 pence per share. This issue took place on 31 December 20X6.

The directors propose to transfer £200,000 from retained profits to the general reserve.

Required:

Prepare a statement showing the movement on share capital and reserves during the year.

Solution

Movements on share capital and reserves

	Share capital	Share premium	General reserve	Retained profits	Total
	£	£	£	£	£
Opening balances	100,000	50,000	350,000	275,000	775,000
Share issue	200,000	150,000	–	–	350,000
Retained profit for the year	–	–	–	400,000	400,000
Transfer	–	–	200,000	(200,000)	–
Closing balances	300,000	200,000	550,000	475,000	1,525,000

ACTIVITY 3

ZZ Ltd's summarised balance sheet at 31 December 20X7 showed:

	£
Net assets	280,000
Capital and reserves	
Called up share capital	
- 50p ordinary shares	75,000
- £1 8% preference shares	60,000
Share premium account	25,000
Plant replacement reserve	30,000
Profit and loss account	90,000

The operating profit for the year to 31 December 20X8 has been computed as £180,000.

The following additional information is available:

(a)　Corporation tax is estimated at £70,000.

(b)　An interim dividend of 2p has been paid on the ordinary shares, and one half of the dividend on the preference shares.

(c)　It is proposed to pay the remaining dividend on the preference shares and a final dividend of 5p on the ordinary shares.

(d)　£20,000 is to be transferred to the plant replacement reserve.

Required:

(a)　Construct the profit and loss account for the year.

(b)　Show the balance sheet at the end of the year to the extent that information is available.

For a suggested answer, see the 'Answers' section at the end of the book.

5 DEBENTURES AND OTHER LOANS

5.1 DEBENTURES

Debentures are long-term loans. A typical debenture will be for a period of 15 years or more. It will be secured on the fixed assets of the company and it will pay a fixed rate of interest. The interest must be paid, even if the company is making a loss. If the interest is not paid then the debenture holders can appoint a receiver to sell off the company's assets in order to pay off the outstanding interest and capital. This makes debentures a safe investment for the lenders, which in turn means that they will be prepared to accept a relatively low rate of interest. A low interest rate will obviously benefit the borrower who issued the debentures.

Debentures may be long-term loans, but they will eventually be repaid. This means that they are recognised as liabilities in the balance sheet. They will be classified as *Creditors, amounts due after more than one year* until they are within a year of repayment.

5.2 LOANS AND SHARES COMPARED

A company can raise finance by issuing shares or by raising loans. There are advantages and disadvantages of both forms of finance, and so most large companies will have a mix of both. Ordinary shares and loans are compared below.

Repayment

A loan will eventually have to be repaid. This means that a company will have to generate enough cash over the life of a loan in order to pay it back at the end. If a company cannot repay its loan then the company is insolvent.

Ordinary shares do not have to be repaid. From the company's point of view, this makes shares a lower risk option compared with loans.

Servicing of finance

Loan interest must be paid as it falls due. If a company defaults on its interest payments then the lender can normally demand repayment of the loan as well as any outstanding interest.

On the other hand, an ordinary dividend is discretionary. Although most companies pay a regular dividend, there is always the option to suspend dividend payments if profits are low or if the company wishes to spend the cash on, say, fixed assets rather than dividends. This also reduces the risks of share finance in comparison with loans.

Cost of finance

We have seen that, from the company's point of view, shares are lower risk than loans. This means that from the investor's point of view shares must be a higher risk than loans. When a company becomes insolvent the shareholders normally lose their entire investment, whereas lenders will normally recover all or part of the money owed to them.

This in turn means that shareholders demand a higher return on their investment than lenders do. This means that companies often find it cheaper to borrow than to raise new share capital. There is also a tax advantage from borrowing; interest is allowed as a charge against profits, whereas dividends are an appropriation of profits after tax has been charged and deducted.

Summary

Companies have to balance the advantages of low risk (but high cost) share capital against the advantages of low cost (but high risk) loans. The balance between capital and loans is called the *debt equity ratio*. It is studied in the chapter on ratio analysis.

6 TAXATION

6.1 INTRODUCTION

Paper 6 is mainly concerned with corporation tax. The accounting treatment for corporation tax is set out in FRS 16 *Current Taxes* and in the Companies Act. A brief overview of deferred tax is also needed. Calculating corporation tax or deferred tax is not on the syllabus.

6.2 PROVISION FOR CORPORATION TAX

Corporation tax is payable nine months after the year-end. When the accounts are published the final assessment has not normally been agreed. Therefore the balance sheet liability and P&L charge are based on an estimated provision for Corporation Tax. Because tax rates may vary, the tax rate used for the provision must be disclosed. Obviously this provision will never be exactly correct, and sometimes it might be deliberately underestimated.

The notes to the P&L tax charge shows the charge for this years provision and any correction to last year's provision. The tax rates used when making this year's provision should also be disclosed. This enables the reader to estimate the reliability of the Directors' tax estimates.

Example

Extracts from Crowbar Ltd's trial balance for the year-ending 31 December 20X6 are noted below:

	Debit £	Credit £
Profits for 20X6		435,000
Under provision for corporation tax in 20X5	23,000	

The Directors estimate that the corporation tax charge for 20X6 will be £130,000.

Task

Show how these balances will be presented in the profit and loss account and balance sheet.

Crowbar Ltd: Profit and loss account

	£
Profit before tax	435,000
Taxation Note 1	(153,000)
Profit after tax	282,000

Note 1   Tax charge

	£
Corporation tax charge on the profits for the year at XX %	130,000
Under provision for corporation tax in prior years	23,000
	153,000

Crowbar Ltd: Balance sheet

	£
Included within creditors due within 12 months	
Corporation tax	130,000

The tax balance in the trial balance normally relates to the previous year. In this example the tax left over from last year was a debit, an under-provision. This debit has to be charged this year to make up for last year's under provision.

If the balance were a credit it would show that last year's provision was too high, too prudent. This over provision would be released the following year, reducing the tax charge.

ACTIVITY 4

A company has operating profits before tax of £200,000 and the estimated corporation tax charge for the current year is £56,000. In the previous year the estimated corporation tax charge was £49,000 and the eventual corporation tax payment was £47,000. In the current year the directors have paid an interim dividend of £5,000 and are proposing a final dividend of £17,000.

Required:

Show the figures that would appear in the profit and loss account and the notes that would be required for corporation tax and dividends.

For a suggested answer, see the 'Answers' section at the end of the book.

6.3   DEFERRED TAX

Deferred tax is tax that *may* become payable in the future as a result of accounting profits claimed in the past. It is shown as a provision in the balance sheet. Deferred tax arises because some profits are claimed in the financial statements before they become liable for tax. Deferred tax itself is an accounting estimate, it is not a tax levied (charged) and collected by the Government.

6.4   ACCOUNTING FOR DEFERRED TAX

The calculation of the deferred tax provision is not on the syllabus. In the exam there may be an increase (or decrease) in the deferred tax provision. This will be adjusted for by an extra charge (or credit) in the tax section of the profit and loss account.

Example

Dither Ltd: Deferred tax 20X1

Dither Ltd is preparing its accounts for 20X1, which is its first year of trade. A summarised trial balance is noted below:

	£000	£000
Profits before tax and dividends		953
Sundry fixed assets	816	
Sundry current assets	687	
Sundry current liabilities		250
Long term loan		200
Ordinary shares		100
	1,503	1,503

Notes

(a)   No dividends have been paid or proposed.

(b)   A provision for corporation tax of £213,000 is required.

(c)   A provision for deferred tax of £47,000 is required.

Required:

Prepare a profit and loss account and balance sheet with supporting notes for Dither Ltd for 20X1.

Solution

Dither Ltd: Profit and loss account of 20X1

	£000
Profit before tax	953
Taxation *Note 1*	(260)
Profit after tax	693

Note 1   Tax charge

	£000
Corporation tax charge on the profits for the year at XX %	213
Deferred tax charge	47
	260

Dither Ltd: Balance sheet for 20X1

	£000	£000
Fixed assets		816
Current assets	687	
Creditors due within one year *Note 2*	(463)	
Net current assets		224
		1,040

Creditors due after one year: Long-term loan	(200)
Provision for deferred tax *Note 3*	(47)
	793

Share capital and reserves	
Ordinary shares	100
Retained profits	693
	793

Note 2   Creditors due within one year

	£000
Sundry	250
Corporation tax	213
	463

Note 3   Provision for deferred tax

	£000
Opening provision	–
Charge (Credit) for the year	47
Closing provision	47

ACTIVITY 5

Dither Ltd is preparing its accounts for 20X2. A summarised trial balance is noted below:

	£000	£000
Profits before tax and dividends		1,036
Sundry fixed assets	1,369	
Sundry current assets	923	
Sundry current liabilities		241
Corporation tax	25	
Provision for deferred tax		47
Long-term loan		200
Ordinary shares		100
Retained profits brought forward		693
	2,317	2,317

Notes

(a)   No dividends have been paid or proposed.

(b)   A provision for corporation tax of £353,000 is required.

(c)   Last year's corporation tax was settled at £238,000. The under provision is noted on the trial balance.

(d)   The provision for deferred tax should be adjusted to a closing balance of £33,000.

Required:

Prepare a profit and loss account and balance sheet with supporting notes for Dither Ltd for 20X2.

For a suggested answer, see the 'Answers' section at the end of the book.

6.5 SUMMARY OF THE P&L TAX CHARGE

There will normally be three components to the profit and loss account tax charge. These components must be disclosed in a note to the financial statements. The proforma note below illustrates this.

		£
Corporation tax charge for the year	This will be given to you in the notes to the question.	X
(Over) under provision for taxation in the previous year.	This will be shown in the trial balance. An over provision will be a credit and an under provision will be a debit.	(X)
Increase (decrease) in deferred tax	The opening provision will be in the trial balance. The closing provision will be given to you in the notes to the question.	X
Tax charge in the profit and loss account		XX

6.6 VALUE ADDED TAX (VAT)

Value added tax is levied on all sales made by VAT registered traders. The VAT on sales is called **output VAT**. A VAT registered trader can also reclaim any VAT on its purchases. The VAT on purchases is known as **input VAT**. The trader must then pay over the net amount (output VAT less input VAT) to HM Revenue and Customs. This is normally done on a monthly or quarterly basis.

The trader is basically acting as an unpaid tax collector. The VAT collected from customers is not income for the business, and the VAT recoverable on purchases is not an expense. Therefore all items of income and expenditure are shown net of VAT in the financial statements of a VAT registered business. Fixed Assets and stocks will also be shown net of VAT. However, debtors and creditors will be shown gross, and there will normally be a balance of VAT owing to HM Revenue and Customs.

Example

Barrel Ltd is a VAT registered business. During March 20X9 it made net sales of £10,000 (plus VAT of £1,750) and net purchases and expenses of £7,000 (plus £1,135 VAT).

At the end of the month there was no stock. All sales and purchases were on credit, and there had been no receipts or payments during the month.

Required:

Prepare the profit and loss account and balance sheet for Barrel Ltd for the month of March 20X9.

Solution

Barrel Ltd: Profit and loss account for March 20X9

			£
Sales	*(net of VAT)*		10,000
Purchases and expenses	*(net of VAT)*		(7,000)
Profit			3,000

Balance sheet as at 31 March 20X9

			£
Current Assets	Trade debtors	*(gross of VAT)*	11,750
Creditors	Trade creditors	*(gross of VAT)*	8,135
	Amount owing to HMRC	*(£1,750 less £1,135)*	615

Exam questions at this level (and at the professional level) tend to ignore VAT.

6.7 VALUE ADDED TAX FOR NON-VAT REGISTERED TRADERS

If a trader is not registered for VAT then there will be no VAT levied on sales, but the trader will not be able to reclaim any of the input VAT on purchases. All purchases, expenses, fixed assets, stocks and creditors will be shown gross of VAT. There will be no VAT on sales and no balance of VAT owed to or from HM Revenue and Customs.

KEY TERMS

Ordinary shares – represent the ownership interest of a company. They are the last shares to be repaid. Ordinary shares are usually the only shares with voting rights.

Members – the owners of the ordinary shares.

Authorised share capital – the authorised share capital is the maximum number of shares that a company may issue.

Issued share capital – the actual number of shares in issue at any point in time.

Share premium – the difference between the proceeds of issue and the nominal value is called the share premium.

Rights issue – in a rights issue existing shareholders have the right to purchase enough shares to maintain their original percentage shareholding.

Bonus issue – in a bonus issue a part of the company's existing reserves are reclassified as share capital. Bonus issues are also known as *capitalisation issues* and *scrip issues*.

Revenue reserve – this is also called retained profits, accumulated profits, P&L account or P&L reserve. These are the distributable reserves of the company out of which dividends will be paid.

Corporation tax – the tax levied on the profits made by a limited company.

Deferred tax – tax that *may* become payable in the future as a result of accounting profits claimed in the past.

SELF TEST QUESTIONS

Paragraph

1	What are the ordinary shareholders also called?	1.1
2	What is the difference between authorised and issued share capital?	1.2
3	What is the difference between the nominal value of a share and the share proceeds?	1.4
4	What are the differences between preference shares and ordinary shares?	3.1
5	How might an over provision for corporation tax arise and how and when will it be corrected?	6.2
6	What is deferred tax?	6.3
7	Will a VAT registered company include VAT in its turnover and cost of sales?	6.6

PRACTICE QUESTION

X LTD 20X6

X Ltd is preparing its accounts for the year ended 31 December 20X6. The deferred tax account as at 31 December 20X5 was £50,000. The current corporation tax charge for the year is £60,000 and a transfer of £20,000 is required to the deferred tax account. Prepare the relevant extracts from the profit and loss account, the balance sheet and the notes to the accounts.

(5 marks)

EXAM-STYLE QUESTION

RESERVES

(a)   The term 'reserves' is frequently found in company balance sheets.

Required:

(i)   Explain the meaning of 'reserves' in this context.

(ii)   Give two examples of reserves and explain how each of your examples comes into existence.   **(6 marks)**

(b)   A company's issued share capital may be increased by a bonus (capitalisation) issue or by a rights issue.

Required:

Define 'bonus issue' and 'rights issue' and explain the fundamental difference between these two types of share issue.   **(5 marks)**
(Total: 11 marks)

For suggested answers, see the 'Answers' section at the end of the book.

Chapter 6

FIXED ASSETS

This chapter explains the difference between capital and revenue expenditure. It also sets out the rules for calculating the cost, depreciation, amortisation and (where appropriate) valuation of tangible and intangible fixed assets. This chapter covers syllabus areas 1(f), 2(a) and 2(c).

CONTENTS

1   Assets and expenses

2   Initial cost and subsequent expenditure

3   Depreciation

4   Disposals

5   Revaluation

6   Intangible fixed assets

7   SSAP 13 *Accounting for Research and Development*

8   FRS 10 *Accounting for Goodwill*

LEARNING OUTCOMES

At the end of this chapter you should be able to:

- distinguish between capital and revenue expenditure

- explain, calculate and demonstrate the inclusion of the profit or loss on disposal in the profit and loss account

- account for the revaluation of fixed assets and for gains and losses on the disposal of revalued assets

- account for depreciation – definition, reasons and methods, including straight line, reducing balance and sum of digits

- account for changes in the useful economic life or residual value of assets

- explain how fixed asset balances and movements are disclosed in the financial statements

---

- define and calculate goodwill and distinguish between purchased and internally generated goodwill

- explain and apply the accounting treatment for both types of goodwill

- explain and apply the requirements of accounting standards for research and development.

1 ASSETS AND EXPENSES

1.1 CAPITAL AND REVENUE EXPENDITURE

Expenditure can either be charged to the profit and loss account as an expense or capitalised as an asset in the balance sheet. Expenditure charged to the profit and loss account is known as revenue expenditure. Expenditure capitalised in the balance sheet is known as capital expenditure.

For an item to be capitalised as an asset it must meet the definition and recognition criteria for an asset. If it does not meet these criteria then it must be charged to the profit and loss account as an expense.

Definition   An **asset** is an item arising from a past transaction or event that will bring economic benefits to the business in the future.

An asset will be recognised in the balance sheet if its cost (or value) can be measured with reasonable certainty.

Assets themselves are further classified between current assets and fixed assets, and tangible assets and intangible assets.

1.2 CURRENT ASSETS AND FIXED ASSETS

Current assets

Definition   A **current asset** is an asset which will be converted into money soon within the normal course of the business's trading cycle. Normally, it will be converted into cash within the next 12 months.

There are three items that have been looked at so far which fall into this sub-category:

- Stock   will be sold in the near future.

- Debtors   will be collected in the near future.

- Cash and bank   is already money.

Fixed assets

Definition   A **fixed asset** is an asset purchased not for resale, but for use within the business in the generation of profits over more than one accounting period.

Definition   **Capital expenditure** is expenditure on fixed assets.

Usually, the classification of an item will depend on the management's intentions. For example, if a furniture removal company buys a van, then it is probably going to be used in the business over many years for transporting furniture. Therefore it is a fixed asset.

If a motor dealership purchases a van then it is probably intending to sell it on to a customer, so the van will be the current asset of stock. (Of course, from time to time the dealership will have to purchase a van for its own use – say for parts delivery – and these vans would then be fixed assets.)

1.3 TANGIBLE AND INTANGIBLE FIXED ASSETS

Definition   **Tangible fixed assets** are assets that can be physically touched.

Examples of tangible fixed assets are:

- property

- vehicles

- machines

- tools

- office equipment.

Definition   **Intangible fixed assets** are assets that cannot be physically touched. These assets may not exist in a physical sense, but, money has been spent on them and hopefully they will generate profits in the future.

Examples of intangible fixed assets are:

- goodwill

- development costs.

Goodwill arises when a business is bought. The amount paid for the business is often more than the market value of the physical assets within that business. The difference is known as goodwill. Goodwill represents reputation, the quality of the staff, customer contacts, and many, many other factors. In this paper you will meet goodwill in the context of partnership accounts and group accounts.

Development costs arise when money is spent on developing new products. These new products will hopefully create profitable sales in the future.

Tangible and intangible assets will be discussed in more detail in the following chapters.

1.4 FRS 15 *TANGIBLE FIXED ASSETS*

FRS 15 sets out the accounting treatment for:

- establishing the initial cost of tangible fixed assets and how to account for subsequent expenditure

- depreciation

- revaluation.

These are looked at in detail over the following sections.

2 INITIAL COST AND SUBSEQUENT EXPENDITURE

2.1 INITIAL COST

All fixed assets must initially be recognised at cost. The cost of a fixed asset is its purchase price (after deducting any trade discounts and rebates) and any costs directly attributable to bringing it into working condition for its intended use.

The initial cost specifically excludes administration costs, general overheads, abnormal costs and any costs incurred after the asset is ready for use.

Example

Head Ltd incurred the following costs when installing a new machine at their factory:

	£
Purchase price	234,500
Transport costs form the supplier to the factory.	12,746
Construction of plinth to stand the machine on:	
materials	9,283
own labour (from job cards)	4,751
administrative overheads	1,500
Repair to machine. The damage was caused when the machine was being set on its plinth.	19,456
Rebate received from the supplier	(2,345)
Commissioning work done up to the date the machine was ready for use.	12,846
Further work done after the machine was ready for use	7,263
Total	300,000

Required:

What will be the initial capital cost of this fixed asset?

Solution

	Total	Capitalise	Charge to P&L
	£	£	£
Purchase price	234,500	234,500	
Transport costs	12,746	12,746	
Construction of plinth:			
materials	9,283	9,283	
own labour	4,751	4,751	
overheads	1,500		1,500
Repair to machine	19,456		19,456
Rebate	(2,345)	(2,345)	
Commissioning before the machine was ready for use.	12,846	12,846	
Work done after the machine was ready for use	7,263		7,263
Total	300,000	271,781	28,219

2.2   SUBSEQUENT EXPENDITURE

Subsequent expenditure can only be capitalised if it enhances the economic benefits of an asset. The old rule of thumb that improvements can be capitalised but repairs must be expensed still holds true.

Economic performance can be enhanced by improving the quality of a product or process, extending **an asset's life, or by improving efficiency.**

2.3   SEPARATE COMPONENTS

Certain large assets do not fit easily into these rules. For example, aeroplanes have quite a long life, but their engines and avionics will be replaced a number of times throughout the plane's useful life. To charge the huge costs of these events to the P & L account as repairs and maintenance would distort the reported profits.

The solution to this problem is to treat the engines and avionics as separate components of the aeroplane, with their own costs. useful lives and depreciation. When the components are replaced the event will be treated as a normal disposal, and the new component purchased will be capitalised. Although this technique was first applied to machines, etc by FRS 15, it is in fact an old idea. Land and buildings have been treated as separate components for years.

Example

During 20X8 Star Airlines Ltd purchased a Douglas DC 3 for £500,000. The cost included £100,000 for the engines (with a remaining life of ten years) and £30,000 for avionics (with a remaining life of two years). The rest of the aeroplane has a remaining life of 25 years.

At the end of 20X9 the avionics were scrapped and new equipment costing £125,000 was bought. This should last for ten years. During 20X9 repairs to the airframe and engines totalled £25,000.

Required:

(a)   Prepare the fixed asset schedules for Star Airlines Ltd for 20X8 and 20X9.

(b)   Summarise the P&L charges for 20X8 and 20X9 in respect of this aeroplane.

Solution

Fixed asset schedule for 20X8

		Airframe £	Engines £	Avionics £	Total £
Cost					
Opening and closing	(a)	370,000	100,000	30,000	500,000
Depreciation					
Charge and closing balance	(b)	14,800	10,000	15,000	39,800
Closing Net Book Value		355,200	90,000	15,000	460,200

Fixed asset schedule for 20X9

	Airframe £	Engines £	Avionics £	Total £
Cost				
Opening balance	370,000	100,000	30,000	500,000
Additions	–	–	125,000	125,000
Disposals	–	–	(30,000)	(30,000)
Closing balance	370,000	100,000	125,000	595,000

Depreciation

Opening balance	14,800	10,000	15,000	39,800
Charge for the year	14,800	10,000	12,500	37,300
Disposals	–	–	(15,000)	(15,000)
Closing balance	29,600	20,000	12,500	62,100
Closing Net Book Value	340,400	80,000	112,500	532,900

(a) The cost of the airframe is the remaining cost of the aeroplane after separating out the other components.

(b) Each component is depreciated over its own useful life.

(c) The old avionics are retired.

(d) The new component is capitalised and depreciated over its useful life.

Summary of P&L charges

	20X8	20X9
	£	£
Depreciation	39,800	37,300
Loss on disposal	–	15,000
Repairs	–	25,000
	39,800	77,300

ACTIVITY 1

QG Jones plc owns and operates a chain of department stores in London. It has just built a new store costing £140m. The property is on a leasehold site with 90 years lease remaining. The building itself cost £80m and has been engineered to last for 150 years, but changes in retail habits will probably mean that the building will be obsolete within fifty years. The £80m cost of the building excludes the frontage. The frontage is very modernistic and cost £15m. It will probably go out of fashion within 10 years and need replacing. The balance of the cost relates to the land.

Required:

What will the annual depreciation charge be on this store?

For a suggested answer, see the 'Answers' section at the end of the book.

3   DEPRECIATION

The mechanics of depreciation have been covered many times during your studies. This section concentrates on some key provisions of FRS 15 and the Companies Act.

3.1   WHAT IS DEPRECIATION?

The depreciation charge in the profit and loss account represents the cost of using a fixed asset. If a fixed asset costs £1m and will be used for four years, then the cost of using that asset in each year is £250,000.

Definition   **Depreciation** is the measure of the cost of the economic benefits of the fixed asset that have been consumed during the period.

Consumption includes:

- the wearing out

- using up; or

- other reduction in the useful economic life of a tangible fixed asset.

This can arise from:

- use

- the effluxion of time; or

- obsolescence caused by changes in technology or demand.

(Taken from the official definition in FRS 15. Examples are given in 3.3 below.)

It is important to remember that depreciation does not represent the fall in value of an asset. Fixed assets are held for use, not for resale, and so their market values are not relevant. The 'net book value' left in the balance sheet after depreciation has been charged does not represent market values. As a separate exercise fixed assets may be revalued to reflect changes in their market values. This is covered at the end of this chapter.

3.2 DEPRECATION AND ACCRUALS

Depreciation is based on the accruals concept. Costs are matched to the benefits that they help to create. Because a fixed asset will help to generate profits over a number of periods, then its cost is capitalised and spread over those periods.

3.3 WHICH FIXED ASSETS SHOULD BE DEPRECIATED?

All fixed assets with a finite life must be depreciated. Because nothing lasts forever, all fixed assets should be depreciated. The only exception to this rule is freehold land. Land lasts forever, and so it should not be depreciated, unless it is being used as a mine or quarry in which case the land will eventually be consumed.

The following table summarises the situation.

Freehold land	Don't depreciate	Land does not normally wear out. It has an infinite life.
Freehold land used for quarrying	Depreciate	The economic value of the land will lie in the minerals being extracted. Once the minerals in the quarry have been used up then its useful life will be over.
Leasehold land	Depreciate	The lease will be for a fixed period. The lease will be consumed due to the effluxion of time.
Freehold building	Depreciate	Buildings may last for a long time, but they do not last forever. Commercial premises often have a shorter life than, say, houses because they may be replaced after a few years with bigger or better premises.
Machinery, vehicles, computers, etc	Depreciate	Machines will obviously get worn out as they are used. They may also suffer from obsolescence. Either the product they are making will be discontinued (market obsolescence), or a new machine will be invented that can do the same job more efficiently (technological obsolescence).

3.4 DEPRECIABLE AMOUNT AND USEFUL ECONOMIC LIFE

The *depreciable amount* of a fixed asset is written off over its *useful economic life*.

Definition	The **depreciable amount** is the cost of a tangible fixed asset (or, where an asset is revalued, the revalued amount) less its *residual value*.
Definition	The **residual value** of an asset is the net realisable value of an asset at the end of its useful economic life. Residual values are based on prices prevailing at the date of the acquisition (or revaluation) of the asset and do not take account of expected future price rises.
Definition	The **useful economic life** of a tangible fixed asset is the period over which the entity expects to derive economic benefit from that asset.

Example

An asset costs £100,000 and has an expected useful life of ten years. The purchaser intends to use the asset for six years at which point the expected residual value will be £40,000 (at current prices). If inflation is taken into account the residual value is expected to be £55,000. What is the depreciable amount?

The depreciable amount is £(100,000 – 40,000) £60,000 spread over six years. Which method of depreciation is used to allocate the charge is left for the purchaser to decide.

3.5 ALLOWABLE DEPRECIATION METHODS

An appropriate method should be selected and then applied consistently. The standard does not favour any method over another. Current practice is to use the straight line method unless another method is more appropriate. For example, if a machine wears out after a certain number of hours of use, then a machine hours method may be appropriate. If an asset is more productive in earlier years than later years, then a reducing balance or a sum of the digits method may be appropriate. The straight line and reducing balance methods are on the Paper 3 Syllabus and so they are not covered in detail here. However, Activity 2 below will help to refresh your memory of these methods.

ACTIVITY 2

Straight line method

Calculate the annual depreciation charge from the following information:

Original cost of asset	£4,200
Estimated useful life	4 years
Estimated scrap value	£200

Reducing balance or decreasing charge method

An asset cost £1,000. Its estimated useful life was four years with a scrap value at the end of four years of approximately £60.

Calculate the depreciation charge for each of the four years on a reducing balance basis at a rate of 50%.

For a suggested answer, see the 'Answers' section at the end of the book.

3.6   THE MACHINE HOURS DEPRECIATION METHOD

The machine hours method charges depreciation over the expected operational life of an asset. For example, if an aircraft component cost £150,000 and could be used for 10,000 flying hours before it needed replacing, then depreciation would be charged at £15 per flying hour. If the plane flew for 2,300 hours in the year then the annual charge would be £34,500.

ACTIVITY 3

The useful life of a machine is estimated to be 60,000 hours of use with a nil scrap value at the end of its life. The cost of the machine is £1,800. The expected usage of this machine is 12,000 hours in Year 1 and 9,000 hours in Year 2. What is the depreciation charge for these two years?

For a suggested answer, see the 'Answers' section at the end of the book.

3.7   THE SUM OF THE DIGITS DEPRECIATION METHOD

The sum of the digits method is useful for an asset that will be used more heavily in the earlier years of its life than in the later years. The sum of the digits will weight the depreciation charge towards the earlier years when the machine is used more and (in theory) should earn more revenue.

Example

Trendy Ltd is an internet service provider. It has just spent £3m on new hardware that should last for four years. The hardware will rapidly become obsolete, and so the economic benefits of the hardware will be concentrated in the earlier years of the asset's life. Therefore the hardware will be depreciated over four years using the sum of the digits method.

The sum of the digits for four years is ten $(4 + 3 + 2 + 1)$

The charge in the first year will be £1.2m $(£3m \times 4/10 = £1.2m)$

The charge in the second year will be £0.9m $(£3m \times 3/10 = £0.9m)$

The charge in the third and fourth years will be £0.6m and £0.3m respectively.

ACTIVITY 4

Groovy Ltd pays £72,000 for a machine with a five-year useful life. The machine is depreciated using the sum of the digits method.

Calculate the depreciation charge in each of the five years of the machine's life.

For a suggested answer, see the 'Answers' section at the end of the book.

4   DISPOSALS

4.1   INTRODUCTION

When a fixed asset is sold or scrapped the cost and accumulated depreciation must be removed from the accounting records. Any proceeds of disposal are matched against the net book value of the asset sold in order to calculate the profit or loss on disposal.

4.2 EXAMPLE

Discard Ltd sells a fixed asset for £24,000. The asset cost £143,000 and the cumulative depreciation was £75,000.

Step 1 The cost and accumulated depreciation are cleared out of the fixed asset ledger accounts and into the *Disposals Account*. The journal entry and the disposal account are noted below:

Journal		Debit £	Credit £
Debit	Fixed asset disposals account	143,000	
Credit	Fixed assets at cost		143,000
Debit	Accumulated depreciation	75,000	
Credit	Fixed asset disposals account		75,000

Fixed assets disposal account

	£		£
Fixed assets at cost	143,000	Accumulated depreciation	75,000

Step 2 Match the proceeds of disposal to the net book value of the asset being disposed of. The journal entry and the disposal account are noted below:

Journal		Debit £	Credit £
Debit	Cash book	24,000	
Credit	Fixed asset disposals account		24,000

Fixed assets disposal account

	£		£
Fixed assets at cost	143,000	Accumulated depreciation	75,000
		Proceeds of disposal	24,000

Step 3 Balance off the disposal account. The double entry for the balancing figure will be the profit or loss on disposal. The disposal account and the journal entry are noted below:

Fixed assets disposal account

	£		£
Fixed assets at cost	143,000	Accumulated depreciation	75,000
		Proceeds of disposal	24,000
	———		———
	143,000		99,000
		Loss on disposal	44,000
	———		———
	143,000		143,000

Journal		Debit £	Credit £
Debit	Profit and loss account: Loss on disposal	24,000	
Credit	Fixed asset disposals account		24,000

If the balancing figure is on the debit side of the Disposal Account, then the proceeds are greater than the net book value of the asset and a profit has been made.

If the balancing figure is on the credit side of the Disposal Account then a loss has been made.

ACTIVITY 5

On 1 January 20X1 Zenith Ltd bought an asset costing £39,000. It was expected to have a five-year life and a residual value of £4,000. The asset was sold for £12,300 during 2004. Zenith has a 31 December year-end and charges a full year's depreciation in the year of acquisition and none in the year of disposal.

Required:

(a)   Prepare the T accounts to record the disposal of this asset.

(b)   Draft the journal to record this transaction.

For a suggested answer, see the 'Answers' section at the end of the book.

4.3   DISPOSALS AND PART-EXCHANGE

Sometimes when a new fixed asset is purchased, the fixed asset that it is replacing is given in part-exchange. This is particularly common with motor vehicles. The new asset will have a list price which, instead of being satisfied in full by a cash payment will be satisfied partly by cash and partly in the form of the old asset. In this way the purchase of the new asset and the disposal of the old asset are linked.

In terms of the disposal of the old asset, the same principles apply as before. However, the proceeds of disposal of the old asset are the part-exchange value (see definition below) given against the cost of the new asset.

For the new fixed asset, the main thing to remember is that the figure recorded in the fixed asset cost account is the full list price of the asset, comprising cash and the part exchange value.

Example

A car has a list price of £8,000. An older car is offered in part-exchange and as a result the business only pays £6,000 for the new car.

The part-exchange value is calculated as:

	£
List price	8,000
Less: part-exchange value	(2,000)
Cash paid	6,000

The steps in accounting for a disposal of a fixed asset with a part-exchange are as follows:

Step 1   Set up the Disposal of fixed assets T account.

Step 2   Remove the cost of the old fixed asset from its nominal ledger account

Dr   Disposal of fixed asset account

Cr   Fixed asset cost account

Step 3   Remove the accumulated depreciation on the old fixed asset from its nominal ledger account

Dr   Accumulated depreciation

Cr   Disposal of fixed asset account

Step 4   Bring down the balance on the disposal of fixed asset account

(Note: the above steps are identical to the basic disposal of a fixed asset.)

Account for the disposal proceeds of the old asset, which is linked with the purchase of the new asset:

			£	£
Debit	B/S	Fixed assets at cost	8,000	
Credit	P&L	Disposal of fixed assets		2,000
Credit	B/S	Cash at bank		6,000

This double entry deals neatly with both the purchase of the new asset at its full cost of £8,000 and the disposal of the old asset.

Step 5   Balance up the disposal account and work out the profit or loss

This is the same final step as in the basic disposal.

4.4   EXAMPLE

Hammer Ltd is to buy a new motor van, which has a list price of £9,000. The new van is to replace a van which cost £7,500 four years ago, and has accumulated depreciation of £6,000 on it.

Hammer Ltd will pay the motor van dealer £7,000 for the new van and therefore the part exchange value is (£9,000 – £7,000) £2,000.

Step 1   Set up a T account called 'disposal of fixed assets'

Step 2   Remove the cost of the fixed asset from its nominal ledger account

Van account   (B/S)

	£		£
Balance b/d	7,500	Disposal a/c	7,500

Disposal of fixed assets account   (P&L)

	£		£
Van at cost	7,500		

Step 3   Remove the accumulated depreciation on the fixed asset from its nominal ledger account

Disposal of fixed assets account   (P&L)

	£		£
Van at cost	7,500	Provision for deprecation	6,000

Van provision for depreciation account (B/S)

	£		£
Balance b/d	6,000	Disposal a/c	6,000

Step 4   Bring down the balance on the disposal of fixed assets account

Disposal of fixed assets account (P&L)

	£		£
Van at cost	7,500	Provision for deprecation	6,000
		Balance c/d	1,500
	7,500		7,500
Balance b/f	1,500		

Step 5   Account for the disposal proceeds of the old asset, and the purchase of the new asset

Disposal of fixed assets account (P&L)

	£		£
Van at cost	7,500	Provision for deprecation	6,000
		Balance c/d	1,500
	7,500		7,500
Balance b/f	1,500		
		Proceeds: Part-exchange	2,000

Cash at bank account (B/S)

	£		£
		Cost of fixed asset	7,000

Fixed asset cost account (B/S)

	£		£
Balance b/d	7,500	Disposal a/c	7,500
Cost of fixed asset: Part-exchange	2,000		
Cost of fixed asset: Cash	7,000	Balance c/d	9,000
	16,500		16,500
Balance b/f	9,000		

Step 6   Balance the disposal account and work out the profit or loss

Disposal of fixed assets account (P&L)

	£		£
Van at cost	7,500	Provision for deprecation	6,000
		Balance c/d	1,500
	7,500		7,500
Balance b/f	1,500	Proceeds: Part-exchange	2,000
Profit on disposal	500		2,000
	2,000		

ACTIVITY 6

In 20X3 Armand Ltd bought an elevator for £45,000. It was to have a twenty year life and a £5,000 residual value. In 20X9 Armand decided to upgrade their elevator for a new one with a list price of £99,000. This will have a useful life of 30 years and a residual value of £9,000. The supplier will give Armand a £20,000 trade in allowance on their old elevator.

Charge a full year's depreciation in the year of acquisition and none in the year of disposal.

Required:

Prepare the following accounts for the year ending 31 December 20X9:

Elevators at cost, provision for depreciation on elevators and disposals account.

For a suggested answer, see the 'Answers' section at the end of the book.

5 REVALUATION

5.1 PURPOSE

The net book value of assets with long lives will soon become unrealistic in comparison with their market value. This also means that the depreciation charge in the profit and loss account no longer reflects the cost of using those assets. The solution to these problems is to revalue these assets and to charge depreciation on the revalued amount.

5.2 REVALUATION RULES IN FRS 15 AND THE COMPANIES ACT

There is no requirement to revalue fixed assets. If a company chooses to revalue assets then it must revalue all assets in a particular class, but it need not revalue all of its fixed assets. For example, the most common approach is to revalue all freehold properties and to leave all other assets at historic cost.

Once assets have been revalued then the revaluations must be kept up to date. Full valuations must be held every five years at least, with additional revaluations whenever there are material changes in value.

5.3 VALUATION METHODS

The main valuation method is the **existing use** basis. This means that a warehouse will be valued on the assumption that it will be used as a warehouse. There may be alternative uses for the premises (such as housing) and these may give different values, but these values are not relevant.

Properties *surplus to requirements* should be valued on an **open market** basis. For example if the warehouse above were surplus to requirements then it could be sold off to a property developer at its market value. This value is therefore the most relevant for surplus properties.

5.4   REVALUATION GAINS AND LOSSES

Revaluation gains are taken directly to the Revaluation Reserve. They are reported in the Statement of Total Recognised Gains and Losses, not in the P&L account, as they are not realised. The Revaluation Reserve represents unrealised gains. They cannot be used to pay a dividend.

Revaluation losses are dealt with in a number of ways, depending on the circumstances. These are as follows:

If a property has been revalued upwards in the past, then any revaluation losses are taken directly to the Revaluation Reserve, until the revaluation reserve for that asset is exhausted. Any further losses must be taken to the profit and loss Account.

If a fall in value has been caused by damage, then this should always be taken to the profit and loss account.

5.5   DEPRECIATION ON REVALUED ASSETS

The depreciation charge on revalued assets is calculated as follows:

$$\frac{\text{Revalued amount less revised residue value}}{\text{Remaining useful life of the asset}}$$

5.6   BOOKKEEPING ENTRIES

(1)   The cost/valuation of the asset is increased to its new value.

		Debit	Credit
Debit	Fixed assets at cost / valuation	X	
Credit	Revaluation reserve		X

with the difference between the historic cost and the revalued amount

(2)   The accumulated depreciation is transferred to the revaluation reserve.

		Debit	Credit
Debit	Accumulated depreciation	X	
Credit	Revaluation reserve		X

with the difference between the historic cost and the revalued amount

(3)   The revaluation reserve is balanced off. It will be included as part of capital and reserves in the balance sheet

(4)   Depreciation will now be charged on the revalued amount.

Example

A company's building is currently included in the balance sheet at its original cost as follows:

	£
Cost	200,000
Depreciation	40,000
Net book value	160,000

It is being depreciated over its useful economic life of 50 years and it has already been owned for 10 years.

It is now to be revalued to its current existing use value of £450,000.

Write up the accounting entries for this revaluation and explain how the building will be depreciated from now on.

Solution

Step 1   Bring the fixed asset – cost account up to the revalued amount.

Fixed asset – cost

	£		£
Balance b/d	200,000	Balance c/d	450,000
Revaluation reserve	250,000		
	450,000		450,000

Step 2   Remove the accumulated depreciation already charged on the asset.

Fixed asset – accumulated depreciation

	£		£
Revaluation reserve	40,000	Balance b/d	40,000

Step 3   Write up the revaluation reserve account.

Revaluation reserve

	£		£
Balance c/d	290,000	Fixed asset – cost	250,000
		Fixed asset – accumulated depreciation	40,000
	290,000		290,000

The balance on the revaluation reserve is the amount required to take the building from its current carrying value of £160,000 to its revalued figure of £450,000 (£290,000).

The depreciation charge for the building for each year will now be based upon the carrying value on the balance sheet, £450,000, and the remaining useful life, 40 years.

Annual depreciation charge   = $\dfrac{£450,000}{40 \text{ years}}$

£11,250 per annum

ACTIVITY 7

Ten years ago Increment Ltd paid £300,000 for a building. It had an expected useful life of 50 years, and 10 years' depreciation has now been charged on it. The directors wish to revalue the property to its current existing use value of £720,000. There has been no change to its expected useful life, and there will be no residual value.

Required:

(a)   Prepare the T accounts to record this revaluation.

(b)   Calculate the revalued depreciation charge.

For a suggested answer, see the 'Answers' section at the end of the book.

6   INTANGIBLE FIXED ASSETS

Fixed assets are assets that are held for use rather than for resale. Intangible fixed assets are fixed assets without physical substance. They include patents, licences, franchises, development costs and goodwill.

Patents, licences, franchises and so on are normally purchased. They will be capitalised at cost and amortised over the life of the asset. Amortisation is the name for the depreciation charge on an intangible asset. It is calculated in the same way as for a tangible asset. The maximum life of the asset is normally set out in the terms of the purchase agreement; for example you might purchase a four year patent. However, circumstances might cause this life to be reduced; for example you might have the marketing rights to a footballer who changes club and country, and thereby reduces the value of his marketing rights.

Research and development costs, and goodwill, are not quite so straightforward. The accounting treatments for these items are explained in the following sections.

7   SSAP 13 *ACCOUNTING FOR RESEARCH AND DEVELOPMENT*

7.1   DEFINITIONS

The term **research and development** can be used to cover a wide range of activity. The following definitions are simplified versions of those in SSAP 13:

- **Research**, whether **pure** or **applied**, is work undertaken to gain new scientific or technical knowledge. There may, or may not, be a commercial use for this knowledge.

- **Development** is the use of existing scientific or technical knowledge to produce new or improved materials, devices, products, services or processes.

For example, the work undertaken inventing the technology for CD ROM computer games would be classified as research. The work undertaken today to write a new computer game using the existing technology would be classified as development.

7.2   THE ACCOUNTING PROBLEM

The costs of research and development today can run into hundreds of millions. However, it may be many years before the new technology or product is commercially viable. Following the accruals concept, the cost of research and development should be capitalised when incurred, and them amortised when the products are eventually marketed. This would then match the costs with the benefits.

However, prudence would say that the eventual profits are so uncertain and so far away that it would be better to write off all research and development expenditure when it is incurred.

7.3   THE ACCOUNTING SOLUTION

SSAP 13 finds a compromise between accruals and prudence.

All research expenditure must be charged to the P&L account as it is incurred. This is because there is such a long time gap between research commencing and a profitable product being launched. In fact in many high tech industries (such as the pharmaceutical industry) the vast majority of research projects will never produce a viable product.

*Development expenditure **may** be capitalised.* Theoretically this is the correct thing to do, because this will match the costs to the hoped for benefits. However, in practice very few companies capitalise their development expenditure. There are strict rules restricting the situations when development expenditure can be capitalised, and what costs can be capitalised. These are looked at in the next sections.

The annual charge for research and development must be disclosed.

7.4   CRITERIA FOR CAPITALISATION

Development expenditure can only be capitalised if the project meets all of the following criteria:

(1)   The project is clearly defined.

(2)   The costs are separately identifiable.

(3)   The project is technically feasible.

(4)   The project is commercially viable.

(5)   The expected revenues will exceed all costs to date plus any future costs.

(6)   The company has the financial resources needed to complete the project.

7.5   DEVELOPMENT COSTS

If a project meets the criteria for capitalisation than all costs allocated to that specific project may be (but are not required to) be capitalised. These costs will include materials, wages and salaries, depreciation of scientific equipment and facilities, a proportion of overheads and any other direct costs.

7.6   AMORTISATION

Capitalised development expenditure can be carried forward until the product being developed is ready for commercial production. At this point it must be amortised over the expected commercial life of the product. The amortisation method used must match the costs of the project with the benefits from selling or using the product. This could be over a set number of years or it may be tied into the level of production or sales.

Example

Improve plc has deferred development expenditure of £600,000 relating to the development of New Miracle Brand X. It is expected that the demand for the product will stay at a high level for the next three years. Annual sales of 400,000, 300,000 and 200,000 units respectively are expected over this period. Brand X sells for £10.

Required:

How might this expenditure be amortised?

Solution

There are two possibilities for writing off the development expenditure:

(a)   in equal instalments over the three year period i.e. £200,000 pa; or

(b)   in relation to total sales expected (900,000 units):

Year 1 $\dfrac{400,000}{900,000}$ × £600,000 = £266,667

Year 2 $\dfrac{300,000}{900,000}$ × £600,000 = £200,000

Year 3 $\dfrac{200,000}{900,000}$ × £600,000 = £133,333

8   FRS 10 *ACCOUNTING FOR GOODWILL*

8.1   INTRODUCTION

Goodwill is rare in company financial statements, but is very common in group situations. The mechanics of calculating and amortising goodwill in group situations will be covered in the chapters on group accounts. This chapter outlines the requirements of FRS 10 in respect of goodwill.

8.2   THE NATURE OF GOODWILL

Any successful and profitable business will have goodwill of its own. This goodwill will arise because of the quality of the business's products and staff, its reputation, its technical know-how, the loyalty of its customers and the reliability of its suppliers. In short, anything that makes a company successful is part of its goodwill.

The goodwill that a business generates through its own efforts is known as **inherent goodwill**. Inherent goodwill is **never capitalised** in corporate financial statements. It has no cost and it is impossible to value.

When one company purchases another company part of the price paid will represent the value of the goodwill in the company being acquired. This is known as **purchased goodwill**. The cost of this purchased goodwill can be calculated accurately and reliably, and this purchased goodwill **must be capitalised**.

8.3   CALCULATING THE COST OF PURCHASED GOODWILL

Purchased goodwill is the difference between the fair value of the consideration given and the fair value of the net assets acquired. For example. if X plc paid £1m for Y Ltd, and Y Ltd had a fair value of £800,000, then purchased goodwill of £200,000 would be recognised.

It must be remembered that goodwill is a balancing figure. The two parties agree a price for the shares being bought; the fair value of the net assets acquired is then calculated; the goodwill is the difference between the two. This does mean that the goodwill will be affected by the bargaining skills of the two parties, and/or the state of the stock market as a whole.

8.4 CAPITALISATION AND AMORTISATION

All purchased goodwill must be capitalised.

FRS 10 assumes that goodwill will be amortised over a period not exceeding 20 years. In practice, the nature of goodwill means that the amortisation period will be less than this. With the pace of change in business being so fast, it is unlikely that goodwill will remain intact for as long as 20 years.

FRS 10 does allow a longer period to be used, but this is only allowed if the reasons for doing so are disclosed and the balance of goodwill is reviewed regularly for impairment.

FRS 10 also allows goodwill to be held in the balance sheet indefinitely, without any amortisation. This is only allowed if the balance of goodwill is reviewed for impairment annually. It also requires the true and fair view override to be invoked because all fixed assets with a finite life should be depreciated or amortised. In practice, very few companies adopt this non-amortisation policy.

8.5 IMPAIRMENT

Goodwill is more susceptible to impairment than most assets. Reputations and customers are easily lost. For example, within the space of a few months, as the result of the Enron accounting scandal, the good name of Arthur Andersen disappeared altogether. It is therefore important to review goodwill regularly to ensure that the profits generated by the related businesses are sufficient to recover the net book value of the goodwill in the balance sheet.

8.6 PRESENTATION

The movements in the carrying value of goodwill should be disclosed by note, along with details of the amortisation policy.

8.7 NEGATIVE GOODWILL

Negative goodwill arises when the price paid for a business is less than the fair value of the net assets acquired. This is rare, and only usually happens if there has been a forced sale of a business.

Negative goodwill is capitalised as a negative fixed asset. It is deducted from the total of positive goodwill. The negative goodwill is then released to the profit and loss account as income over the periods expected to benefit from its use.

8.8 EXAMPLE OF CAPITALISATION, AMORTISATION, AND PRESENTATION.

On 1 January 20X1 Able plc purchased Baker, an unincorporated business, for £5m. The net assets of Baker were £4,460,000. Goodwill is to be amortised over six years on a straight line basis.

Required:

(a) Calculate the cost of goodwill in 20X1.

(b) Calculate the expected annual amortisation charge.

Present the results in the form of the goodwill disclosure note for 20X1 and 20X2.

Solution

Able plc   **Extracts from the balance sheet – goodwill**

		20X1 £000	20X2 £000
Opening balance		–	450
Acquisitions	(a)	540	–
Amortisation	(b)	(90)	(90)
Closing balance		450	360

Goodwill is capitalised and amortised over six years.

(a)	Calculation of the cost and amortisation	£
	Fair value of the consideration	5,000,000
	Less: Fair value of the net assets acquired	(4,460,000)
	Goodwill at cost	540,000
(b)	Annual amortisation charge over six years	90,000

ACTIVITY 8

On 1 January 20X1 Charlie plc purchased Dude, an unincorporated business, for £9m. The net assets of Dude were £6m. Dude's business is old fashioned and well established, and so a 25-year amortisation period is considered to be appropriate.

Required:

(a) Calculate the cost of goodwill in 20X1.

(b) Calculate the expected annual amortisation charge.

Present the results in the form of the goodwill disclosure note for 20X1 and 20X2.

For a suggested answer, see the 'Answers' section at the end of the book.

KEY TERMS

Current assets – an asset which will be converted into cash within the next 12 months.

Fixed assets – an asset purchased not for resale, but for use within the business in the generation of profits over more than one accounting period.

Capital expenditure – expenditure on fixed assets.

Tangible fixed assets – assets that can be physically touched.

Intangible fixed asset – assets that cannot be physically touched.

Depreciation – the measure of the cost of the economic benefits of the fixed asset that have been consumed during the period.

Amortisation – depreciation charge on an intangible asset.

Useful economic life – the period over which the entity expects to derive economic benefit from that asset.

Development – the use of existing scientific or technical knowledge to produce new or improved materials, devices, products, services or processes.

Purchased goodwill – the difference between the fair value of the consideration given and the fair value of the net assets acquired.

SELF TEST QUESTIONS

		Paragraph
1	What is a tangible fixed asset?	1.3
2	When can subsequent expenditure on a fixed asset be capitalised?	2.2, & 2.3
3	What is the purpose of depreciation?	3.1
4	How are revaluation gains dealt with?	5.4
5	How should research costs be accounted for?	7.3
6	What are the two alternative ways in which development costs can be accounted for?	7.3
7	What criteria must be met before development expenditure can be capitalised?	7.4
8	What is the difference between inherent and purchased goodwill?	8.2
9	What is the accounting treatment for inherent goodwill?	8.2
10	What is the accounting treatment for purchased goodwill?	8.2
11	Under what conditions can purchased goodwill be amortised for a period in excess of 20 years?	8.4
12	How might negative goodwill arise?	8.7

EXAM-STYLE QUESTION

ARBALEST

The summarised balance sheet of Arbalest Limited at 30 September 20X6 was as follows:

	Cost	Aggregate depreciation	Net book value
	£000	£000	£000
Fixed assets			
Land	2,000	nil	2,000
Buildings	1,500	450	1,050
Plant and machinery	2,800	1,000	1,800
	6,300	1,450	4,850
Current assets		3,180	
Less: Current liabilities		2,070	1,110
			5,960
Capital and reserves			
Called-up share capital			
3,000,000 ordinary shares of 50p each			1,500
Share premium account			400
Profit and loss account			4,060
			5,960

During the year ended 30 September 20X7 the company had the following transactions:

(1)   1 November 20X6:

A rights issue of one share for every three held at a price of £1.50 per share. All the rights issue shares were taken up.

(2)   1 December 20X6:

Sale for £70,000 of plant and machinery which had cost £1,000,000 and had a book value of £200,000.

(3)   1 March 20X7:

A bonus (capitalisation) issue of one share for every one held at that date using the share premium account as far as possible for the purpose.

(4)   1 June 20X7:

Purchased a new factory block for £3,000,000 (including land £600,000).

(5)   1 July 20X7:

Purchased plant and machinery for £1,600,000.

(6)   30 September 20X7:

The company decided to revalue the freehold land held at 30 September 20X6 from £2,000,000 to £2,500,000.

The company depreciation policies are:

Land	no depreciation
Buildings	2% per annum on cost, straight-line basis
Plant and machinery	10% per annum on cost, straight-line basis

Proportionate depreciation is provided in the year of purchase of an asset, with none in the year of disposal. The retained profit for the year was £370,000.

Required:

Prepare the notes required for the company's balance sheet for publication at 30 September 20X7 detailing:

(a)   movements on reserves

(b)   movements on fixed assets.

Ledger accounts for the transactions are not required.   **(15 marks)**

For a suggested answer, see the 'Answers' section at the end of the book.

Chapter 7

STOCKS

This chapter revises the accounting treatment of stocks. It covers syllabus areas 2(a) and 2(d).

CONTENTS

1   Stocks

2   Stock valuation methods

LEARNING OUTCOMES

At the end of this chapter you should be able to:

*   calculate the cost and net realisable value of stocks.

1   STOCKS

1.1   THE REASON FOR RECOGNISING STOCK IN THE BALANCE SHEET

Profit is calculated by matching costs with revenues. Revenues are normally claimed when a sale is made, and all related costs and expenses are then matched to that revenue. As stock is bought it is charged to the P&L as purchases. There is nearly always a time lag between purchasing stock and selling it, and so at the year-end there will be unsold stock on hand. This unsold stock must be carried forward in the balance sheet so that it can be matched with next year's revenues. This is applying the accruals concept.

1.2   VALUING STOCK IN THE BALANCE SHEET

Stocks are valued at the lower of cost and net realisable value. This is an application of the prudence concept. Most items will be valued at cost, which excludes any future profits. However, if any losses are foreseen then they will be recognised immediately. Valuation is a two stage process; firstly the costs is calculated and then it is compared with its net realisable value.

1.3 THE COST OF STOCK

SSAP 9 states that the cost of stock includes all costs that have been incurred in the normal course of business in bringing the product or service to its present condition and location. (This rule is similar to that for calculating the cost of a tangible fixed asset.)

These costs will include the costs of purchase and the costs of conversion.

(a) **Costs of purchase**: material costs, import duties, freight.

(b) **Costs of conversion**: this includes direct costs and production overheads.

Example

Head Ltd incurred the following costs in respect of some stock:

	£
Invoice price of raw materials	123,456
Transport costs from the supplier to the factory	5,283
Repair to damaged materials	15,389
Own labour (from job cards)	18,627
Production overheads	12,634
Administration and marketing overheads	24,611
Total	200,000

Task

What will be the cost of this stock?

Solution

	Total	Stock	
	£	£	
Invoice price	123,456	123,456	Purchase cost
Transport costs	5,283	5,283	Purchase cost
Repair	15,389		
Own labour	18,627	18,627	Conversion cost
Production overheads	12,634	12,634	Conversion cost
Administration and marketing	24,611		
Total	200,000	160,000	

The repair costs are not in the normal course of business (unless there is a steady amount of wastage in the production process). The stock will be valued at £160,000.

1.4 METHODS OF CALCULATING THE COST OF PURCHASE

There are different ways in which the cost of stock can be calculated. FIFO (first in first out) is by far the most common and the most accurate. This, and other methods are discussed in section 2.

1.5 NET REALISABLE VALUE

Having calculated the cost of stock, it is then compared with its net realisable value. This is done on a line-by-line basis (or by categories) in accordance with the principle of separate valuation. The expected profit on one item cannot be offset against the expected loss on another item.

Definition **Net realisable value** is the estimated proceeds of sale less any further costs to completion and all costs to be incurred in distributing, marketing and selling.

Example – Net realisable value

A product sells for £2,000. The costs incurred so far total £987 and the costs to complete the product are estimated at £126. Marketing costs will be about £47. The manufacturer delivers the products to the customer for free, and this normally costs £66. The administrative costs of sale (invoicing and so on) amount to £58.

Required:

Calculate the cost, net realisable value and balance sheet value for this item of stock.

Solution

Cost	£987	
Net realisable value	£1,703	£(2,000 – 126 – 47 – 66 – 58)
Balance sheet value	£987	

Example – Cost and net realisable value

Charles Smart runs a sweet shop. His annual stock count in December revealed a few seasonal items of stock which would have to be reduced in price in the new year. These were as follows:

Range	Number of boxes	Cost	Normal retail price	Expected selling price
Venus	35	£5.30	£8	£4
Earth	54	£5.70	£9	£6
Saturn	85	£7.80	£11	£8
Pluto	47	£9.90	£14	£8
Jupiter	72	£6.50	£10	£8

Task

Calculate the balance sheet value of his closing stock. (Assume that selling costs are immaterial.)

Solution

Range	Number of boxes	Cost	Expected selling price	Lower of cost & NRV	Valuation £
Venus	35	£5.30	£4	£4	140.00
Earth	54	£5.70	£6	£5.70	307.80
Saturn	85	£7.80	£8	£7.80	663.00
Pluto	47	£9.90	£8	£8	376.00
Jupiter	72	£6.50	£8	£6.50	468.00
					1,954.80

The balance sheet value of these stock items is £1,954.80.

ACTIVITY 1

The following information relates to five dissimilar stock items:

Range	Cost	NRV
	£	£
Alpha	480	510
Beta	220	200
Gamma	170	220
Delta	150	200
Epsilon	600	450
	1,620	1,580

Required:

What will be the total balance sheet value of this stock?

For a suggested answer, see the 'Answers' section at the end of the book.

1.6 DISCLOSURE REQUIREMENTS – SSAP 9

Stocks and work-in-progress should be sub-classified in the notes to the financial statements in an appropriate manner.

The accounting policies used to value stock should be disclosed.

The following would be a typical example:

Note X Stocks	£
Raw materials	19,273
Work-in-progress	4,927
Finished goods	43,568
	67,768

Stocks are valued at the lower of cost and net realisable value.

Cost is calculated on a First in First out basis.

2 STOCK VALUATION METHODS

There are several allowable ways of valuing stocks. These include:

(a) identified, actual or unit cost

(b) average cost

(c) first-in-first-out (FIFO).

Some countries use the *last-in-first-out* (LIFO) method, but this is not allowed in the UK.

2.1 IDENTIFIED, ACTUAL OR UNIT COST

Unsold or unused stocks are linked with their purchase. This method is limited to large or valuable items where individual units can be easily identified with their cost of acquisition e.g. diamonds. This method, therefore, has limited usefulness in practice, but is acceptable under SSAP 9.

2.2 AVERAGE COST

Where raw materials or goods go, for example, into a bin, e.g. grain, it may be impossible or impracticable to identify particular items. All units going into and out of the store are pooled and an average price determined. This average price should be calculated as a weighted average (this is preferable to a simple average).

Example

200 units	Purchased	Day 1 at £15 per unit
100 units	Purchased	Day 2 at £21 per unit
200 units	Sold	Day 3 at £25 per unit

Calculate the gross profit earned on Day 3 and the valuation of stock remaining at the end of Day 3, using the weighted average method.

Solution

Weighted average price at end of Day 2 $= \dfrac{(200 \times £15) + (100 \times £21)}{300}$

$= £17$ per unit

Calculation of gross profit

		£
Proceeds of sale	200 × £25 =	5,000
Less: Cost of goods sold	200 × £17 =	3,400
Gross profit		1,600

Calculation of stock in the balance sheet

		£
100 units stated at	100 × £17 =	1,700

Note: Calculations based on a simple average would give a different gross profit of £1,400.

The aim of the weighted average method is to even out price fluctuations. It is complex to operate, but acceptable under SSAP 9.

2.3 FIRST-IN-FIRST-OUT (FIFO)

This is the most common method in practice. This method assumes that goods are sold or used in production in the order in which they are brought into stock. The first items sold will be the earliest purchases.

Example

Using the figures from the previous activity calculate the gross profit on Day 3 and the value of stock at the end of Day 3 using FIFO.

Solution

The assumption here is that the 200 units sold on Day 3 were the 200 units acquired on Day 1.

Calculation of gross profit

		£
Proceeds of sale	200 × £25 =	5,000
Less: Cost of goods sold	200 × £15 =	3,000
Gross profit		2,000

Calculation of stock in the balance sheet

		£
100 units stated at	100 × £21 =	2,100

One of the features of FIFO is that stock in the balance sheet tends to be stated at the most recent values, whereas cost of goods sold is based on the more historical values. In a period of inflation FIFO tends to overstate gross profit because current revenues are matched with historical costs.

KEY TERMS

Cost of stock – SSAP 9 states that the cost of stock includes all costs that have been incurred in the normal course of business in bringing the product or service to its present condition and location

Net realisable value – the estimated proceeds of sale less any further costs to completion and all costs to be incurred in distributing, marketing and selling.

FIFO – (First in First Out) – the most common method of estimating the cost of stock. This method assumes that goods are sold or used in production in the order in which they are brought into stock. The first items sold will be the earliest purchases.

SELF TEST QUESTIONS

Paragraph

1	Which two accounting concepts are most relevant to the accounting treatment of stocks?	1.1 & 1.2
2	What is the SSAP 9 definition of the cost of stocks?	1.3
3	What is the net realisable value of stocks?	1.5
4	What is the assumption behind a FIFO cost valuation for stocks?	2.3
5	What effect does the FIFO method of stock valuation have on reported profits?	2.3

EXAM-STYLE QUESTION

SAMPI

Sampi is a manufacturer of garden furniture. The company has consistently used FIFO (first in, first out) in valuing stock, but it is interested to know the effect on its stock valuation of using weighted average cost instead of FIFO.

At 28 February 20X8 the company had a stock of 4,000 standard plastic tables, and had computed its value on each of the three bases as:

Basis	Unit cost £	Total value £
FIFO	16	64,000
Weighted average	13	52,000

During March 20X8 the movements on the stock of tables were as follows:

Received from factory

Date	Number of units	Production cost per unit £
8 March	3,800	15
22 March	6,000	18

Sales

Date	Number of units
12 March	5,000
18 March	2,000
24 March	3,000
28 March	2,000

Required:

Compute what the value of the stock at 31 March 20X8 would be using:

(a)   FIFO   **(5 marks)**

(b)   Weighted average cost.   **(5 marks)**

In arriving at the total stock values you should make calculations to three decimal places (where necessary) and deal with each stock movement in date order.

(Total: 10 marks)

For a suggested answer, see the 'Answers' section at the end of the book.

Chapter 8

PROVISIONS, CONTINGENCIES AND EVENTS AFTER THE BALANCE SHEET DATE

This chapter explains provisions, contingent liabilities, contingent assets, and events after the balance sheet date. It covers syllabus areas 1(f), 2(a), 2(g) and 2(h).

CONTENTS

1   FRS 12 *Provisions, Contingent Liabilities and Contingent Assets*

2   FRS 21 *Events After the Balance Sheet Date*

LEARNING OUTCOMES

At the end of this chapter you should be able to:

*   prepare the financial statements for a limited company from a trial balance, including adjustments for items including provisions

*   prepare the following notes to the financial statements:

    (i)   events after the balance sheet date

    (ii)   contingent liabilities and contingent assets

*   define an event after the balance sheet date and distinguish between adjusting and non-adjusting events

*   account for each category of event in the financial statements

*   define and account for a provision, contingent liability and contingent asset.

1 FRS 12 *PROVISIONS, CONTINGENT LIABILITIES AND CONTINGENT ASSETS*

1.1 PROVISIONS

The term provision has two different meanings in UK GAAP.

(1) Provisions can be used to **reduce the carrying value of an asset**. For example, the provision for depreciation reduces the net book value of fixed assets. The allowance for doubtful debts is sometimes called a provision.

(2) Provisions can also be used to recognise a **liability of uncertain timing or amount**. For example, a warranty provision will be based on estimates of how much the company expects to pay out in warranty costs. There is no certainty as to how much will be payable or when it will be paid.

This section deals with the second type of provision, the liability of uncertain timing or amount.

1.2 RECOGNISING PROVISIONS

A provision is a liability of uncertain timing or amount. This means that a provision can only be recognised if it meets the definition and recognition criteria of a liability. These are as follows:

(1) an **obligation** must exist at the balance sheet date as a result of a **past** transaction or event

(2) a transfer of economic benefits to settle the liability is **probable**; and

(3) a **reliable estimate** can be made of the amount of the obligation

Examples

Provisions for repairs and maintenance

These were very common before FRS 12 was published. In the interest of prudence, companies would make a provision for the repairs and maintenance that they intended to do in the next year or so. However, these do not meet the recognition criteria. This old provision is based on intentions rather than obligations. The directors can change their minds and not carry out the work. Also, the intended repairs and maintenance relate to future events, not past events. These provisions are no longer allowed.

Warranties

Many companies give warranties on their products. The company is then obliged to carry out repair work if the product breaks within a certain period of time. These costs meet the recognition criteria for a provision. There is an obligation to carry out the repairs and suffer the costs. The obligation arose from events in the past (a sale). The transfer of economic benefits is probable (unless the products are perfect and never fail). A reliable estimate can be made of the obligation on the basis of past experience. Warranty obligations must be provided for.

1.3 MEASURING, REVIEWING AND USING PROVISIONS

A provision should be based on the best estimate of the expenditure required to settle the provision. This will take into account risks and uncertainties. Typically it will be based on past experience and probabilities.

Provisions should be reviewed and adjusted at each balance sheet date. If they are no longer needed then they should be released back to the P&L account.

Provisions should only be used for their intended purpose.

1.4 DISCLOSURE OF PROVISIONS

The following should be disclosed for each class of provision:

(a)   the opening and closing balance on the provision and details of any movements during the year

(b)   a brief description of the nature of the obligation and the expected timing of the cash flows

(c)   an indication of the uncertainties surrounding the amount or timing.

1.5 CONTINGENT LIABILITIES

There are two types of contingent liability:

(1)   obligations dependent on uncertain future events

(2)   obligations where the transfer of economic benefits is not probable or the amount of the obligation cannot be measured reliably.

Contingent liabilities are not recognised in the financial statements. Instead they are disclosed in the notes. A brief description of the nature of the contingent liability should be given, an estimate of its financial effect and an indication of the uncertainties surrounding its amount or timing. If the possibility of a contingent liability crystallising is remote, it can be ignored.

1.6 OBLIGATIONS DEPENDENT ON UNCERTAIN FUTURE EVENTS

The definition of these liabilities is 'a possible obligation arising from past events whose existence will be confirmed only by the occurrence of one or more uncertain future events not wholly within the entity's control'.

Example

At the year-end Omicron plc is defending itself in a court case. If Omicron loses, then they will have to pay out £3m in fines and court fees. If they win, then they will not have to pay a penny. Their lawyers have advised them that the verdict could go either way.

The £3m fine is a possible obligation arising from past events (otherwise they would not have been in court at the year-end) but the obligation will only be confirmed by the verdict of the jury. The jury's verdict is beyond the control of Omicron.

Omicron will not recognise the £3m. Instead it will disclose details of the court case and the amounts involved in the notes to the accounts.

1.7 OBLIGATIONS WHERE THE TRANSFER OF ECONOMIC BENEFITS IS NOT PROBABLE OR THE AMOUNT OF THE OBLIGATION CANNOT BE MEASURED RELIABLY

The definition of these liabilities is 'a present obligation that arises from past events but is not recognised because it is not probable that a transfer of economic benefits will be required to settle the obligation or because the amount of the obligation cannot be measured with sufficient reliability'.

Example – Transfer not probable

Kappa Ltd has guaranteed the overdraft of Lambda Ltd. Lambda is a profitable company and it is in excellent financial health. Its overdraft currently stands at £32,000.

An obligation exists as a result of Kappa having offered to guarantee Lambda's overdraft, and the obligation can be measured exactly (£32,000). However, because Lambda is in excellent financial health it is not probable that Kappa will be required to pay out any money. Therefore this will be disclosed as a contingent liability. (If Lambda was in serious difficulties and the Banks were likely to call in the guarantee, then the £32,000 would have to be recognised as a liability in the balance sheet.)

Example – Cannot be measured with sufficient reliability

Shortly after the 1997 UK General Election, the new Government announced that there would be a Windfall Tax on the past profits of the privatised utilities. However, the amount of tax was not confirmed until the Budget, which was some months later. Utilities reporting their results in the period between the announcement and the budget knew that they would have to pay more tax, but they were unable to estimate how much tax that would be payable. Therefore, the obligation to pay the Windfall Tax was disclosed, but no attempt was made to measure the amount or recognise any provision in the balance sheet.

1.8 CONTINGENT ASSETS

A contingent asset is a possible asset arising from past events whose existence will be confirmed only by the occurrence of one or more uncertain future events not wholly within the entity's control.

A contingent asset should never be recognised. Details of any contingent asset should only be disclosed where the inflow is probable.

Example

Shortly before the year-end Pye Ltd submitted an application for a £5m Government grant. Pye meet all the criteria for receiving the grant and Government approval for the grant should be a formality. This approval is not expected to be received until after the accounts have been published.

Pye cannot recognise the grant as a debtor, but because the receipt of cash is probable it can be disclosed as a contingent asset.

1.9 DISCLOSURE

Because provisions and contingencies involve a lot of judgement, and because the outcome of the events in question are so uncertain, there are extensive disclosure requirements for these items. These are noted below:

Provisions

For each class of provision, disclose:

(a)   carrying amount at the beginning and end of the period

(b)   additional provisions made in the period

(c)   amounts used during the period

(d)   unused amounts reversed during the period

(e)   effect of discounting during the period

(f)   a brief description of the nature of the obligation and expected timing of any resulting transfers of economic benefit

(g)   an indication of the uncertainties about the amount or timing of those transfers of economic benefit

(h)   the amount of any expected reimbursement.

Contingent liabilities

For each class of contingent liability (unless remote) disclose:

(a)   an estimate of its financial effect

(b)   an indication of the uncertainties relating to the amount or timing of any outflow

(c)   the possibility of any reimbursement.

Contingent assets

For contingent assets (only where probable) disclose:

(a)   a brief description of their nature

(b)   where practicable, an estimate of their financial effect.

ACTIVITY 1

Should a provision be recognised in the accounts of Prudence Ltd for the following items? If not, how should they be treated in the financial statements?

(a)   Prudence Ltd is a retail store and has a policy of refunding purchases by dissatisfied customers, even though there is no legal obligation to do so. Its policy of making refunds is generally known.

(b)   Prudence Ltd is being sued for £100,000 damages. Counsel assesses the chances of losing the case as fifty fifty.

(c)   Prudence Ltd is suing another company for £50,000 damages. At the date on which the financial statements are approved, counsel's opinion is that Prudence Ltd is likely to win the case and receive the damages.

For a suggested answer, see the 'Answers' section at the end of the book.

---

2 FRS 21 *EVENTS AFTER THE BALANCE SHEET DATE*

2.1 INTRODUCTION

Between the year-end and the date that the financial statements are approved for publication, events will occur and information come to light that may be relevant to the year just ended. The question is, should the financial statements be adjusted for events and information that arise after the year-end?

The answer is to divide these events into two categories, **adjusting** and **non-adjusting** events.

- **Adjusting events** are events which provide evidence of conditions existing at the balance sheet date.

- **Non-adjusting events** are events which concern conditions which did not exist at the balance sheet date.

- **Events after the balance sheet date** are those events, both favourable and unfavourable, which occur between the balance sheet date and the date on which the financial statements are authorised for issue.

2.2 ROUTINE ADJUSTING EVENTS

Many of these items have been adjusted for as part of normal bookkeeping procedures for generations. Some examples are noted below:

Event after the balance sheet date	Adjustment
Slow payment or non-payment by year-end trade debtors.	Increase the doubtful debt provision.
Invoices received in respect of goods or services received before the year-end.	Accrue.
Year-end stock is selling at below cost.	Revise stock valuation (stock is valued at the lower of cost and net realisable value).
The tax rates applicable to the financial year are announced.	Base the tax charge on these revised rates. (This is no longer an issue in the UK because rates are now announced in advance.)
An insurance claim (applied for before the year-end) is received.	Recognise a debtor at the year-end.
The auditors submit their fee.	Accrue.

In theory the event after the balance sheet date merely provides new evidence for conditions that already existed at the year-end. The event often provides more accurate information about the valuation of assets or liabilities that would have been recognised in the balance sheet anyway.

2.3 GOING CONCERN

Events may occur after the year-end that call into doubt the ability of the company to continue in business. If these events mean that the going concern concept is no longer applicable, then the financial statements must be redrawn on a break-up basis. This rule applies even if the events causing the company's problems clearly arose after the year-end. This is because the accounts would be meaningless if they were to be drawn up on a going concern basis when the company was insolvent.

2.4   NON-ADJUSTING EVENTS

These are events arising after the balance sheet date but which, unlike those events above, do **not** concern conditions existing at the balance sheet date. These in turn are divided into two categories:

- **Non-adjusting events not requiring disclosure**

   This accounts for the vast majority of events after the balance sheet date. These events will be reported in the year in which they occurred in the normal way.

- **Non-adjusting events requiring disclosure**

   These are discussed in more detail below.

2.5   NON-ADJUSTING EVENTS REQUIRING DISCLOSURE

In respect of each material non-adjusting event, the following information should be stated by way of notes in financial statements:

- the nature of the event

- an estimate of the financial effect, or a statement that such an estimate cannot be made.

Material non-adjusting events require disclosure because non-disclosure would affect the ability of the users of financial statements to reach a proper understanding of the financial position. This could influence the economic decisions of users taken on the basis of the financial statements.

For example, if a factory burns down after the year-end, or the stock is destroyed by flood, then these are non-adjusting events. At the year-end these assets existed and so it would be incorrect to remove them from the year-end balance sheet. However, if the shareholders were not informed of these events they would have a misleading impression of the health of their company. Therefore, these events must be disclosed.

If a company acquires another company after the year-end, or gets taken over itself, then these are non-adjusting events. The takeovers cannot be back-dated. However, as before, the shareholders would not be able to assess the performance of their directors or the future of their company if they were not informed of these events. Therefore they must be disclosed.

FRS 21 gives some specific examples of other events that normally require disclosure:

- announcing a plan to discontinue an operation

- major purchases and disposals of assets

- announcing a major restructuring

- major ordinary share transactions (e.g. an issue of new shares or a bonus or rights issue)

- commencing major litigation arising out of events that occurred after the balance sheet date.

ACTIVITY 2

Kamoso Ltd has just prepared its draft accounts for the year-ending 31 December 20X5. These are noted below. The accounts will not be audited and approved by the Board for another three weeks. During this period the following information comes to light:

(1)   In January 20X6 a building with a net book value of £250,000 burnt down. It was not insured.

(2)   In February 20X6 stocks with a year-end cost of £79,000 were sold for £65,000.

(3)   In March 20X6 a major customer went bankrupt owing £235,000. The debt was made up as follows:

Date of invoices	£
December 20X5	64,000
January 20X6	123,000
February 20X6	48,000
	235,000

(4)   In April 20X6 Kamoso Ltd repaid a £500,000 ten-year loan. The loan was from a business owned by Kamoso's Managing Director. It was taken out in December 20X5.

The draft balance sheet of Kamoso Ltd is as follows:

Kamoso Ltd Balance Sheet as at 31 December 20X5

	£000	£000
Fixed assets		1,126
Current assets		
Stocks	238	
Trade debtors	436	
Cash	400	
	1,074	
Current liabilities	700	
Net current (liabilities) assets		374
Capital employed		1,500
Ten year loan		(500)
Net assets		1,000

Required:

(a)   Explain how each of these events will be accounted for.

(b)   Redraft the balance sheet to incorporate all the adjusting events.

For a suggested answer, see the 'Answers' section at the end of the book.

KEY TERMS

Contingent liability

(a)   a possible obligation that arises from past events and whose existence will be confirmed only by the occurrence of one or more uncertain future events not wholly within the entity's control; or

(b)   a present obligation that arises from past events but is not recognised because:

    (i)   it is not probable that a transfer of economic benefits will be required to settle the obligation; or

    (ii)   the amount of the obligation cannot be measured with sufficient reliability.

Contingent asset – a possible asset that arises from past events and whose existence will be confirmed only by the occurrence of one or more uncertain future events not wholly within the entity's control.

Provision – a liability of uncertain timing or amount.

Events after the balance sheet date – events, both favourable and unfavourable, which occur between the balance sheet date and the date on which the financial statements are authorised for issue.

Adjusting events – events which provide additional evidence of conditions existing at the balance sheet date.

Non-adjusting events – events that concern conditions which did not exist at the balance sheet date.

SELF TEST QUESTIONS

		Paragraph
1	State two distinct meanings for the term 'provision'.	1.1
2	What conditions must exist before a provision is recognised as a liability?	1.2
3	State two types of contingent liability.	1.5
4	Should contingent liabilities be recognised in the balance sheet?	1.5
5	What is an adjusting event after the balance sheet date?	2.1 & 2.2
6	What possible accounting treatments are there for non-adjusting events after the balance sheet date?	2.4

EXAM-STYLE QUESTION

GERMAINE LTD

(a) The financial position of an entity as revealed by its financial statements may be seriously affected by events occurring after the balance sheet date and contingencies. For this reason FRS 21 *Events After the Balance Sheet Date* and FRS 12 *Provisions, Contingent Liabilities and Contingent Assets* lay down rules to ensure that such events and contingencies are properly reflected in financial statements.

Required:

(i) What factors determine whether events after the balance sheet date require adjustment to the financial statements, according to FRS 21 *Events After the Balance Sheet Date*? **(3 marks)**

(ii) Explain the meaning of the term 'contingent liability'. **(2 marks)**

(iii) Explain the different accounting treatments required for contingent liabilities and contingent assets depending on their degree of probability. **(4 marks)**

(iv) Up to what date would it normally be necessary to adjust for or disclose events after the balance sheet date or to disclose contingent liabilities and contingent assets? **(2 marks)**

(b) Germaine Limited prepared its draft financial statements for the year ended 31 March 20X9 shortly after the balance sheet date. They showed a profit of £980,000. After they were prepared and before the directors formally approved them, the following events took place:

(i) A customer commenced an action against the company to recover £120,000 of losses incurred as a result of Germaine's alleged supply of faulty components in February 20X9. Germaine Limited intends to defend the case vigorously. The company's legal advisers consider it has a 70% chance of successfully defending the action. If the customer's action is successful, damages and costs are expected to amount to £180,000. If Germaine successfully defends the action, non-recoverable legal costs of £30,000 will be incurred. **(6 marks)**

(ii) A trade debtor, for whose balance a full specific provision had been made at 31 March 20X9, paid the account of £84,000 in full. **(3 marks)**

Required:

Advise the directors of Germaine Limited as to the correct accounting treatment of these items, giving your reasons. If you consider that the financial statements require adjustment, draft journal entries with narrations to give effect to the adjustment. If you consider that a note to the financial statements is required, draft a suitable disclosure note.

(Total: 20 marks)

For a suggested answer, see the 'Answers' section at the end of the book.

Chapter 9

REPORTING FINANCIAL PERFORMANCE

This chapter explains the purpose and outlines the disclosures required by FRS 3 *Reporting Financial Performance*. It covers syllabus areas 1(f), 2(f) and 2(i).

CONTENTS

1   The all inclusive approach to reporting profit

2   Exceptional and extraordinary items

3   Prior year adjustments

4   Additional notes

LEARNING OUTCOMES

At the end of this chapter you should be able to:

- prepare a statement of total recognised gains and losses

- prepare the following notes to the financial statements:

    (i)   statement of movements in reserves

    (ii)   exceptional items

- distinguish between extraordinary and exceptional items, including their accounting treatment and disclosure requirements.

1   THE ALL INCLUSIVE APPROACH TO REPORTING PROFIT

FRS 3 was introduced to solve two problems:

1   to prevent companies from hiding bad news in reserves (reserve accounting) or in extraordinary items; and

2   to provide a fuller analysis of a company's performance during the year.

Its aim is to help users to have a better understanding of past performance so that they will be able to make better estimates of future performance.

UK GAAP adopts the all inclusive approach to reporting financial performance which states that all profits and losses should be reported as part of the profit on ordinary activities for the year. This approach is objective and ensures consistency between companies. However, it does mean that the profit for the year might be distorted by unusual events.

This contrasts with the opinion that ordinary profit should only show the results of normal activities, with any unusual items shown as extraordinary items in the profit and loss account or hidden in reserves. In theory, this has the advantage that the ordinary profit reports the regular profit that can be achieved year after year. However, in practice, companies would be likely to treat unusual profits as part of their ordinary activities, and any unusual losses as extraordinary items or as movements on reserves.

FRS 3 favours the all inclusive approach because it is more objective. The only exception to this rule (relevant to this unit) is that revaluation gains are taken straight to the revaluation reserve. Under FRS 3 the profit on ordinary activities includes just about everything, as is shown by its definition of ordinary activities:

Ordinary activities are any activities which are undertaken by a reporting entity as part of its business and such related activities in which the reporting entity engages in furtherance of, incidental to, or arising from, these activities. Ordinary activities include the effects on the reporting entity of any event in the various environments in which it operates, including the political, regulatory, economic and geographical environments, irrespective of the frequency or unusual nature of the events.

This can lead to fluctuations in the profit for the year, and so FRS 3 has additional disclosure requirements. These explain the causes and report the effects of unusual events. These are covered in the sections below.

2 EXCEPTIONAL AND EXTRAORDINARY ITEMS

2.1 INTRODUCTION

FRS 3 requires *exceptional items* to be highlighted on the face of the profit and loss account or disclosed in the notes. It has, however, virtually abolished the use of *extraordinary items*.

2.2 EXCEPTIONAL ITEMS: DEFINITION

Exceptional items are **material** items which derive from events or transactions that fall within the **ordinary** activities of the company, and which **individually or**, if of a similar type, **in aggregate**, need to be disclosed by virtue of their **size or incidence** if the financial statements are to give a true and fair view.

If an unusual item is not **material** then there is no need to report it. It will not affect the reader's decisions.

Exceptional items are part of the **ordinary** activities of the business.

An **individual** item can be exceptional because of its **size**. For example, a single bad debt may be so large that it materially reduces the business's profits.

Smaller items can be classified as exceptional in **aggregate** because of their **incidence**. For example, poor economic conditions may cause a business to have three times the level of bad debts in one particular year as compared with normal. Even if no bad debt is particularly large, in aggregate they have made an exceptionally large dent in the company's profits.

2.3 EXCEPTIONAL ITEMS: EXAMPLES

The following items may be exceptional when they are material. This list is not exhaustive:

- redundancy costs

- reorganisation costs

- profits and losses on disposal of assets

- impairment losses

- provisions against stocks or debtors

- insurance claims.

2.4 EXCEPTIONAL ITEMS: TREATMENT AND PRESENTATION

Exceptional items are usually charged (or credited) to the P&L in the normal way, included under the appropriate cost headings. However, they will be disclosed and explained in the notes to the accounts. For example, if there had been an exceptional provision for the write off of obsolete stock, then this would be accounted for in the normal way, decreasing the value of closing stock and increasing cost of sales. The notes would then explain and quantify the effects of this exceptional item.

There are three exceptional items that must be disclosed on the face of the profit and loss account:

(1) profits or losses on the sale or termination of an operation

(2) costs of a fundamental reorganisation or restructuring having a material effect on the nature and focus of the company's operations

(3) profits or losses on the disposal of fixed assets. (This refers to the material profits or losses when, say a property is sold, rather than the pennies gained or lost when the office typewriter is scrapped.)

These will be shown as part of ordinary activities immediately after operating profit and before interest.

Example – Exe Ltd

Noted below is the draft profit and loss account for Exe Ltd for 20X7:

	£
Turnover	976,000
Cost of sales	(276,000)
Gross profit	700,000
Selling and distribution costs	(180,000)
Administration costs	(120,000)
Operating profit	400,000
Interest payable	(50,000)
Profit before tax.	350,000

The following adjusting events have just been brought to the attention of the accounts department:

(1) One major stock line has become obsolete and so a provision for £124,000 to write it down to net realisable value is needed.

(2)   The entire distribution network has been outsourced. This has resulted in redundancy costs of £176,000.

(3)   A surplus plot of land was sold just before the year-end yielding a profit of £345,000.

Required:

(a)   Explain how each item will be classified in the revised financial statements.

(b)   Redraft the P&L to take these adjustments into account.

Solution

(a)   (1)   This is an exceptional item requiring disclosure only. The additional cost of £124,000 will be included in cost of sales.

(2)   These redundancy costs of £176,000 have probably been caused by a fundamental reorganisation of the business and so they can be treated as an exceptional item to be disclosed on the face of the profit and loss account after operating profit. Further information will be disclosed in the notes.

(3)   The £345,000 profit on disposal will be treated as an exceptional item to be disclosed on the face of the P&L.

(b)   **Exe Ltd – Revised profit and loss account for 20X7**

			£
Turnover			976,000
Cost of sales	Note a	(276,000 + 124,000)	(400,000)
Gross profit			576,000
Selling and distribution costs			(180,000)
Administration costs			(120,000)
Operating profit			276,000
Exceptional items			
Reorganisation and redundancy	Note b		(176,000)
Profit on disposal of fixed assets	Note c		345,000
Operating profit after exceptional items			445,000
Interest payable			(50,000)
Profit before tax			395,000

Note a   One major stock line has become obsolete. As a result cost of sales includes a £124,000 exceptional charge for stock write-offs.

Note b   The entire distribution network has been outsourced. This has resulted in an exceptional redundancy charge of £176,000.

Note c   A surplus plot of land has been sold yielding an exceptional profit of £345,000.

2.5   EXTRAORDINARY ITEMS

Definition   **Extraordinary items** are material items possessing a high degree of abnormality which arise from events or transactions that fall outside the ordinary activities of the company and which are not expected to recur. They do not include exceptional items nor do they include prior period items merely because they relate to a prior period.

Extraordinary items were heavily misused in the past, with any bad news being classified as extraordinary. Current practice is to have no extraordinary items. The definition of ordinary activities is now so broad that no events will ever fall outside the ordinary activities of the company. As Sir David Tweedie said, 'Martians walking down the street will be extraordinary, everything else exceptional'. No examples of extraordinary items are given in FRS 3 and the ASB hopes that extraordinary items have been killed off and will never be seen again.

3 PRIOR YEAR ADJUSTMENTS

3.1 PRIOR PERIOD ITEMS

There are many items in the financial statements that relate to prior periods. For example, many accruals are based on estimates. In the following year the actual amount paid may be quite different from the estimate. Strictly speaking, the difference between the actual amount paid and the accrual relates to the previous year. Similar situations arise with doubtful debt allowances, estimated useful lives and so on. FRS 3 upholds traditional accounting practice on these items. This is that estimates are a normal part of accounting, and that any changes in estimates should be dealt with in the year that they are identified. No adjustments should be made to prior period financial statements for these items.

However, there are two situations where an adjustment has to be made to previously published financial statements, these are the correction of fundamental errors and changes in accounting policy. A prior period adjustment is accounted for by adjusting the company's opening reserves.

These rules are summed up in FRS 3's definition of a prior period adjustment:

'**Prior period adjustments** are those material adjustments applicable to prior periods arising from changes in accounting policies or from the correction of fundamental errors. They do not include normal recurring adjustments or corrections of accounting estimates made in prior periods.'

3.2 CHANGES IN ACCOUNTING POLICIES

The consistency concept means that companies should apply the same accounting concepts from year to year. However, accounting policies should be changed if the directors consider that a different policy would be more appropriate, or if a new standard has been published.

When an accounting policy is changed, consistency requires that previously published financial statements should be amended in line with the new policy. This enables valid comparisons to be made between the current year and previous years.

The cumulative affect on profits of the changes are adjusted for by restating the opening balance of retained profits.

3.3 CORRECTIONS OF FUNDAMENTAL ERRORS

Very occasionally, financial statements may be published that contain such fundamental errors that the accounts do not show a true and fair view. When these errors are noticed they are corrected by adjusting the previously published financial statements. The opening balance of retained profits will also have to be adjusted.

Example – Wye Ltd

Below are summary financial statements for Wye Ltd. The 20X3 statements were prepared and published last year. The 20X4 statements are still in draft format.

		20X4 Draft £000	20X3 Published £000
Turnover		1,235	1,437
Cost of sales	Note 1	(1,135)	(807)
Gross profit		100	630
Expenses		(250)	(280)
Net (loss) profit for the year		(150)	350
Opening revenue reserves		1,300	950
		1,150	1,300

Whilst preparing the 20X4 accounts the financial director noted the following errors in the 20X3 accounts:

(1)   The closing stock figure was twice what it should have been. Owing to an administrative mistake stock was counted and valued twice. The correct closing stock figure for 20X3 is £234,000.

The cost of sales calculation for the two years is as follows:

	20X4 Draft £000	20X3 Published £000
Opening stock	468*	298
Add: purchases	916	977
Less: closing stock	(249)	(468)*
Cost of sales	1,135	807

*The closing stock for 20X3 and the opening stock for 20X4 is incorrect.

(1)   The doubtful debt provision in 20X3 was understated. The provision was £23,000 whereas £30,000 of the year-end debtors failed to pay up. The charge for these bad debts has been included in the operating expenses in the draft accounts for 20X4. The closing provision for 20X4 is considered to be reasonable.

Required:

(a)   Explain how these items will be accounted for in 20X4.

(b)   Revise the financial statements for 20X3 and 20X4 in accordance with FRS 3.

Solution

(a)   **Accounting treatment**

The error in the stock valuation is a fundamental error. The previously reported profits for 20X3 are roughly twice what they should have been. Also, if the error is adjusted for in 20X4 (as has happened in the draft accounts) then these accounts too will be incorrect. Therefore the previous accounts need to be restated and the opening reserves adjusted. The difference between the estimated doubtful debt provision and the actual bad debt charge is just a normal accounting adjustment. This does not need a prior year adjustment and it is not really material enough to be disclosed as an exceptional item.

(b)   **Revised financial statements**

The published financial statements for 20X4 will be as follows:

Profit and loss account		20X4 Revised £000	20X3 Restated £000
Turnover		1,235	1,437
Cost of sales	(W1)	(901)	(1,041)
Gross profit		334	396
Expenses		(250)	(280)
Net (loss) profit		84	116

Movement on reserves	20X4 £000
Opening reserves as previously published	1,300
Correction of fundamental error	(234)
Restated opening reserves	1,066
Net profit for the period	84
Closing reserves	1,150

(W1) **Cost of sales**	20X4 £000	20X3 £000
Opening stock	234	298
Add: purchases	916	977
Less: closing stock	(249)	(234)
Cost of sales	901	1,041

4   ADDITIONAL NOTES

4.1   INTRODUCTION

FRS 3 introduced a range of new disclosures. These are:

- the statement of total recognised gains and losses

- the note of historical cost profits and losses

- the reconciliation of movements in shareholders' funds

- the reserves note.

These are discussed below.

4.2   STATEMENT OF TOTAL RECOGNISED GAINS AND LOSSES

This is a primary statement, and ranks alongside the profit and loss account, balance sheet and cash flow statement in importance. The statement of total recognised gains and losses brings together all the gains and losses for the period, including items which do not pass through the profit and loss account.

The most common example of an item which does not pass through the profit and loss account is a gain on the revaluation of a fixed asset. Revaluation gains cannot be taken to the profit and loss account because they are unrealised, but nevertheless, they may form an important part of a company's overall performance. Before the introduction of FRS 3, revaluation gains and losses were required to be disclosed as a movement on reserves and within the tangible fixed asset note. However, it was often difficult for users of the financial statements to appreciate their impact upon the company's overall financial performance. The statement of total recognised gains and losses highlights the effect of revaluations and other items such as prior period adjustments.

Example

Stergel plc reported profits for the financial year of £42m. During the year some freehold land with a book value of £2m was revalued upwards to £7m. There was also a prior year adjustment that decreased the opening reserves by £2m.

Statement of total recognised gains and losses

	£m
Profit for the financial year *(from the profit and loss account)*	42
Unrealised surplus on revaluation of properties	5
Total recognised gains and losses relating to the year	47
Prior year adjustment (See Note XX)	(2)
Total gains and losses recognised since the last annual report	45

4.3 NOTE OF HISTORICAL COST PROFITS AND LOSSES

When an asset is revalued then the depreciation charge is based on the revalued amount. This tends to result in a higher depreciation charge and lower profits than if the asset had been left at historical cost. The note of historical cost profits and losses is designed to enable users of the financial statements to make fair comparison between the results of different entities.

Example

Wesley plc has revalued some machinery and some land. The machinery is being depreciated and the land was sold during the year.

(1) Wesley has revalued some major pieces of plant and machinery. These machines had a cost of £30m and they were being depreciated over 15 years at £2m per annum. The assets have been revalued to £49m, and they have seven years useful life remaining. The revalued depreciation charge is £7m per annum.

(2) Land with a cost of £3m was sold during the year for £17m. However, the land had previously been revalued to £12m and so only £5m of profit could be claimed on disposal.

Wesley's profits before tax (taking the revaluations into account) were £23m. The tax charge was £7m. The tax charge will not be affected by these items. There were no dividends.

Note of historical cost profits and losses

		£m
Reported profit on ordinary activities before taxation		23
Difference between the historic cost depreciation charge and the reported charge based on the revaluation	(7 – 2)	5
Realisation of property revaluation gains of previous years	(12 – 3)	9
Historic cost profit on ordinary activities before taxation		37
Historic cost profit on ordinary activities after taxation and dividends	(37 – 7)	30

4.4 RECONCILIATION OF MOVEMENTS IN SHAREHOLDERS' FUNDS

FRS 3 requires financial statements to include a note reconciling the opening and closing shareholders' funds (share capital and reserves). This can be presented either as a primary statement or as a note to the accounts.

The profit and loss account and the statement of total recognised gains and losses together reflect the performance of an entity in a period. However, there may be other items which affect shareholders' funds, such as issues of share capital or the payment of dividends. The reconciliation highlights these items and brings them together into one statement.

Example

Recomove Ltd made a profit for the year of £53m. Dividends for the year were £18m. During the year ten million £1 ordinary shares were issued at a premium of £1.50. The total other recognised gains and losses (all relating to revaluations) amounted to £4m. Opening shareholders' funds were £99m.

Reconciliation of movements in shareholders' funds

	£m
Profit for the financial year	53
Dividends	(18)
	35
Other recognised gains and losses relating to the year	4
New share capital subscribed 10m @ (£1 + £1.50)	25
	64
Opening shareholders' funds	99
Closing shareholders' funds	163

Example – Strathdon Ltd

Strathdon Ltd had the following share capital and reserves at 1 January 20X3:

	£000
Share capital (£1 ordinary shares)	100
Share premium	50
Revaluation reserve	225
Profit and loss account	200
	575

During the year ended 31 December 20X3, the company issued a further 50,000 £1 ordinary shares at a market price of £1.60.

On 31 December 20X3 it disposed of a property for £450,000. The property had originally cost £300,000 and was revalued to £500,000 on 1 January 20X1, when it was four years old and its net book value was £250,000. From that date depreciation was charged on a straight line basis over its estimated remaining useful economic life of 20 years.

On 31 December 20X3 another property was revalued at £400,000 and this valuation was incorporated into the financial statements. This property had previously been stated at historic cost of £250,000 less accumulated depreciation of £50,000.

All other fixed assets were included in the financial statements at historical cost less accumulated depreciation.

Dividends of £10,000 were paid during the year.

An extract from the profit and loss account of Strathdon Ltd for the year ended 31 December 20X3 is shown below:

	£000
Profit on ordinary activities before taxation	100
Tax on profit on ordinary activities	(40)
Profit on ordinary activities after taxation	60

You are required to prepare:

(a)   the statement of total recognised gains and losses

(b)   the note of historical cost profits and losses

(c)   the reconciliation of movements in shareholders' funds

(d)   the reserves note

for the year ended 31 December 20X3.

Solution

(a)   **Statement of total recognised gains and losses for the year ended 31 December 20X3**

	£000
Profit for the financial year (Note 1)	60
Unrealised surplus on revaluation of properties (Note 2)	
(400 – 200)	200
Total recognised gains and losses relating to the year	260

(b)   **Note of historical cost profits and losses**

	£000
Reported profit on ordinary activities before taxation	100.0
Realisation of property revaluation gains of previous years	
(Note 3) (W1)	212.5
Difference between a historical cost depreciation charge and the actual depreciation charge of the year calculated on the revalued amount (W2)	12.5
Historical cost profit on ordinary activities before taxation	325.0
Historical cost profit for the year retained after taxation and dividends (50 + 212.5 + 12.5)	275.0

(c)   **Reconciliation of movements in shareholders' funds**

	£000
Profit for the financial year (Note 1)	60
Dividends	(10)
	50
Other recognised gains and losses relating to the year (revaluation)	200
New share capital subscribed (50,000 × £1.60)	80
Net addition to shareholders' funds	330
Opening shareholders' funds	575
Closing shareholders' funds	905

(d)   **Reserves**

	Share premium account	Revaluation reserve	Profit and loss account	Total
	£000	£000	£000	£000
At the beginning of the year	50	225	200	475
Premium on issue of shares (50,000 × 60p)	30			30
Transfer from profit and loss account of the year (60 – 10)			50	50
Transfer of realised profit (Notes 3 and 4)		(225)	225	
Surplus on property revaluation (Note 2)		200		200
At end of year	80	200	475	755

Notes:

(1)   Both the statement of total recognised gains and losses and the reconciliation of movements in shareholders' funds start with profit for the year. This is the amount which is available for distribution to shareholders.

(2)   The surplus on revaluation appears in the statement of total recognised gains and losses for the accounting period in which the revaluation takes place. Because it is unrealised, it does not pass through the profit and loss account, but the gain is recognised in the financial statements and taken to the revaluation reserve.

(3)   Where a fixed asset has been revalued, FRS 3 requires the profit or loss on disposal of a fixed asset to be calculated as the difference between the sales proceeds and the net book value based on the revalued amount. The disposal realises the surplus that was recognised at the time the revaluation took place. This accounting treatment is confirmed by FRS 15 *Tangible Fixed Assets*.

(4)   The disposal of the revalued property causes the unrealised revaluation surplus to become realised. The surplus is transferred from the revaluation reserve to the profit and loss account reserve. Only amounts relating to assets that the company still holds should remain in the revaluation reserve.

At its simplest level, this transfer would be equal to the original surplus on revaluation, in this case, £250,000. The actual amount transferred is £225,000, which is made up of the two reconciling items in the note of historical cost profits and losses. These are the difference between the profit based on the revalued amount and the profit based on the original cost (W1) and the difference between the annual depreciation charge based on the revalued amount and that based on the historic cost (W2). (The disposal took place on the final day of the accounting period.) In previous accounting periods, the company has made an annual transfer of £12,500 from revaluation reserve to profit and loss account reserve. This is the figure which would have been disclosed in the note of historical cost profits and losses for 20X1 and 20X2 and represents the additional depreciation charged on the revalued amount.

Where assets are carried at a valuation, FRS 15 states that depreciation must be based on the revalued amount and that the whole charge must pass through the profit and loss account. It is not acceptable to split the charge between the reserves so that only depreciation charged on historic cost passes directly through the profit and loss account while the additional depreciation on the revalued amount is set against the revaluation reserve. However, it has become normal practice to make an annual reserve transfer equal to the difference between depreciation on the revalued amount and depreciation on the original cost. The illustrative examples included in FRS 3 adopt this treatment, thereby legitimising it.

Workings

(W1) **Realisation of property revaluation gains**

Profit on disposal (included in profit on ordinary activities before taxation):

	£000	£000
Sale proceeds		450
Valuation at 1 January 20X1	500	
Less:		
Accumulated depreciation (500/20 × 3)	(75)	
		425
		25

Profit on disposal (based on historic cost):

	£000	£000
Sale proceeds		450.0
Cost	300.0	
Less:		
Accumulated depreciation to 31 December 20X0 (300/24 × 4)	(50.0)	
Accumulated depreciation from 1 January 20X1(300/24 × 3)	(37.5)	
		212.5
		237.5
Difference between historical cost profit and profit based on the revalued amount (realised gain) (237.5 – 25)		212.5

(W2) **Difference between historical cost depreciation and depreciation based on the revalued amount**

	£000
Annual depreciation based on revalued amount (500/20)	25.0
Annual depreciation based on historic cost (300/24)	12.5
Difference	12.5

(W3) **Revaluation reserve**

	£000	£000
Revalued amount		500
Historic cost	300	
Less: Accumulated depreciation	(50)	
		(250.0)
Unrealised surplus at 1 January 20X1		250.0
Less: Additional depreciation (3 × 12.5)		(37.5)
		212.5

ACTIVITY 1

The following figures have been calculated for Phibbs plc for the year ended 31 December 20X9, together with comparatives for the previous year.

	20X9 £m	20X8 £m
Profit before tax	50	35
Tax	(12)	(7)
Profit for the financial year	38	28
Dividends	(18)	(15)
Retained profit	20	13
Unrealised surplus on revaluation of property	2	1
Opening shareholders' funds	222	204
Share capital issued during the year		
Par value	10	3
Premium	2	1
Additional depreciation charged on property revaluations	3	2
(i.e. over and above what would have been charged on their historical cost)		

You are required to draft the following statements for Phibbs plc for inclusion in the 20X9 accounts:

(a)   statement of total recognised gains and losses

(b)   reconciliation of movements in shareholders' funds

(c)   note of historical cost profits and losses.

For a suggested answer, see the 'Answers' section at the end of the book.

KEY TERMS

Ordinary activities – any activities which are undertaken by a reporting entity as part of its business and such related activities in which the reporting entity engages in furtherance of, incidental to, or arising from, these activities. Ordinary activities include the effects on the reporting entity of any event in the various environments in which it operates, including the political, regulatory, economic and geographical environments, irrespective of the frequency or unusual nature of the events.

Exceptional items – material items which derive from events or transactions that fall within the ordinary activities of the company, and which individually or, if of a similar type, in aggregate, need to be disclosed by virtue of their size or incidence if the financial statements are to give a true and fair view.

Extraordinary items – material items possessing a high degree of abnormality which arise from events or transactions that fall outside the ordinary activities of the company and which are not expected to recur. They do not include exceptional items nor do they include prior period items merely because they relate to a prior period.

Prior period adjustments – those material adjustments applicable to prior periods arising from changes in accounting policies or from the correction of fundamental errors. They do not include normal recurring adjustments or corrections of accounting estimates made in prior periods.

SELF TEST QUESTIONS

		Paragraph
1	What is the all inclusive approach to reporting financial performance?	1
2	What are the ordinary activities of a business?	1
3	What is an exceptional item?	2.2
4	Which three exceptional items need to be shown in the profit and loss account?	2.4
5	What type of prior period item will not be adjusted for?	3.1
6	What type of prior period item will be adjusted for?	3.1
7	Name four additional notes and statements required by FRS 3.	4.1

EXAM-STYLE QUESTION

LEONARDO LTD

The trial balance of Leonardo Ltd at 30 September 20X8 included the following items:

	Dr	*Cr*
	£000	£000
Turnover		6,840
Opening stock	1,200	
Purchases	3,670	
Distribution costs	880	
Administrative expenses	590	
Interest payable	300	
Costs of a fundamental reorganisation of the company's operations	560	
Profit on sale of head office building (the company plans to move its central administration into a rented building)		1,200
Provision for doubtful debts 1 October 20X7		150

In preparing the company's profit and loss account the following further information is to be taken into account:

(i) The closing stock was counted on 27 September 20X8 (all valued at cost) and amounted to £950,000. Between that date and the close of business on 30 September 20X8, goods costing £68,000 were sold and there were no further receipts of goods. These sales are included in the turnover total of £6,840,000.

(ii) During the year a debt of £400,000 proved to be irrecoverable and is to be written off. The provision for doubtful debts is to be increased to £200,000.

(iii) The corporation tax expense on the profit from ordinary activities was £300,000.

Required:

(a)   Prepare the company's profit and loss account for the year ended 30 September 20X8 for inclusion in the company's annual report and complying, so far as the information permits, with the requirements of FRS 3 *Reporting Financial Performance*.   **(10 marks)**

(b)   FRS 3 requires companies to produce several other statements or notes in addition to the profit and loss account and balance sheet. Name and briefly describe the contents of these statements or notes.   **(5 marks)**
    (Total: 15 marks)

For a suggested answer, see the 'Answers' section at the end of the book.

Chapter 10

CASH FLOW STATEMENTS

This chapter explains the need for a cash flow statement, how to prepare a cash flow statement in accordance with FRS 1, and how to interpret a cash flow statement. It covers syllabus areas 3(a), 3(b) and 3(c).

CONTENTS

1   Cash flow statements

2   Preparing a cash flow statement

3   Incomplete information

4   Usefulness of the cash flow statement

5   Interpretation of cash flow data

LEARNING OUTCOMES

At the end of this chapter you should be able to:

- explain the need for a cash flow statement

- prepare a cash flow statement including relevant notes for a single company in accordance with accounting standards

- appraise the usefulness of, and interpret the information in a cash flow statement.

1   CASH FLOW STATEMENTS

1.1   CASH AND PROFIT

The profit reported in the profit and loss account is calculated using the accruals concept. Income arises when sales are invoiced and expenses are charged when they are incurred. The profit for the year represents the increase in the net assets of the company during the year, but it does not represent the increase in cash. Some of these profits are represented by increases in fixed assets, stocks and debtors rather than in cash. The business may also use some of the cash generated to reduce its loans and trade creditors.

It is important to know how much profit a business is making. However, it is equally important to know how much cash a business is generating, and how that cash is being used. This information is reported in the *cash flow statement*.

1.2 STANDARD HEADINGS

FRS 1 requires a cash flow statement to be presented using standard headings that highlight the major components of cash flow. The standard headings shown in the statement are:

(a) operating activities

(b) dividends received from associates (not examinable)

(c) returns on investments and servicing of finance

(d) taxation

(e) capital expenditure and financial investment

(f) acquisitions and disposals (not examinable)

(g) equity dividends paid

(h) management of liquid resources

(i) financing.

The bottom line of the cash flow statement is the increase or decrease in cash during the accounting period. Cash includes deposits and overdrafts that are repayable on demand. This means that money tied up in a 30-day account would not be considered as cash. Instead it would be classified as a liquid resource. This is discussed in more detail later.

1.3 PROFORMA CASH FLOW STATEMENT

A simplified version of the FRS 1 format is shown below. Section 3 explains how each part of the cash flow statement is prepared.

Cash flow statement for the year ended 31 December 20X0

	£000	£000
Net cash inflow from operating activities *Note 1*		6,889
Returns on investments and servicing of finance		
Interest received	2,911	
Dividends received	100	
Interest paid	(12)	
		2,999
Taxation		(2,922)
Capital expenditure		
Payments to acquire:		
intangible fixed assets	(71)	
tangible fixed assets	(1,496)	
Proceeds from sale of tangible fixed assets	42	
		(1,525)
		5,441
Equity dividends paid		(2,417)
		3,024
Management of liquid resources		
Purchase of current asset investment		(450)
Financing		
Issue of ordinary share capital	206	
Redemption of debentures	(149)	
		57
Increase in cash *Note 2*		2,631

Note 1   Reconciliation of operating profit to net cash inflow from operating activities

	£000
Operating profit	6,022
Depreciation charges	850
Loss on disposal of fixed assets	49
Increase in stocks	(194)
Increase in debtors	(72)
Increase in creditors	234
Net cash inflow from operating activities	6,889

Note 2   Analysis of changes in net debt

	At 1 Jan 20X0 £000	Cash flows £000	Other changes £000	At 31 Dec 20X0 £000
Cash in hand, at bank	42	847		889
Overdrafts	(1,784)	1,784		
Increase in cash		**2,631**		
Debt due within 1 year	(149)	149	(230)	(230)
Debt due after 1 year	(1,262)		230	(1,032)
Current asset investments	250	450		700
Total	(2,903)	3,230	–	327

1.4   NET CASH INFLOW FROM OPERATING ACTIVITIES

The first line of the statement shows the net cash inflow from operating activities. This reports the cash generated from the business's day-to-day trade. There are two ways in which this can be calculated; the *direct method* and the *indirect method*.

The direct method

The direct method calculates the net cash inflow from operating activities using information about sales and purchases and other payments taken directly from the cash book. An example is noted below.

Net cash inflow from operating activities: Direct method

	£000
Cash received from customers	15,424
Cash payments to suppliers	(5,824)
Cash paid to and on behalf of employees	(2,200)
Other cash payments	(511)
Net cash inflow from operating activities	6,889

Companies are encouraged (but not required) to disclose this information.

Most questions are based on the indirect method rather than the direct method. This chapter concentrates on the indirect method.

The indirect method

This method reconciles the operating profit to the net cash inflow from operating activities. It adjusts the operating profit for non-cash items (such as depreciation) and for changes in cash flows caused by movements in working capital (such as delays in receiving cash from customers).

This reconciliation must be published as part of the financial statements. It is called the *Reconciliation of operating profit to net cash inflow from operating activities.* An example is shown as Note 1 to the cash flow statement above.

The two methods give the same answer. In practice very few companies use the optional direct method.

1.5 THE ANALYSIS OF CHANGES IN NET DEBT

This reconciliation shows the movements in cash and debt during the year. The most important part of this analysis for you is the third line which shows the increase or decrease in cash. It nets off the movements in positive bank and cash balances against any overdrafts. It links together the balances shown in the opening and closing balance sheets with the bottom line of the cash flow statement. In this example the £2,631 increase in cash in the *cash flow statement* agrees with the net increase in bank, cash and overdrafts shown in the *analysis of changes in net debt.*

2 PREPARING A CASH FLOW STATEMENT

This section looks at each component of the cash flow statement in turn. It outlines the purpose of each section and explains how to calculate the information in it.

2.1 NET CASH INFLOW FROM OPERATING ACTIVITIES: INDIRECT METHOD

As mentioned above, under the indirect method the net cash inflow from operating activities is calculated in the *Reconciliation of operating profit to net cash inflow from operating activities.* The reconciliation adjusts for non-cash items and for movements in working capital.

Example – Non-cash items

Ormond plc makes an operating profit of £345,000. This is after charging £79,000 of depreciation and claiming a £23,000 profit on disposal of some fixed assets.

Solution

The £79,000 depreciation charge is a bookkeeping adjustment. It does not represent an outflow of cash. Therefore it must be added back to the £345,000 operating profit as part of the reconciliation of profit to cash flows. The cash outflows relating to fixed assets occur when fixed assets are purchased. This is reported in the *capital expenditure* section of the cash flow statement.

The £23,000 gain on disposal is merely a bookkeeping entry to adjust for an over-provision of depreciation in the past. This gain must be deducted from the operating profit in the reconciliation. The cash inflows relating to fixed assets occur when fixed assets are sold. This is reported in the *capital expenditure* section of the cash flow statement.

If there is a loss on disposal, then it is treated as an additional depreciation charge. A loss is added back to the operating profit.

The first few lines of the reconciliation will look as follows:

	£
Operating profit	345,000
Add back depreciation	79,000
Less profit on disposal of fixed assets	(23,000)
	401,000

In some questions the depreciation charge and/or the profit on disposal will not be given to you. In these situations the charges, gains and loss have to be calculated. The techniques for doing this are illustrated in Section 3 below.

Under the standard format for the profit and loss account as set out in FRS 3, material profits or losses on the disposal of fixed assets are shown as exceptional items *after* operating profit. If this is the case, then the profit or loss will *not* appear in the reconciliation. You must check each question carefully to see whether the operating profit is stated before or after claiming profits (or charging losses) on disposal.

Example – Movements in working capital

Working capital absorbs cash. Stocks have to be paid for and customers are slow in paying for the goods they have bought. If working capital increases then more cash will have to be invested in it. The extra cash required to fund working capital will decrease the amount of cash generated through trade. The *Reconciliation* reduces the operating profit by the increase in working capital in order to calculate the cash generated from operations.

Continuing with the Ormond plc example, the balance sheet shows the following working capital balances:

	This year	Last year
	£	£
Stocks	85,000	67,000
Trade debtors and prepayments	123,000	104,000
Trade creditors and accruals	139,000	113,000

Stocks

Stocks bought and *used* during the year are charged to the profit and loss account as part of the cost of goods sold. However, any cash flows arising from the increase in stocks is excluded from the cost of sales by the adjustments for opening and closing stock. The cash flow statement must recognise the cash paid for these extra stock items. Therefore any *increase* in stocks will be *deducted* from the reported operating profit figure in the reconciliation.

In this example the £18,000 increase in stocks is deducted from operating profits.

If there is a decrease in stocks then this will be added on to the operating profit. This is because the charge in the profit and loss account is greater than the cost of the stock purchased.

Trade debtors and prepayments

The profit and loss account recognises turnover on the basis of sales made during the year. For most businesses there will be a delay between making a sale and collecting the cash in from their customers. This means that in any year there will be some cash received in respect of opening debtors (relating to the previous year's sales), and some of this year's sales will not be received until the following year (giving rise to closing debtors). The reconciliation adjusts for the net affect of the delay caused by opening and closing debtors.

If debtors *increase*, then the cash received is less than the turnover claimed. Therefore, an increase in debtors will be *deducted* from operating profit in the reconciliation.

In this example the £19,000 increase in debtors and prepayments is deducted from operating profits.

If debtors decrease, then the cash received from customers must have been greater than the turnover claimed in the profit and loss account. A decrease in debtors is added to the operating profit in the reconciliation.

Trade creditors and accruals

All goods and services purchased during the year are charged to the profit and loss account. However, there is normally a delay between making purchases and paying for them. In any year, some payments are made in respect of opening creditors (goods and services charged in the previous year's accounts), and some of this year's purchases will not be paid for until the following year (giving rise to closing creditors).

If creditors and accruals *increase*, then the cash paid is less than the amounts charged. Therefore, an increase in creditors will be *added* to operating profit in the reconciliation.

In this example the £26,000 increase in creditors and accruals is added to operating profits.

The reconciliation is now complete. It will look as follows:

Ormond plc
Reconciliation of operating profit to net cash inflow from operating activities

		£
Operating profit		345,000
Add back depreciation		79,000
Less profit on disposal of fixed assets		(23,000)
		401,000
Increase in stocks	(85 – 67)	(18,000)
Increase in debtors	(123 – 104)	(19,000)
Increase in creditors	(139 – 113)	26,000
Net cash inflow from operating activities		390,000

ACTIVITY 1

Barts Ltd makes an operating profit of £436,000. This profit is after charging £153,000 of depreciation and claiming a £47,000 gain on disposal of some fixed assets. The opening and closing balances on its working capital is as follows;

	This year	Last year
	£	£
Stocks	64,000	78,000
Trade debtors and prepayments	83,000	59,000
Trade creditors and accruals	157,000	102,000

Required:

Prepare Bart Ltd's *Reconciliation of operating profit to net cash inflow from operating activities.*

For a suggested answer, see the 'Answers' section at the end of the book.

2.2 RETURNS ON INVESTMENTS AND SERVICING OF FINANCE

For most companies the most important item in this section is the interest paid on its borrowings. This section also covers preference dividends paid and investment income received.

Interest paid

Interest is charged in the profit and loss account on an accruals basis. There may be a delay between the interest charge and the interest being paid. The cash flow statement obviously shows the cash paid rather than the accrued charge. The cash paid is calculated by adding the opening accrued interest (charged last year but paid this year) and deducting the closing accrued interest (charged this year but not paid until next year).

Example

Ormond charges £43,000 of interest. Its opening accrual for interest is £14,000 and the closing accrual is £21,000. What is the cash payment for interest?

Solution

This can be calculated by taking into account the charge and the opening and closing accruals.

		£
Opening accrual	*from the balance sheet*	14,000
Add: Interest charge	*from the profit and loss account*	43,000
Less: Closing accrual	*from the balance sheet*	(21,000)
Cash paid		36,000

Interest and other investment income received

Investment income is often accounted for on a received basis, and so in many questions the investment income in the profit and loss account will be the same as the investment income received in the cash flow statement.

However, if the investment income is claimed on a receivable basis, then the cash received during the year is calculated by adjusting for opening and closing debtors.

Example

Ormond claims £22,000 of investment income in its profit and loss account. Investment income receivable in the opening balance sheet is £5,000, and the closing debtor is £2,000. How much investment income has been received in cash?

Solution

Enter the income from the profit and loss account charge and the opening and closing debtors from the question. The cash received will be the balancing figure.

		£
Opening debtor	*from the balance sheet*	5,000
Add: Investment income	*from the profit and loss account*	22,000
Less: Closing debtor	*from the balance sheet*	(2,000)
Cash received		25,000

Preference dividends paid

Only the preference dividend paid appears in this section. The equity (ordinary) dividend has a section to itself. Normally, the preference dividend will be the same from one year to the next, and so any accrued charges will cancel each other out. The preference dividend paid in the cash flow statement will usually be the same as the preference dividend charge in the profit and loss account. If there are any differences then the dividend paid is calculated in the same way as for interest paid.

Example

Ormond charges £90,000 for preference dividends. The opening creditor for preference dividends is £15,000 and the closing creditor £40,000. What is the cash paid?

Solution

		£
Opening creditor	*from the balance sheet*	15,000
Add: Dividend charge	*from the profit and loss account*	90,000
Less: Closing creditor	*from the balance sheet*	(40,000)
Cash paid		65,000

The *Returns on investments and servicing of finance* section is now complete. It will look as follows:

Ormond plc – Returns on investments and servicing of finance

	£
Investment income received	25,000
Interest paid	(36,000)
Preference dividends paid	(65,000)
	(76,000)

ACTIVITY 2

The following items of income and expenditure appeared in Charring Ltd's financial statements:

Investment income of £19,000. The opening debtor for investment income was £12,000, and the closing debtor is £7,000.

An interest charge of £55,000. The opening accrual is £19,000 and the closing accrual is £32,000.

A £40,000 charge for preference dividends. The opening proposed preference dividend is £35,000 and the closing proposed dividend is £22,000.

Required:

Prepare the *Returns on investments and servicing of finance* section of the cash flow statement for Charring Ltd.

For a suggested answer, see the 'Answers' section at the end of the book.

2.3   TAXATION

The tax charge in the profit and loss account is an estimate of the tax that will be paid nine months after the year end. This means that there is always a delay between tax being charged and tax being paid, and there is normally a small difference between the tax creditor and the amount eventually paid.

The tax paid during the year will, roughly speaking, be last year's tax provision. The exact amount can be calculated using a table similar to that used for calculating interest paid.

Example

The tax charge for Ormond plc is £90,000. The opening provision for tax is £79,000 and the closing provision is £65,000. How much tax was paid during the year?

Solution

		£
Opening provision	*from the balance sheet*	79,000
Add: Tax charge	*from the profit and loss account*	90,000
Less: Closing provision	*from the balance sheet*	(65,000)
Cash paid		104,000

ACTIVITY 3

The tax charge for Cross Ltd is £135,000. The opening provision for tax is £163,000 and the closing provision is £148,000. How much tax was paid during the year?

For a suggested answer, see the 'Answers' section at the end of the book.

2.4   CAPITAL EXPENDITURE AND FINANCIAL INVESTMENT

The capital expenditure element of this section looks at the cash payments and proceeds from buying and selling plant and machinery, land and buildings and so on. The financial investment element covers the cash flows arising from buying and selling stocks and shares, government securities, etc.

Capital expenditure: Payments to acquire fixed assets

The cash paid to acquire fixed assets will usually be the cost of additions shown in the fixed asset note to the balance sheet. The cash paid might be different if some of the assets are paid for in instalments.

Example

The fixed asset note for Ormond plc shows additions of £300,000, and there is a year-end creditor for £34,000 relating to capital items. The cash paid for fixed assets is £266,000.

Capital expenditure: Proceeds of disposal

The profit and loss account reports the profit or loss on disposal, rather than the proceeds. The fixed asset note will show the net book value of the assets sold during the year. The proceeds will have to be calculated from this information.

Example

Ormond plc claims a £23,000 profit on disposal of fixed assets. The fixed asset note shows that the net book value of assets disposed of during the year was £43,000. What were the cash proceeds?

Solution

You will already be familiar with the calculation of profit on disposal; proceeds less net book value equals profit on disposal. This formula can be rearranged as follows to calculate the proceeds of disposal:

- net book value plus profit on disposal equals proceeds; and

- net book value less loss on disposal equals proceeds.

In this example the proceeds are £66,000 calculated as follows:

NBV of £43,000　　**+**　　Profit of £23,000　　**=**　　Proceeds of £66,000

ACTIVITY 4

(a)　Westminster Ltd claims a £66,000 profit on disposal of fixed assets. The fixed asset note shows that the assets disposed of during the year had a cost of £143,000 and related depreciation of £57,000. What were the cash proceeds?

(b)　Hammersmith Ltd charges a loss of £64,000 on the disposal of fixed assets. The fixed asset note shows that the assets disposed of had a cost of £199,000 and related depreciation of £78,000. What were the cash proceeds?

For a suggested answer, see the 'Answers' section at the end of the book.

Financial investment

Calculating the cash flows arising from buying and selling financial investments can be complicated. However, a common situation in questions is a straight forward purchase of new investments. The purchase, and the cash outflow, will be the increase in the balance sheet value of the investments.

Example

Ormond plc has opening investments at cost of £42,000, and closing investments at cost of £55,000. In the absence of other information, the purchases during the year must have been £13,000.

The capital expenditure note can now be completed.

Ormond plc – Capital expenditure and financial investment

	£
Proceeds from the disposal of fixed assets	66,000
Payments to acquire fixed assets	(266,000)
Payments to acquire investments	(13,000)
	(213,000)

2.5 EQUITY DIVIDENDS PAID

The equity dividend is the dividend paid on the ordinary shares. The dividend will vary from year to year in response to the amount of profit made by the company. The dividend is normally paid in two instalments. The interim dividend is paid and charged in the same year, while the final dividend is charged in one year but paid in the next. The equity dividend is almost always recognised on a cash basis and so there is no need to adjust the reported dividend payment.

2.6 MANAGEMENT OF LIQUID RESOURCES

Companies place surplus cash on short-term deposits or in Government bonds so that it can earn interest until it is needed These deposits do not meet the FRS 1 criteria for cash, which must be available on demand. Instead they are classified as liquid resources. For example, a 30-day deposit with a reputable bank would be classified as a liquid resource.

If cash is transferred from a current account to a deposit account, then it is treated as a reduction in the cash available. During the course of a year, there may be many transfers to and from such accounts. In an exam question, the net movement is reported in the cash flow statement. Any increase in the balance of liquid resources represents a decrease in cash, and vice versa.

Example

Ormond plc has £50,000 of liquid resources at the start of the year and £85,000 at the end of the year. The *management of liquid resources* section of the cash flow statement shows an outflow of £35,000.

2.7 FINANCING

This section covers the long-term financing of a company. Loans received and repaid will be recorded here, along with the issue and redemption of share capital.

Loans

When you take out a loan you receive cash, and when you repay a loan you pay out cash. Therefore an increase in loans represent an inflow of cash, and vice versa. When calculating the increase or decrease in loans you must be careful to take into account loans due within one year and loans due after one year. These are recognised separately on the balance sheet.

Example

Ormond plc's balance sheet shows the following loans:

	This year £	Last year £
Creditors due within one year		
Loans	25	75
Creditors due after one year		
Loans	150	230

The total increase or decrease in loans is:

	Current	+	Deferred	£
Opening loans	75	+	230	305
Closing loans	25	+	150	175
Decrease	An outflow of cash			130

Share capital

The proceeds of a share issue will cause an increase in the balance on the share capital and share premium accounts and an inflow of cash. (The repayment of share capital is not needed for this paper.)

The cash inflow will be the increase in the combined balances on the share capital and share premium accounts.

Example

Ormond plc's capital and reserves are as follows:

	This year £	Last year £
Ordinary share capital	350	190
Share premium	235	45
Revenue reserves	209	185
	794	420

The proceeds from the issue of shares is:

	This year £	Last year £
Ordinary share capital	350	190
Share premium	235	45
	585	235
Increase (Proceeds of issue)	**350**	

The financing section is now complete. The financing section in the cash flow statement will look as follows:

Ormond plc – Financing

	£
Proceeds from share issues	350
Payments to redeem loans	(130)
	220

ACTIVITY 5

A summary balance sheet for Guy Ltd is noted below.

Required:

Prepare the financing section for Guy Ltd's cash flow statement.

	This year £		Last year £	
Fixed assets		656		796
Current assets		364		413
Creditors due within one year				
Loans	55		190	
Sundry	356		453	
		(411)		(643)
Total assets less current liabilities		609		566
Long term loans		(120)		(350)
Net assets		489		216
Ordinary share capital		200		80
Share premium		100		40
Revenue reserves		189		96
		489		216

For a suggested answer, see the 'Answers' section at the end of the book.

2.8 INCREASE OR DECREASE IN CASH

The cash flow statement adds down to the increase or decrease in cash. This should be proved by calculating the increase or decrease in the combined cash, bank and overdraft balances. In an exam it is a good idea to do this calculation first because it gives you a target figure to work towards.

Example

Ormond's cash balances are as follows:

	This year	Last year
	£	£
Current assets		
Bank and cash	<u>17</u>	<u>12</u>
Creditors due within one year		
Overdrafts	<u>3</u>	<u>35</u>

Solution

	Bank & Cash	Less	Overdrafts	£
Opening balance	12	Less	35	(23)
Closing balance	17	Less	3	<u>14</u>
Increase				<u>37</u>

2.9 THE COMPLETED CASH FLOW STATEMENT

The examples have been based on the accounts of Ormond plc. The full cash flow statement for Ormond plc is noted below:

Ormond: Cash flow statement

	£000	£000
Net cash inflow from operating activities *Note 1*		390
Returns on investments and servicing of finance		
Interest received	25	
Interest paid	(36)	
Preference dividend paid	<u>(65)</u>	
		(76)
Taxation		(104)
Capital expenditure and financial investment		
Receipts from sale of tangible fixed assets	66	
Payments to acquire tangible fixed assets	(266)	
Payments to acquire investments	<u>(13)</u>	
		(213)
Equity dividends paid		<u>(145)</u>
Cash inflow (outflow) before financing		(148)
Management of liquid resources		
Payments to acquire liquid resources		(35)
Financing		
Net proceeds from issue of shares	350	
Loans repaid	<u>(130)</u>	
		<u>220</u>
Increase in cash *Note 2*		<u>37</u>

Note 1   The net cash inflow from operating activities is reconciled to the operating profit. The reconciliation is published as part of the cash flow statement.

Note 2   The increase in cash is reconciled back to the cash balances in the balance sheet in the *analysis of net debt*.

2.10 THE ANALYSIS OF NET DEBT

The analysis of net debt shows the movement in bank, overdraft and loan balances during the year. The information comes straight from the balance sheets. The example below is for Ormond plc, and is based on the information used to calculate the cash flow statement.

Analysis of net debt

	Opening balance sheet	Cash flow	Closing balance sheet
	£000	£000	£000
Cash at bank	12	5	17
Overdrafts	(35)	32	(3)
Net bank and cash	(23)	37	14
Liquid resources	50	35	85
Investments	42	13	55
Debt due within one year	(75)	50	(25)
Debt due after one year	(230)	80	(150)
Net funds (debt)	(236)	215	(21)

The first three lines adding down to the net bank and cash figure (highlighted) are the most important lines for you. These tie in the net increase in cash from the cash flow statement to the bank, cash and overdraft balances in the balance sheet.

This analysis shows that Ormond has reduced its net debt figure by £215,000 from £236,000 down to £21,000.

2.11 NET CASH INFLOW FROM OPERATING ACTIVITIES: DIRECT METHOD

The most common way to calculate the net cash flow from operating activities is to use the indirect method. The direct method calculates the same figure by summarising the relevant entries from the cash book. If you are asked to prepare the net cash inflow from operating activities using the direct method then the question will have to give you the appropriate information.

Example

The following is a summary of Boston Ltd's cash book.

	£
Opening balance	(110,000)
Loans received	200,000
Loans repaid	(45,000)
Cash received from customers	423,000
Cash payments to suppliers	(132,000)
Cash paid to and on behalf of employees	(98,000)
Other operating cash payments	(34,000)
Capital expenditure	(174,000)
Dividends paid	(24,000)
Tax paid	(39,000)
Closing balance	(33,000)

Required:

Calculate the net cash inflow from operating activities.

Only the operating cash receipts and payments are relevant.

Solution

	£
Cash received from customers	423,000
Cash payments to suppliers	(132,000)
Cash paid to and on behalf of employees	(98,000)
Other cash payments	(34,000)
Net cash inflow from operating activities.	159,000

3 INCOMPLETE INFORMATION

3.1 INTRODUCTION

You will often come across incomplete information in a cash flow statement question. You will then be required to calculate the missing information by using balancing figures. Strictly speaking this is testing you on your knowledge and understanding of the profit and loss account and balance sheet rather than of the cash flow statement. There are two areas where you are likely to be given incomplete information; operating profit and capital expenditure. The techniques for obtaining this information are covered below.

3.2 CALCULATING OPERATING PROFIT

If the operating profit is not given to you then it is calculated from the increase or decrease in the revenue reserves, as adjusted for dividends, tax and interest.

Example

Ormond plc's opening revenue reserves are £185,000 and the closing reserves are £209,000.

The total dividend charge for the year is £210,000, the tax charge is £90,000 and the net finance costs are £21,000.

Required:

What is Ormond's operating profit?

Solution

Prepare a proforma profit and loss account, starting with operating profit and ending with the movement on reserves. Enter the information given to you onto the proforma and the operating profit will be the balancing figure.

		£
Operating profit	4	?
Less: Interest charge	3	(21,000)
Less: Tax charge	3	(90,000)
Less: Dividend charge	3	(210,000)
Retained profit	2	24,000
Add: Opening reserves	1	185,000
Closing reserves	1	209,000

Method

(1) Enter the opening and closing reserves.

(2) Calculate the retained profit for the year. This will be the increase in reserves.

(3) Add back the dividend, tax and interest charges for the year.

(4) Calculate the operating profit as a balancing figure. The operating profit is £345,000.

ACTIVITY 6

Arnos Ltd makes a profit after tax of £100,000. The dividend charge for the year is £67,000, the tax charge is £35,000 and the net finance costs are £52,000.

Required:

What is the operating profit? Be careful to adjust the profit after tax for the correct items.

For a suggested answer, see the 'Answers' section at the end of the book.

3.3 CAPITAL EXPENDITURE AND INCOMPLETE INFORMATION

It has become traditional in cash flow statement questions for the examiner to give you incomplete information in respect of capital expenditure. The examiner then expects you to calculate *either* the acquisitions for the year, *or* the depreciation charge, *or* the net book value of any disposals. The question can only have one missing figure, as the answer is based on a balancing figure. The technique is to schedule out the movements for the year on the basis of all the information given to you in the question, and then identify the missing line and the missing number. The examples below set out the basic techniques.

Example A – Information based on cost

Middlesex plc has opening fixed assets at cost of £645,000 and closing fixed assets at cost of £457,000. The cost of assets disposed of during the year was £423,000 with related depreciation of £97,000.

A loss on disposal of £73,000 was reported.

Required:

Prepare the capital expenditure section of the cash flow statement.

Solution

(1) Schedule out the movements on fixed assets entering the information given in the question about opening and closing balances, and disposals. The missing figure must be the additions for the year.

Fixed assets at cost		£
Opening		645,000
Additions	balancing figure	235,000
Disposals		(423,000)
Closing balance		457,000

(2)   Calculate the proceeds of disposal from the information about cost, accumulated depreciation and loss on disposal.

		£
Cost of disposals		423,000
Less: depreciation		(97,000)
NBV of disposals		326,000
Less: Loss on disposal		(73,000)
Proceeds of disposal		253,000

(3)   Prepare the capital expenditure note.

	£
Proceeds from the disposal of fixed assets	253,000
Payments to acquire fixed assets	(235,000)
	18,000

Example B – Calculating depreciation from information based on net book values

Thomas Ltd has opening fixed assets at net book value of £444,000 and closing fixed assets at net book value of £563,000. The cost of assets purchased during the year was £231,000 and there were no disposals during the year. What was the depreciation charge for the year?

Solution

Schedule out the movements on fixed assets entering the information given in the question about opening and closing balances, and additions. With no disposals the missing figure must be the depreciation charge for the year.

Fixed assets at net book value		£
Opening		444,000
Additions		231,000
Depreciation	*balancing figure*	(112,000)
Closing balance		563,000

Example C – Additions, revaluations and net book values

Revaluations increase the book value of fixed assets, but there is no related cash payment. Additions need to be calculated after taking into account any revaluation.

LSTM Ltd has opening fixed assets at net book value of £364,000 and closing fixed assets at net book value of £993,000. Assets with a net book value of £123,000 were sold during the year yielding a profit of £17,000. The depreciation charge for the year is £154,000. The opening balance on LSTM's revaluation reserve is £200,000, and the closing balance is £500,000.

Required:

(1)   Calculate the proceeds of disposal.

(2)   Calculate the revaluation gain for the year.

(3)   Schedule out the movement in the net book value of fixed assets. This should include a line for additions and for revaluations.

(4)   Calculate the additions for the year as a balancing figure.

(5)   Prepare the capital expenditure section of LSTM's cash flow statement.

Solution

(1)   Calculate the proceeds of disposal.

NBV of   +   Profit of £17,000   =   Proceeds of £140,000
£123,000

(2)   Calculate the revaluation gain for the year.

This is the £300,000 increase in the revaluation reserve. (£500,000 –
£200,000)

(3)   Schedule out the movement in the net book value of fixed assets.

(4)   Calculate the additions as a balancing figure.

Fixed assets at Net book value		£
Opening balance at NBV		364,000
Add: Additions at cost	balancing figure	606,000
Add: Revaluation		300,000
Less: Disposals at NBV		(123,000)
Less: Depreciation		(154,000)
Closing balance at NBV		993,000

(5)   Prepare the capital expenditure section of LSTM's cash flow statement.

	£
Proceeds from the disposal of fixed assets	140,000
Payments to acquire fixed assets	(606,000)
	(466,000)

ACTIVITY 7

Harley Ltd has opening fixed assets at net book value of £900,000 and closing fixed
assets at net book value of £800,000. Assets with a net book value of £253,000 were
sold during the year causing a loss of £67,000. The additions for the year are
£224,000.

The opening balance on Harley's revaluation reserve is £150,000, and the closing
balance is £280,000.

Required:

(1)   Calculate the proceeds of disposal.

(2)   Calculate the revaluation gain for the year.

(3)   Schedule out the movement in the net book value of fixed assets.

(4)   Calculate the depreciation charge the year as a balancing figure.

(5)   Prepare the capital expenditure section of LSTM's cash flow statement.

For a suggested answer, see the 'Answers' section at the end of the book.

Example

The previous sections have looked at the individual elements of the cash flow statement. This section works through a full example.

Information and task

The balance sheets of Fox Limited as at 31 December were as follows:

	20X8		20X7	
	£000	£000	£000	£000
Fixed assets				
Freehold property (as revalued)		22,000		12,000
Plant and machinery				
Cost	10,000		5,000	
Depreciation	2,250	7,750	2,000	3,000
		29,750		15,000
Trade investment at cost		_____		7,000
		29,750		22,000
Current assets				
Stock	16,000		11,000	
Debtors	9,950		2,700	
Cash	–		1,300	
	25,950		15,000	
Less:				
Creditors due within one year				
Trade creditors	(8,000)		(11,000)	
Bank overdraft	(11,700)	6,250	–	4,000
		36,000		26,000
Less:				
Creditors due over one year				
10% debentures		(6,000)		(10,000)
		30,000		16,000
Called up share capital		16,000		14,000
Revaluation reserve		4,000		-
Profit and loss account		10,000		2,000
		30,000		16,000

Notes:

(1)   At the beginning of the year machinery which had cost £1,000,000 and which had a book value of £250,000, was sold for £350,000.

(2)   In addition to the interest on the debentures, interest paid on the overdraft amounted to £800,000.

(3)   £4,000,000 of debentures were redeemed on 31 December 20X8.

(4)   The trade investment was sold for £10,000,000 during the year. No dividends were received from it.

(5)   The operating profit for the year before interest but after profits/losses on sale of fixed assets was £9,800,000.

Required:

Prepare a cash flow statement for the company for the year ended 31 December 20X8 complying with the requirements of FRS 1.

Solution

Fox Ltd
Cash flow statement for the year ended 31 December 20X8

Reconciliation of operating profit to net cash inflow from operating activities

	£000
Operating profit (given in note 5)	9,800
Depreciation charges (W2)	1,000
Profit on sale of plant (W3)	(100)
Profit on sale of investment (10,000 – 7,000)	(3,000)
Increase in stocks (16,000 – 11,000)	(5,000)
Increase in debtors (9,950 – 2,700)	(7,250)
Decrease in creditors (8,000 – 11,000)	(3,000)
Net cash outflow from operating activities	(7,550)

Cash flow statement

	£000	£000
Net cash outflow from operating activities		(7,550)
Returns on investments and servicing of finance		
Interest paid (W4)		(1,800)
Capital expenditure		
Payments to acquire tangible fixed assets:		
plant and machinery (W1)	(6,000)	
freehold property (10,000 – 4,000) (revaluation)	(6,000)	
Receipts from sale of investments	10,000	
Receipts from sale of plant	350	(1,650)
		(11,000)
Financing		
Issue of ordinary share capital (16,000 – 14,000)	2,000	
Redemption of debentures (6,000 – 10,000)	(4,000)	(2,000)
Reduction in cash (1,300 + 11,700)		(13,000)

Workings

(W1)   **Plant and machinery – cost**

	£000		£000
Balance b/d	5,000	Transfer – disposal	1,000
Additions during			
Year (balancing figure)	6,000	Balance c/d	10,000
	11,000		11,000

(W2) **Plant and machinery – aggregate depreciation**

	£000		£000
Depreciation: disposals during		Balance b/d	2,000
year £(1,000 – 250)	750		
		Depreciation provided	
Balance c/d	2,250	for year (bal fig)	1,000
	3,000		3,000

(W3) **Plant and machinery – disposal**

	£000		£000
Cost of disposals	1,000	Depreciation on disposals	750
Profit on sale	100	Sale proceeds	350
	1,100		1,100

(W4) The fact that the debentures were redeemed at the end of the year means that debenture interest at 10% must have been paid on the whole £10,000,000. Therefore debenture interest paid was £1,000,000 plus overdraft interest (note 2) of £800,000.

Note: Analysis of changes in net debt:

	At 1 Jan 20X8 £000	Cash flows £000	At 31 Dec 20X8 £000
Cash at bank	1,300	(1,300)	–
Overdraft	–	(11,700)	(11,700)
Debt	(10,000)	4,000	(6,000)
Total	(8,700)	(9,000)	(17,700)

Tutorial note: The debt was all shown in the opening balance sheet as falling due after more than one year. Nevertheless, £4,000,000 was repaid during the year. This is perfectly possible, but we may find questions in which some of the debentures are shown as current liabilities.

4 USEFULNESS OF THE CASH FLOW STATEMENT

4.1 ADVANTAGES OF THE CASH FLOW STATEMENT

A cash flow statement can provide information which is not available from balance sheets and profit and loss accounts.

(a) It may assist users of financial statements in making judgements on the amount, timing and degree of certainty of future cash flows.

(b) It gives an indication of the relationship between profitability and cash generating ability, and thus of the quality of the profit earned.

(c) A cash flow statement in conjunction with a balance sheet provides information on liquidity, viability and adaptability. The balance sheet is often used to obtain information on liquidity, but the information is incomplete for this purpose as the balance sheet is drawn up at a particular point in time.

(d) Cash flow cannot easily be manipulated and is not affected by judgement or by accounting policies.

4.2 LIMITATIONS OF THE CASH FLOW STATEMENT

Cash flow statements should normally be used in conjunction with profit and loss accounts and balance sheets when making an assessment of future cash flows.

(a) Cash flow statements are based on historical information and therefore do not provide complete information for assessing future cash flows.

(b) There is some scope for manipulation of cash flows. For example, a business may:

- delay paying creditors until after the year end

- offer incentives to debtors to pay early

- make particular efforts to collect amounts due from debtors just before the year end

- dispose of assets just before the year end, or

- otherwise structure transactions so that the cash balance is favourably affected.

It can be argued that cash management of this kind is an important aspect of stewardship and therefore desirable. However, more deliberate manipulation is possible (e.g. assets may be sold and then immediately repurchased after the year end).

(c) Cash flow is necessary for survival in the short term, but in order to survive in the long term a business must be profitable. It is often necessary to sacrifice cash flow in the short term in order to generate profits in the long term (e.g. by investment in fixed assets). A huge cash balance is not a sign of good management if the cash could be invested elsewhere to generate profit.

Neither cash flow nor profit provide a complete picture of a company's performance when looked at in isolation.

5 INTERPRETATION OF CASH FLOW DATA

5.1 INTRODUCTION

The estimation of the future cash flows is very important in determining the solvency or otherwise of a business. This section summarises some areas to consider.

5.2 INTERPRETATION OF THE CASH FLOW STATEMENT

Points to watch for within the various headings in the cash flow statement include:

(a) **Cash inflow/outflow from operating activities**

The figure should be compared to the operating profit. The reconciliation note to the cash flow statement is useful in this regard.

Overtrading may be indicated by:

(i)   high profits and low cash generation

(ii)   large increases in stock, debtors and creditors.

(b)   **Dividend and interest payouts**

These can be compared to cash generated from trading operations to see whether the normal operations can sustain such payments. In most years they should.

(c)   **Capital expenditure and financial investment**

The nature and scale of a company's investment in fixed assets is clearly shown.

(d)   **Management of liquid resources and financing**

The subtotal 'cash inflow/outflow before use of liquid resources and financing' indicates the financing required unless existing cash is available. The changes in financing (in pure cash terms) are clearly shown. There may be a note to the cash flow statement provided which links the inflows/outflows with the balance sheet movement.

(e)   **Cash flow**

The statement clearly shows the end result in cash terms of the company's operations in the year. Do not overstate the importance of this figure alone, however. A decrease in cash in the year may be for very sound reasons (e.g. there was surplus cash last year) or may be mainly the result of timing (e.g. a new loan was raised just after the end of the accounting period).

To help in determining the future cash position other areas of the published accounts should be considered as illustrated below.

KEY TERMS

Cash – cash and bank balances. The bank balances must be available on demand. It includes overdrafts that are repayable on demand.

Liquid resources – bank and other balances that are not available on demand, for example, a 30-day deposit account.

Net cash inflow from operating activities – the cash generated by a business from its day-to-day trading activities. It must be reconciled back to the operating profit reported in the profit and loss account.

Direct method – the method of deriving the net cash flow from operating activities directly from the cash book.

Indirect method – the method of deriving the net cash flow from operating activities by adjusting the operating profit for non-cash items and for movements in working capital.

SELF TEST QUESTIONS

Paragraph

1	Why is cash flow information important to users of financial statements?	1.1
2	What are the standard headings in a cash flow statement?	1.2
3	What are the main categories of items to adjust profit for in order to arrive at net cash flow from operating activities?	2.1
4	Is an increase in stocks a deduction or addition to operating profit in the reconciliation note?	2.1
5	Is a decrease in creditors a deduction or addition to operating profit in the reconciliation note?	2.1
6	How would net cash flow from operating activities be determined using the direct method?	2.11

EXAM-STYLE QUESTION 1

CHARLTON LTD

The summarised financial statements of Charlton Ltd are as follows:

(a) **Balance sheets at 31 December**

	20X5 £	20X6 £
Fixed assets (net book value)	40,406	47,759
Stock	27,200	30,918
Debtors	15,132	18,363
Bank	4,016	2,124
	86,754	99,164
Share capital	40,000	50,000
Share premium	8,000	10,000
Profit and loss account	19,933	22,748
Debenture stock	10,000	–
Creditors	3,621	10,416
Taxation	5,200	6,000
	86,754	99,164

(b)   **Profit and loss account for the year ended 31 December 20X6**

	£	£
Trading profit (after charging depreciation of £2,363 and interest of £900)		17,215
Taxation		6,000
Profit after tax		11,215
Dividends		8,400
Retained profit		2,815
Balance b/d		19,933
Balance c/d		22,748

An item of machinery with a net book value of £1,195 was sold for £1,614. The depreciation charge of £2,363 does not include the profit/loss on the sale of the fixed asset.

Task

Prepare a cash flow statement for the year ended 31 December 20X6.   **(20 marks)**

Guidance

Step 1   Allocate a page to the cash flow statement so that easily identifiable cash flows can be inserted. Allocate a further page to workings.

Step 2   Go through the balance sheets and take the balance sheet movements to the cash flow statement, the reconciliation note or to workings as appropriate. Tick off the information in the balance sheets once it has been used.

Step 3   Go through the additional information provided and deal with as per Step 2.

Step 4   The amounts transferred to workings can now be reconciled so that the remaining cash flows can be inserted on the statement or in the profit reconciliation note.

Step 5   The profit reconciliation note can now be totalled, the operating cash flow transferred to the cash flow statement and the cash flow statement completed.

Step 6   Prepare the analysis of net debt if required in the question.

EXAM-STYLE QUESTION 2

BOGDANOVITCH PLC

The summarised financial statements of Bogdanovitch plc are as follows.

(a)   **Balance sheet as at 31 December**

	20X8		20X9	
	£	£	£	£
Fixed assets:				
Plant and machinery		2,086		2,103
Fixtures and fittings		1,381		1,296
		3,467		3,399
Current assets:				
Stock	1,292		1,952	
Debtors	1,763		2,086	
Cash	197		512	
		3,252		4,550
Creditors: Amount falling due within one year:				
Taxation	257		312	
Trade creditors	899		903	
		(1,156)		(1,215)
		5,563		6,734
Capital and reserves:				
Share capital		4,200		4,500
Share premium		800		900
Profit and loss account		563		1,334
		5,563		6,734

(b)   **Profit and loss account for year ended 31 December 20X9**

	£	£
Profit before taxation		1,381
Taxation		310
Profit after taxation		1,071

You are informed that:

(a)   Plant and machinery with a net book value of £184 was disposed of for £203, whilst a new item of plant was purchased for £312.

(b)   Fixtures and fittings with a net book value of £100 were disposed of for £95. Depreciation provided on fixtures and fittings amounted to £351.

(c)   Dividends of £300,000 were paid during the year.

You are required to prepare a cash flow statement for the year ended 31 December 20X9. The reconciliation of net cash flow to the movement in net debt is not required.

(20 marks)

EXAM-STYLE QUESTION 3

WEASEL PLC

The balance sheets of Weasel plc at 31 August 20X8 and 20X9 are given below:

	Reference to notes	Year ended 31 August 20X8		Year ended 31 August 20X9	
		£000	£000	£000	£000
Fixed assets	1		6,400		8,500
Current assets					
Stock		1,200		1,400	
Debtors		1,500		1,400	
Cash at bank		200		300	
		2,900		3,100	
Creditors – amounts falling due within one year					
Trade creditors		(800)		(700)	
Taxation		(400)		(500)	
Bank overdraft		(360)		(200)	
Net current assets			1,340		1,700
Total assets less current liabilities			7,740		10,200
Creditors – amounts falling due after more than one year					
10% debentures 20Y5	3		(1,000)		(1,500)
			6,740		8,700
Capital and reserves					
Called up share capital			2,000		2,200
Share premium account			2,340		2,540
Revaluation reserve			–		1,000
Profit and loss account			2,400		2,960
			6,740		8,700

Notes:

(1)   Movements in fixed assets:

	Land	Buildings	Plant and equipment	Total
	£000	£000	£000	£000
Cost or valuation				
At 1 September 20X8	2,000	3,000	3,400	8,400
Additions			2,500	2,500
Disposals			(1,000)	(1,000)
Revaluation	1,000			1,000
At 31 August 20X9	3,000	3,000	4,900	10,900
Accumulated depreciation				
At 1 September 20X8		400	1,600	2,000
Provision for year		60	1,140	1,200
Disposals			(800)	(800)
At 31 August 20X9		460	1,940	2,400
Net book amounts				
At 31 August 20X9	3,000	2,540	2,960	8,500
At 1 September 20X8	2,000	2,600	1,800	6,400

(2)   Dividends paid during the year amounted to £500,000.

(3)   Issue of debentures – a further £500,000 of 10% debentures was issued at par on 1 September 20X8. Interest on all debentures is paid on 28 February and 31 August each year.

(4)   Plant sold during the year realised £250,000.

(5)   The tax charge for the year in the profit and loss account was £500,000.

Required:

Prepare a cash flow statement for Weasel plc for the year ended 31 August 20X9, complying as far as possible with FRS 1 *Cash flow statements*, using the indirect method.

The note reconciling operating profit to operating cash flows must be shown, but no other notes are required.   **(25 marks)**

For suggested answers, see the 'Answers' section at the end of the book.

Chapter 11

INTERPRETATION OF FINANCIAL STATEMENTS

Financial statements are prepared for a variety of people and purposes. For example:

- shareholders need to assess the stewardship of their directors

- investors need to assess the investment potential of a company's shares

- managers need to assess the past and potential performance of individual products or departments.

These different needs require the financial statements to be analysed and interpreted. Part of this analysis will involve the calculation of ratios, but the key performance criteria at this stage is to interpret those ratios. In an exam situation this will involve outlining the possible causes of change within a business, and then outlining the possible effects of those changes. This chapter covers syllabus areas 5(a) and 5(b).

CONTENTS

1 Analysis of accounting statements and use of ratios

2 Ratio calculation and analysis

3 Profitability ratios

4 Working capital ratios

5 Solvency ratios

6 Investor ratios

7 Interpretation of financial statements

LEARNING OUTCOMES

At the end of this chapter you should be able to:

- calculate the following ratios: profitability, liquidity, efficiency, investor, financial

- analyse and interpret the ratios to give an assessment of a company's performance in comparison with:

    (i)   a company's previous period's financial statements

    (ii)   another similar company for the same period

    (iii)   industry average ratios

- identify and discuss the limitations of ratio analysis

- prepare a financial analysis report of a company in a suitable format.

1 ANALYSIS OF ACCOUNTING STATEMENTS AND USE OF RATIOS

1.1 THE INTERNAL AND EXTERNAL USERS OF ACCOUNTING INFORMATION

Users of accounting information have been discussed in an earlier chapter. The main users we will normally be concerned with are management, lenders and shareholders (including potential shareholders).

1.2 RELEVANT INFORMATION

The various users of financial statements require information for quite different purposes. There are a large number of ratios, not all of which will be relevant to a particular situation. It is therefore important to determine the precise information needs of the user, and the decisions he has to take after analysing the relevant information.

The needs of the three particular users may be summarised:

User	Required for
Management	Control of costs, improved profitability
Lenders	Borrowing and credit purposes
Shareholders and investment analysts	Investment decisions – buying and selling shares

Ask yourself the questions 'What decision is being made?' and 'What information is relevant to that decision?'.

1.3 THE SHORTCOMINGS OF INTERPRETATION

The main function for many users is to estimate the future. However, an estimation can only be made by interpretation of the past. There is thus a significant shortcoming in any interpretation as to its effectiveness in estimating the future.

Even if the needs of the user are more concerned with historical stewardship of the business, there are limitations of interpretation as the information presented to the user is of necessity summarised in some form. The summarisation process may have the effect of distorting the nature of some of the information. For example, creditors will be classified into those payable within one year and those payable beyond one year. Two loans which have two days difference in their payment date may well as a consequence be classified under separate headings. The user, unless he is provided with further information will tend to take the two resultant totals at face value.

Finally, it should be noted that the emphasis on information produced by an undertaking is financial. In many cases, non-financial data would be useful in order to see a complete picture of the state of the organisation. Non-financial data includes for example the number of employees in the organisation and the type of skills they possess or indicators of efficiency with which the organisation addresses complaints from customers.

1.4 TECHNIQUES OF INTERPRETATION

The syllabus at this level of accounting emphasises the use of ratios to interpret information but this is only one stage in the interpretation process. A most important first step is to understand the environment in which the business operates.

Factors that need to be considered include:

- markets in which the business operates
- general economic conditions
- size of business in relation to competitors.

1.5 RATIO CALCULATION

In the context of examination questions much of this information is not available and thus we start at the calculation of ratios stage.

When calculating ratios, the two main points to bear in mind are:

- calculate only those ratios which are relevant to the needs of the user
- state the definitions used.

Some ratios can be calculated in alternative ways and therefore it is important to define the terms used.

1.6 RATIO ANALYSIS

Having calculated the ratios, the results must be analysed. Consideration needs to be given to such matters as:

- If a ratio has been computed over a number of time periods does it show a worsening or an improving situation?
- Can the ratio be compared to an objective standard? That is can it be compared with an 'ideal' ratio?
- Do all the ratios when taken together support the conclusions drawn from each individual ratio?

The final stage of interpretation is the critical review.

The limitations of the data used to calculate the ratios need to be considered so that a prudent overall conclusion can be reached.

The information gathered by calculating ratios will allow comparisons with:

(a) the performance of the business in previous years

(b) the budgeted or planned performance in the current year

(c) the performance of similar businesses.

The ratios themselves do not tell one what to do, but they do help to point one in the right direction. Ratios should, therefore, make it easier to make better decisions.

1.7 SHORTCOMINGS OF RATIO ANALYSIS

It must be emphasised that accounting ratios are only a means to an end; they are not an end in themselves. By comparing the relationship between figures, they merely highlight significant features or trends in the accounts. Indeed, they may well create more problems than they solve. The real art of interpreting accounts lies in defining the reasons for the features and fluctuations disclosed. To do this effectively, the interested party may need more information and a deeper insight into the affairs of the business.

He should also bear in mind the following:

(a)   The date at which the accounts are drawn up. Accurate information can only be obtained with any degree of certainty from up-to-date figures. Furthermore, seasonal variations in the particular trade should be taken into account. Final accounts tend to be drawn up at the end of seasonal trade when the picture they present is of the business at its strongest point financially.

(b)   The accuracy of the position shown in the balance sheet. The arrangement of certain matters can be misleading and present a more favourable picture e.g. such 'window-dressing' operations as:

(i)   making a special effort to collect debts just before the year-end in order to show a larger cash balance and lower debtors than is normal

(ii)   ordering goods to be delivered just after the year-end so that stocks and creditors can be kept as low as possible.

(c)   Interim accounts. Whenever possible interested parties should examine accounts prepared on a monthly basis, as a clearer picture of the trends and fluctuations will emerge from these than from the annual financial statements.

(d)   Accounting ratios are based on accounting information and are, therefore, only as accurate as the underlying accounting information. At a time, as at present, when traditional accounting procedures are coming in for heavy criticism, students should remember that ratios based on those procedures can be easily criticised.

(e)   Ratios based on historic cost accounts do not give a true picture of trends from year to year. An apparent increase in profit may not be a 'true' increase, because of the effects of inflation.

(f)   Financial statements only reflect those activities that can be expressed in money terms. They do not give a complete picture of the activities of a business.

(g)   The accounting ratios of one company must be compared with those of another similar company in order to draw meaningful conclusions. These conclusions will only be meaningful if that other company's trade is similar.

However, even comparing the financial statements of apparently similar businesses can be misleading because:

(a)   Businesses may use different accounting policies. For example, some businesses measure fixed assets at historic cost while others revalue them.

(b)   Ratios may not be calculated according to the same formula. For example, there are several possible definitions of gearing and return on capital employed.

(c)   Large organisations can achieve economies of scale (e.g. by negotiating extended credit periods or discounts for bulk buying with suppliers). These measures may not be available to smaller businesses.

(d)   Companies within the same industry can serve completely different markets and there may be differences in sales mix and product range. These can affect profitability ratios such as profit margin and expenses to sales.

1.8 INTERPRETATION AND 'NOT-FOR-PROFIT' ORGANISATIONS

Most public sector bodies now prepare commercial style accounts and may be required to comply with generally accepted accounting principles and applicable accounting standards. These accounts can be interpreted using ratio analysis and observation in exactly the same way as the accounts of a commercial organisation.

When interpreting the accounts of a public sector body you should bear in mind the following major differences between private sector and public sector organisations.

	Private sector	*Public sector*
Primary objective	To make profits	To provide a service (economy, effectiveness, efficiency)
Stewardship responsibilities	To investors (shareholders)	To the general public

The main users of the accounts of private sector organisations are investors and potential investors, lenders and potential lenders and management. The main users of the accounts of public sector organisations are:

(a)   taxpayers

(b)   those who benefit from their activities

(c)   electors.

Other users may include:

(a)   central government

(b)   employees

(c)   lenders of funds

(d)   pressure groups.

As always, you should interpret the accounts in the light of the objective of the organisation and the needs of those who are interested in its accounts (these should normally be stated or implied in the question).

Conclusion   When calculating ratios:

–   be aware of the needs of the users of the accounts

–   calculate only those ratios relevant to those needs

–   always state the definitions used.

Remember that ratios cannot be used in isolation. They must always be interpreted in relation to other information e.g.:

–   comparative figures

–   budgeted figures

–   performance of similar businesses.

2 RATIO CALCULATION AND ANALYSIS

2.1 TYPES OF RATIOS

Ratios fall into several groups, the relevance of particular ratios depending on the purpose for which they are required. The groups to be considered here are:

- profitability ratios

- working capital ratios

- medium- and long-term solvency ratios

- investor ratios.

2.2 ILLUSTRATION

Each of the above ratios will be illustrated by reference to the following example. In each case the ratio will be defined and explained, calculated and then interpreted.

Summarised balance sheets at 30 June

	20X7		20X6	
	£000	£000	£000	£000
Fixed assets (net book value)		130		139
Current assets:				
Stock	42		37	
Debtors	29		23	
Bank	3		5	
	74		65	
Creditors: Amounts falling due within one year:				
Trade creditors	36		55	
Taxation	10		10	
	46		65	
Net current assets		28		–
Total assets less current liabilities		158		139
Creditors: Amounts falling due after more than one year:				
5% secured loan stock		40		40
8% Preference shares (£1 shares)		25		25
		93		74
Ordinary share capital (50p shares)		35		35
Share premium account		17		17
Revaluation reserve		10		–
Profit and loss account		31		22
		93		74

Summarised profit and loss account for the year ended 30 June

	20X7		20X6	
	£000	£000	£000	£000
Sales		209		196
Opening stock	37		29	
Purchases	162		159	
	199		188	
Closing stock	42		37	
		157		151
Gross profit		52		45
Interest	2		2	
Preference share dividend	2		2	
Depreciation	9		9	
Sundry expenses	14		11	
		27		24
Net profit		25		21
Taxation		10		10
Net profit for the year		15		11
Dividends paid		6		5

3 PROFITABILITY RATIOS

3.1 INTRODUCTION

There are several ratios which attempt to assess the profitability of a business. These are more conveniently expressed in percentage form and look at various aspects of a business's operations.

3.2 GROSS PROFIT PERCENTAGE

Definition   **Gross profit** is expressed as a percentage of sales. It is also known as the **gross profit margin**.

This is a very popular ratio and is used by even the smallest of businesses. In the illustration the ratios for the two years are as follows:

20X7   *20X6*

$$\frac{52}{209} \times 100 = 24.9\% \qquad \frac{45}{196} \times 100 = 23.0\%$$

What can be learned from these figures? Clearly, the gross profit percentage has improved but it is not known why. Nor is it obvious whether these figures are better or worse than those which would be expected in a similar type of business. Before coming to definite conclusions one would need further information. For example, most businesses sell a wide range of products, usually with different gross profit percentages (or profit margins). It may be that in 20X7 the sales mix changed and that a larger proportion of items with a high profit percentage were sold, thus increasing the overall gross profit percentage of the business.

3.3 PERCENTAGE CHANGE IN SALES

Definition   Increase or decrease in sales/turnover expressed as a percentage of the earliest year's turnover.

It is relevant to consider the change in sales at this point. The percentage growth in sales is:

$$\frac{209 - 196}{196} \times 100 = 6.6\%$$

This may not be a significant increase. A larger increase might have given some evidence of the type of changes in trading conditions that have occurred.

3.4 NET PROFIT PERCENTAGE

Definition $\dfrac{\text{Net profit}}{\text{Sales}} \times 100$. This is also known as the **net profit margin**.

20X7   *20X6*

$$\frac{25}{209} \times 100 = 11.9\%$$ $$\frac{21}{196} \times 100 = 10.7\%$$

What conclusions can be drawn from this apparent improvement? Very few! Since net profit equals gross profit less expenses, it would be useful to tabulate, for each of the two years, the various expenses and express them as a percentage of sales. A suitable tabulation might be:

	20X7		*20X6*	
	£000	%	£000	%
Sales	209	100.0	196	100.0
Cost of sales	157	75.1	151	77.0
Gross profit	52	24.9	45	23.0
Interest	(2)	(1.0)	(2)	(1.1)
Preference dividend	(2)	(1.0)	(2)	(1.1)
Depreciation	(9)	(4.3)	(9)	(4.5)
Sundry expenses	(14)	(6.7)	(11)	(5.6)
Net profit	25	11.9	21	10.7

Given a detailed trading and profit and loss account, the above type of summary could be very useful. Care must be taken in interpreting the results, particularly since sales (£) are used as the denominator. An increase in sales (£) could be due to a combination of price and quantity effects.

3.5 RETURN ON CAPITAL EMPLOYED (ROCE)

Definition   Profit is expressed as a percentage of the capital invested in the business. Due to its importance the **ROCE** is sometimes referred to as the **primary ratio**.

This is an important ratio as it relates profit to the capital invested in a business. Finance for a business is only available at a cost – loan stock finance requires interest payments and further finance from shareholders requires either the immediate payment of dividends or the expectation of higher dividends in the future. Therefore a business needs to maximise the profits per £ of capital employed.

There are several ways of measuring ROCE, but the essential point is to relate the profit figure used to its capital base. The profit figure used must match with the capital employed figure.

Definition   **Total capital employed** in the business

$$\frac{\text{Profit before interest and tax}}{\text{Share capital} + \text{Reserves} + \text{Long term liabilities}} \times 100$$

The denominator could alternatively be calculated as total assets less current liabilities. This is the profit available for all of the providers of finance as a percentage of all of the sources of finance.

Definition   **Equity shareholders' capital employed**

$$\frac{\text{Profit after interest and preference dividend but before tax}}{\text{Ordinary share capital} + \text{Reserves}} \times 100$$

This is the profit available to the ordinary shareholder (before tax) as a percentage of the ordinary shareholder's capital. This is sometimes called **return on owner's equity** (ROOE).

Example

Using the figures in the illustration in Section 2.2, calculate ROCE for 20X6 and 20X7 using each of these alternatives.

Solution

Total capital employed

20X7   *20X6*

$\dfrac{29}{158} \times 100 = 18.4\%$ $\dfrac{25}{139} \times 100 = 18.0\%$

Equity capital employed

20X7   *20X6*

$\dfrac{25}{93} \times 100 = 26.9\%$ $\dfrac{21}{74} \times 100 = 28.4\%$

(The ordinary shareholders' funds is the capital and reserves total minus the preference shares.)

There is a slight improvement in total ROCE and a falling off in equity ROCE.

A reason for the variation is the revaluation of fixed assets during the year. This has the effect of increasing the denominator in 20X7 relative to 20X6 and creates an unfair comparison as it is likely that the fixed assets were worth more than their book value last year as well. It is not common, however, for UK companies to revalue their assets every year so that comparisons from year to year can be difficult.

The differences in returns for equity compared to total capital employed are large. It means that equity shareholders have had a significant increase in their return because of the company's using fixed interest finance to enlarge the capital employed in the business.

3.6   STRUCTURE OF OPERATING RATIOS

ROCE can be broken down into a further pattern of operating ratios as shown in the diagram below:

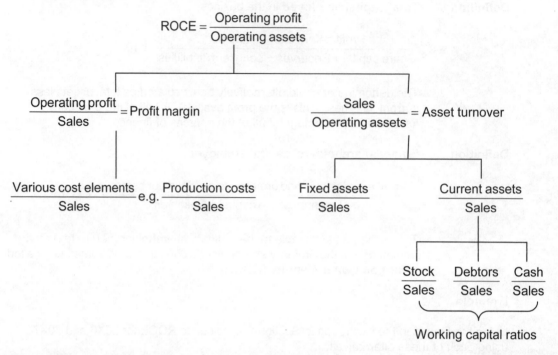

3.7   ANALYSIS OF ROCE

As can be seen from the diagram the initial breakdown of ROCE is into two further ratios:

- profit margin

- rate of asset utilisation or asset turnover.

Note: The product of these two gives the return on capital employed:

$$\frac{\text{Operating profit}}{\text{Sales}} \times \frac{\text{Sales}}{\text{Operating assets}} = \frac{\text{Operating profit}}{\text{Operating assets}} = \text{ROCE}$$

In the example for 20X7 using total capital employed:

$$\text{ROCE} = \frac{£29,000}{£158,000} = 18.3\%$$

$$\text{Profit margin} = \frac{\text{Operating profit}}{\text{Sales}} = \frac{£29,000}{£209,000} = 13.9\%$$

$$\text{Asset turnover} = \frac{\text{Sales}}{\text{Operating assets}} = \frac{£209,000}{£158,000} = 1.32$$

$13.9\% \times 1.32 \times 100 = 18.3\%$

As ROCE is made up of the product of profit margin and asset turnover then any initial analysis of ROCE over a period will normally involve calculation of these two further ratios.

Conclusion $\quad \dfrac{\text{Operating profit}}{\text{Sales}} \times \dfrac{\text{Sales}}{\text{Operating assets}} = \dfrac{\text{Operating profit}}{\text{Operating assets}} = \text{ROCE}$

3.8 ASSET TURNOVER

Definition   **Asset turnover** is calculated as $\dfrac{\text{Sales}}{\text{Operating assets}}$

The resultant figure indicates how many £s of sales are being made for every £1 of operating assets or capital employed.

In our example asset turnover for each of the two years is:

20X6 $=$ $\dfrac{£196,000}{£139,000} = 1.41$

20X7 $=$ $\dfrac{£209,000}{£158,000} = 1.32$

This shows that for every £1 invested in the business in 20X6 £1.41 of sales were being made whilst this has fallen to £1.32 of sales for every £1 invested in 20X7.

The profit margin can also be considered for each of the two years:

20X6 $=$ $\dfrac{£25,000}{£196,000} = 12.8\%$

20X7 $=$ $\dfrac{£29,000}{£209,000} = 13.9\%$

The initial analysis of ROCE (using total capital employed) might therefore be that it has increased over the two year period due to an increase in profit margin and indeed despite a reduction in the efficient use of the assets as measured by asset turnover.

Tutorial note: If this analysis of ROCE is to be carried out it is important that the same profit figure and capital employed figure is used in all three ratios otherwise the result will be meaningless.

3.9 FIXED ASSET TURNOVER

Definition   **Fixed asset turnover** is calculated as $\dfrac{\text{Sales}}{\text{Fixed assets}}$

The resultant figure indicates the amount of £ sales being made for every £1 investment in fixed assets.

This measures the efficiency of just the fixed asset utilisation rather than all of the assets in total.

In our example the fixed asset turnover is:

20X6 $=$ $\dfrac{£196,000}{£139,000} = 1.41$

20X7 $=$ $\dfrac{£209,000}{£130,000} = 1.61$

This indicates that there has been a substantial increase in the efficiency of the utilisation of the fixed assets although not of the overall assets over the two year period. This is also despite the fact that there has been a revaluation of the fixed assets in 20X7.

Conclusion   From the analysis it becomes clear that the subdivision of the key ratio, return on capital employed, is limited only by the detail in the data available. The important point to remember is that if ROCE is to be subanalysed care must be taken with the profit and capital employed figures used.

4   WORKING CAPITAL RATIOS

4.1   INTRODUCTION

The working capital (net current assets) of a business can be considered in total and also broken down into their component elements.

4.2   THE CURRENT RATIO

Definition   The **current ratio** is the ratio of current assets to current liabilities.

20X7   *20X6*

$$\frac{74}{46} = 1.61 \qquad\qquad \frac{65}{65} = 1.0$$

The current ratio is sometimes referred to as the working capital ratio.

4.3   THE LIQUIDITY (OR QUICK) RATIO (ACID TEST RATIO)

Definition   The **liquidity ratio** is the ratio of current assets excluding stock to current liabilities.

20X7   *20X6*

$$\frac{32}{46} = 0.7 \qquad\qquad \frac{28}{65} = 0.43$$

Stock is excluded from this ratio as it is much less liquid than cash and even debtors.

4.4   ANALYSIS

Both of these ratios show a strengthening.

The extent of the change between the two years seems surprising and would require further investigation.

It would also be useful to know how these ratios compare with those of a similar business, since typical ratios for supermarkets are quite different from those for heavy engineering firms.

What can be said is that in 20X7 the current liabilities were well covered by current assets. Liabilities payable in the near future (creditors), however, are only half covered by cash and debtors (a liquid asset, close to cash).

Conventional wisdom has it that an ideal current ratio is 2 and an ideal quick ratio is 1. It is very tempting to draw definite conclusions from limited information or to say that the current ratio **should** be 2, or that the liquidity ratio **should** be 1. However, this is not very meaningful without taking into account the type of ratio expected in a similar business.

It should also be noted that a high current or liquidity ratio is not necessarily a good thing. It may indicate that working capital is not being used efficiently. This in itself can be investigated by calculation of ratios for each individual element of working capital.

4.5 STOCK TURNOVER RATIO

Companies have to strike a balance between being able to satisfy customers' requirements out of stock and the cost of having too much capital tied up in stock.

Definition The **stock turnover ratio** is the cost of sales divided by the average level of stock during the year. Using the example:

20X7	20X6

$$\frac{157}{\frac{1}{2}(37+42)} = 4.0 \text{ times pa} \qquad \frac{151}{\frac{1}{2}(29+37)} = 4.6 \text{ times pa}$$

The stock turnover ratio has fallen.

Note: The average of opening and closing stocks is used here, but examination questions frequently do not provide the opening stock figure and the **closing** stock has to be taken instead of the average stock. In any case, the average of opening and closing stock will not necessarily give the true average level of stock during the year if the stock fluctuates a lot from month to month.

Unless the nature of the business is known, it is not possible to say whether either 4.6 or 4.0 is satisfactory or unsatisfactory. A jeweller will have a low stock turnover ratio, but it is hoped that a fishmonger selling fresh fish has a very high turnover ratio.

An alternative calculation of the stock turnover ratio is to show the result in days. The calculation is:

$$\frac{\text{Average stock during the accounting period}}{\text{Cost of sales}} \times 365 \text{ (i.e. length of accounting period)}$$

20X7	20X6

$$\frac{\frac{1}{2}(37+42)}{157} \times 365 = 92 \text{ days} \qquad \frac{\frac{1}{2}(29+37)}{151} \times 365 = 80 \text{ days}$$

4.6 DEBT COLLECTION PERIOD (OR AVERAGE PERIOD OF CREDIT ALLOWED TO CUSTOMERS)

Businesses which sell goods on credit terms specify a credit period. Failure to send out invoices on time or to follow up late payers will have an adverse effect on the cash flow of the business.

Definition The **debt collection period** relates closing trade debts to the average daily credit sales. It shows the number of days that debtors are outstanding on average.

In the example:

	20X7	20X6
Credit sales per day	$\dfrac{£209,000}{365} = £573$	$\dfrac{£196,000}{365} = £537$
Closing trade debtors	£29,000	£23,000
Debt collection period	$\dfrac{£29,000}{£573} = 50.6 \text{ days}$	$\dfrac{£23,000}{£537} = 42.8 \text{ days}$

Compared with 20X6 the debt collection period has worsened in 20X7.

If the average credit allowed to customers was, say, 30 days, then something is clearly wrong. Further investigation might reveal delays in sending out invoices or failure to 'screen' new customers.

The quickest way to compute the debt collection period is to use the formula:

$$\frac{\text{Closing trade debtors}}{\text{Credit sales for year}} \times 365$$

20X7	20X6
$\dfrac{29,000}{209,000} \times 365 = 50.6 \text{ days}$	$\dfrac{23,000}{196,000} \times 365 = 42.8 \text{ days}$

Tutorial note: In this example it has been assumed that all sales are on credit.

4.7 AVERAGE PERIOD OF CREDIT ALLOWED BY SUPPLIERS

Definition This relates closing creditors to average daily credit purchases. It shows the number of days it takes the business to pay its creditors.

	20X7	20X6
Credit purchases per day	$\dfrac{162,000}{365} = £444$	$\dfrac{159,000}{365} = £436$
Closing trade creditors	£36,000	£55,000
Average period of credit allowed by suppliers	81.1 days	126.3 days

Tutorial note: Again it has been assumed here that all purchases are on credit.

The average period of credit allowed has fallen substantially from last year. It is, however, in absolute terms still a high figure.

Often, suppliers request payment within 30 days. The company is taking nearly three months. Trade creditors are thus financing much of the working capital requirements of the business which is beneficial to the company.

However, there are three potential disadvantages of extending the credit period:

(i)   future supplies may be endangered

(ii)   possibility of cash discounts is lost

(iii)   suppliers may quote a higher price for the goods knowing the extended credit taken by the company.

The quick calculation is:

$$\frac{\text{Closing trade creditors}}{\text{Credit purchases for year}} \times 365$$

20X7	*20X6*

$$\frac{36{,}000}{162{,}000} \times 365 = 81.1 \text{ days} \qquad\qquad \frac{55{,}000}{159{,}000} \times 365 = 126.3 \text{ days}$$

4.8   THE WORKING CAPITAL CYCLE

The investment made in working capital is largely a function of sales and, therefore, it is useful to consider the problem in terms of a firm's working capital (or **cash operating**) cycle.

The cash operating cycle

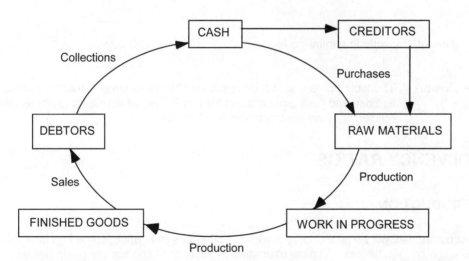

The cycle reflects a firm's investment in working capital as it moves through the production process towards sales. The investment in working capital gradually increases, firstly being only in raw materials, but then in labour and overhead as production progresses. This investment must be maintained throughout the production process, the finished goods holding period and up to the final collection of cash from trade debtors. Note that the net investment can be reduced by taking trade credit from suppliers.

The faster a firm can 'push' items around the operating cycle the lower its investment in working capital will be. However, too little investment in working capital can lose sales since customers will generally prefer to buy from suppliers who are prepared to extend trade credit, and if items are not held in stock when required by customers, sales may be lost.

With some fairly basic financial information it is possible to measure the length of the working capital cycle for a given firm.

Example

Using the example in Section 2.2, determine the working capital cycle for 20X7.

Solution

(1)   Creditors:

Average payment collection period

$$\left(365 \times \frac{\text{Creditors}}{\text{Purchases}}\right) \qquad 365 \times \frac{36}{162} = \qquad (81 \text{ days})$$

(2)   Debtors:

Average collection period

$$= \left(365 \times \frac{\text{Debtors}}{\text{Sales}}\right) \qquad 365 \times \frac{29}{209} = \qquad 51 \text{ days}$$

(3)   Stock turnover:

$$= 365 \times \frac{\text{Stock}}{\text{Cost of goods sold}} \qquad 365 \times \frac{\frac{1}{2}(37 + 42)}{157} \qquad 92 \text{ days}$$

Length of working capital cycle   62 days

Conclusion   The working capital of a business can be considered in total to assess liquidity and then broken down into its individual elements to assess the efficiency of the control of these elements.

5   SOLVENCY RATIOS

5.1   INTRODUCTION

Most companies will be financed by a variety of sources of finance, some by share capital and some by loan finance. Typical examples of sources of finance are given below:

Source of finance	Priority in relation to profit	Priority on liquidation
Secured loan stock (debentures)	Interest must be paid whether or not the company makes a profit	Secured by a fixed or floating charge – first claim on assets
Unsecured loan stock	Interest must be paid whether or not the company makes a profit	Ranks as unsecured creditor
Preference share capital (assumed non-participating)	If the company makes a profit, the preference dividend has a priority over the ordinary dividend	Cannot be repaid until all liabilities have been met. Has priority over ordinary shareholders

Ordinary share capital	Dividends paid after debenture interest and fixed preference dividends have been paid	Ranks behind all the above but usually entitled to surplus assets in a liquidation

The aim of solvency ratios is to assess how much a business is financed by loan capital rather than owners' capital.

5.2 CAPITAL GEARING

Gearing is one of the most widely used terms in accounting. Unfortunately it can be defined and calculated in several different ways. It is essential to state the definition used.

Gearing is relevant to the long-term financial stability of a business. Two possible definitions will be considered, both based on book values of assets. Both of these consider the relationship between:

(a) ordinary shareholders' funds (or equity interest)

(b) fixed return capital – comprising loans and preference share capital.

5.3 EQUITY GEARING

Definition $\dfrac{\text{Preference share capital plus loans}}{\text{Ordinary share capital and reserves}}$

20X7 *20X6*

$$\frac{25+40}{118-25} \times 100 = 69.9\% \qquad \frac{25+40}{99-25} \times 100 = 87.8\%$$

5.4 TOTAL GEARING

Definition $\dfrac{\text{Preference share capital plus loans}}{\text{Total long - term capital}}$

20X7 *20X6*

$$\frac{65}{158} \times 100 = 41.1\% \qquad \frac{65}{139} \times 100 = 46.8\%$$

There is no real difference between the two types of calculation as the components of the numerator remain the same. Some prefer to use the equity gearing as it shows a more pronounced change if either fixed return capital or equity capital changes. Most use the second calculation as it is perhaps clearer to note the relationship of fixed interest finance to total finance.

There is no immediate cut-off between a low-geared company and a highly-geared company. Gearing is a matter of degree.

In our example there has been no increase or decrease in the amount of fixed interest finance. The only reason for the change in ratio is due to retained profit and revaluation for 20X7.

5.5 THE ADVANTAGES AND DISADVANTAGES OF RAISING FINANCE BY ISSUING DEBENTURES

Gearing may have an important effect on the distribution of profits. For example, consider two companies with the same profit record but different capital structures. The return of the ordinary shareholders can vary considerably.

	A Ltd £	B Ltd £
Capital structure:		
10% Loan stock	20,000	–
Ordinary share capital and reserves	10,000	30,000
	30,000	30,000

	Highly geared	No gearing
Year 1 – Profits £4,000 before interest		
∴ Returns:		
10% Interest	2,000	–
Ordinary shares – balance	2,000	4,000
	4,000	4,000
Year 2 – Profits double to £8,000 before interest		
∴ Returns:		
10% Interest	2,000	–
Ordinary shares – balance	6,000	8,000
	8,000	8,000
Therefore, increase in return to ordinary shareholders	3 times	2 times

Thus, the doubling of the profits in year 2 has the effect of tripling the return to the equity shareholders in the highly-geared company. The effect would be even more dramatic if the profits fell below £2,000 because then there would be no return at all to the ordinary shareholders in A Ltd. Thus an investment in ordinary shares in a highly-geared company is a far more speculative investment than a purchase of ordinary shares in a low-geared company.

5.6 INTEREST COVER

Definition $\dfrac{\text{Profit before interest and tax}}{\text{Interest}}$

Interest on loan stock (debenture stock) must be paid whether or not the company makes a profit. The ratio emphasises the cover (or security) for the interest by relating profit before interest and tax to interest paid.

20X7	*20X6*
$\dfrac{29}{2}$ i.e. 14.5 times	$\dfrac{25}{2}$ i.e. 12.5 times

From the point of view of medium- and long-term solvency, the company is in a strong position as regards the payment of interest. Profit would have to drop considerably before any problem of paying interest arose.

(It is assumed that the company could delay paying the preference dividend.)

Conclusion   The medium- to long-term solvency of a business will be of concern to most users of the financial statements. Therefore gearing ratios will be very important but to avoid confusion any calculation must be defined.

6 INVESTOR RATIOS

6.1 INFORMATION REQUIRED BY INVESTORS

An investor is interested in the income earned by the company for him and the return on his investment (the income earned related to the market price of the investment).

An investor in ordinary shares can look to the earnings of the company available to pay the ordinary dividend or to the actual ordinary dividend paid as a measure of the income earned by the company for him. The ratios he would compute in each case would be:

Dividends	Earnings
Dividends per share	Earnings per share
Dividend cover	Price earnings ratio
Dividend yield	

Suppose that the company in the illustration is quoted on the Stock Exchange and that the market value of each ordinary share is 204 pence.

6.2 DIVIDEND PER SHARE

Definition $\dfrac{\text{Total ordinary dividend}}{\text{Total number of ordinary shares}}$

20X7	20X6
$\dfrac{£6,000}{70,000} = 8.6$ pence per share	$\dfrac{£5,000}{70,000} = 7.1$ pence per share

Tutorial note: The ordinary share capital of the company is made up of £35,000 of 50p shares. Therefore a total of 70,000 shares.

6.3 DIVIDEND COVER

Definition **Dividend cover** is a measure of how many times the profit covers the ordinary dividend payment.

This is calculated by dividing profit available for ordinary shareholders (i.e., after preference dividend) by the dividend for the year (i.e. interim plus final):

20X7	20X6
$\dfrac{£17,000 - £2,000}{£6,000} = 2.5$ times	$\dfrac{£13,000 - £2,000}{£5,000} = 2.2$ times

Note: The profits available for ordinary shareholders are after the deduction of the preference dividend. The cover represents the 'security' for the ordinary dividend – in this company the cover is reasonable.

6.4 DIVIDEND YIELD

Definition **Dividend yield** expresses dividend per share as a percentage of the current share price.

The net yield at today's date is:

$\dfrac{8.6p}{204p} \times 100 = 4.2\%$

6.5 EARNINGS PER SHARE (EPS)

When a company pays a dividend, the directors take many factors into account, including the need to retain profits for future expansion. Earnings per share looks at the profits which could in theory be paid to each ordinary shareholder.

Definition   EPS =

$$\frac{\text{Net profit or loss attributable to ordinary shareholders}}{\text{Weighted average number of ordinary shares outstanding during the period}}$$

FRS 14 requires earnings per share to be disclosed on the face of the profit and loss account of quoted companies.

20X7	20X6
$\dfrac{£17,000 - £2,000}{70,000}$ = 21.4p per share	$\dfrac{£13,000 - £2,000}{70,000}$ = 15.7p per share

6.6 PRICE EARNINGS RATIO (P/E RATIO)

Definition   P/E ratio $= \dfrac{\text{Current share price per share}}{\text{EPS}}$

This is often regarded as the most important ratio. It expresses the current share price (market value) as a multiple of the earnings per share. For 20X7, the price earnings ratio is:

$$\frac{204p}{21.4p} = 9.5$$

The ratio of 9.5 implies that if the current rate of EPS is maintained it will take nine and a half years to repay the cost of investing. The higher the PE ratio the longer the payback period. Thus we could conclude that the lower the PE ratio, the better investment it is. However, this is not generally the case. **High** PE ratios are generally viewed as better than low ones.

The apparent paradox is resolved if the forward-looking nature of stock exchange investments is considered. The PE ratio is based on **current** EPS but the stock market is pricing the share on expectations of **future** EPS. If the market considers that a company has significant growth prospects, the market price of the share will rise giving a higher P/E ratio.

6.7 EARNINGS YIELD

Definition $\dfrac{\text{EPS}}{\text{Current share price per share}} \times 100$

This term is not often referred to these days. It expresses the earnings per share as a percentage of the current share price i.e.:

Earnings yield $=$ $\dfrac{21.4p}{204p} \times 100$

                      $=$ 10.5%

It is merely the reciprocal of the PE ratio:

$$\frac{1}{\text{PE ratio}} = \text{Earnings yield}$$

$$\frac{1}{9.5} = 0.105 \text{ i.e. } 10.5\%$$

Conclusion   An investor or potential investor in a company will be concerned with the return that he is receiving or is likely to receive on that investment. This may be measured in terms of the actual return, dividend paid, or the potential return, and earnings for the year.

ACTIVITY 1

Calculate the earnings per share based on the following information:

	£000
Profit on ordinary activities	7,692
Tax on profit on ordinary activities	1,004
Profit after taxation	6,688
Dividends *Note 1*	1,200

Note 1

Dividends	Ordinary	1,000
	Preference	200
		1,200

There are 10,000,000 shares in issue throughout the year.

For a suggested answer, see the 'Answers' section at the end of the book.

7   INTERPRETATION OF FINANCIAL STATEMENTS

7.1   INTRODUCTION

So far this chapter has concentrated on the calculation of a variety of ratios for different purposes and provision of information. It is now important to consider using these ratios in order to interpret a set of financial statements and to draw valid conclusions from the information contained in a set of financial statements.

7.2 EXAMPLE

A Ltd has been trading steadily for many years as ski boot manufacturers. In 20X4 a surge in skiing increased the level of A Ltd's turnover significantly. The summarised balance sheets of the last two years are given below:

	20X4		20X3	
	£000	£000	£000	£000
Fixed assets:				
Intangible assets		30		40
Tangible assets:				
Property		640		216
Plant		174		142
		844		398
Current assets:				
Stock	540		140	
Debtors	440		170	
Investments	–		120	
Cash at bank	4		150	
	984		580	
Creditors – Amounts falling due within one year:				
Trade creditors	520		250	
Taxation	70		80	
Dividend proposed	60		20	
	650		350	
Net current assets		334		230
Total assets less current liabilities		1,178		628
Creditors – Amounts falling due after more than one year:				
10% debentures		120		–
		1,058		628
Capital and reserves:				
Called up share capital:				
Ordinary 50p shares		300		250
Revaluation reserve		270		–
Capital redemption reserve		–		50
Profit and loss account		488		328
		1,058		628

Sales for 20X4 and 20X3 respectively were £1,600,000 and £1,150,000. Cost of goods sold for 20X4 and 20X3 respectively were £1,196,000 and £880,000.

Given that this is the only information available, you are required to comment as fully as you can on A Ltd's financial position.

7.3 SOLUTION

Comments on A Ltd – Financial position

Profitability and growth

Profit and loss accounts have not been given but laying these out as far as they are available:

	20X4	20X3
	£	£
Sales	1,600,000	1,150,000
Cost of sales	1,196,000	880,000
Gross profit	404,000	270,000

Profit margin:

$$\frac{\text{Gross profit}}{\text{Sales}} \times 100 \qquad\qquad 25.25\% \qquad\qquad 23.48\%$$

Return on capital employed:

$$\frac{\text{Gross profit}}{\text{Share capital} + \text{Reserves} + \text{Debt}} \times 100 \qquad \frac{404,000}{1,178,000} \qquad \frac{270,000}{628,000 + 270,000}$$

(see note below)

$$= 34.30\% \qquad\qquad = 30.07\%$$

(Average capital employed should be used but year-end figures have been taken so that a figure for 20X3 can be computed. It is assumed that property was worth £270,000 more than its book value in 20X3 also.)

Asset turnover:

$$\frac{\text{Sales}}{\text{Share capital} + \text{Reserves} + \text{Debt}} \times 100 \qquad \frac{1,600,000}{1,178,000} \qquad \frac{1,150,000}{898,000}$$

$$= 1.36 \qquad\qquad = 1.28$$

The ROCE figures have been computed in a rough and ready fashion but they indicate an improvement in 20X4 compared with 20X3. The gross profit/sales shows a (slight) improvement as does the efficiency measure of asset turnover. This would appear to be encouraging as the sales have grown considerably.

20X4 Sales	£1,600,000
20X3 Sales	£1,150,000
Percentage increase	39.13%

Solvency: long term

Gearing

There was no debt in 20X3. The 10% debentures issued in 20X4 were to enable the investment to be made to finance growth. The year-end gearing is:

$$\frac{\text{Debt}}{\text{Capital employed (as above)}} \times 100 \quad = \quad \frac{120,000}{1,178,000} \times 100$$

$$= \quad 10.19\%$$

In absolute terms this is a low figure.

Solvency: short term

	20X4	20X3

Current ratio

$$\frac{\text{Current assets}}{\text{Current liabilities}} \qquad \frac{984,000}{650,000} = 1.5 \qquad \frac{580,000}{350,000} = 1.7$$

Quick ratio

$$\frac{\text{Current assets - Stock}}{\text{Current liabilities}} \qquad \frac{444,000}{650,000} = 0.7 \qquad \frac{440,000}{350,000} = 1.3$$

Both ratios have shown a decline – particularly the quick ratio. Conventional opinion states that for many businesses an ideal current ratio is 2 and an ideal quick ratio is 1. However, the ideal ratio will depend on the type of business of a company. More important is the constancy of the ratio over time (assuming that the ratios reflect the efficient use of working capital).

The decline should not be viewed with alarm, particularly as the 20X3 figures include current assets which were surplus to the working capital requirements of the business at that time i.e., the investments and cash. Both these items have been spent in purchasing new fixed assets. The quick ratio is, however, now low and should be watched carefully.

Working capital efficiency

	20X4	20X3

Stock turnover

$$\frac{\text{Cost of sales}}{\text{Year - end stocks}} \qquad \frac{1,196,000}{540,000} = 2.2 \text{ times pa} \qquad \frac{880,000}{140,000} = 6.3 \text{ times pa}$$

Year-end stock has been taken so that the 20X3 figure can be computed.

A very significant fall in stock turnover. This may indicate that:

(a)   the growth in sales has been made by offering many more types of boots, some of which are not selling quickly; or

(b)   further growth in sales is expected so that the company has stepped up production to anticipate this.

A closer look at this area is required.

	20X4	20X3

Debtor collection period

$$\frac{\text{Year - end trade debtors}}{\text{Sales}} \times 365 \qquad \frac{440,000}{1,600,000} = 100.4 \text{ days} \qquad \frac{170,000}{1,150,000} = 54.0 \text{ days}$$

54 days to collect debts is not very impressive – 100 days is potentially disastrous. Immediate action is required to ensure prompter payment although the situation may not be as bad as it appears if it is the case that the growth in sales took place shortly before the year end rather than throughout the year. Debtors at the year end would then not be typical of the sales throughout the whole year.

Creditor collection period

(Cost of sales will have to be used in this example in the absence of purchases figures.)

	20X4	*20X3*

$$\frac{\text{Year - end trade creditors}}{\text{Cost of sales}} \times 365 \qquad \frac{520,000}{1,196,000} \times 365 = 159 \text{ days} \qquad \frac{250,000}{880,000} \times 365 = 104 \text{ days}$$

The creditor collection period was high in 20X3 but is now even higher. Clearly one of the ways in which the company's considerable growth has been financed has been through taking long periods of credit from its suppliers. This area may need further investigation as this policy may backfire at some point in the future.

Working capital cycle

	20X4	*20X3*

Stock turnover in days

$$\frac{540,000}{1,196,000} \times 365$$
$$165 \text{ days}$$

$$\frac{140,000}{880,000} \times 365$$
$$58 \text{ days}$$

	20X4	20X3
Debtors turnover in days	100 days	54 days
Creditors turnover in days	(159 days)	(104 days)
	106 days	8 days

Overall analysis

The company has quite clearly had considerable growth over the past year. This has been financed by a small amount of loan capital but largely by a reduction in overall short-term liquidity and in particular an increase in time taken to pay creditors. This can be further seen from the drastic increase in the working capital cycle.

The growth appears to be worthwhile as the company continues to be profitable, indeed the ROCE has increased as has the profit margin.

The major concern for this company would therefore appear to be regarding its working capital control.

ACTIVITY 2

The outline balance sheets of the Nantred Trading Co Ltd were as shown below:

Balance sheets as at 30 September

	20X5		20X6	
	£	£	£	£
Fixed assets				
(at written down values):				
Premises	40,000		98,000	
Plant and equipment	65,000		162,000	
		105,000		260,000
Current assets:				
Stock	31,200		95,300	
Trade debtors	19,700		30,700	
Bank and cash	15,600		26,500	
	66,500		152,500	
Current liabilities:				
Trade creditors	23,900		55,800	
Corporation tax	11,400		13,100	
Sundry	17,000		17,000	
	52,300		85,900	
Working capital		14,200		66,600
Net assets employed		119,200		326,600
Financed by:				
Ordinary share capital	100,000		200,000	
Reserves	19,200		26,600	
Shareholders' funds		119,200		226,600
7% debentures		–		100,000
		119,200		326,600

The only other information available is that the turnover for the years ended 30 September 20X5 and 20X6 was £202,900 and £490,700, respectively, and that net profit before tax for 20X5 and 20X6 respectively was £21,500 and £37,500.

Required:

(a)   Calculate, for each of the two years, six suitable ratios to highlight the financial stability, liquidity and profitability of the company.

(b)   Comment on the situation revealed by the figures you have calculated in your answer to (a) above.

For a suggested answer, see the 'Answers' section at the end of the book.

KEY TERMS

Gross profit margin – gross profit expressed as a percentage of sales. It is also known as the gross profit margin.

Percentage change in sales – increase or decrease in sales/turnover expressed as a percentage of the earliest year's turnover.

Net profit percentage – $\dfrac{\text{Net profit}}{\text{Sales}} \times 100$. This is also known as the net profit margin.

Return on capital employed (ROCE) – profit is expressed as a percentage of the capital invested in the business. Due to its importance the ROCE is sometimes referred to as the primary ratio.

Total capital employed in the business – the profit available for all of the providers of finance as a percentage of all of the sources of finance.

Equity shareholders' capital employed – the profit available to the ordinary shareholder (before tax) as a percentage of the ordinary shareholder's capital.

Asset turnover – indicates how many £s of sales are being made for every £1 of operating assets or capital employed.

Fixed asset turnover – indicates the amount of £ sales being made for every £1 investment in fixed assets.

Current ratio – the ratio of current assets to current liabilities.

Liquidity (or quick) ratio – the ratio of current assets (excluding stock) to current liabilities.

Stock turnover ratio – the cost of sales divided by the average level of stock during the year.

Debt collection period – relates closing trade debts to the average daily credit sales. It shows the number of days that debtors are outstanding on average.

Average period of credit allowed by suppliers – relates closing creditors to average daily credit purchases.

Working capital cycle – the period of time which elapses between the point at which cash begins to be expended on the production of a product and the collection of cash from the purchaser.

Gearing – relationship between a company's borrowings and its shareholder funds.

Dividend cover – a measure of how many times the profit covers the ordinary dividend payment.

Dividend yield – this expresses dividend per share as a percentage of the current share price.

Price earnings ratio (P/E ratio) – expresses the current share price as a multiple of the earnings per share.

SELF TEST QUESTIONS

Paragraph

1	Name three different user groups of financial statements and state the particular interests of each group.	1.2
2	Distinguish between the gross profit margin and the net profit margin.	3.2 & 3.4
3	How do you calculate the return on capital employed for a company?	3.5
4	Which two ratios can be multiplied together to give the return on capital employed?	3.7
5	What does fixed asset turnover represent?	3.9
6	What are the two key ratios to assess a company's liquidity?	4.2 & 4.3
7	How would you assess whether a company's debt collection procedures were improving or deteriorating?	4.6
8	How is capital gearing determined?	5.2
9	What is the formula to calculate the dividend yield?	6.4
10	How is the P/E ratio of a company calculated?	6.6

PRACTICE QUESTION

ELECTRICAL ENGINEERING

You are given summarised results of an electrical engineering business, as follows. All figures are in £000.

Profit and loss account

	Year ended	
	31.12.X1	*31.12.X0*
Turnover	60,000	50,000
Cost of sales	42,000	34,000
Gross profit	18,000	16,000
Operating expenses	15,500	13,000
	2,500	3,000
Interest payable	2,200	1,300
Profit before taxation	300	1,700
Taxation	350	600
(Loss) profit after taxation	(50)	1,100

Dividends of £600,000 were paid in each year.

Balance sheet

Fixed assets		
Intangible	500	–
Tangible	12,000	11,000
	12,500	11,000
Current assets		
Stocks	14,000	13,000
Debtors	16,000	15,000
Bank and cash	500	500
	30,500	28,500
Creditors due within one year	24,000	20,000
Net current assets	6,500	8,500
Total assets less current liabilities	19,000	19,500
Creditors due after one year	6,000	5,500
	13,000	14,000
Capital and reserves		
Share capital	1,300	1,300
Share premium	3,300	3,300
Revaluation reserve	2,000	2,000
Profit and loss	6,400	7,400
	13,000	14,000

Required:

(a) Prepare a table of the following 12 ratios, calculated for both years, clearly showing the figures used in the calculations:

> current ratio
>
> quick assets ratio
>
> stock turnover in days
>
> creditors turnover in days
>
> gross profit %
>
> net profit % (before taxation)
>
> interest cover
>
> dividend cover
>
> ROOE (before taxation)
>
> ROCE
>
> gearing **(12 marks)**

(b) Making full use of the information given in the question, of your table of ratios, and your common sense, comment on the actions of the management.

(8 marks)
(Total: 20 marks)

EXAM-STYLE QUESTION

HAWK

The directors of Hawk Limited wish to compare the company's most recent financial statements with those of the previous year. The company's financial statements are given below.

Hawk Limited
Profit and loss accounts

	Year ended	
	31 March 20X1 £000	31 March 20X2 £000
Sales revenue (80% on credit and 20% cash)	1,800	2,500
Cost of sales (see note below)	(1,200)	(1,800)
Gross profit	600	700
Distribution costs	(160)	(250)
Administrative expenses	(200)	(200)
Operating profit	240	250
Interest payable	(50)	(50)
Profit before tax	190	200
Taxation	(44)	(46)
Retained profit	146	154

Note: Cost of sales figures are made up as follows:

	Year ended	
	31 March 20X1 £000	31 March 20X2 £000
Opening stock	180	200
Purchases (all on credit)	1,220	1,960
	1,400	2,160
Less closing stock	(200)	(360)
Cost of sales	1,200	1,800

Balance sheets

	As at			
	31 March 20X1		31 March 20X2	
	£000	£000	£000	£000
Fixed assets – cost	3,100		3,674	
Less accumulated depreciation	1,214		1,422	
		1,886		2,252
Current assets				
Stock	200		360	
Debtors – trade	400		750	
Cash at bank	100		120	
	700		1,230	
Less current liabilities				
Creditors – trade	(210)		(380)	
– sundry	(260)		(430)	
Taxation	(48)		(50)	
	(518)		(860)	
Net current assets		182		370
Total assets less current liabilities		2,068		2,622
10% debentures		500		500
		1,568		2,122
Capital and reserves				
Issued ordinary share capital*	1,000		1,200	
Share premium account*	400		600	
Profit and loss account	168		322	
		1,568		2,122
		1,568		2,122

*The additional share capital was issued on 1 April 20X1

Required:

(a) Calculate, for each of the two years, eight accounting ratios which should assist the directors in their comparison, using closing figures for balance sheet items needed.

(8 marks)

(b) Suggest possible reasons for the changes in the ratios between the two years.

(12 marks)
(Total: 20 marks)

For suggested answers, see the 'Answers' section at the end of the book.

Chapter 12

CONSOLIDATION PRINCIPLES

This chapter introduces group accounting. It explains how groups arise, why consolidated group accounts are needed and which methods of group accounting are acceptable. This chapter covers syllabus areas 5(a) and 5(b).

CONTENTS

1   Consolidation

LEARNING OUTCOMES

At the end of this chapter you should be able to:

*   describe and be able to identify the general characteristics of a parent company, investment, and subsidiary undertaking

*   describe the concept of a group and the objective of consolidated financial statements

*   describe the circumstances and reasoning for subsidiaries to be excluded from consolidated financial statements.

1   CONSOLIDATION

1.1   CONTROL

A group of companies arises when one company takes control of another. This can happen in a number of ways. The most common way in the UK is when one company (the parent) acquires more than 50% of the equity shares of another company (the subsidiary). This gives the parent the majority of the votes, which enables it to appoint the Board of Directors, which in turn means that it controls the day to day affairs of the company. The other shareholders will normally own 49% or less of the equity shares, and collectively they are known as the 'minority interest'.

There are other ways in which a parent can control a subsidiary. FRS 2 *Accounting for Subsidiary Undertakings* states that an entity is the parent of a subsidiary undertaking if:

*   it holds a majority of the voting rights

*   it is a member and has the right to appoint or remove directors holding a majority of the voting rights

- it has the right to exercise a dominant influence over the subsidiary undertaking (for example, as the result of a legal agreement)

- it is a member and controls alone, or in agreement with other shareholders, a majority of the voting rights

- it has the power to exercise, or actually exercises dominant influence or control over the undertaking **or** it and the subsidiary are managed on a unified basis

- a parent undertaking is also treated as the parent of the subsidiary undertakings of its subsidiary undertakings.

If an entity has a dominant influence over another, it is able to give directions with respect to its operating and financial policies and the directors are obliged to comply.

However, all of these situations are based on the idea that one company controls another. It is just the methods used that are different. These situations are unusual in the UK. In the exam you will only be set a computational question on a typical group situation where the parent owns the majority of the ordinary shares in the subsidiary.

1.2 GROUP STRUCTURE

The group structure is often shown diagrammatically as follows:

This shows that Big plc owns 51% of the ordinary shares of Small Ltd. Big plc is the parent of Small Ltd, its subsidiary. Together they form the 'The Big Group'. In practice group structures can be a lot more complicated than this, but this paper only covers simple groups.

1.3 THE NEED FOR GROUP ACCOUNTS

Each member company of a group is a legally independent company in its own right, with its own shareholders and own board of directors. Each company enjoys limited liability, and one group member has no obligation to settle the debts of another group member (although companies occasionally guarantee each others debts). Each company is required to prepare and file its own statutory financial statements for each year.

When groups were first established this legal situation meant that group accounts were not prepared. If an investor wanted to assess the overall performance of a group then they had to read the individual accounts for each group company.

This was obviously inconvenient, but it had other drawbacks as well. These were:

- A group normally acts as a single economic entity, not as a collection of individual companies. For example, one subsidiary may manufacture cars, a second subsidiary operate car showrooms in the home market, and a third subsidiary arrange all of the exports. The parent itself is often a shell company which does nothing but hold shares in the subsidiaries.

- The parent company will only show the dividend income received from its subsidiaries. This will not necessarily reflect the profitability of the subsidiary. For example dividends could be increased even though profits have turned to losses.

- The parent company's balance sheet will show the subsidiary as an investment at historic cost. After a few years the real value of a subsidiary will normally be much greater than this.

- Each company's accounts will include inter-company transactions, for example when the manufacturing subsidiary sells its output to the retailing subsidiary. From the group point of view these are not sales, merely a change of location. These transactions, along with any related profits and losses, have to be eliminated in order to assess the performance of the group as a whole.

- The directors of the parent company act as stewards for the funds entrusted to them by the shareholders. Some of this money will have been invested directly in the parent company's own trade, but a large part of these funds will have been invested through the subsidiaries. The directors should be held to account for all of the funds under their control, wherever they have invested it.

At best, the above problems mean that the parent company's financial statements will be an incomplete record of the group's activities. At worst they can be deliberately misleading.

Therefore, group accounts are needed to show the complete picture of the group's activities. FRS 2 *Accounting for Subsidiary Undertakings* describes the purpose of group accounts as follows:

'to present financial information about a parent undertaking and its subsidiary undertakings as a single economic entity to show the economic resources controlled by the group, the obligations of the group and the results the group achieves with its resources.'

1.4 GROUP ACCOUNTING METHODS

There are various ways in which group accounts could be prepared. These are outlined below:

The equity method

Under the equity method the parent accounts for its share of the net profit and net assets of its subsidiaries. So, the Big Group would claim 51% of Small's net assets and net profit. Details of turnover and expenses, assets and liabilities would not be shown. In the UK this method is not allowed for subsidiaries, but it is used for associates.

Proportional consolidation

Under proportional consolidation the parent accounts for its share of each asset and liability, income and expense. The Big Group would claim 51% of Small's turnover, cost of sales etc, and 51% of each item of plant, 51 % of each trade debtor and so on. This method is not allowed by the Companies Act.

Consolidation

Consolidated accounts aggregate each item of income and expenditure, asset and liability in full. The Big Group would claim 100% of each item in Small's accounts. This is done on the basis of control. The parent controls the entire subsidiary and so it should consolidate the entire subsidiary.

However, the parent might not own 100% of the subsidiary. In The Big Group 49% of Small is owned by minority interests. The capital and reserves section of the balance sheet will credit the minority interests with 49% of the net assets of Small. Likewise in the profit and loss account the minority will claim 49% of Small's profits after tax.

The following key rules apply under the consolidation method:

- uniform accounting policies will be applied across the group

- inter-company transactions and profits will be eliminated

- the same year-end will be used across the group. (Sometimes this is not possible for legal reasons. In these cases the consolidated accounts would be based upon interim accounts drawn up to the group balance sheet date.)

This is the method of group accounting required by FRS 2. This method will be studied in detail over the next few chapters.

1.5 CONSOLIDATION METHODS

There are two ways in which a business combination can occur, and this gives rise to two ways in which consolidated accounts can be prepared. These are as follows:

The acquisition method

This method assumes that one company buys another and takes control of it. This is the basic method of consolidation, and is the only method that you will be set a computational question on. Under the acquisition method the companies are consolidated from the date that control passes.

The merger method

This method assumes that two companies join together as equal partners. It is only allowed in situations where the shareholders of one company swap their shares for new shares in the other company. This is known as a share for share exchange. Merged companies are assumed to have been merged forever, and their previous accounts from before the merger are restated as if the merger had already taken place.

This method is very rare in practice, and will almost certainly be outlawed in the near future. It is not allowed in international accounting standards, which are becoming more widely used. You will not be set a computational question on merger accounting.

1.6 EXEMPTIONS FROM CONSOLIDATION

Group accounts do not have to be prepared in the following situations:

The parent company is itself a subsidiary.

The ultimate parent will prepare one set of group accounts for the whole group.

The group is classified as a small group.

A parent company need not prepare group accounts if the group headed by that parent satisfies at least two of the following conditions:

Annual turnover	not more than £6.72m gross or £5.6m net
Balance sheet assets	not more than £3.36m gross or £2.8m net
Average employees	not more than 50

The 'gross' figures are those calculated prior to any consolidation adjustments whereas the 'net' figures are those after the consolidation adjustments, such as the elimination of intra-group balances, have been made. A company may satisfy the relevant limits on either a net or a gross basis or by a mixture of the two.

The purpose of allowing the calculations to be made using the higher gross figures is to prevent a parent company from having to prepare group accounts in order to discover that it does not need to prepare group accounts.

These exemptions remove the burden of preparing group accounts from many small family businesses.

1.7 EXCLUDED SUBSIDIARIES

The Companies Act and FRS 2 have restricted the occasions when a subsidiary can be excluded from consolidation.

FRS 2 states that subsidiaries **must** be excluded from consolidation in the following situations:

- The subsidiary operates under **severe long-term restrictions**. If there are restrictions over a subsidiary's activities then the parent cannot claim to control it. Therefore it will not be consolidated. This is rare within the UK, but it might arise if a company has a subsidiary in an unstable third world country.

- The subsidiary is a **temporary investment** held exclusively with a view to resale. It must not have been consolidated in previous years. In this case, a subsidiary is excluded because control is only intended to be temporary.

The Companies Act states that subsidiaries **may** be excluded from consolidation for the following reasons:

- The subsidiary is **immaterial**. This might apply to certain dormant subsidiaries that have a nominal amount of share capital and no assets or liabilities. FRS 2 (like all accounting standards) does not apply to immaterial items, so in theory it would be possible to exclude a subsidiary for this reason.

- Consolidation would entail **disproportionate expense** or **undue delay**. In practice this would probably only apply to a small and virtually immaterial subsidiary. However, FRS 2 states that this is not a valid reason for excluding a subsidiary.

KEY TERMS

Group – a group of subsidiary companies under the control of the same parent company.

Control – the ability to control the operating and financial policies of an investment to the benefit of the investor. This is normally evidenced by being able to appoint a majority of the Board of Directors.

Parent company – a company that controls another company. Control is normally obtained by owning 50% or more of the ordinary shares of a company.

Subsidiary company – a company under the control of a parent.

Consolidated accounts – a single set of financial statements that combine the assets, liabilities, income and expenditure of a parent company and its subsidiaries.

Acquisition method – the basis of consolidation used in the UK. This assumes that the parent has bought the underlying assets and liabilities of the subsidiary on the date that it obtained control of the subsidiary.

Minority interests – the minority interest represents other shareholders in a subsidiary. The parent may own between 50% and 100% of the shares in its subsidiaries. Any shares that it does not own form part of the minority interest.

Excluded subsidiaries – subsidiary companies that are not included in the consolidated financial statements. These situations are very rare.

SELF TEST QUESTIONS

Paragraph

1	What one thing must one company have in order to treat another company as its subsidiary?	1.1
2	In the UK, how does a parent / subsidiary relationship normally arise?	1.1
3	If a parent owns 60% of a subsidiary, who owns the other 40%?	1.1
4	What problems might arise if group accounts were not prepared?	1.3
5	State three different methods for preparing group accounts.	1.4
6	State two situations in which a parent would not have to prepare group accounts.	1.6
7	State two situations in which a subsidiary must be excluded from consolidation.	1.7

PRACTICE QUESTION

IDENTIFYING SUBSIDIARIES

Polyglot plc has connections with each of the companies below. For each of them **state** with **explanations**, whether or not they should be treated as subsidiaries of Polyglot plc.

(a) Polyglot owns 1,000,000 £1 25% preference shares in Welsh Ltd. Welsh Ltd's share capital consists of 2 ordinary shares of 10p each and one million Preference Shares.

(b) Polyglot owns two $12^1/_2$p ordinary shares in Gaelic Ltd. Gaelic Ltd's share capital consists of three $12^1/_2$p ordinary shares and one million preference shares.

(c) Polyglot owns 4,500 ordinary shares in English Ltd. English Ltd has 10,000 ordinary shares. The shares not held by Polyglot are shared equally between 44 other shareholders.

(d) Polyglot holds one share in Scotch Ltd. Scotch Ltd's share capital consists of one hundred $12^1/_2$p ordinary shares and one million preference shares. Polyglot supplies all the raw materials for Scotch Ltd and markets its output. Also, many of Scotch's technical and managerial staff are on secondment from Polyglot plc.

(12 marks)

For a suggested answer, see the 'Answers' section at the end of the book.

Chapter 13

CONSOLIDATED BALANCE SHEET

This chapter explains how a consolidated balance sheet is prepared under the acquisition method of accounting for a subsidiary as set out in FRS 2 *Accounting for Subsidiary Undertakings*. This chapter covers syllabus areas 5(a) and 5(b).

CONTENTS

LEARNING OUTCOMES

At the end of this chapter you should be able to:

- prepare a consolidated balance sheet for a simple group including adjustments for pre and post acquisition profits, minority interests and consolidated goodwill

- explain why intra-group transactions should be eliminated on consolidation

- account for the effects in the balance sheet of intra-group trading and other transactions including:

    (i)   unrealised profits in stock and fixed assets

    (ii)   intra-group loans and interest and other intra-group charges.

1 THE CONSOLIDATED BALANCE SHEET

The consolidated balance sheet combines the assets and liabilities of the parent and its subsidiaries on a line by line basis. This recognises all the assets and liabilities under the *control* of the Group.

The cost of the parent's investment in its subsidiary is eliminated. The consolidated balance sheet recognises the underlying assets and liabilities of the subsidiary, and so it would be double counting to show the cost of the investment as well.

The parent company's shareholders are the ultimate source of control within the group, and so the share capital (and share premium) of the Group is the share capital and premium of the parent only.

Reserves represent the retained profits of a business. The reserves of the group will therefore represent the retained profits of the parent and its subsidiaries. The subsidiaries' reserves will only be consolidated from the date that they became subsidiaries.

Example – Paul plc and Saul Ltd

This first example illustrates the basic concepts of:

- aggregating the assets and liabilities

- eliminating the cost of the investment in the subsidiary from the parent's balance sheet

- eliminating the capital and reserves of the subsidiary. (Future examples will keep a portion of the subsidiary's post acquisition reserves.)

Noted below are the company balance sheets of Paul plc and its subsidiary Saul Ltd. Paul plc acquired all the shares in Saul Ltd on 31 December 20X4 for a cost of £50,000.

Company balance sheets at 31 December 20X4

	Paul plc		Saul Ltd	
	£000	£000	£000	£000
Tangible fixed assets		60		40
Investment in Saul at cost		50		–
Current assets	45		38	
Current liabilities	(25)		(28)	
		20		10
Net assets		130		50
Ordinary share capital (£1 Shares)		100		50
Revenue reserves		30		–
		130		50

Required:

Prepare a consolidated balance sheet.

Solution

(1) The Paul Group consolidated balance sheet will differ from that of Paul plc's own company balance sheet, in that the cost of the investment in the subsidiary account will be replaced by the underlying net assets which the investment represents. The cost of the investment in the subsidiary is cancelled with the ordinary share capital and reserves of the subsidiary. In this simple case, it can be seen that the relevant figures are equal and opposite, and therefore cancel directly. The cost of the investment in S Ltd is £50,000 and the share capital of S Ltd acquired is £50,000.

(2) All other assets and liabilities are aggregated.

(3) The share capital (and share premium) of the group is always that of the parent alone. This represents the ultimate control of the group.

(4) The group reserves are the parent's reserves plus the Group's share of the post acquisition reserves of the subsidiary. In this case the balance sheet is being drawn up on the date of acquisition and so there are no post acquisition reserves.

The Paul Group balance sheets at 31 December 20X4

		£000	£000
Tangible fixed assets	*60 + 40*		100
Current assets	*45 + 38*	83	
Current liabilities	*(25 + 28)*	(53)	
			30
Net assets			130
Ordinary share capital	*parent only*		100
Revenue reserves			30
			130

In this example the £50,000 cost of the investment equals the £50,000 fair value of the investment.

This simplifies the accounting by preventing any goodwill from arising. Goodwill is introduced in Section 4.

2 POST ACQUISITION RESERVES

In the above example the consolidated balance sheet was prepared on the same day that the acquisition took place. When the balance sheet is drawn up in a few year's time the subsidiary will have generated some post acquisition reserves. These profits will have been earned while the subsidiary was part of the group and so they will be included as part of the group reserves.

Example – Paul plc and Saul Ltd 20X6

Noted below are the company balance sheets of Paul plc and its subsidiary Saul Ltd as at 31 December 20X6. As before, Paul plc acquired all the shares in Saul Ltd on 31 December 20X4 for a cost of £50,000. Saul Ltd's reserves at acquisition were £Nil.

Company balance sheets at 31 December 20X6

	Paul plc		Saul Ltd	
	£000	£000	£000	£000
Tangible fixed assets		135		287
Investment in Saul at cost		50		–
Current assets	99		364	
Current liabilities	(64)		(195)	
		35		169
Net assets		220		456
Ordinary share capital (£1 shares)		100		50
Revenue reserves		120		406
		220		456

Required:

Prepare a consolidated balance sheet.

Solution

(1)   The cost of the investment is eliminated.

(2)   All other assets and liabilities are aggregated.

(3)   The share capital of the group is that of the parent alone

(4)   The Group reserves are the parent's reserves plus the Group's share of the post acquisition reserves of the subsidiary.

The Paul Group balance sheet at 31 December 20X6

		£000	£000
Tangible fixed assets	*135 + 287*		422
Current assets	*99 + 364*	463	
Current liabilities	*(64 + 195)*	(259)	
			204
Net assets			626
Ordinary share capital (£1 shares)			100
Revenue reserves			526
			626

Workings – Group reserve calculation

		£000	£000
(W1)	The parent's own reserves at the balance sheet date		120
(W2)	The subsidiary's own reserves at the balance sheet date	406	
	Less the subsidiary's reserves at acquisition	–	
	Subsidiary's post acquisition reserves		406
(W3)	Total group reserves		526

3   PRE AND POST ACQUISITION RESERVES

Subsidiaries have usually traded on their own account before they are acquired by their new parent, and so they will already have a balance on their revenues reserves. On acquisition, this balance is frozen and does not form part of the group reserves. This is because these profits have been bought rather than earned. Only the post acquisition reserves have been earned by the group.

Example – Michael plc and Luke Ltd 20X8

Noted below are the company balance sheets of Michael plc and its subsidiary Luke Ltd as at 31 December 20X8. Michael plc acquired all the shares in Luke Ltd on 31 December 20X4 for a cost of £90,000. Luke Ltd had already been trading for many years, and its reserves at acquisition were £60,000.

Company balance sheets at 31 December 20X8

	Michael	Luke
	£000	£000
Tangible fixed assets	333	287
Investment in Luke at cost	90	–
Net current assets	114	169
Net assets	537	456
Ordinary share capital (£1 shares)	50	30
Revenue reserves	487	426
	537	456

Required:

Prepare a consolidated balance sheet.

Solution

The only complication is in the reserves calculation. This will be as follows:

Group reserve calculation

		£000	£000
(i)	The parent's own reserves at the balance sheet date		487
(ii)	The subsidiary's own reserves at the balance sheet date	426	
	Less the subsidiary's reserves at acquisition	(60)	
	Subsidiary's post acquisition reserves		366
(iii)	Total group reserves		853

The Michael Group balance sheet at 31 December 20X8

		£000
Tangible fixed assets	*333 + 287*	620
Net current assets	*114 + 169*	283
Net assets		903
Ordinary share capital (£1 shares)		50
Revenue reserves		853
		903

4 GOODWILL ARISING ON CONSOLIDATION

Definition **Goodwill** is the difference between the fair value of the consideration and the fair value of the net assets acquired.

Companies usually have to pay a premium in order to purchase another successful company from its existing shareholders. This premium is known as goodwill.

Goodwill is a term used to describe all those things that make a company successful. Goodwill will include the quality of the products, the staff, the way in which the business is organised, the loyalty of the customers, the reliability of the suppliers and many more things. It is impossible to value. You will know from an earlier chapter that the goodwill inherent in all successful businesses must *not* be capitalised. Purchased goodwill, however, **must** be capitalised, because the cost of this goodwill has been fixed by a business transaction.

When one company purchases another, the purchase price will include an element in respect of goodwill. This goodwill is a balancing figure. It can only be calculated in relation to the purchase price of the business and the net assets acquired.

4.1 BASIC RULES

The accounting treatment for goodwill is set out in FRS 10 *Goodwill and Intangible Assets*. Goodwill, like almost all other assets, is normally capitalised and amortised over its useful life. The goodwill will be capitalised at its cost as calculated on the day of acquisition.

Original cost

The original cost of goodwill is the difference between the fair value of the consideration paid to acquire the subsidiary and the fair value of the net assets acquired.

In order to calculate the goodwill you need to know what the fair value of the net assets were at the date of acquisition. This will be based on their book value. This can be calculated from the subsidiary's share capital plus its reserves at the date of acquisition.

Example – Peter plc and Simon Ltd 20X1

On 1 January 20X1 Peter plc paid £250,000 for all of the ordinary shares in Simon Ltd. Simon Ltd's share capital and reserves on that date were as follows:

	£
£1 ordinary shares	50,000
Share premium account	30,000
Reserves	140,000
Total shareholders' funds	220,000

The accounting equation tells us that shareholders' funds equals the net assets of the business, so Simon's net assets must be £220,000.

Goodwill can now be calculated as follows:

		£
(i)	Fair value of the consideration	250,000
(ii)	Less: the fair value of the net assets acquired	(220,000)
(iii)	Goodwill at cost	30,000

On 1 January the Peter Group will capitalise this goodwill as an intangible fixed asset at its cost of £30,000.

Amortisation

There is a *rebuttable presumption* that the useful economic life of goodwill does not exceed 20 years. Therefore goodwill will normally be amortised over 20 years or less. The goodwill should be reviewed regularly for impairment, and written down if the carrying value exceeds its recoverable amount. The amortisation charge is normally shown as a separate line within group operating expenses on the face of the P&L.

There are two alternatives to the above rules:

- goodwill may be amortised over a period exceeding 20 years; and

- goodwill may be carried at its cost indefinitely, without any amortisation.

These policies are only allowed if the group can prove that the goodwill still exists. To do this they must:

- perform annual impairment reviews

- be able to measure the value of the goodwill throughout its life

- be able to justify the estimate of the useful economic life of the goodwill.

As before, the value of the goodwill should be written down if its carrying value exceeds its recoverable amount. These alternative treatments are very rarely used.

Example – Peter plc and Simon Ltd 20X3

This example follows on from the previous one. It illustrates the normal treatment of goodwill, including:

- the amortisation of goodwill

- the presentation of goodwill in the balance sheet

- the deduction of the cumulative amortisation charge from group reserves

- the calculation of the post acquisition reserves in a subsidiary.

Situation

As before, on 1st January 20X1 Peter plc paid £250,000 for all of the ordinary shares in Simon Ltd. Simon Ltd's reserves on that date were £140,000. Goodwill of £30,000 arose, and this is to be amortised over ten years on a straight line basis.

The balance sheets of these two companies three years later on 31 December 20X3 are noted below.

Company balance sheets at 31 December 20X3

	Peter £000	Simon £000
Tangible fixed assets	127	403
Investment in Simon at cost	250	–
Net current assets	59	241
Net assets	436	644
Ordinary share capital (£1 shares)	100	50
Share premium	45	30
Revenue reserves	291	564
	436	644

Required:

(1)   Calculate the cumulative amortisation and net book value of the goodwill as at 31 December 20X3.

(2)   Calculate the group's revenue reserves as at 31 December 20X3.

(3)   Prepare the consolidated balance sheet for the Peter Group as at 31 December 20X3.

Solution

(1)   The amortisation and net book value will be calculated in the same way as for any other fixed asset.

	£	
Goodwill at cost	30,000	
Three years amortisation at £3,000 pa	(9,000)	Deduct from group reserves. See below.
Net book value	21,000	Recognise as a fixed asset.

(2)   The £9,000 cumulative amortisation charged will be deducted from the parent's reserves in the group reserves calculation.

Group reserve calculation

			£000	£000
(i)	The parent's own reserves at the balance sheet date			291
(ii)	Less: cumulative amortisation of goodwill			(9)
(iii)	The subsidiary's own reserves at the balance sheet date		564	
	Less the subsidiary's reserves at acquisition		(140)	
	Subsidiary's post acquisition reserves			424
(iv)	Total group reserves			706

The Peter Group balance sheet at 31 December 20X3

		£000
Goodwill at NBV	*See above*	21
Tangible fixed assets	*(127 + 403)*	530
Net current assets	*(59 + 241)*	300
Net assets		851
Ordinary share capital (£1 shares)	*Parent only*	100
Share premium account	*Parent only*	45
Revenue reserves	*See above*	706
		851

ACTIVITY 1

On 1st January 20X2 George plc paid £357,000 for all of the ordinary shares in Albert Ltd. Albert Ltd's reserves on that date were £189,000.

The balance sheets of these two companies six years later on 31 December 20X7 are noted below.

Company balance sheets at 31 December 20X7

	George	Albert
	£000	£000
Tangible fixed assets	22	425
Investment in Albert at cost	369	–
Net current assets	17	478
Net assets	408	903
Ordinary share capital (£1 Shares)	200	80
Share premium	50	40
Revenue reserves	158	783
	408	903

Required:

(1) Calculate the cost of the goodwill arising on the acquisition of Albert Ltd on 1 January 20X2.

(2) Calculate the cumulative amortisation and net book value of the goodwill as at 31 December 20X7. Goodwill is to be amortised over ten years on a straight line basis.

(3) Calculate the group revenue reserves as at 31 December 20X7.

(4) Prepare the consolidated balance sheet for the George Group as at 31 December 20X7.

For a suggested answer, see the 'Answers' section at the end of the book.

4.2 NEGATIVE GOODWILL

Sometimes a company may be purchased for less than the fair value of its net assets. This may happen if the company is in financial difficulties and the only option for the present owners is to sell the company as quickly as possible. In these situations negative goodwill arises. This is treated as a negative fixed asset, to be netted off any positive goodwill balances.

5 MINORITY INTERESTS

The consolidation method of group accounting combines the assets and liabilities of the parent and its subsidiaries on the basis of control. The parent need only own 51% of a subsidiary in order to control and consolidate it. The remaining 49% of the subsidiary is then owned by the minority interests.

This has three effects on the way in which the balance sheet is prepared:

(1)   The Minority's ownership interest in the net assets of the subsidiary needs to be recognised in the capital and reserves section of the group balance sheet.

(2)   When goodwill is being calculated the purchase price is compared with the percentage share of the net assets acquired.

(3)   In the group reserves calculation, the Group will only claim its share of the post acquisition profits of the subsidiary.

Example – Edward Ltd and David Ltd

On 1 January 20X4 Edward plc paid £153,000 for 12,000 £1 ordinary shares in David Ltd. David Ltd's reserves on that date were £140,000. Any goodwill arising is to be amortised over eight years.

The balance sheets of these two companies five years later on 31 December 20X8 are noted below.

Company balance sheets at 31 December 20X8

	Edward	David
	£000	£000
Tangible fixed assets	45	106
Investment in David at cost	153	–
Net current assets	71	179
Net assets	269	285
Ordinary share capital (£1 shares)	50	20
Share premium	25	15
Revenue reserves	194	250
	269	285

Required:

(1)   Calculate the ownership interest that Edward has in David. Is it a subsidiary?

(2)   Calculate the cost of the goodwill arising on the acquisition of David Ltd on 1 January 20X4.

(3)   Calculate the cumulative amortisation and net book value of the goodwill as at 31 December 20X8.

(4)   Calculate the minority interest in David as at 31 December 20X8.

(5)   Calculate the Group's revenue reserves as at 31 December 20X8.

(6)   Prepare the consolidated balance sheet for the Edward Group as at 31 December 20X8.

Solution

Most of the workings will be familiar to you. The new stages in the calculations have been **highlighted**.

(1)   *Ownership interest.* Edward owns 12,000 £1 ordinary shares out of a total of 20,000. This is a 60% interest. Because this is more than 50% then Edward will be able to appoint David's board of directors and control the company. This makes David a subsidiary of Edward. There is also a 40% minority interest.

(2)   *Goodwill at cost*

		£000	£000
(i)	Fair value of the consideration		153
(ii)	Fair value of the net assets acquired		
	Ordinary shares	20	
	Share premium	15	
	Revenue reserves at acquisition	140	
		175	
	Group share @ 60%		105
	Goodwill at cost		48

There is one new line on this calculation. Only the group share (60%) of the net assets of the subsidiary are included in the goodwill calculation. This is 60% × £175,000 = £105,000.

This goodwill is being amortised over eight years at £6,000 per annum.

(3)   *Goodwill: Amortisation and NBV*

	£000	
Goodwill at cost	48	
Five years amortisation at £6,000 pa	(30)	Deduct from group reserves.
Net book value	18	Recognise as a fixed asset.

(4)   *The minority interest in the balance sheet*

This will represent the 40% of the net assets owned by outside shareholders. The minority interest is recalculated at each balance sheet date. It is based on the subsidiary's net assets at the balance sheet date.

In this example, the minority own 40% of David's net assets of £285,000. Therefore the minority interest on 31 December 20X8 is £114,000.

(5)   *Group reserves*

		£000	£000
(i)	The parent's own reserves at the balance sheet date		194
(ii)	Less: cumulative amortisation of goodwill *(See above)*		(30)
(iii)	The subsidiary's own reserves at the balance sheet date	250	
	Less the subsidiary's reserves at acquisition	(140)	
	Subsidiary's post acquisition reserves	110	
	Group share @ 60%		66
(iv)	Total group reserves		230

The only change to this calculation is in respect of the subsidiary's reserves. Only the group's 60% share of the post acquisition reserves can be included as part of the group reserves. The other 40% belongs to the minority interests, and was accounted for as part of the calculation in part (4) above.

(6)   **Edward Group balance sheet at 31 December 20X7**

		£000
Goodwill at NBV	(3) above	18
Tangible fixed assets	(45 + 106)	151
Net current assets	(71 + 179)	250
Net assets		419
Ordinary share capital (£1 shares)	Parent only	50
Share premium account	Parent only	25
Revenue reserves	(5) above	230
Group shareholders' funds		305
Minority interests	(4) above	114
		419

The net assets under the control of the Edward Group total £419,000. Of this, £305,000 is owned by the Parent Company shareholders, and £114,000 is owned by minority interests.

ACTIVITY 2

On 1 July 20X3 Henry plc paid £345,000 for 24,000 £1 Ordinary Shares in Arthur Ltd. Arthur Ltd's reserves on that date were £220,000. Any goodwill arising is to be amortised over eight years. The Group year-end is December. Henry charges a full year's amortisation in the year of acquisition.

The balance sheets of these two companies on 31 December 20X9 are noted below:

Company balance sheets at 31 December 20X9

	Henry	Arthur
	£000	£000
Tangible fixed assets	54	246
Investment in Arthur at cost	352	
Net current assets	101	399
Net assets	507	645
Ordinary share capital (£1 shares)	90	30
Share premium	49	20
Revenue reserves	368	595
	507	645

Required:

(1)   Calculate the ownership interest that Henry has in Arthur. Is it a subsidiary?

(2)   Calculate the cost of the goodwill arising on the acquisition of Arthur Ltd on 1 July 20X3.

(3)   Calculate the cumulative amortisation and net book value of the goodwill as at 31 December 20X9. Remember to charge a full year's amortisation in the year of acquisition.

(4)   Calculate the minority interest in Arthur as at 31 December 20X9.

(5)   Calculate the group's revenue reserves as at 31 December 20X9.

(6)   Prepare the consolidated balance sheet for the Henry Group as at 31 December 20X9.

For a suggested answer, see the 'Answers' section at the end of the book.

6   INTER-COMPANY BALANCES, UNREALISED PROFITS, AND THE CONSOLIDATION SCHEDULE

6.1   INTER-COMPANY TRADE

It is normal for group companies to trade with each other. Sometimes it is essential because one subsidiary might provide the components or raw materials used by another company. Also, parent companies often provide services (such as marketing) that benefit the whole group. The cost of these services will then be recharged to the other companies in the group. Sometimes the parent will make loans to their subsidiaries as well.

The income and expense resulting from this trade will be dealt with in the next chapter. This section will look at the debtor and creditor balances arising, and the next section will look at unrealised profit.

6.2   DEBTOR AND CREDITOR BALANCES

Inter-company trade can be dealt with either through the normal trade debtors ledger and trade creditors ledger, or through specific inter-company accounts. Either way, these balances do not represent debtors or creditors from the group point of view, and so they must be cancelled out on consolidation. If the balances agree, then this procedure is easy. Sometimes though they do not agree, and then the balances must be reconciled before they are cancelled.

6.3   RECONCILING INTER-COMPANY ACCOUNTS

Every group will have its own procedures for reconciling inter-company accounts. The key issue is that any procedure must be applied consistently otherwise the situation will get worse instead of better.

Differences between the parent's and the subsidiary's records can arise for two reasons:

(1)   mistakes made by either party; or

(2)   goods or cash in transit.

These are dealt with as follows:

(1)   If a mistake has been made then the mistake must be corrected permanently.

(2)   If there are goods or cash in transit between companies then a temporary adjustment will be made for year-end purposes. (These adjustments will be reversed after the year-end when the actual goods, invoices or cash are received. This stage of the process though is not on your syllabus.)

Exam questions tend to concentrate on the items in transit.

6.4   GOODS AND CASH IN TRANSIT – RECONCILIATION AND CANCELLATION

Example – Parcel plc and String Ltd

Parcel plc has one wholly owned subsidiary, String Ltd. Parcel has owned String since incorporation and there is no goodwill. Parcel transfers goods to String at cost price. These transfers are recorded in an inter-company account. The cash payments that String makes to Parcel are also recorded in this account.

At the year-end the balance sheets of the two companies were as follows:

	Parcel		String	
	£	£	£	£
Tangible fixed assets		132,956		243,856
Investment in String at cost		20,000		–
Current assets				
Stocks	25,385		32,957	
Debtors	65,283		23,475	
Bank and cash	9,384		44,857	
Inter-company account	30,611		–	
	130,663		101,289	
Current liabilities				
Sundry	56,392		36,826	
Inter-company account	–		18,916	
	56,392		55,742	
Net current assets		74,271		45,547
Net assets		227,227		289,403
£1 ordinary shares		50,000		20,000
Revenue reserves		177,227		269,403
		227,227		289,403

From this you can see that the inter company accounts are not in agreement:

Parcel's balance sheet	Inter-company debtor	Amount owed by String	£30,631
String's balance sheet	Inter-company creditor	Amount owed to Parcel	£18,916

The following information is relevant:

(1)   Shortly before the year-end Parcel sent goods with a cost of £4,933 to String. String had not received these goods at the year-end.

(2)   Shortly before the year-end String sent a cheque for £6,762 to Parcel. Parcel had not received this money at the year-end.

Solution

For consolidation purposes these half-completed transactions can be reversed, and then the inter-company balances will agree and can be cancelled out. This cancelling out is known as a contra. Remember that these adjustments will not be made in the books of the individual companies. They are only adjusted for on the consolidation working papers.

The adjustments can be recorded in journal format as follows:

Goods in transit

Debit	Stocks	£4,933	
Credit	Inter company debtors		£4,933

With the stocks in transit. This removes the stocks from Parcel's inter-company account and puts them back in the warehouse as part of stock.

Cash in transit

Debit	Bank and cash	£6,762	
Credit	Inter company creditors		£6,762

With the cash in transit. This removes the cheque payment from the inter-company account, and puts the money back in the bank account.

The inter-company balances will be amended as follows:

Parcel's own balance sheet	£	
Inter company debtor	30,611	Dr
Less: Goods in transit	4,933	Cr
Revised balance	25,678	Dr
Contra	25,678	Cr
Consolidated balance	Nil	

String's own balance sheet		
Inter-company creditor	18,916	Cr
Add: Cash in transit	6,762	Cr
Revised balance	25,678	Cr
Contra	25,678	Dr
Consolidated balance	Nil	

The consolidated balance should always be £Nil. The Group cannot owe money to and from itself.

6.5   THE CONSOLIDATION SCHEDULE

Now that the number of consolidation adjustments is increasing, it is useful to record all of these changes on a consolidation schedule. The consolidation schedule for the Parcel and String example is shown below:

Consolidation schedule for the Parcel Group

	(a) Parcel £	(a) String £	(b) Adjustments	(c) Group £
Tangible fixed assets	132,956	243,856		376,81
Investment in String	20,000	–	Cancelled	
Current assets				
Stocks	25,385	32,957	4,933 Dr goods in transit	63,275
Debtors	65,283	23,475		88,758
Bank and cash	9,384	44,857	6,762 Dr Cash in transit	61,003
Inter-company account	30,611	–	4,933 Cr Goods in transit, 25,678 Contra	–
				213,036
Current liabilities				
Sundry	56,392	36,826		93,218
Inter-company account	–	18,916	6,762 Cr Cash in transit, 25,678 Contra	–
				93,218
Net current assets				119,818
Net assets				496,630
£1 ordinary shares	50,000	20,000	Parent only	50,000
Revenue reserves	177,227	269,403	All post acquisition, no minority	446,630
				496,630

(a) All of the line items for the parent and the subsidiary are entered into the left hand columns of the schedule. Do not bother with the sub-totals, because these will not add across.

(b) The adjustments are recorded in the middle of the schedule. These will be entered onto the schedule as you work through an example. Do not add across until you have dealt with all of the information in the question and entered all of the individual adjustments onto the schedule.

(c) Finally, add each line across to create the group balance sheet.

(d) This approach is used by most businesses. In practice it may be performed on a spread-sheet, but the underlying techniques are exactly the same, whether it is done electronically or in ink.

In an exam it will give you an orderly and methodical approach to your answer. It also means that if exam nerves cause you to make any mathematical errors, the marker will be able to see that you were following the correct method and using the right information.

7 PROVISION FOR UNREALISED PROFIT

7.1 INTRODUCTION

In the last section goods were transferred between the two companies at cost. However, sometimes group companies will trade with each other on normal commercial terms. This means that the selling company will have made a profit, and the cost of the stock in the buying company's books will also include an element of profit. This is correct, as far as the individual companies are concerned. However, for group purposes this inter company profit must be eliminated. This is for two reasons:

(1)   a group cannot make a profit by trading with itself

(2)   stock must be stated at its cost to the group. This will exclude any profit made by one group company at the expense of another.

7.2   BASIC RULES – WHOLLY OWNED SUBSIDIARIES

The most important rule to remember is that these rules only apply to stock on hand at the year-end. Inter-company profits on goods that have eventually been sold onto third parties will have been realised by the year-end and do not cause a problem.

The rules are:

(1)   The consolidated stock value will be reduced by the element of unrealised profit at the year-end. This is known as the *provision for unrealised profit*, or PuP.

(2)   This unrealised profit will also be deducted from the **selling** company's revenue reserves in the group reserve calculation.

Example – Wholly owned subsidiary sells goods to the parent

Paper Ltd has one wholly owned subsidiary, Scissors Ltd. Paper paid £33,000 for String when String's reserves were £25,000. No goodwill arose on acquisition.

During the year-ending 31 March 20X2 Paper purchased £100,000 of goods from Scissors. Scissors made £40,000 profit on these goods, which had cost Scissors £60,000 to make. At the year-end Paper had £25,000 of these goods left in stock, which included £10,000 of profit.

The balance sheets of these two companies as at 31 March 20X2 are as follows:

	Paper £	Paper £	Scissors £	Scissors £
Tangible fixed assets		22,000		175,000
Investment in Scissors		33,000		
Current assets				
Stocks	138,000		76,000	
Sundry	224,000		212,000	
	362,000		288,000	
Current liabilities	183,000		63,000	
Net current assets		179,000		225,000
Net assets		234,000		400,000
£1 ordinary shares		5,000		8,000
Revenue reserves		229,000		392,000
		234,000		400,000

Solution

Paper's stocks of £138,000 includes some items bought from Scissors. These items include £10,000 of unrealised profit. This profit must be eliminated, reducing the stock value to £128,000.

Scissors reserves of £390,000 includes £10,000 of profit which has not been realised from the group point of view. This must be eliminated reducing Scissors' reserves to £380,000.

This can be set out as a journal as follows:

Debit	Subsidiary's revenue reserves	£10,000	
Credit	Stocks		£10,000

The consolidation schedule will look as follows:

	Paper	Scissors	Adjustments		Group
	£	£		£	£
Tangible fixed assets	22,000	175,000			197,000
Investment in Scissors	33,000	–	Cancelled		–
Current assets					
Stocks	138,000	76,000	£10,000 Cr	204,000	
Sundry	224,000	212,000		436,000	
				640,000	
Current liabilities	183,000	63,000		246,000	
Net current assets					394,000
Net assets					591,000
£1 ordinary shares	5,000	8,000	Parent only		5,000
Revenue reserves	229,000	392,000	Working		586,000
					591,000

Working for the group reserves	£	£
The parent's own reserves at the balance sheet date		229,000
The subsidiary's own reserves at the balance sheet date	392,000	
Less the subsidiary's reserves at acquisition	(25,000)	
Less Provision for unrealised profits	(10,000)	
Subsidiary's post acquisition reserves		357,000
Total group reserves		586,000

7.3 UNREALISED PROFITS AND PARTLY OWNED SUBSIDIARIES

The rules set out in Section 7.2 above apply equally to partly and wholly owned subsidiaries. However, the procedure for partly owned subsidiaries needs some clarification.

The full amount of the provision is always deducted from the stock value in the top half of the balance sheet.

The effect on reserves will depend on who was selling the goods.

The parent sold the goods:

- The provision will be deducted from the parent's reserves.

The subsidiary sold the goods:

- The provision will be deducted from the subsidiary's reserves. The Group will then claim its share of these revised reserves.

- The provision will also be deducted from the net assets of the subsidiary when calculating the minority interests in the subsidiary.

Example – Partly owned subsidiary sells goods to the parent

Many years ago, Phantom Ltd paid £90,000 for 60% of the shares in Spirit Ltd. Spirit Ltd's reserves at that time were £130,000 and no goodwill arose on the acquisition.

On 30 June 20X5 Phantom had £70,000 worth of stock on hand which it had purchased from Spirit. Spirit had made a £30,000 profit on these items.

The balance sheets of these two companies as at 30 June 20X5 are as follows:

	Phantom		Spirit	
	£000	£000	£000	£000
Tangible fixed assets		210		278
Investment in Spirit		90		–
Current assets				
Stocks	182		98	
Sundry	535		235	
	717		333	
Current liabilities	317		111	
Net current assets		400		222
Net assets		700		500
£1 ordinary shares		100		20
Revenue reserves		600		480
		700		500

Solution

The £30,000 Provision for Unrealised Profits will have the following effects on the group balance sheet:

- reduce Group stocks by £30,000

- reduce the subsidiary's reserves by £30,000 when calculating the group reserves

- reduce the subsidiary's net assets by £30,000 when calculating the minority interests.

The consolidation schedule will look as follows:

	Phantom £000	Spirit £000	Adjustments	Group £000	£000
Tangible fixed assets	210	278			488
Investment in Spirit	90	–	Cancelled		–
Current assets					
Stocks	182	98	£30 Cr PUP	250	
Sundry	535	235		770	
				1,020	
Current liabilities	317	111		428	
Net current assets					592
Net assets					1,080
£1 ordinary shares	100	20	Parent only		100
Revenue reserves	600	480	Working 1 below		792
Group shareholders' funds					892
Minority interests			Working 2 below		188
					1,080

(W1) **Group reserves**	£000	£000
The parent's own reserves at the balance sheet date		600
The subsidiary's own reserves at the balance sheet date	480	
Less the subsidiary's reserves at acquisition	(130)	
Less provision for unrealised profits	(30)	
Subsidiary's post acquisition reserves	320	
The group's 60% share		192
Total group reserves		792

(W2) **Minority interests**	£000
The subsidiary's net assets from its own balance sheet	500
Less: Provision for unrealised profits	(30)
The revised net assets	470
The Minority's 40% share of these net assets	188

ACTIVITY 3

Many years ago, Planet Ltd paid £210,000 for 70% of the shares in Star Ltd. Star Ltd's reserves at that time were £250,000 and no goodwill arose on the acquisition.

On 30 June 20X5 Planet had £200,000 worth of stock on hand which it had purchased from Star. Star had made a £80,000 profit on these items.

The balance sheets of these two companies as at 30 June 20X5 are as follows:

	Planet		Star	
	£000	£000	£000	£000
Tangible fixed assets		384		130
Investment in Star		210		–
Current assets				
Stocks	468		235	
Sundry	579		654	
	1,047		889	
Current liabilities	841		419	
Net current assets		206		470
Net assets		800		600
£1 ordinary shares		10		50
Revenue reserves		790		550
		800		600

Required:

Prepare the consolidation schedule for the Planet Group as at 30th June 20X5, along with the supporting workings for the group reserves and minority interests.

For a suggested answer, see the 'Answers' section at the end of the book.

ACTIVITY 4

Pluto sold £62,660 worth of goods to Saturn. Calculate the profit in cash terms assuming:

(1)   a 30% gross profit margin

(2)   a 30% mark-up on cost.

For a suggested answer, see the 'Answers' section at the end of the book.

ACTIVITY 5

P Ltd owns 90% of S Ltd. S Ltd sells goods to P Ltd at cost plus 25%. At the year end P Ltd's stock includes £8,000 of goods at invoice value from S Ltd.

What is the consolidation adjustment required?

For a suggested answer, see the 'Answers' section at the end of the book.

ACTIVITY 6

Balance sheets at 31 December 20X4

	P Ltd £	S Ltd £
Investment in S Ltd (at cost)	75,000	
Stock	12,000	5,000
Other net assets	83,000	95,000
	170,000	100,000
Share capital (£1 ord)	50,000	40,000
Profit and loss account	120,000	60,000
	170,000	100,000

P Ltd acquired 32,000 shares in S Ltd on 1 January 20X4 when the balance on the profit and loss account of S Ltd was £50,000. During the year S Ltd sold goods to P Ltd for £80,000 making a standard mark up of 25%. At 31 December 20X4, P Ltd included in its stock value £5,000, being the price paid for goods purchased from S Ltd. Goodwill is to be written off over 3 years.

Prepare the consolidated balance sheet at 31 December 20X4.

For a suggested answer, see the 'Answers' section at the end of the book.

7.4 SALES OF FIXED ASSETS

Sometimes one group company sells a fixed asset to another. The principles are the same as for sales of goods. Any profit made by the selling company is unrealised and must be eliminated from the consolidated financial statements.

Example

Perch Ltd owns 60% of Salmon Ltd. At the beginning of the year Salmon Ltd transfers an item of plant costing £20,000 to Perch Ltd. Perch Ltd pays £25,000 for the plant, depreciating over five years with a nil scrap value at the end of the period using the straight line basis.

Solution

There are two problems here:

(a)   There is an unrealised profit of £5,000 in the transfer price of the fixed asset.

(b)   During the first year in which the plant is used Perch incurs a depreciation charge of 20% of £25,000. Had the asset been transferred at cost, the depreciation charge would have been only £4,000.

Step 1

Calculate the cost and accumulated depreciation on the transferred asset as it stands in the balance sheet.

	Per balance sheet £
Cost	25,000
Accumulated depreciation	5,000
NBV	20,000

Step 2

Compare these figures with how the non-current asset would appear had there been no transfer (i.e. how the asset should appear).

	Per balance sheet £	Should be £
Cost	25,000	20,000
Accumulated depreciation	5,000	4,000
	20,000	16,000

Step 3

Calculate the adjustments required.

	Per balance sheet £	Should be £	Adjustment £
Cost	25,000	20,000	5,000
Accumulated depreciation	5,000	4,000	1,000
NBV	20,000	16,000	

Step 4

Deal with the adjustments

The unrealised profit of £5,000 reduces the cost of the fixed asset from its transfer value to the original cost to the group. The subsidiary has made the profit and so the adjustment is shared between the group and minority interest:

	£	£
Dr Consolidated profit and loss account (60% × 5,000)	3,000	
Dr Minority interest (40% × 5,000)	2,000	
Cr Tangible fixed asset cost(allowance for unrealised profit)		5,000

There must also be an adjustment for the excess depreciation of £1,000. As Perch has the asset, Perch has suffered the additional depreciation and so the adjustment is:

	£	£
Dr Accumulated depreciation (allowance for unrealised profit)	1,000	
Cr Consolidated profit and loss account		1,000

Step 5

The tangible fixed assets section of the balance sheet will show:

	Cost	Dep'n	
	£	£	£
Tangible assets			
Plant	20,000	4,000	16,000

If Perch had sold the plant to Salmon, Perch would have made the unrealised profit and Salmon would have suffered the additional depreciation. Therefore the adjustments would have been:

	£	£
Dr Consolidated profit and loss account (100%))	5,000	
Cr Tangible fixed asset cost (allowance for unrealised profit)		5,000
Dr Accumulated depreciation (allowance for unrealised profit)	1,000	
Cr Consolidated profit and loss account (60% × 1,000)		600
Cr Minority interests (40% × 1,000)		400

8 PREFERENCE SHARES AND DEBENTURES IN SUBSIDIARIES

8.1 PREFERENCE SHARES AND CONTROL

Normally, preference shares do not carry any votes and so they are not relevant when identifying a parent/subsidiary relationship.

Preference shares are only entitled to a return of their capital. They are not entitled to a share of the net assets of the company. This affects the calculation of goodwill and of minority interests.

Preference shareholders are only entitled to their preference dividend. They are not entitled to any further share of the profits. This means that the preference shares will be ignored when the group reserves are being calculated.

8.2 PREFERENCE SHARES AND GOODWILL

The fair value of the net assets acquired will be the parent's share of the equity (ordinary share capital, premium and revenue reserves etc) plus the nominal value of the preference shares acquired.

Example – Prefect and Monitor 20X4

On 1 January 20X4 Prefect paid £424,000 for 60,000 £1 ordinary shares and 40,000 £1 preference shares in Monitor Ltd. The balance sheet of the two companies immediately after the purchase was as follows:

	Prefect	Monitor
	£000	£000
Investment in Monitor Ltd	424	
Sundry net assets	456	700
£1 preference shares	(90)	(160)
Net assets	790	540
£1 ordinary shares	50	100
Share premium	125	70
Revenue reserves	615	370
	790	540

Required:

(1)   Calculate Prefect's share of Monitor's equity, and decide whether or not this gives Prefect control over Monitor.

(2)   Calculate the goodwill arising on the purchase.

Solution

(1)   Prefect owns 60,000 out of 100,000 ordinary shares in Monitor. This means that Prefect has 60% of the votes in Monitor, appoints the board of directors and controls Monitor absolutely. The fact that Prefect only owns 40,000 out of 160,0000 preference shares (25%) is irrelevant, because preference shares do not normally carry any voting rights.

(2)   Goodwill

- The fair value of the consideration will be the cash paid £424,000.

- The fair value of the net assets acquired will be Prefect's 60% interest in Monitor's equity. Monitor's equity is the ordinary share capital, Share premium (unless told otherwise) and revenue reserves. These total £540,000.

- Prefect also bought £40,000 of preference shares.

	£000	£000
Fair value of the consideration		424
Less: The fair value of the net assets acquired:		
Ordinary shares	100	
Share premium	70	
Revenue reserves	370	
	540	
Group share (60%)		(324)
Less: The nominal value of preference shares acquired		(40)
Goodwill at cost		60

8.3 PREFERENCE SHARES, MINORITY INTERESTS, AND GROUP RESERVES

- When the group reserves are calculated, the group will claim its share of post acquisition profits in proportion to its equity interest. The percentage holding of preference shares is irrelevant.

- The minority interest will consist of the minority's share of the equity.

- The subsidiary's preference shares owned by the parent will be cancelled out on consolidation.

- The subsidiary's preference shares not owned by the parent will remain in the balance sheet as a liability.

Example – Prefect and Monitor (continued)   20X5

The previous example established that Monitor was a 60% subsidiary of Prefect, and that the goodwill on consolidation was £60,000. This will be amortised over six years on a straight line basis.

This example looks at the same group two years later on 31 December 20X5. The balance sheets at that date are noted below:

	Prefect £000	Monitor £000
Tangible fixed assets	250	680
Investment in Monitor Ltd	424	–
Net current assets	326	290
£1 preference shares	(90)	(160)
Net assets	910	810
£1 ordinary shares	50	100
Share premium	125	70
Revenues reserves	735	640
	910	810

Required:

(1) Calculate the minority interests in the Prefect group on 31 December 20X5.

(2) Calculate the Prefect group reserves on 31 December 20X5.

(3) Prepare the Prefect group balance sheet on 31 December 20X5.

Solution

(1) *Minority interests*

	£000	£000
Share of equity		
£1 ordinary shares	100	
Share premium	70	
Revenue reserves	640	
	810	
Minority interest @ 40%		324

(2) *Group reserves*

	£000	£000
The parent's own reserves at the balance sheet date		735
Cumulative amortisation of goodwill (2 years @ £10,000 pa)		(20)
The subsidiary's own reserves at the balance sheet date	640	
Less the subsidiary's reserves at acquisition	(370)	
Subsidiary's post acquisition reserves	270	
The group's 60% share of equity		162
Total group reserves		877

(3) *Group balance sheet*

	Prefect £000	*Monitor* £000		*Group* £000
Goodwill			60 – 20	40
Tangible fixed assets	250	680		930
Investment in Monitor	424	–	Cancelled	–
Net current assets	326	290		616
Total assets less current liabilities				1,586
£1 preference shares	(90)	(160)	40	(210)
				1,376
£1 ordinary shares	50	100	Parent only	50
Share premium	125	70	Parent only	125
Revenue reserves	735	640	2 above	877
Group shareholders' funds				1,052
Minority interests			1 above	324
				1,376

ACTIVITY 7

The draft balance sheet of S Ltd at 31 January 20X5 is as follows:

	£		£
Net assets	180,000	Ordinary share capital	100,000
		Profit and loss account	30,000
		Preference share capital	50,000
	180,000		180,000

At 31 January 20X5 P Ltd has reserves of £150,000 on the profit and loss account. During the previous year P Ltd acquired 70% of the ordinary share capital of S Ltd at a cost of £90,000 when the reserves of S Ltd amounted to £10,000 and 40% of the preference share capital at a cost of £22,000. Goodwill is to be written off over five years.

Show the consolidation schedules and shareholdings in S Ltd workings.

For a suggested answer, see the 'Answers' section at the end of the book.

8.4 DEBENTURES IN A SUBSIDIARY COMPANY

Debentures do not normally have any voting rights and so they will not affect the identification of a parent / subsidiary relationship.

Debenture holders are only entitled to the payment of interest and the repayment of capital. Therefore, they will not affect the minority interests or the group reserves.

If a parent holds debentures in a subsidiary then the proportion of the debenture held by the parent will be cancelled out, just as for an inter-company trade debtor or trade creditor. The balance of the debenture owed to third parties will be recognised in the balance sheet as a liability.

The balance sheet may also hold some accrued interest payable by one company and receivable by the other company. The inter-company element will be cancelled, leaving a third party accrual for the balance.

Example

The Preston Group is preparing its group accounts for the year-ending 31 May 20X6. Preston plc owns 100% of the share capital in Sean Ltd. The shares in Sean were purchased at par on incorporation.

Preston also owns £40,000 worth of Sean's 15% debentures. The interest on these debentures is paid annually in arrears. At 31 May Sean had accrued for one year's interest (for the year to 31 May 20X6) which would be paid in June. This accrual is included in creditors. Preston has also accrued for its share of the interest as income. This is included within debtors.

The balance sheets of the two companies as at 31 May 20X6 are noted below:

	Preston		Sean	
	£000	£000	£000	£000
Tangible fixed assets		45		438
Investments in Sean				
Ordinary shares	20			
Debentures	40			
		60		
Current assets				
Debtors	26		351	
Sundry	31		235	
	57		586	
Current liabilities				
Creditors	32		76	
Sundry	14		64	
	46		140	
Net current assets		11		446
15% debenture		–		(100)
Net assets		116		784
£1 ordinary shares		5		20
Revenue reserves		111		764
		116		784

Required:

(1)   Calculate the inter-company interest receivable and payable at the year-end.

(2)   Prepare the consolidated balance sheet for the Preston Group.

Solution

(1)   The inter-company interest will be based on the inter-company capital.

£40,000 × 15% =   £6,000

This will be deleted from both debtors and creditors. It will leave a balance of £9,000 owing to third parties.

(2)   The Preston Group consolidated balance sheet as at 31 December 20X6

	Preston £000	Sean £000	Adjustments	£000	£000
Tangible fixed assets	45	438			483
Investments in Sean					
Ordinary shares	20		Cancelled		–
Debentures	40		40 Cr; Contra with liability		–
Current assets					
Debtors	26	351	6 Cr; Contra with accrual	371	
Sundry	31	235		266	
				637	
Current liabilities					
Creditors	32	76	6 Dr; Contra with debtor	102	
Sundry	14	64		78	
				180	
Net current assets					457
15% debenture		100	40 Dr; Contra with asset		(60)
Net assets					880
£1 ordinary shares	5	20			5
Revenue reserves	111	764			875
					880

9   DIVIDENDS AND INTEREST NOT ACCRUED FOR

9.1   INTRODUCTION

In the example above, the parent and subsidiary had both dealt with the interest correctly, and so the cancellation was straight forward. Sometimes interest will not have been accounted for by one or other of the companies. In these situation the individual company accounts will have to be corrected before the consolidation can take place.

If a dividend has been declared before the year-end but has not been paid, the individual company accounts will have to be corrected for this also. However, it is unlikely that you will have to deal with this situation in the exam.

9.2 INTEREST AND DIVIDENDS RECEIVABLE NOT ACCOUNTED FOR

In these situations the receiving company's balance sheet must be updated to include the interest or dividends receivable. This is in two stages:

(1) The debtor balances should be updated. These revised balances can then be cancelled against the related creditor balances.

(2) The receiving company's reserves will also have to be increased by the new income recognised.

Example

Portsmouth Ltd has owned 70% of Southampton Ltd's ordinary shares for many years. The shares were purchased when Southampton's reserves were £50,000. No goodwill arose.

Portsmouth also owns £60,000 of Southampton's 10% Debentures. Interest on these debentures is paid half yearly in arrears. At 31 December 20X5 Southampton had accrued for six months interest payable, but Portsmouth had not yet accounted for its share of this interest.

At 31 December 20X5 Southampton had proposed and accrued for a £200,000 dividend. Portsmouth has not accounted for its share of this dividend.

The balance sheets of the two companies at 31 December 20X5 are shown below:

	Portsmouth		Southampton	
	£000	£000	£000	£000
Tangible fixed assets		20		636
Investments in Southampton				
Ordinary shares	105			
Debentures	60			
		165		
Current assets				
Debtors	34		266	
Sundry	156		351	
	190		617	
Current liabilities				
Creditors and accruals	168		493	
Net current assets		22		124
10% debenture		–		(200)
Net assets		207		560
£1 ordinary shares		10		100
Revenue reserves		197		460
		207		560

Required:

(1) Calculate the share of Southampton's accrued debenture interest that Portsmouth should recognise as a debtor at the year-end.

(2) Calculate the Group Reserves as at 31 December 20X5 taking into account the above adjustments.

(3)   Calculate the minority interest at the year-end.

(4)   Prepare a consolidation schedule and put through the adjustments necessary to account for the above items.

(5)   Complete the consolidation schedule and prepare the consolidated balance sheet of the Portsmouth Group.

Solution

(1)   *Debenture interest*   £60,000 × 6/12 × 10% = £3,000

(2)   *Group reserves*

The subsidiary's balance sheet and reserves are correct. However, the Parent's reserves need to be increased by the accrued income calculated above.

	£000	£000
The parent's own reserves at the balance sheet date		197
Add: Accrued interest receivable		3
The subsidiary's own reserves at the balance sheet date	460	
Less the subsidiary's reserves at acquisition	(50)	
Subsidiary's post acquisition reserves	410	
The group's 70% share of equity		287
Total group reserves		487

(3)   *Minority interests*   Net assets of £560,000 × 30% = £168,000

(4) & (5) *Consolidation schedule*

	P	S		Group	
	£000	£000		£000	£000
Tangible fixed assets	20	636			656
Investments in S					
Ordinary shares	105		Cancelled		–
Debentures	60		60 Cr; Contra with liability		–
Current assets					
Debtors	34	266	(£3 Dr), (£3 Cr)	300	
Sundry	156	351		507	
				807	
Current liabilities					
Creditors and accruals	168	493	3 Dr (inter-company)	658	
Net current assets					149
10% debenture		(200)	60 Dr; Contra with asset		(140)
Net assets					665
£1 ordinary shares	10	100	Parent only		10
Revenue reserves	197	460	(3) above		487
Group shareholders' funds					497
Minority interests			(4) above		168
					665

10 FAIR VALUE ADJUSTMENTS

10.1 INTRODUCTION

Earlier we said that goodwill was the difference between the fair value of the consideration and the fair value of the net assets acquired. Complicated situations involving the fair valuing of the consideration are not on the syllabus, but you must be able to fair value the net assets acquired.

10.2 TYPICAL SITUATION

In our previous goodwill calculations we have used the net book value of the assets acquired. The values may be out of date in respect of freehold properties, and the purchasing company may give a lower value to stocks and trade debtors than was shown in the balance sheet. The net book value will be adjusted for the increase or decrease caused by these items.

Example

Five years ago Pilot plc paid £456,000 for 68% of the ordinary shares of Soldier Ltd. The Soldier Ltd has £40,000 of ordinary shares, £30,000 of share premium and its reserves at the date of acquisition were £346,000.

Pilot carried out a careful review of the fair value of Soldier's net assets and identified the following changes:

(a)   Stocks with a book value of £77,000 only had a realisable value of £22,000.

(b)   Soldier owned freehold land which was carried at its cost of £45,000. Its market value was £234,000.

Tasks

(1)   Calculate the goodwill arising at acquisition.

(2)   Calculate the minority interest in Soldier at the date of acquisition.

Solution

(1)   *Goodwill*

	£000	£000
Fair value of the consideration		456
Less: The fair value of the net assets acquired:		
Ordinary shares	40	
Share premium	30	
Revenue reserves	346	
Book value of net assets at acquisition	416	
Fair value adjustments		
Stock write off (77 – 22)	(55)	
Increase in land value (234 – 45)	189	
Fair value of net assets at acquisition	550	
Group share @ 68%		(374)
Goodwill at cost		82

(2) Minority interest

The new values will be incorporated into the balance sheet, and so the minority interest will be credited with their share of these fair valued net assets as follows

£550,000 × 32% = £176,000

ACTIVITY 8

X plc acquired 80% of the ordinary share capital of Y Ltd on 30 September 20X4 for £320,000.

The net assets of Y Ltd at that date had a book value of £350,000.

The following information is relevant:

(a)   Y Ltd's freehold factory is included in the accounts at £100,000 and no adjustment has been made to recognise the valuation of £120,000 put on the property when it was professionally revalued on 15 September 20X4.

(b)   The fair value of Y Ltd's stock at 30 September 20X4 is estimated to be £4,000 less than its book value at that date.

Calculate:

(i)   goodwill arising on the acquisition of Y Ltd

(ii)   minority interest at 30 September 20X4.

For a suggested answer, see the 'Answers' section at the end of the book.

11   SUMMARY

This has been a long chapter on a new topic. Consolidated balance sheets are fairly straightforward to prepare if you take a methodical approach. A step-by-step summary to consolidation is noted below:

1   Establish the group structure. What percentage holding does the parent have in the subsidiary?

2   Set out a consolidation schedule leaving room for adjustments and the group balance sheet. You should leave spare lines for goodwill and minority interests.

3   Enter the parent and subsidiary balances onto the schedule straight from their own company balance sheets.

4   Note any adjustments on the consolidation schedule, for example:

   •   inter-company balances

   •   unrealised profits

   •   cash and goods in transit

   •   fair valuations.

5   Add across the assets and liabilities in the balance sheet, taking into account the adjustments noted on the schedule. Don't total the balance sheet just yet.

6   Calculate the goodwill at cost, cumulative amortisation, and net book value. Enter the net book value into the group balance sheet.

7   Enter the parent's share capital and share premium into the group balance sheet.

8   Calculate the group reserves. This consists of:

- the parent's reserves

- less the cumulative amortisation of goodwill

- less unrealised profit on good's sold by the parent to its subsidiary

- plus the group's share of the post acquisition reserves of the subsidiary. (These may be reduced by unrealised profits on goods sold by the subsidiary.)

9   Calculate the minority interest.

10 The consolidation schedule should now be complete and the balance sheet can be added down and balanced.

ACTIVITY 9

Revision Ltd has been trading for many years as an accountancy tuition college. On 1 January 1999 it paid £145,000 for 25,000 ordinary shares of 25 pence each in Homework Ltd, a human resources consultancy. At that time the retained profits of Homework Ltd stood at £170,000.

Noted below are the balance sheets of the two companies at 31 March 2007:

	Revision Ltd		Homework Ltd	
	£	£	£	£
Fixed assets				
Tangible fixed assets		230,000		189,000
Investment in Homework Ltd		145,000		–
		375,000		189,000
Current assets				
Stocks	45,000		12,000	
Trade and other debtors	87,000		154,000	
Inter-company	12,000		–	
Cash	3,000		15,000	
	147,000		181,000	
Creditors				
Trade and other creditors	73,000		15,000	
Inter-company	–		9,000	
	73,000		24,000	
Net current assets		74,000		157,000
NET ASSETS		449,000		346,000
Capital and reserves				
Called up share capital		100,000		10,000
P&L reserves		349,000		336,000
		449,000		346,000

Notes:

(a)   At the year end Revision Ltd had £15,000 of goods in stock bought from Homework Ltd. Homework Ltd prices sales on a 60% mark-up on cost.

(b)   At the year end Homework Ltd had £2,000 of goods in stock bought from Revision Ltd. Revision Ltd makes a 60% gross profit on sales.

(c)   On 30 March Homework sent Revision a cheque for £3,000 in respect of the inter-company account. Revision had not received this cheque at the year-end.

(d)   Goodwill is to be capitalised and amortised over 15 years.

Required:

Prepare the consolidated balance sheet for the Revision Group as at 31 March 2007.

For a suggested answer, see the 'Answers' section at the end of the book.

KEY TERMS

Consolidated balance sheet – the consolidated balance sheet combines the assets and liabilities of the parent and its subsidiaries on a line by line basis. This recognises all the assets and liabilities under the *control* of the Group.

Group reserves – the retained profits of the parent combined with the post acquisition retained profits of its subsidiaries.

Post acquisition profits – profits earned by the subsidiary since it became part of the group, and so they will be included as part of the group reserves.

Pre acquisition profits – profits earned by the subsidiary before it became part of the group. On acquisition, this balance is frozen and does not form part of the group reserves.

Goodwill – the difference between the fair value of the consideration for a subsidiary and the fair value of the net assets acquired.

Minority interests – the percentage share of the net assets owned by minority shareholders in the subsidiary.

Inter-company balances – debtor and creditor balances between the companies in a group. These are cancelled on consolidation.

Provision for unrealised profits – profits arising on trade between members of the same group. The profits are legitimately earned by the individual companies, but no profit has been earned from the group point of view. These profits are eliminated on consolidation.

SELF TEST QUESTIONS

Paragraph

1	On what bases are assets and liabilities recognised in a group balance sheet?	1
2	Why must a distinction be drawn between a subsidiary's pre acquisition and post acquisition reserves?	3
3	How are pre acquisition reserves treated?	3
4	What is represented by the excess of the price paid for a business over the fair value of the net assets acquired?	4.1
5	How should goodwill on consolidation be treated according to FRS 10?	4.1
6	What affect do minority interests have on the preparation of the group balance sheet?	5
7	How are current account balances made to balance for consolidation purposes?	6.3 & 6.4
8	How should unrealised profits in year-end stocks be accounted for?	7.2
9	If P holds 100% of S's ordinary shares but only 10% of S's preference shares, is S still a subsidiary of P?	8.1
10	If the parent owns debentures in a subsidiary, how should this be accounted for?	8.4
11	Do fair value adjustments affect the minority interests?	10.2

PRACTICE QUESTION

HANSON LTD

Five years ago, Hanson Ltd acquired the following shares in Pickford Ltd:

	£
75,000 ordinary shares of £1 – cost	93,100
15,000 6% preference shares of £1 – cost	16,050
	109,150

At the date of acquisition, the accumulated profits of Pickford Ltd amounted to £11,000. The summarised balance sheets of the two companies at 31.12.X8 were as follows:

	Hanson Ltd £	Pickford Ltd £
Ordinary shares of £1	350,000	100,000
6% preference shares of £1	–	60,000
Profit and loss account	348,420	132,700
Sundry creditors	93,400	51,150
	791,820	343,850

	£	£
Fixed assets	431,100	219,350
Investments	109,150	–
Stock	143,070	71,120
Debtors	89,200	36,230
Cash at bank	19,300	17,150
	791,820	343,850

During the year, Hanson Ltd sold goods whose invoice value was £24,000 to Pickford Ltd. These goods were invoiced at cost plus 25%, and one-quarter were still in Pickford's stock at the year end.

Goodwill should be amortised over a period of ten years.

You are required to prepare the consolidated balance sheet of Hanson Ltd as at 31 December 20X8.

(20 marks)

EXAM-STYLE QUESTION

SHOPAN

You have been asked to assist in the preparation of the consolidated accounts of the Shopan Group. Set out below are the balance sheets of Shopan Ltd and its subsidiary undertaking Hower Ltd, as at 30 September 20X9:

Balance sheets as at 30 September 20X9

	Shopan Ltd		Hower Ltd	
	£000	£000	£000	£000
Fixed assets		6,273		1,633
Investment in Hower Ltd		2,100		
Current assets				
Stocks	1,901		865	
Debtors	1,555		547	
Cash	184		104	
	3,640		1,516	
Current liabilities				
Trade creditors	1,516		457	
Taxation	431		188	
	1,947		645	
Net current assets		1,693		871
Long-term loan		(2,870)		(400)
		7,196		2,104
Capital and reserves				
Called up share capital		2,000		500
Share premium		950		120
Profit and loss account		4,246		1,484
		7,196		2,104

Further information:

- The share capital of both Shopan Ltd and Hower Ltd consists of ordinary shares of £1 each.

- Shopan Ltd acquired 375,000 shares in Hower Ltd on 30 September 20X9.

- The fair value of the fixed assets of Hower Ltd at 30 September 20X9 was £2,033,000.

Required:

(a) Prepare a consolidated balance sheet for Shopan Ltd and its subsidiary undertaking as at 30 September 20X9. **(10 marks)**

(b) FRS 2 states that 'a parent undertaking should prepare consolidated financial statements for its group'. Give two of the criteria that, according to FRS 2, determine whether an undertaking is the parent undertaking of another undertaking.
(5 marks)
(Total: 15 marks)

For suggested answers, see the 'Answers' section at the end of the book.

Chapter 14

CONSOLIDATED PROFIT AND LOSS ACCOUNT AND ASSOCIATES

This chapter explains how a consolidated profit and loss account is prepared under the acquisition method of accounting for a subsidiary as set out in FRS 2 *Accounting for Subsidiary Undertakings.* The accounting treatment of associates is also looked at briefly. This chapter covers syllabus areas 5(a) and 5(b).

CONTENTS

1   The consolidated profit and loss account

2   Inter-company trade and unrealised profit

3   Preference shares in the subsidiary company

4   Associates

5   Equity accounting for associates

LEARNING OUTCOMES

At the end of this chapter you should be able to:

- prepare a consolidated profit and loss account for a simple group including adjustments for pre and post acquisition profits, minority interests and consolidated goodwill

- explain why intra-group transactions should be eliminated on consolidation

- account for the effects (in the profit and loss account and balance sheet) of intra-group trading and other transactions including:

    (i)   unrealised profits in stock and fixed assets

    (ii)   intra-group loans and interest and other intra-group charges.

1 THE CONSOLIDATED PROFIT AND LOSS ACCOUNT

1.1 INTRODUCTION

The consolidated profit and loss account combines the income and expenses of the parent and its subsidiaries in full on a line by line basis. This recognises all the income and expenditure under the control of the group. Inter company trading and profits must be eliminated.

The dividend income from the parent's investment in its subsidiary is eliminated. The consolidated balance sheet recognises the underlying profits of the subsidiary, and so it would be double counting to show the dividend income as well.

The consolidated profit and loss account has an additional expense; the amortisation of the goodwill arising on consolidation. This was calculated in the last chapter.

These accounts are prepared for the parent company's shareholders, and so the dividend shown in the profit and loss account is the parent's dividend only.

Not all subsidiaries are wholly owned. If there is a minority interest then some of the profits earned by the subsidiary and reported in the group profit and loss account belong to them. Their minority interest in the profit after tax of the subsidiary is shown as a deduction from the post-tax profit.

The reserves are the link between the P&L account and the balance sheet. The calculation of the group reserves was covered in the last chapter. When preparing the profit and loss account the opening and closing reserves may need to be calculated in order to prove the movement on reserves.

1.2 PREPARATION OF CONSOLIDATED PROFIT AND LOSS ACCOUNT

As for a balance sheet, the easiest way to produce a consolidated profit and loss account is to use a consolidation schedule. The income and expense items from each of the individual companies are entered into the left hand columns, the adjustments are recorded in the centre as you work through the question, and the group profit and loss account will be prepared by cross-casting the individual lines.

1.3 EXAMPLE – WHOLLY OWNED SUBSIDIARY

Situation

On 1 July 20X4 Plastic plc paid £280,000 for the entire share capital of Steel Ltd. Steel's share capital consisted of 40,000 shares of 50 pence each. Its reserves at the date of acquisition were £165,000. Any goodwill arising will be written off over five years.

This example looks at the profit and loss accounts for the two companies for the year-ending 30 June 20X7.

Plastic has no other subsidiaries or investments. It has recorded its dividend income from Steel correctly.

During the year-ending 30 June 20X7 Plastic sold goods worth £138,000 to Steel. These had all been sold onto third party customers by the year-end.

Company profit and loss accounts for the year ending 30 June 20X7

	Plastic	Steel
	£000	£000
Turnover	457	613
Cost of sales	(212)	(376)
Gross profit	245	237
Operating expenses	(197)	(85)
Dividend income from Steel	63	–
Profit before tax	111	152
Taxation	(14)	(45)
Profit for the year	97	107
Opening reserves	63	256
Profit for the year	97	107
Dividends	(60)	(63)
Closing reserves	100	300

Required:

(1)   Prepare the consolidation schedule for Plastic plc and its subsidiary Steel Ltd for the year ending 30 June 20X7 and record the consolidation adjustments.

(2)   Calculate the goodwill and the amortisation charge.

(3)   Calculate the opening and closing balances for the group reserves. Ensure that they reconcile with the profit and loss account.

Solution

(1)   Consolidation schedule

	Plastic	Steel	Adjustments	Group
	£000	£000		£000
Turnover	457	613	£138 Dr inter-company sale	932
Cost of sales	(212)	(376)	£138 Cr inter-company purchase	(450)
Gross profit				482
Operating expenses	(197)	(85)		(282)
Amortisation charge			**Working 1**	**(19)**
Dividend from Steel	63	–	Cancelled	–
Profit before tax				181
Taxation	(14)	(45)		(59)
Profit for the year	97	107		122
Opening reserves	63	256	Working 2	116
Profit for the year	97	107	See above	122
Dividends	(60)	(63)	Parent only	(60)
Closing reserves	100	300	Working 2	178

(W1) Goodwill

	£000	£000
Fair value of the consideration		280
Fair value of the net assets acquired		
Ordinary shares (40,000 shares @ 50 pence)	20	
Revenue reserves at acquisition	165	
		(185)
Goodwill at cost		95

Amortisation over five years

Opening balance (X4 – X5 & X5 – X6)	38	Deduct from opening reserves
Charge for this year	19	Charge to the P&L
Closing balance	57	Deduct from closing reserves

(W2) Group reserve

	Closing		Opening	
	£000	£000	£000	£000
The parent's own reserves		100		63
Less: cumulative amortisation of goodwill		(57)		(38)
The subsidiary's own reserves				
Less the subsidiary's reserves at acquisition	300		256	
Subsidiary's post acquisition reserves	(165)		(165)	
		135		91
Total group reserves		178		116

The movement on reserves at the bottom of the group profit and loss account show that the opening and closing balances reconcile.

1.4   MINORITY INTERESTS

The top half of the profit and loss account (down to profit after tax) records all of the income and expenditure under the control of the group in full. However, profits after tax belong to the shareholders, and so the subsidiary's profit after tax must be shared between the group interest and the minority interests.

Example

Pork plc has owned 60% of Sausage Ltd since incorporation.

A summarised profit and loss account for the two companies for the current year is set out below:

	Pork	Sausage
	£000	£000
Profit before tax	150	400
Taxation	(40)	(130)
Profit after tax	110	270

In the absence of any unrealised profits or fair value adjustments, the minority interest in Sausage's profits after tax is £108,000 (£270,000 × 40%)

The summarised group profit and loss account will be as follows:

	P	S	Adjustments	Group
	£000	£000		£000
Profit before tax	150	400	less £60 inter-company dividend	490
Taxation	(40)	(130)		(170)
Profit after tax	110	270		320
Minority interest			as above	(108)
Profit for group shareholders				212

The minority interest of £108,000 includes the minority's share of the dividend as well as the minority's share of the retained profits.

ACTIVITY 1

The draft profit and loss accounts for Tree Ltd and its subsidiary Wood Ltd for the year ended 31 March are as follows:

	T Ltd	W Ltd
	£	£
Turnover	216,300	24,400
Cost of sales	136,269	15,372
Gross profit	80,031	9,028
Distribution costs	(21,630)	(2,440)
Income from shares in group companies	1,464	–
Net profit before taxation	59,865	6,588
Taxation	28,119	3,172
Net profit after taxation	31,746	3,416
Reserves brought forward	36,728	7,076
Net profit after taxation	31,746	3,416
Dividends	(20,000)	(1,952)
Reserves carried forward	48,474	8,540

Tree Ltd bought 75% of the ordinary shares (the only type) in Wood Ltd several years ago for £48,000 when that company's reserves amounted to £5,124. The issued share capital of W Ltd is 50,000 £1 shares. The goodwill on acquisition has already been written off through the profit and loss account.

Required:

Prepare the consolidated profit and loss account for the year ended 31 March 20X7.

For a suggested answer, see the 'Answers' section at the end of the book.

2 INTER-COMPANY TRADE AND UNREALISED PROFIT

2.1 INTRODUCTION

In Section 1 we cancelled out trade between group companies. The whole amount of the inter-company trade was deducted from both sales and purchases (cost of sales). An additional problem can arise if some of this stock is unsold at the year-end. The previous chapter covered the treatment of this unrealised profit in stock from the balance sheet point of view. This section will look at its impact on the profit and loss account.

2.2 BASIC RULES – UNREALISED PROFITS IN CLOSING STOCK

The provision for unrealised profit is calculated in the same way for both the P&L and balance sheet. The effect on the profit and loss account is that the reduction in the value of closing stock will increase the cost of sales, and thereby reduce the group's profits.

When the group reserves are calculated the reserves of the **selling** company will be reduced by the provision for unrealised profit.

If the subsidiary sold the goods then the minority interest will also be reduced in respect of their share of the provision for unrealised profit.

Example – Parent sells goods to the subsidiary

Phillip plc owns 70% of the ordinary shares of Macedon Ltd. The shares were bought when Macedon's reserves were £40,000. No goodwill arose on the acquisition.

During the current year Phillip sold £78,000 of goods to Macedon making a profit of £26,000. At the year-end £42,000 of these goods had not been sold onto third parties. These stocks included £14,000 of unrealised profit.

There was no other inter-company trade. There were no dividends.

The profit and loss accounts for the two companies are noted below.

	Phillip	Macedon
	£000	£000
Turnover	900	400
Cost of sales	(600)	(210)
Gross profit	300	190
Operating expenses	(160)	(90)
Profit before tax	140	100
Taxation	(45)	(20)
Profit after tax	95	80
Opening reserves	349	200
Closing reserves	444	280

Required:

Prepare the consolidated profit and loss account for the Phillip Group.

Solution

Consolidation schedule

	Phillip £000	Macedon £000	Adjustments	Group £000
Turnover	900	400	78 Dr inter-company trade	1,222
Cost of sales			78 Cr inter-company trade	
	(600)	(210)	14 Dr unrealised profit	(746)
Gross profit				476
Operating expenses	(160)	(90)		(250)
Profit before tax				226
Taxation	(45)	(20)		(65)
Profit after tax				161
Minority interests		–	Working 3	(24)
Group retained profit				137
Opening reserves	349	200	Working 4	461
Closing reserves	444	280	Working 4	598

(1)   Eliminate the inter company trade

     Debit   Turnover   £78,000

     Credit   Cost of sales   £78,000

(2)   Increase cost of sales by the closing provision for unrealised profit

     Debit   Cost of sales   £14,000

     (The credit entry reduces the value of stocks in the balance sheet.)

(3)   Minority interests

     Profit after tax of £80,000 × 30% = £24,000

(4)   Group reserve

	Closing £000	£000	Opening £000	£000
The parent's own reserves		444		349
Less: provision for unrealised profit		**(14)**		
The subsidiary's own reserves	280		200	
Less the subsidiary's reserves at acquisition	(40)		(40)	
Subsidiary's post acquisition reserves	240		160	
Group share @ 70%		168		112
Total group reserves		598		461

Example – Subsidiary sells goods to the parent

The situation is the same as before, except that Macedon (the subsidiary) sold £78,000 of goods to Phillip (the parent). As before, closing stocks will include £14,000 of unrealised profit.

Solution

(1)   The elimination of the £78,000 inter-company trade and the £14,000 increase in cost of sales in respect of the unrealised profit will be as before. The profit and loss account will be the same down to the Profit after Tax of £161,000.

(2)   The minority interest will be affected by their share of the unrealised profit.

	£000
Subsidiary's profit after tax	80
Less: Closing provision for unrealised profit	(14)
Revised profit after tax	66
Minority's 30% share	20

(3)   The subsidiary's closing reserves will be reduced by the provision for unrealised profit

	Closing	
	£000	£000
The parent's own reserves		444
The subsidiary's own reserves	280	
Less: provision for unrealised profit	(14)	
Less the subsidiary's reserves at acquisition	(40)	
Subsidiary's post acquisition reserves	226	
Group share @ 70%		158
Total group reserves		602

Consolidation schedule

		Group
		£000
Profit after tax	*As before*	161
Minority interests	*Working 2 above*	(20)
Group retained profit		141
Opening reserves	*As before*	461
Closing reserves	*Working 3 above*	602

ACTIVITY 2

Plate plc owns 60% of the ordinary shares of Saucer Ltd. The shares were bought when Saucer's reserves were £62,000. No goodwill arose on the acquisition.

During the current year Saucer sold £323,000 of goods to Plate making a profit of £120,000. At the year-end £142,000 of these goods were still in stock. These stocks included £48,000 of unrealised profit.

There was no other inter-company trade.

Plate has accounted for all dividend's receivable from Saucer.

The profit and loss accounts for the two companies are noted below.

	Plate	Saucer
	£000	£000
Turnover	999	750
Cost of sales	(427)	(260)
Gross profit	572	490
Operating expenses	(252)	(140)
Dividend from Saucer	120	–
Profit before tax	440	350
Taxation	(130)	(62)
Profit after tax	310	288
Opening reserves	506	312
Profit after tax	310	288
Dividends	(150)	(200)
Closing reserves	666	400

Required:

(1)   Prepare the consolidated profit and loss account for the Plate Group.

(2)   Calculate the opening and closing group reserves.

For a suggested answer, see the 'Answers' section at the end of the book.

3   PREFERENCE SHARES IN THE SUBSIDIARY COMPANY

Preference shares are normally recognised as a liability in the balance sheet and preference dividends are normally recognised as an expense in the profit and loss account.

If the parent owns preference shares, then the parent's preference dividend income will be netted off the subsidiary's preference dividend expense. The third party element of the dividend will be shown as an expense in the group profit and loss account.

Example

A Ltd owns 75% of the ordinary £1 shares of B Ltd and 40,000 of the 100,000 £1 6% preference shares of B Ltd.

Summarised profit and loss accounts for the two companies and the group are noted below:

		A £	B £		Group £
Operating profit		85,000	90,000		175,000
Finance charge	Preference dividend	–	(6,000)	*Third party*	(3,600)
Finance income	Preference dividend	2,400	–		–
Profit before tax		87,400	84,000		171,400
Tax		(30,000)	(20,000)		(50,000)
Profit after tax		57,400	64,000		121,400
Minority interest				*$64,000@25%*	(16,000)
					105,400

4   ASSOCIATES

4.1   INTRODUCTION

There are a number of levels of investment that one company can have in another.

A simple trade investment would be for a small proportion of the shares in a company. The investing company would account for the investment at cost in its balance sheet and record its share of any dividends received in the profit and loss account.

A subsidiary undertaking is where the investing company controls its investment. Group accounts are prepared, consolidating all of the assets, liabilities, income and expenditure of the subsidiary with those of the parent. Any minority interest is dealt with as a one line deduction from post-tax profits, and as a single line in the ownership section of the balance sheet.

However, in practice there are many investments that are half way between these two extremes. These are major long term investments over which the investing company has *significant influence* but not control. These are called associates and they are accounted for using the equity method.

4.2 DEFINITION OF AN ASSOCIATE

FRS 9 defines an associate as follows:

'An associate is an entity (other than a subsidiary) in which another entity (the investor) has a **participating interest** and over whose operating and financial policies the investor exercises a **significant influence**.'

A participating interest is a long-term interest in the equity shares of another company.

An entity can exercise significant influence over another (an investee) if it is actively involved in directing its investee by taking part in policy decisions, including decisions on strategic issues such as:

- the expansion or contraction of the business, investing in other entities or changes in products, markets and activities of its investee

- determining dividend policy.

The Companies Act assumes that there is significant influence if the investor holds between 20% and 50% of the voting power (equity) of another company, unless it can be shown that this is not the case. You should follow this assumption in all exam questions unless you have been given information that suggests otherwise.

Significant influence is often indicated by the investing company being represented on the board of directors of the other company. This enables the investing company to participate and vote on all important decisions. (Note that the investor will still be in a minority on the associate's board of directors. This gives them influence but not control.)

Significant influence can also be indicated by:

- material transactions between the investor and the investee

- interchange of managerial personnel; and

- provision of essential technical information.

The Companies Act, and common practice, assumes that an associate exists when one company owns between 20% and 50% of the equity of another. You should follow this assumption in all exam questions.

5 EQUITY ACCOUNTING FOR ASSOCIATES

5.1 INTRODUCTION

In the investing company's own financial statements an investment in an associate would be recorded at cost in the balance sheet, and the profit and loss account would show the dividends received. If the investing company is already preparing group accounts for its subsidiaries, then it must also account for its associates using the equity method.

5.2 EQUITY METHOD

Under the equity method the investing group accounts for its share of the profits and net assets of the associate. The method is similar to that used when calculating the minority interest in a subsidiary. Goodwill may also arise, and this will be recognised as an asset in the balance sheet and amortised through the profit and loss account.

The rules are summarised below:

Associate companies in the group balance sheet

The cost of the investment is replaced by the group's share of the associate's net assets, calculated as follows:

	£
Percentage share of the associate's net assets	X
Plus, goodwill at its net book value	X
Carrying value of the associate in the balance sheet	XX

Associate companies in the group profit and loss account

The dividend income from the associate is eliminated. It is replaced by the group's share of the associate's profits, calculated and analysed as follows:

The profit and loss account will record the group's share of the associate's:

- operating profit (less any amortisation of goodwill)
- financial income and expenditure (e.g. interest paid)
- exceptional items
- taxation.

The share of the operating profit and taxation are the most common items.

The cost of the investment in the associate and the dividend income from the associate are eliminated, but any other inter-company items are not cancelled. The profit and loss account will recognise trade to and from the associate, and the balance sheet will recognise any inter-company debtors and creditors between the associate and the group. This is because only a share of the net assets and profits of the associate are recorded under the equity method, which makes cancellation impossible.

Associate companies in the group reserves

The group reserves will include the group's share of the associate's post acquisition reserves. These are calculated in the normal way.

As with all goodwill, the cumulative amortisation will be deducted from the parent's reserves in the group reserves calculation.

Example – Balance sheet presentation

On 1 January 20X1 E plc acquired 25% of the ordinary share capital of A plc for £640,000 when the reserves of A plc stood at £720,000. The Goodwill was being amortised over five years. E plc appointed two directors to the board of A plc and the investment is regarded as long-term. Both companies prepare accounts to 31 December each year. The summarised balance sheet of A plc on 31 December 20X4 is as follows:

	£000
Sundry net assets	2,390
Capital and reserves	
Called up share capital	800
Share premium	450
Profit and loss account	1,140
	2,390

A plc has made no new issues of shares nor has there been any movement in the share premium account since E plc acquired its holding.

Show at what amount the investment in A plc will be shown in the consolidated balance sheet of E plc as on 31 December 20X4.

Solution

The group balance sheet will recognise the associate at a value of £627,000 made up as follows:

		£
Group share of A plc's net assets	£2,390,000 × 25%	597,500
Goodwill at net book value		29,500
		627,000

The group reserves will record the following:

	£	£
Cumulative amortisation of goodwill		(118,000)
Group share of A plc's post acquisition reserves		
Reserves in today's balance sheet	1,140	
Less: reserves at acquisition	(720)	
Post acquisition reserves	420	
Group share	25%	105,000
		(13,000)

Workings

(W1) **Goodwill**

		£	£
Cost			640,000
Less:			
Share of net assets at acquisition			
Share capital		800,000	
Share premium		450,000	
Reserves		720,000	
	25% ×	1,970,000	(492,500)
Goodwill arising			147,500
Cumulative amortisation	£147,500 × 4 years/5 years		£118,000
Net book value			£29,500

Example – profit and loss account

Continuing with the two companies used in the previous example the consolidated profit and loss account of E group and the profit and loss account of A plc for the year ended 31 December 20X4 are as follows.

The E group has accounted for A plc as a trade investment, and has recognised the dividend income alone rather than its share of A plc's profits.

	E group £000	A plc £000
Turnover	11,000	4,000
Cost of sales	(6,500)	(3,000)
Gross profit	4,500	1,000
Distribution costs	(1,000)	(400)
Administrative expenses	(700)	(300)
Dividend from associate (50 × 25%)	12	–
Profit on ordinary activities before taxation	2,812	300
Taxation	(1,200)	(60)
Profit on ordinary activities after taxation	1,612	240
Minority interests	(300)	–
Profit attributable to the group	1,312	240

Required:

Show the amounts to be included in the consolidated profit and loss account of E plc for the year ended 31 December 20X4.

Solution

	£000	£000
Turnover		11,000
Cost of sales		(6,500)
Gross profit		4,500
Distribution costs		(1,000)
Administrative expenses		(700)
Group operating profit		2,800
Share of operating profit in associate (25% × £300)		75
Less: amortisation of goodwill (W1)		(30)
Profit on ordinary activities before taxation		2,845
Taxation – group	(1,200)	
– associate (25% × £60)	(15)	(1,215)
Profit on ordinary activities after taxation		1,630
Minority interests		(300)
Profit attributable to the members of E plc		1,330

Workings

(W1) **Amortisation charge** £147,500 / 5 years = £29,500, rounded to £30K.

KEY TERMS

Consolidated profit and loss account – the consolidated profit and loss account combines the income and expenses of the parent and its subsidiaries on a line by line basis.

Minority interest – the minority interest's percentage share of the subsidiary's profit after tax.

Inter-company trade – trade between group companies. The income and expenditure is cancelled on consolidation.

Associated undertaking – a company over which the group has significant influence but not control.

Significant influence – the ability to influence the operating and financial policies of an investment for the benefit of the investor. This is normally evidenced by representation on the Board of Directors.

Equity accounting – the way in which an associated undertaking is accounted for in the consolidated financial statements. The group's share of the net assets and profits are claimed by the group.

SELF TEST QUESTIONS

Paragraph

1	How is a dividend received during the year from a subsidiary company treated in the consolidated profit and loss account?	1.1
2	If a subsidiary has been 80% owned all year how much of its taxation charge should appear in the consolidated profit and loss account?	1.4
3	If a sale of goods is made between a holding company and subsidiary during a year but the goods do not remain in stock at the year end, what is the consolidation adjustment required?	1.3, 2.1
4	If a sale of goods is made between a holding company and a subsidiary during a year and the goods are still in stock at the year end, what is the consolidation adjustment?	2.2
5	Is it an intra-group sale from holding company to subsidiary or subsidiary to holding company that affects the minority interest calculation if the goods are still in stock at the year end?	2.2
6	How is the minority interest figure for the consolidated profit and loss account calculated if the subsidiary company has preference shares in issue?	3

PRACTICE QUESTION

E LTD AND F LTD

The profit and loss accounts of E Ltd and F Ltd for the year ended 31 July 20X7 are as follows:

	E Ltd £	F Ltd £
Turnover	6,956	3,290
Cost of sales	3,108	1,470
Gross profit	3,848	1,820
Administrative expenses	(1,184)	(560)
Net profit on ordinary activities before taxation	2,664	1,260
Tax on profit on ordinary activities	1,258	595
Net profit after taxation	1,406	665

Statement of reserves

	E Ltd £	F Ltd £
As at 31 July 20X6	797	3,955
Profit for the year	1,406	665
Dividends paid	(800)	–
As at 31 July 20X7	1,403	4,620

Further information

(a)   E Ltd acquired 6,000 of the issued 10,000 ordinary shares in F Ltd several years ago when the reserves of F Ltd were £980. There was no goodwill on acquisition.

(b)   In the year ended 31 July 20X7 F Ltd sold to E Ltd goods costing £500 for £625 (25% profit margin on cost).

(c)   At 31 July 20X7 E Ltd had sold 40% of these goods for £300.

Required:

Prepare the consolidated profit and loss account of E Ltd and its subsidiary for the year ended 31 July 20X7.

(25 marks)

EXAM-STYLE QUESTION

JESSOP AND GRIFFIN

You are provided with the following summarised financial information for Jessop Ltd and Griffin Ltd.

Profit and loss account for the year ended 31 December 20X4

	Jessop Ltd £000	Griffin Ltd £000
Turnover	1,200	300
Cost of sales	(780)	(216)
Gross profit	420	84
Distribution costs	(90)	(18)
Administrative expenses	(72)	(24)
Operating profit	258	42
Investment income	17	–
Profit on ordinary activities before taxation	275	42
Tax on profit on ordinary activities	(84)	(12)
Profit for the year	191	30

Balance sheet as at 31 December 20X4

	Jessop Ltd £000	Jessop Ltd £000	Griffin Ltd £000	Griffin Ltd £000
Fixed assets				
Tangible assets		420		90
Investment				
Shares in Griffin Ltd at cost		120		
Current assets				
Stock	216		54	
Debtors	174		66	
Bank	84		26	
	474		146	
Creditors: amounts falling due within one year				
Creditors	60		39	
Corporation tax	84		12	
	144		51	
Net current assets		330		95
		870		185
Capital and reserves				
£1 ordinary shares		600		120
Profit and loss account		270		65
		870		185

The following information is also available:

(1) Jessop Ltd purchased 80% of the issued ordinary share capital of Griffin Ltd on 1 January 20X3 when the profit and loss account of Griffin Ltd was £25,000. Goodwill is amortised over its estimated useful life of four years.

(2) Jessop Ltd sold goods costing £120,000 to Griffin Ltd for £200,000 during the year ended 31 December 20X4. At 31 December 20X4, 25% of these goods remained in Griffin Ltd's stocks.

(3) Jessop has paid an ordinary dividend of £96,000 and Griffin has paid an ordinary dividend of £15,000 during the year.

Required:

Prepare the following statements for Jessop Ltd:

(a) the consolidated profit and loss account for the year ended 31 December 20X4

(12 marks)

(b) the consolidated balance sheet as at 31 December 20X4. **(10 marks)**

Disclosure notes are not required. **(Total: 22 marks)**

For suggested answers, see the 'Answers' section at the end of the book.

Chapter 15

PARTNERSHIP ACCOUNTS

With partnerships, there is some new terminology to learn but more importantly there are a number of special accounting entries that have to be dealt with.

Partnership accounts are covered by three chapters. Firstly, the basic techniques specific to partnership accounting are looked at. These basics are then built upon in subsequent chapters when various changes in partnerships are investigated.

This chapter covers syllabus area 2(a).

CONTENTS

1   Partnerships – key features, advantages and disadvantages

2   Division of profits and the partners' capital and current accounts

3   The appropriation account

4   Drafting the financial statements for a partnership from the trial balance

LEARNING OUTCOMES

At the end of this chapter you should be able to:

- identify the key features of a partnership

- outline the advantages and disadvantages of operating as a partnership, compared with operating as a sole trader or limited company

- outline the conventional methods of dividing profit and maintaining equity between partners

- draft an appropriation account for a partnership

- distinguish between partners' capital and current accounts

- record the partners' share of profits and losses and their drawings in the ledger accounts

- record introductions and withdrawals in the ledger accounts

- draft the trading and profit and loss account and appropriation account and the balance sheet for a partnership from a trial balance incorporating period end adjustments including:

  - accruals and prepayments

  - depreciation

  - irrecoverable debts and provisions for debtors

  - closing stock.

1 PARTNERSHIPS – KEY FEATURES, ADVANTAGES AND DISADVANTAGES

1.1 IDENTIFICATION OF PARTNERSHIP

A partnership exists whenever two or more people trade together with the intention of making a profit. No legal formalities are needed to create a partnership, although most partnerships will have a partnership agreement. If no agreement exists then the partnership agreement set out in the Partnership Act of 1890 comes into affect. This states that all profits and losses should be shared equally between the partners.

1.2 THE PARTNERSHIP AGREEMENT

Definition   A **partnership agreement**, which need not necessarily be in written form, will govern the relationships between the partners.

Important matters to be covered include:

(a)   name of firm, the type of business, and duration

(b)   capital to be introduced by partners

(c)   distribution of profits between partners

(d)   drawings by partners

(e)   arrangements for dissolution, or on the death or retirement of partners

(f)   settling of disputes

(g)   preparation and audit of accounts.

1.3 THE ADVANTAGES AND DISADVANTAGES OF OPERATING AS A PARTNERSHIP, RELATIVE TO SOLE TRADING OR AS A COMPANY

Comparing a partnership to sole trading, the advantages of operating as a partnership are as follows:

(a)   Business risks are spread among more than one person.

(b)   Individual partners can develop special skills upon which the other partners can rely rather than being a jack of all trades.

(c)   Certain partners may be able to draw upon larger capital resources to set up the partnership or expand the partnership.

The disadvantages are:

(a) There may be disputes between partners on such matters as the direction the business is taking or how much money individual partners are taking out of the business. Some partners may feel they are contributing more time and effort to the partnership than others and not being sufficiently financially rewarded as a result.

(b) A partner is 'jointly and severally liable' for his partners. This means that if one partner is being sued in relation to the business of the partnership, the other partners share in the responsibility.

A partnership has some advantages over a company as the arrangement is less formal than setting up a company requiring the issue of shares and the appointment of directors. If the partners wish to dissolve the business that is an easier matter to achieve by a partnership rather than a company.

The advantage of a company is that the owners of the business – the shareholders – may be protected from the creditors of the company as regards the payment of outstanding debts. This point is looked at more closely when we examine company accounts in a later chapter.

1.4 SUMMARY

Relative to sole trading, a partnership can give access to the wider skills and capital resources of several partners, although disputes amongst partners and the problems which can arise from joint and several liability are disadvantages

Partnerships have fewer formalities than companies but do not have the protection of limited liability.

2 DIVISION OF PROFITS AND THE PARTNERS' CAPITAL AND CURRENT ACCOUNTS

2.1 DIVISION OF PROFITS

The partnership agreement will detail how the profits of the firm are to be divided amongst the partners. However, if the partners do not have a partnership agreement, verbal or written, the rules laid down in the Partnership Act 1890 will apply. The rules are:

• residual profits are shared equally

• there are no salaries paid to partners

• there is no interest paid on partners' capital invested in the business

• interest at 5% per annum is payable on partners' loans to the business.

The division of profit stated in the partnership agreement may be quite complex in order to reflect the expected differing efforts and contributions of the partners. For example, some or all of the partners may be entitled to a salary to reflect the differing management involvement in the business. Interest on capital may be provided to reflect the differing amounts of capital contributed. The profit shares may differ to reflect seniority or greater skills.

It is important to appreciate however that all of the above examples are means of dividing the profits of the partnership and are not expenses of the business. A partnership salary is merely a device for calculating the division of profit; it is not a salary in the normal meaning of the term.

2.2 ACCOUNTING DISTINCTIONS BETWEEN PARTNERSHIPS AND SOLE TRADERS

The accounting techniques developed for sole traders are generally applicable to partnerships, but there are certain important differences:

Item	Sole trader's books	Partnership's books
Capital introduced	Capital account	Partners' fixed capital accounts
Drawings and share of the profit	Capital account	Partners' current accounts
Division of profits	Inapplicable – one proprietor only	Appropriation account

2.3 CAPITAL ACCOUNTS

At the commencement of the partnership an agreement will have to be reached as to the amount of capital to be introduced. This could be in the form of cash or other assets. Whatever the form of assets introduced and debited to asset accounts, it is normal to make the credit entry to fixed capital accounts. These are so called because they are not then used to record drawings or shares of profits but only major changes in the relations between partners. In particular, fixed capital accounts are used to deal with:

(a)   capital introduced or withdrawn by new or retiring partners

(b)   revaluation adjustments (these are discussed further in the next chapter).

The balances on fixed capital accounts do not necessarily bear any relation to the division of profits. However, to compensate partners who provide a larger share of the capital, it is common for notional interest on capital accounts to be paid to partners. This is dealt with through the appropriation account (see section 3).

2.4 CURRENT ACCOUNTS

These are used to deal with the regular transactions between the partners and the firm i.e. matters other than those sufficiently fundamental to be dealt with through the capital accounts. Most commonly these are:

(a)   share of profits, interest on capital and partners' salaries usually computed annually

(b)   monthly drawings against the annual share of profit.

2.5 RECORDING THE PARTNERS' SHARES OF PROFITS/LOSSES AND THEIR DRAWINGS IN THE LEDGER ACCOUNTS AND BALANCE SHEET PRESENTATION

Example 1

Nab and Crag commenced business in partnership on 1 January 20X6, contributing as fixed capital £5,000 and £10,000 cash respectively. All profits and losses are shared equally. The profit for the year ended 31 December 20X6 amounted to £10,000. Drawings for Nab and Crag amounted to £3,000 and £4,000 respectively.

You are required to prepare the capital and current accounts and balance sheet extracts.

Partners' capital accounts

		Nab £	Crag £			Nab £	Crag £
				20X6			
				1 Jan	Cash	5,000	10,000

Partners' current accounts

		Nab £	Crag £			Nab £	Crag £
20X6				20X6			
1 Dec	Drawings	3,000	4,000	31 Dec	Share of profits	5,000	5,000
	Balance c/d	2,000	1,000				
		5,000	5,000			5,000	5,000
				20X7			
				1 Jan	Balance b/d	2,000	1,000

The above accounts are presented in a columnar format. This is quite common in a partnership set of books as each partner will have similar transactions during the year. A columnar format allows two (or more) separate accounts to be shown using the same narrative. It is important to remember though that each partner's account is separate from the other partner(s).

Balance sheet at 31 December 20X6 (extract)

	Capital accounts £	Current accounts £	£
Partners' accounts:			
Nab	5,000	2,000	7,000
Crag	10,000	1,000	11,000
	15,000	3,000	18,000

Note that the current account balances of £2,000 and £1,000 will be credited in the following year with profit shares and debited with drawings.

One of the main differences between the capital section of the balance sheet of a sole trader and a partnership is that the partnership balance sheet will often only give the closing balances whereas the sole trader's movements in capital are shown. The main reason for the difference is simply one of space. Movements in the capital and current accounts for a few partners cannot be easily accommodated on the face of the balance sheet.

Example 2

The information is the same as in Example 1, except that Nab's drawings are £5,300. The current accounts now become

Partners' current accounts

		Nab £	Crag £			Nab £	Crag £
20X6				20X6			
	Drawings	5,300	4,000		Share of profits	5,000	5,000
31 Dec	Balance c/d		1,000	31 Dec	Balance c/d	300	
		5,300	5,000			5,300	5,000
20X7				20X7			
1 Jan	Balance b/d	300		1 Jan	Balance b/d		1,000

Note that Nab's current account is overdrawn. How do we present this in the balance sheet?

Balance sheet at 31 December 20X6 (extract)

	Capital accounts £	Current accounts £	£
Partners' accounts:			
Nab	5,000	(300)	4,700
Crag	10,000	1,000	11,000
	15,000	700	15,700

ACTIVITY 1

Tor and Hill have been in partnership for two years, sharing profits in the ratio 2:1. Figures for profit and drawings are as follows:

		Year ending 31 December	
		20X4 £	20X5 £
Drawings:	Tor	2,000	2,500
	Hill	1,500	1,500
Residual profit		9,000	12,000

You are required to prepare the partners' current accounts for 20X4 and 20X5, bringing down balances at the end of each year.

For a suggested answer, see the 'Answers' section at the end of the book.

2.6 SUMMARY

Partners' drawings and share of the annual profit is recorded in their current accounts. Their capital accounts are used to record fixed capital introduced or withdrawn and revaluation adjustments.

3 THE APPROPRIATION ACCOUNT

3.1 INTRODUCTION

Definition   The **appropriation account** is a ledger account dealing with the allocation of net profit between the partners. In practice it is often included as the final part of the trading and profit and loss account.

It can also be presented as a statement in columnar form.

An important point is that all allocations of profit to partners in their capacity as partners, and during the time they actually are partners, are made through the appropriation account. This applies even though such allocations may be described as partners' salaries, interest on capital or a share of profits.

3.2 USING THE APPROPRIATION ACCOUNT

Pike and Scar are in partnership and have the following profit-sharing arrangements:

(a)   interest on capital is to be provided at a rate of 8% pa

(b)   Pike and Scar are to receive salaries of £6,000 and £8,000 pa respectively

(c)   the balance of profit or loss is to be divided between Pike and Scar in the ratio 3 : 2.

Net profit for the year amounts to £20,000 and capital account balances are Pike £12,000 and Scar £9,000.

You are required to prepare:

(a)   a statement showing the allocation of profit between the partners; and

(b)   relevant entries in the trading and profit and loss and appropriation account.

Solution

(a)   **Allocation of net profit of £20,000**

	Pike		Scar		Total
	£		£		£
Interest on capital	960		720		1,680
Salaries	6,000		8,000		14,000
Balance of profits (£20,000 – £15,680)					
In ratio 3 : 2	2,592	(3/5)	1,728	(2/5)	4,320
Totals	9,552		10,448		20,000

Note that this is only a calculation of the allocation of profit and not part of the double entry bookkeeping system, merely providing the figures for the appropriation account.

(b)   Extract from trading and profit and loss and appropriation account for the year ended 20X1

	£	£
Sales		x
Cost of sales		x
Gross profit		x
Expenses		x
Net profit		20,000
Allocated to:		
Pike	9,552	
Scar	10,448	
		20,000

The profit and loss appropriation account is closed by transferring the profit shares to the credit of the partners' current accounts. The double entry is therefore

Debit	Credit	With
Profit and loss appropriation account	Pike's current account	£9,552
Profit and loss appropriation account	Scar's current account	£10,448

For the purposes of examinations (and in practice) parts (a) and (b) above can be amalgamated as follows

Extract from trading and profit and loss and appropriation account for the year ended 20X1

	£	£
Sales		x
Cost of sales		x
Gross profit		x
Expenses		x
Net profit for year		20,000

Appropriation statement

	Pike £		Scar £		Total £
Interest on capital	960		720		1,680
Salaries	6,000		8,000		14,000
Balance of profits (£20,000 – £15,680) in ratio 3 : 2	2,592	(3/5)	1,728	(2/5)	4,320
Totals	9,552		10,448		20,000

The debits actually being made are as before (£9,552 and £10,448).

ACTIVITY 2

Flame and Smoke are in partnership and have the following profit-sharing arrangements:

(a)   Interest on capital is provided at a rate of 8% pa.

(b)   Flame and Smoke are to receive salaries of £6,000 and £8,000 pa.

(c)   The balance of profit or loss is to be divided between Flame and Smoke in the ratio 3:2.

The balances on the capital accounts of the partners stand at Flame: £6,000 and Smoke: £4,000. The net profit for the year is £3,680.

You are required to show the allocation of profit between the partners.

For a suggested answer, see the 'Answers' section at the end of the book.

3.3   PARTNERS' SALARIES

One point which regularly causes difficulties is the partners' salaries. The key is to remember at the outset that a partner's salary is an appropriation of profit, whereas a salary paid to an employee is an expense.

Accordingly a salary to which a partner is entitled is included as part of the appropriation statement. Questions sometimes state that a partner has withdrawn his salary. In this case:

(a)   include the salary in the appropriation statement as usual; and

(b)   quite separately treat the withdrawal of the salary as drawings.

Debit	Credit	With
Partner's current account	Bank	Amount withdrawn

3.4   GUARANTEED MINIMUM PROFIT SHARE

In certain partnership agreements a partner may be guaranteed a minimum share of profits. The appropriation of profit would proceed in the normal way. If the result is that the partner has less than this minimum, the deficit will be made good by the other partners (normally in profit-sharing ratio). Sometimes the guarantee is given by one partner only, who will then bear the whole of the deficit.

Example

Tessa, Laura and Jane are in partnership and have the following profit-sharing arrangements:

(a)   Tessa and Laura are to receive salaries of £20,000 and £30,000 respectively

(b)   the balance of profit or loss is to be divided Tessa 1, Laura 2, Jane 3

(c)   Tessa is guaranteed a minimum profit share of £25,000.

The net profit for the year is £68,000.

You are required to show the appropriation account for the year.

Solution

Appropriation account

	Tessa £	Laura £	Jane £	Total £
Net profit				68,000
Salaries	20,000	30,000		(50,000)
				18,000
Balance of profits in ratio 1 : 2 : 3	3,000	6,000	9,000	(18,000)
	23,000	36,000	9,000	
Adjustment	2,000			
Laura 2/5 × 2,000		(800)		
Jane 3/5 × 2,000			(1,200)	
Totals	25,000	35,200	7,800	68,000

3.5 INTEREST ON DRAWINGS

Occasionally there is a provision in a partnership agreement for a notional interest charge on the drawings by each partner. The interest charges are merely a negative profit share – they are a means by which total profits are allocated between the partners.

The reason for an interest on drawings provision is that those partners who draw out more cash than their colleagues in the early part of an accounting period should suffer a cost.

Example

Dick and Dastardly are in partnership. The capital and current accounts as at 1 January 20X7 show:

	Capital £	Current £
Dick	50,000	2,500
Dastardly	20,000	3,000

The partnership agreement provides for the following:

(a)   profits and losses are shared between Dick and Dastardly in percentages 60 and 40

(b)   interest on capital at 10% per annum is allowed

(c)   interest on drawings is charged at 12% per annum.

Drawings for the year to 31 December 20X7 are:

	Dick	Dastardly
	£	£
1 February 20X7	5,000	2,000
30 September 20X7	2,000	5,000

The profit for the year is £20,000.

You are required to prepare the appropriation account and the current accounts for the year ended 31 December 20X7.

Solution

Appropriation account for the year ended 31 December 20X7

	Dick	Dastardly	
	£	£	£
Profit for the year			20,000
Add: Interest on drawings (see working)	(610)	(370)	980
			20,980
Less: Interest on capital:			
50,000 × 10%	5,000		
20,000 × 10%		2,000	(7,000)
			13,980
Balance in profit-sharing ratio:			
13,980 × 60%	8,388		
13,980 × 40%		5,592	(13,980)
Total allocation	12,778	7,222	20,000

Current accounts

		Dick	Dastardly			Dick	Dastardly
		£	£			£	£
20X7:				20X7:			
1 Feb	Drawings	5,000	2,000		Balance b/d	2,500	3,000
30 Sep	Drawings	2,000	5,000	31 Dec	Share of profits	12,778	7,222
	Balance c/d	8,278	3,222				
		15,278	10,222			15,278	10,222

Workings

		Dick	Dastardly
		£	£
Interest on drawings:			
1 February 20X7	5,000 × 12% × 11/12	550	
	2,000 × 12% × 11/12		220
30 September 20X7	2,000 × 12% × 3/12	60	
	5,000 × 12% × 3/12		150
		610	370

Conclusion   The appropriation account shows how the net profit for the year has been divided amongst the partners. Appropriations may take the form of:

- interest on capital

- 'salaries'

- a share of the remaining profit (in the agreed ratio)

- interest on drawings (occasionally).

4 DRAFTING THE FINANCIAL STATEMENTS FOR A PARTNERSHIP FROM THE TRIAL BALANCE

You should now be in a position to follow through from the trial balance stage a full example of partnership accounts.

Example

You are provided with the following information regarding the partnership of Dacre, Hutton and Tod.

(a) The trial balance at 31 December 20X6 is as follows:

	Dr £	Cr £
Sales		50,000
Stock at 1 January 20X6	6,000	
Purchases	29,250	
Carriage inwards	250	
Carriage outwards	400	
Creditors		4,000
Cash at bank	3,900	
Current accounts:		
Dacre		900
Hutton		750
Tod		1,350
Capital accounts:		
Dacre		4,000
Hutton		5,000
Tod		6,000
Drawings:		
Dacre	2,000	
Hutton	3,000	
Tod	5,000	
Sundry expenses	2,800	
Debtors	13,000	
Shop fittings:		
Cost	8,000	
Accumulated depreciation		1,600
	73,600	73,600

(b)   Closing stock is valued for accounts purposes at £5,500.

(c)   Depreciation of £800 is to be provided on the shop fittings.

(d)   The profit-sharing arrangements are as follows:

    (i)   interest on capital is to be provided at a rate of 10% per annum

    (ii)   Dacre and Tod are to receive salaries of £3,000 and £4,000 per annum respectively

    (iii)   the balance of profit or loss is to be divided between Dacre, Hutton and Tod in the ratio of 3 : 8 : 4.

You are required to prepare final accounts together with current accounts of the partners.

Solution

Dacre, Hutton and Tod
Trading and profit and loss account for the year ended 31 December 20X6

	£	£
Sales		50,000
Opening stock	6,000	
Purchases	29,250	
Carriage inwards	250	
	35,500	
Less: Closing stock	5,500	
		30,000
Gross profit		20,000
Sundry expenses	2,800	
Carriage outwards	400	
Depreciation	800	
		4,000
Net profit		16,000
Allocated to:		
Dacre	4,900	
Hutton	4,500	
Tod	6,600	
		16,000

Balance sheet as at 31 December 20X6

	Cost £	Acc dep'n £	£
Fixed assets			
Shop fittings	8,000	2,400	5,600
Current assets			
Stock		5,500	
Debtors		13,000	
Cash		3,900	
		22,400	
Current liabilities			
Creditors		4,000	
Net current assets			18,400
			24,000

Partners' accounts

	Capital accounts £	Current accounts £	£
Dacre	4,000	3,800	7,800
Hutton	5,000	2,250	7,250
Tod	6,000	2,950	8,950
	15,000	9,000	24,000

Partners' current accounts

		Dacre £	Hutton £	Tod £			Dacre £	Hutton £	Tod £
20X6:					20X6:				
	Drawings	2,000	3,000	5,000	1 Jan	Balance b/d	900	750	1,350
31 Dec	Balance					P&L app	4,900	4,500	6,600
	c/d	3,800	2,250	2,950					
		5,800	5,250	7,950			5,800	5,250	7,950
					20X7:				
					1 Jan	Balance b/d	3,800	2,250	2,950

Workings and commentary

The adjustments for stock and depreciation should be familiar by now.

The new development is that, having calculated the profit for the period, it has to be appropriated between Dacre, Hutton and Tod. To calculate their respective shares an appropriation statement is used

	Dacre	Hutton	Tod	Total
	£	£	£	£
Interest on capital	400	500	600	1,500
Salaries	3,000	–	4,000	7,000
Balance of profit (£16,000 – £8,500)				
in ratio 3 : 8 : 4	1,500	4,000	2,000	7,500
	4,900	4,500	6,600	16,000

This gives us the figures for the double entry

Dr Profit and loss appropriation

Cr Partners' current accounts

A final point

The majority of examination questions specify separate capital and current accounts. Occasionally you may be faced with a question specifying only one account for each partner. Such an account acts as a capital and current account combined.

Conclusion   Adopt a stepwise approach to the preparation of partnership accounts, as follows:

1   Draw up a proforma balance sheet and profit and loss account and enter figures as soon as you calculate them.

2   Work through any adjustments required.

3   Complete the profit and loss account and appropriate the profit as per the partnership agreement.

4   Open up partners' current accounts; enter the opening balances, appropriations of profit and drawings.

5   Find the new balances on the partners' current accounts.

6   Complete the balance sheet.

KEY TERMS

Partnership – exists whenever two or more people trade together with the intention of making a profit.

Partnership agreement – which need not necessarily be in written form, will govern the relationships between the partners.

Joint and several liability – each partner has unlimited liability for all of the losses incurred by the business. Usually losses will be shared in the profit sharing ratio, but if one or more partners become insolvent then the loss must be borne by the other partners.

Partners' capital accounts – records the long-term investment by the partners in the business.

Partners' current accounts – used to deal with the regular transactions between the partners and the firm, such as profits and drawings.

Partners' appropriation account – a ledger account dealing with the allocation of net profit between the partners.

Partners' salaries – an appropriation of profit. They are not an expense of the business.

Profit-sharing ratio – the agreed ratio in which the residual profits of the partnership are shared between the partners.

Residual profits – the net profit of the partnership adjusted for interest on capital and drawings and salaries.

SELF TEST QUESTIONS

		Paragraph
1	What is a partnership?	1.1
2	What are the differences between capital and current accounts?	2.3 & 2.4
3	Is interest on drawings an expense of the partnership?	3.5

EXAM-STYLE QUESTION

OWEN AND GRIFFITHS

Owen and Griffiths are in partnership, sharing profits equally after Owen has been allowed a salary of £5,000 per year. No interest is charged on drawings or allowed on current accounts, but interest of 10% pa is allowed on the opening capital account balances for each year. Their bookkeeper has been having trouble balancing the books and has eventually produced the following list of balances as at 31 December:

	£
Capital account:	
Owen	9,000
Griffiths	10,000
10% loan account:	
Griffiths	5,000
Williams	6,000
Current account balance on 1 January:	
Owen	1,000
Griffiths	2,000
Drawings:	
Owen	6,500
Griffiths	5,500
Sales	113,100
Sales returns	3,000
Closing stock	17,000
Cost of goods sold	70,000
Sales ledger control account	30,000
Purchase ledger control account	25,000
Operating expenses	26,100
Fixed assets at cost	37,000
Provision for depreciation	18,000
Bank overdraft	3,000
Suspense account	

You ascertain the following information:

(a)   The sales ledger control account does not agree with the list of balances from the ledger. The following errors when corrected will remove the difference:

(i)   the sales returns day book has been undercast by £100

(ii)   a contra entry with the creditors ledger for £200 has been omitted from the control accounts

(iii)   an invoice for £2,000 was incorrectly entered in the sales day book as £200.

(b)   A fully depreciated fixed asset, original cost £5,000, was sold during the year. The proceeds of £1,000 were entered in the bank account only, and no other entries in connection with the disposal were made.

(c)   It is agreed that hotel bills for £500 paid by Griffiths from his personal bank account are proper business expenses. Owen has taken goods out of the business for his own use, costing £1,000. No entry has been made for either of these items.

(d)   No interest of any kind has yet been paid or recorded.

(e)   Any remaining balance on the suspense account cannot be traced, and is to be treated in the most suitable manner.

You are required:

(a)   to prepare a trial balance and establish the balance on the suspense account
                                                                                    (4 marks)

(b)   to incorporate the necessary adjustments, showing your workings clearly in any way you feel appropriate   **(8 marks)**

(c)   to prepare final accounts for presentation to the partners.   **(13 marks)**
                                                                            (Total: 25 marks)

For a suggested answer, see the 'Answers' section at the end of the book.

Chapter 16

PARTNERSHIP CHANGES

This chapter covers the accounting techniques to record changes in a partnership. It covers syllabus area 2(a).

CONTENTS

1   Introduction

2   Recording introductions and withdrawals of capital in the ledger accounts

3   Partnership changes requiring revaluations

4   Partnership changes and goodwill

LEARNING OUTCOMES

At the end of this chapter you should be able to:

- explain why a revaluation is required after an admission, a change in the profit sharing ratio or a retirement

- revalue the partnership after such a change and calculate the goodwill

- make appropriate entries in the ledger accounts

- draft the partnership balance sheet after a change in the partnership.

1   INTRODUCTION

1.1   TYPES OF PARTNERSHIP CHANGE

Definition   **Partnership changes** may occur in three quite different situations:

        (a)   when a partner leaves, dies or retires

        (b)   when a new partner enters the partnership

        (c)   when existing partners change their profit-sharing arrangements.

From the accounting viewpoint there are two aspects:

(a) dividing profits between old and new partners when the change occurs during the course of the financial period (covered in this section)

(b) the problem of valuing partnership assets, especially goodwill, at the time of the change (sections 3 and 4).

1.2 DIVISION OF PROFITS IN A PARTNERSHIP CHANGE

There will be many occasions when a partnership change does not take place at a convenient date (such as the accounting year end!).

For the purpose of dividing profits equitably between the partners concerned, it is necessary to apportion (or allocate) profits between those arising before the change, and those arising afterwards.

In most cases where the trade is not of a seasonal nature, sales occur at an even rate during the year. It will then be reasonable to apportion sales on a time basis. Having apportioned the profit between the different parts of the year, it is then allocated between the partners according to their arrangements for sharing profits during those periods. This is demonstrated below.

Example

Gavel and Kirk are in partnership, sharing profits in the ratio 3 : 2, after Gavel has received a salary of £2,000 per annum. The accounting year-end of the partnership is 31 December. On 30 June 20X6 Blea is admitted to the partnership. The new profit-sharing arrangements provide for Gavel's salary of £2,000 per annum to be maintained, and for Blea to receive a salary of £3,000 per annum. The balance is to be shared between Gavel, Kirk and Blea in the ratio 2 : 2 : 1.

The net profit for the year to 31 December 20X6 is £22,000.

You are required to show the transfer to the partners' current accounts for the year ended 31 December 20X6.

Solution

Assuming that the net profit of £22,000 accrues evenly over the year, it may be apportioned on a time basis as follows:

		£
1 January 20X6 to 30 June 20X6	$\frac{6}{12} \times £22,000$	11,000
1 July 20X6 to 31 December 20X6	$\frac{6}{12} \times £22,000$	11,000
		_____
		22,000

The net profit relating to each six-month period is allocated according to the profit-sharing arrangements operating during that period.

Statement of allocation of profit

	Gavel £	Kirk £	Blea £	Total £
Six months to 30 June 20X6				
Salary:				
Gavel 6/12 × £2,000	1,000	–	–	1,000
Balance of profit (£11,000 – £1,000)				
in ratio 3 : 2	6,000	4,000	–	10,000
	7,000	4,000	–	11,000

Six months to 31 December 20X6	Gavel £	Kirk £	Blea £	Total £
Salary:				
Gavel 6/12 × £2,000	1,000	–	–	1,000
Blea 6/12 × £3,000	–	–	1,500	1,500
Balance of profit (£11,000 – £2,500)				
in ratio 2 : 2 : 1	3,400	3,400	1,700	8,500
	4,400	3,400	3,200	11,000
Totals – 12 months	11,400	7,400	3,200	22,000

Remember that the salaries are expressed at an annual rate! Interest on capital percentages are also expressed at an annual rate so a similar problem of time apportionment could apply elsewhere.

Partners' current accounts – Extract

	Gavel £	Kirk £	Blea £		Gavel £	Kirk £	Blea £
				Profit and loss appropriation:			
				To 30 June	7,000	4,000	–
				To 31 Dec 20X6	4,400	3,400	3,200

1.3 APPORTIONMENT OF PROFIT – SOME COMPLICATIONS

Unless otherwise instructed, it is acceptable to apportion profits on a time basis. Occasionally the question may specify some alternative basis.

Example

Assume that in the previous example the net profit of £22,000 was arrived at as follows:

	£	£
Sales (£96,000 in six months to 30 June 20X6)		160,000
Cost of sales		118,000
Gross profit		42,000
Selling and distribution expenses	5,500	
Administrative expenses	12,500	
Financial expenses	2,000	
		20,000
Net profit		22,000

You are required to show the apportionment of profit between the two parts of the year. Assume that gross profit and selling expenses are to be apportioned on a turnover basis and all other items on a time basis. The allocation of profit between the partners is not required.

Solution

	£
Turnover:	
Six months to 30 June 20X6	96,000
Six months to 31 December 20X6	64,000
	160,000

The ratio of turnover is therefore 96 : 64 or 3 : 2. . Costs directly related to sales should be split in this ratio (i.e. cost of sales and selling expenses). Other costs which can be taken to accrue evenly over the year should be split equally.

	Six months to 30 June 20X6		Six months to 31 December 20X6		Total	
	£	£	£	£	£	£
Gross profit (3:2)		25,200		16,800		42,000
Selling expenses (3:2)	3,300		2,200		5,500	
Administrative expenses (1:1)	6,250		6,250		12,500	
Financial expenses (1:1)	1,000		1,000		2,000	
		10,550		9,450		20,000
Net profit		14,650		7,350		22,000

The apportionment of net profit is therefore:

	£
Six months to 30 June 20X6	14,650
Six months to 31 December 20X6	7,350
	22,000

As can be seen, in a seasonal business, where sales fluctuate greatly from month to month, the apportionment of a net profit on a time basis may give a misleading picture.

ACTIVITY 1

The net profit of Harry, Barry and Gary for the year ended 31 December 20X8 was arrived at as follows:

	£
Sales (£30,000 in the 4 months to 1 May 20X8)	180,000
Less: Cost of sales	90,000
	90,000
Gross profit	
Selling and distribution expenses	12,000
Administrative expenses	3,000
	15,000
Net profit	75,000

Gary joined the partnership on 1 May 20X8. The partners have agreed to apportion gross profit and selling and distribution expenses on the basis of sales and administrative expenses on a time basis.

The profit-sharing ratios are:

1 January to 30 April 20X8	Harry 2: Barry 1
1 May to 31 December 20X8	Harry 2: Barry 1 : Gary 1

There are no salaries or interest payable to the partners.

You are required to calculate each partner's share of profit for 20X8.

For a suggested answer, see the 'Answers' section at the end of the book.

1.4 SUMMARY

In the year of a partnership change, the profits for the year have to be split into pre-acquisition and post-acquisition portions with reference to the date of the change. The relevant portions will then be divided amongst the old partners in the old profit-sharing ratio and the new partners in the new profit-sharing ratio.

2 RECORDING INTRODUCTIONS AND WITHDRAWALS OF CAPITAL IN THE LEDGER ACCOUNTS

2.1 INTRODUCTIONS AND WITHDRAWALS OF CAPITAL

Definition   **Introductions of capital** refers to the introduction of cash or other assets into the partnership. This is usual on admission of a new partner who will be expected to 'buy' her way in to the partnership.

Definition   **Withdrawals of capital** refers to cash or other assets taken out of the business in settlement of amounts owing to the partners on their capital and current accounts. This will occur when a partner leaves the partnership.

Partners may need to introduce or withdraw capital at times other than when there are partnership changes and the accounting treatment will be the same.

For the sake of clarity two unrealistic assumptions will be made in this section, namely that at the date of partnership changes:

(a)   all tangible assets (e.g. stock, fixed assets) are stated in the accounts at their current value

(b)   goodwill is ignored.

These unrealistic assumptions will be removed in sections 3 and 4 below, but first two possible causes of a change in the partnership will be considered – the retirement of an existing partner and the admission of a new partner.

2.2 RETIREMENT OF AN EXISTING PARTNER

When a partner retires it is important first of all to ensure that his current account is credited with his share of profits and debited with his drawings up to the date of retirement. The balances on his current and capital accounts are then transferred to a loan account and becomes a liability of the business. The manner and timing of the payment of this liability are likely to be regulated by the partnership agreement. In practice the amount will probably be paid in instalments, with allowance for interest on the unpaid balance. Since the former partner is no longer a partner of the business, the interest cannot be regarded as an appropriation of profit and must be regarded as an expense of the partnership (in the same way as interest on a bank overdraft).

Example

Birk, How and Stile have been in partnership for many years. Birk retired from the partnership on 1 July. At 30 June the summarised balance sheet showed the following position:

			£
Sundry assets			27,296

Partners' accounts	Capital accounts	Current accounts	
	£	£	
Birk	12,000	1,735	13,735
How	8,000	2,064	10,064
Stile	3,000	497	3,497
	23,000	4,296	27,296

It is assumed that the current account balances reflect profit shares and drawings up to 30 June. At that date the balances on Birk's capital and current accounts should be transferred to a loan account and regarded as a liability of the partnership. A balance sheet at 1 July would then appear:

	£
Sundry assets	27,296
Less: Loan account – Birk	13,735
Net assets	13,561

Partners' accounts	Capital accounts	Current accounts	
	£	£	
How	8,000	2,064	10,064
Stile	3,000	497	3,497
	11,000	2,561	13,561

Birk is now a creditor of the partnership as he is no longer a partner.

Example

Strode wishes to retire from his partnership. The balances on his capital and current accounts, after accounting for his share of the profits and his drawings, are £9,000 Cr and £1,000 Cr respectively. He wishes to keep his car, which is in the partnership books at a cost of £8,000 less depreciation of £6,000, to be paid £3,000 in cash and for the rest to remain on loan.

You are required to show the double entry to record the withdrawal of capital by Strode on his retirement.

Solution

		£	£
Dr	Capital account	9,000	
Dr	Current account	1,000	
Dr	Car: depreciation	6,000	
	Cr Car: cost		8,000
	Cr Cash		3,000
	Cr Loan		5,000

The £10,000 owed to Strode is partly settled by means of a car at its net book value of £2,000 and £3,000 cash. Therefore, £5,000 still remains on loan.

2.3 ADMISSION OF A NEW PARTNER

A new partner will often be required to bring in cash as a contribution to the fixed capital of the partnership. This cash is therefore credited to the partner's capital account.

Example

Facts as in the previous Birk, How and Stile example. Tarn is admitted to the partnership on 3 July. He brings in cash of £2,500 as his fixed capital. The partners' current accounts would not be affected, but the capital accounts would appear as follows:

Partners' capital accounts

	Birk £	How £	Stile £	Tarn £		Birk £	How £	Stile £	Tarn £
2 July:					1 July:				
Loan account	12,000	–	–	–	Bal b/d	12,000	8,000	3,000	·
					3 July:				
					Cash	–	–	–	2,500

A summarised balance sheet at 3 July would then show the following position:

	£
Sundry assets (£13,561 + £2,500)	16,061

Partners' accounts	Capital accounts £	Current accounts £	
How	8,000	2,064	10,064
Stile	3,000	497	3,497
Tarn	2,500	–	2,500
	13,500	2,561	16,061

If Tarn had contributed his capital share in the form of an asset other than cash, for example a car valued at £2,500, the double entry would have been:

Debit	Credit	With
Motor car account	Tarn's capital account	£2,500

The only effect on the balance sheet would then be the make-up of the sundry assets figure of £16,061 as between fixed and current assets.

2.4 SUMMARY

Withdrawals of capital are recorded as:

> Dr Capital (and current) account
>> Cr Cash / other assets / loan (if the amount due is to be settled later)

Introductions of capital are recorded as:

> Dr Cash / other assets
>> Cr Capital account

3 PARTNERSHIP CHANGES REQUIRING REVALUATIONS

3.1 INTRODUCTION

Two unrealistic assumptions have been made so far.

(a) No notice was taken of any difference between the current value of individual tangible assets and the amount at which they were stated in the books of account. On a change in partnership-sharing arrangements such account must be taken as partners are entitled to share capital profits in the same ratio as they share revenue profits.

Thus, just as we time-apportion profits between periods before and after the change, so we need to take account of capital gains or losses at the date of change. This topic is explored further in this section.

(b) Goodwill was ignored. Its nature and measurement will be dealt with in the next section.

3.2 WHY A REVALUATION IS REQUIRED ON A PARTNERSHIP CHANGE

Any change in a partnership (and remember a change can be an admission of a new partner, the retirement of an old partner or a change in profit sharing ratios) affects partners' rights to profits and assets. The entitlement to a one third share in profits means an entitlement to a one third share in the assets which exist in the partnership as well.

To the extent that the current worth of the assets is different from their book value a profit or loss will have accrued on the asset from the date of acquisition of the asset to the date of the partnership change. This profit or loss will need to be allocated to each partner in the old profit sharing ratio as the partnership change triggers off new profit sharing ratios.

The gain/loss is computed by revaluing the net assets at the date of change.

3.3 ENTRIES IN THE LEDGER ACCOUNTS IN RESPECT OF REVALUATIONS

Wherever there is a change in profit-sharing arrangements, a partnership will take account of changes in the value of its tangible assets.

In this instance use will be made of a temporary revaluation account to calculate the overall gain or loss on the revaluation; this will then be shared between the old partners in their old profit-sharing ratios in the capital accounts.

The initial bookkeeping entries are as follows:

Debit	Credit	With
Assets	Revaluation	Increases in asset values
Revaluation	Assets	Decreases in asset values
Liabilities	Revaluation	Decreases in liability values
Revaluation	Liabilities	Increases in liability values

At this stage the balance on the revaluation account will represent the overall surplus or deficiency on the revaluation, which will be shared between the old partners in their old profit-sharing ratios, viz:

Debit	Credit	With
Revaluation or	Partner's capital accounts	Surplus on revaluation
Partners' capital accounts	Revaluation	Deficit on revaluation

Example

Trooper, Tremlett and Arkle are in partnership; sharing profits in the ratio 4 : 3 : 3. As at 1 January 20X6 Randall is to be admitted to the partnership, thereafter profits are to be shared equally. Randall is to introduce capital of £30,000.

The partnership's balance sheet as at 31 December 20X5 shows the following:

	£	£
Fixed assets:		
Property		70,000
Plant and machinery		30,000
Fixtures and fittings		25,000
		125,000
Current assets:		
Stock	35,000	
Debtors	28,000	
Bank	17,000	
	80,000	
Less: Current liabilities:		
Creditors	27,250	
		52,750
		177,750

	Capital £	Current £	Total £
Partners' accounts:			
Trooper	50,000	2,000	52,000
Tremlett	53,750	4,000	57,750
Arkle	65,000	3,000	68,000
	168,750	9,000	177,750

For the purposes of the revaluation the assets of the partnership are to be revalued as follows:

	£
Property	80,000
Plant and machinery	27,500
Fixtures and fittings	32,100
Stock	36,350
Debtors	27,750

You are required to show:

(a)   the revaluation account

(b)   the partners' capital accounts

(c)   the balance sheet of the partnership as at 1 January 20X6.

Solution

(a)

Revaluation

	£	£		£
Plant and machinery		2,500	Property	10,000
Debtors		250	Fixtures and fittings	7,100
Profit on revaluation:			Stock	1,350
Trooper (4)	6,280			
Tremlett (3)	4,710			
Arkle (3)	4,710			
		15,700		
		18,450		18,450

(b)

Partners' capital accounts

	Trooper £	Tremlett £	Arkle £	Randall £		Trooper £	Tremlett £	Arkle £	Randall £
Balance					Balance				
c/d	56,280	58,460	69,710	30,000	b/d	50,000	53,750	65,000	
					Revalu-				
					ation	6,280	4,710	4,710	
					Bank				30,000
	56,280	58,460	69,710	30,000		56,280	58,460	69,710	30,000

(c)
Trooper, Tremlett, Arkle and Randall
Balance sheet as at 1 January 20X6

	£	£
Fixed assets:		
Property		80,000
Plant and machinery		27,500
Fixtures and fittings		32,100
		139,600
Current assets:		
Stock	36,350	
Debtors	27,750	
Bank	47,000	
	111,100	
Less: Current liabilities:		
Creditors	27,250	
		83,850
		223,450

	Capital £	Current £	Total £
Partners' accounts			
Trooper	56,280	2,000	58,280
Tremlett	58,460	4,000	62,460
Arkle	69,710	3,000	72,710
Randall	30,000	–	30,000
	214,450	9,000	223,450

Note that the capital accounts were adjusted for the change in asset values as it is a capital transaction. In particular the revaluation does not create realised profits (i.e. they are not in the form of cash) and thus partners cannot increase their drawings out of their current accounts.

ACTIVITY 2

The following revaluations were made to the net assets of Blagden and MacDonald on admission of Kirkman:

		£
Plant and machinery	increased by	5,000
Debtors	decreased by	1,000
Stock	decreased by	1,000
Property	increased by	17,000

The profit-sharing ratio prior to Kirkman's admission was Blagden 3 : McDonald 2. After Kirkman's admission it was Blagden 2 : MacDonald 2 : Kirkman 1.

You are required to write up the revaluation account indicating each partner's share of any profit or loss on revaluation.

For a suggested answer, see the 'Answers' section at the end of the book.

3.4 SUMMARY

All increases and decreases in the value of assets and liabilities at the date of a partnership change are included in the revaluation account:

- increases in assets will be credit entries

- increases in liabilities will be debit entries.

The balance on the revaluation account is shared amongst the old partners in their old profit-sharing ratio.

4 PARTNERSHIP CHANGES AND GOODWILL

4.1 THE NATURE OF GOODWILL

Definition **Goodwill** is the difference between the value of the business as a whole and the aggregate of the fair values of the net assets.

When a business changes hands, the price paid will commonly exceed the value of the net assets owned by the business, even when these are valued at market prices. This difference is an intangible asset referred to as goodwill. It is generated by the business as it continues to operate and comprises a number of factors, such as reputation for quality, a good location, experience and technical know-how. Such factors all mean that the business is in a good position to continue in the future and to make profits, and it is this that a purchaser is prepared to pay for, over and above the value of the net assets of the business.

4.2 MEASUREMENT OF GOODWILL

There can be no precise valuation of goodwill, which has to be essentially the result of an exercise of judgement of the worth of the business as a whole by the parties involved.

In examination questions the examiner will either tell you the valuation to be placed on the goodwill, or give sufficient information to enable you to calculate the figure. The most likely possibilities are as follows.

(a)   Goodwill is valued at £12,000. Self-explanatory.

(b)   X introduces £3,000 in payment for his share of one quarter of the goodwill. If a quarter share is valued at £3,000, then the total value for goodwill is £12,000.

(c)   Goodwill is to be valued at three times last year's profit of £4,000. Three times last year's profit is £12,000, giving the total value for goodwill.

(d)   The business is worth £200,000 and the fair value of the tangible net assets is £160,000. Goodwill is therefore £40,000.

4.3 ADJUSTMENTS IN RESPECT OF GOODWILL

There are two main situations as regards goodwill:

(a)   the partners wish to include goodwill as an asset in their balance sheet; or

(b)   the partners do not wish to include goodwill as an asset in their balance sheet but the effect of goodwill needs to be reflected in their capital accounts. This is more likely to be the requirement in examination questions.

4.4 GOODWILL INCLUDED AS AN ASSET IN THE BALANCE SHEET

In this situation use can be made of the revaluation account in the normal fashion, viz:

Debit	Credit	With
Goodwill	Revaluation	Increase in the value of goodwill
Revaluation	Goodwill	Decrease in the value of goodwill

If goodwill has not previously been incorporated in the books, the entry is:

Debit	Credit	With
Goodwill	Revaluation	The agreed value of goodwill

Again the revaluation account acts as a 'holding account' with the balance being split between the partners in the profit share ratio and cleared out to the capital accounts.

4.5 EXAMPLE

Laid, Back and Gower are in partnership sharing profits 5 : 3 : 2. As at 1 January 20X7 Gooch is to be admitted to the partnership; thereafter profits are to be shared equally. Gooch is to introduce capital of £40,000, of which £10,000 represents a payment for his share of the goodwill, which is subsequently to be disclosed in the books.

The partnership's balance sheet as at 31 December 20X6 shows the following:

	£	£
Fixed assets:		
Property		42,500
Plant and machinery		16,750
Fixtures and fittings		12,800
Current assets:		72,050
Stock	15,800	
Debtors	29,471	
Bank	18,623	
	63,894	
Less: Current liabilities:		
Creditors	24,713	
		39,181
		111,231
Partners' capital accounts:		
Laid		61,237
Back		18,476
Gower		31,518
		111,231

For the purposes of the revaluation the assets of the partnership are to be revalued as follows:

	£
Property	75,000
Plant and machinery	21,250
Fixtures and fittings	11,000

You are required to show:

(a)   the revaluation account

(b)   the partners' capital accounts

(c)   the balance sheet of the partnership as at 1 January 20X7.

Solution

(a)

Revaluation account

	£	£		£
Fixtures and fittings		1,800	Property	32,500
Profit on revaluation:			Plant and machinery	4,500
Laid (5)	37,600		Goodwill	40,000
Back (3)	22,560			
Gower (2)	15,040			
		75,200		
		77,000		77,000

Working – Goodwill

If Gooch is introducing £10,000 for his share of the goodwill (one quarter thereof) the total value of goodwill must be £40,000.

(b)

Partners' capital accounts

	Laid £	Back £	Gower £	Gooch £		Laid £	Back £	Gower £	Gooch £
Balance					Balance				
c/d	98,837	41,036	46,558	40,000	b/d	61,237	18,476	31,518	
					Bank				40,000
					Reval-				
					uation	37,600	22,560	15,040	
	98,837	41,036	46,558	40,000		98,837	41,036	46,558	40,000

Laid, Back, Gower and Gooch
Balance sheet as at 1 January 20X7

	£	£
Fixed assets:		
Goodwill		40,000
Property		75,000
Plant and machinery		21,250
Fixtures and fittings		11,000
		147,250
Current assets:		
Stock	15,800	
Debtors	29,471	
Bank	58,623	
	103,894	
Less: Current liabilities:		
Creditors	24,713	
		79,181
		226,431
Partners' capital accounts:		
Laid		98,837
Back		41,036
Gower		46,558
Gooch		40,000
		226,431

4.6 GOODWILL IS THE ONLY ASSET THAT REQUIRES REVALUATION

Quite often, it is only goodwill which requires to be revalued. The book value of the tangible assets may be fairly close to their market value and thus the time and expense involved in making valuations is too much compared to the benefits.

If only goodwill is being revalued, the revaluation account need not be used. The revaluation increase (or decrease) can be transferred from the goodwill account to the partner's capital accounts.

ACTIVITY 3

The Faldo, Woosnam partnership is to admit Newcomer into the partnership as at 1 July 20X6. Faldo and Woosnam currently share profits 3:1 after annual salaries of £100,000 each.

As from 1 July 20X6 the profit sharing ratio will be Faldo 3, Woosnam 2, Newcomer 2, after annual salaries of £120,000 each.

The partnership balance sheet as at 30 June 20X6 shows:

	£
Net assets	45,000

Partners' accounts	Capital	Current	Total
	£	£	£
Faldo	20,000	8,000	28,000
Woosnam	12,000	5,000	17,000
	32,000	13,000	45,000

Goodwill which does not currently appear on the balance sheet is estimated to be worth £280,000. Newcomer is to pay £90,000 capital into the business. Goodwill is to remain as an asset in the books.

You are required to show the partnership balance sheet as at 1 July 20X6 after the admission of Newcomer.

For a suggested answer, see the 'Answers' section at the end of the book.

4.7 GOODWILL NOT INCLUDED AS AN ASSET IN THE BALANCE SHEET

In many cases goodwill will not be shown on the balance sheet after a partnership change despite the fact that a new partner, for example, has paid for a share. The reasons for this are:

(a) **Subjective nature of valuation**

The value attached to goodwill on a partnership change is either a matter of negotiation between the partners or derived from a formula in the partnership agreement.

It only represents a value attached to the asset at the time of the change. In changing business conditions in the future its value may be very different.

(b) **Taxation**

For capital gains tax purposes it is generally disadvantageous to record partnership goodwill as an asset.

This will not change the need to make entries; the old partners by allowing another person into partnership are sharing their business with him. They are thus selling some of the past goodwill to him and this fact needs to be recorded in the capital accounts.

The approach to be adopted in this instance is to open up temporarily an account for goodwill, using the following journal entries:

Debit	Credit	With
Goodwill	Old partners' capital accounts	Their share of the goodwill (using old profit-sharing ratio)
New partner's capital accounts	Goodwill	Their share of the goodwill (using new profit-sharing ratio)

In simple terms this can be described as:

- write up goodwill in the old profit-sharing ratios (OPSR); and

- write it down in the new profit-sharing ratios (NPSR).

Example

Alpha, Beta and Gamma are in partnership sharing profits 7 : 2 : 1. As at 1 January 20X8 Delta is to be admitted to the partnership; thereafter profits are to be shared 3 : 3 : 3 : 1. Delta is to introduce capital of £50,000, of which £12,000 represents a payment for his share of the goodwill, not to be disclosed in the books.

An extract from the partnership balance sheet as at 31 December 20X7 shows the following:

	£
Capital accounts:	
Alpha	36,761
Beta	27,304
Gamma	29,287
	93,352

Assuming that there are no other revaluations necessary to other assets you are required to show:

(a) partners' capital accounts; and

(b) goodwill account.

Solution

(a) **Partners' capital accounts**

	Alpha £	Beta £	Gamma £	Delta £		Alpha £	Beta £	Gamma £	Delta £
					Balance				
Goodwill	36,000	36,000	36,000	12,000	b/d	36,761	27,304	29,287	
Balance					Bank				50,000
c/d	84,761	15,304	5,287	38,000	Goodwill	84,000	24,000	12,000	
	120,761	51,304	41,287	50,000		120,761	51,304	41,287	50,000

(b) **Goodwill**

	£		£
Alpha (7)	84,000	Alpha (3)	36,000
Beta (2)	24,000	Beta (3)	36,000
Gamma (1)	12,000	Gamma (3)	36,000
		Delta (1)	12,000
	120,000		120,000

Working

If Delta is introducing £12,000 for his share of the goodwill (one-tenth thereof) the total value of goodwill must be £120,000.

Commentary

Goodwill invariably appears as a complication in questions involving partnerships. The key is to follow the requirements of the question.

Confusion often arises in the case of goodwill not shown in the books in the sense that it appears most unfair that Delta, in the previous example, for instance pays in £50,000 on admission to the partnership and yet ends up with only £38,000 on his capital account. However, the point to remember is that the balance sheet does not include goodwill.

If goodwill were subsequently to be included in the books, say on 2 January 20X8, Delta's capital account would be credited with his share of the goodwill (1/10 × £120,000 = £12,000).

Similarly, if the partnership were dissolved, Delta would be entitled to a one-tenth share in the profit on the disposal of the partnership, which would include the valuation placed on the goodwill.

In any event the key is to follow the requirement in the question, which is likely to treat the partners fairly.

ACTIVITY 4

The balances on Ratner's and Hogg's capital accounts are £12,500 and £8,600 when they take on a third partner, Friar. Friar contributes £10,000 in cash as her fixed capital. Goodwill is valued at £20,000 at the date of Friar's admission, and is to remain in the books as an asset.

The partners have agreed to share profits and losses equally after Friar is admitted, as was the case prior to the partnership change.

You are required to write up the partners capital accounts and the goodwill account, bringing down balances after the partnership change.

For a suggested answer, see the 'Answers' section at the end of the book.

4.8   SUMMARY

The double entries in respect of goodwill are as follows:

If goodwill is to remain as an asset in the balance sheet:

> Dr Goodwill
>
> > Cr Revaluation (if other assets are being revalued)
>
> > or
>
> > Cr Capital accounts in the old profit-sharing ratio

If goodwill is not to remain as an asset in the balance sheet:

> Dr Capital accounts in the new profit-sharing ratio
>
> > Cr Capital accounts in the old profit-sharing ratio

SELF TEST QUESTIONS

Paragraph

1   What are the three types of partnership change?   1.1

2   Where does the capital account of a partner go to when he retires?   2.2

3   Why is it necessary to revalue assets at the date of the partnership change?   3.2

4   If goodwill is to be valued at three times last year's profit of £4,000, what is the value of goodwill?   4.2

EXAM-STYLE QUESTION 1

AL, BERT AND HALL

Al and Bert are in partnership, sharing profits equally. At 30 June they have balances on their capital accounts of £12,000 (Al) and £15,000 (Bert). On that day they agree to bring in their friend Hall as a third partner. All three partners are to share profits equally from now on. Hall is to introduce £20,000 as capital into the business. Goodwill on 30 June is agreed at £18,000.

You are required:

(a)   to show the partners' capital accounts for 30 June and 1 July on the assumption that the goodwill, previously unrecorded, is to be included in the accounts

(3 marks)

(b)   to show the additional entries necessary to eliminate goodwill again from the accounts   **(4 marks)**

(c)   to explain briefly what goodwill is. Why are adjustments necessary when a new partner joins a partnership?   **(8 marks)**
(Total: 15 marks)

EXAM-STYLE QUESTION 2

RED, BLUE AND YELLOW

Red, Blue and Yellow are in partnership. Red has decided to retire from the partnership at the end of the day on 31 March 20X9. You have been asked to finalise the partnership accounts for the year ended 31 March 20X9 and to make the entries necessary to account for the retirement of Red from the partnership on that day.

You have been given the following information:

(a)   The profit for the year ended 31 March 20X9 was £53,060.

(b)   The partners are entitled to the following salaries per annum:

Red   £9,000

Blue   £8,000

Yellow   £6,500

(c)   Interest on capital is to be paid at a rate of 12% on the balance at the beginning of the year on the capital accounts. No interest is paid on the current accounts.

(d)   Cash drawings in the year amounted to:

Red   £19,000

Blue   £15,000

Yellow   £14,500

(e)   The balances on the current and capital accounts at 1 April 20X8 were as follows:

Capital accounts		Current accounts	
Red	£14,000 Cr	Red	£1,250 Cr
Blue	£13,000 Cr	Blue	£1,080 Cr
Yellow	£11,000 Cr	Yellow	£935 Cr

(f)   The profit-sharing ratios in the partnership are currently:

Red   4/10

Blue   3/10

Yellow   3/10

On the retirement of Red, Blue will put a further £20,000 of capital into the business. The new profit-sharing ratios will be:

Blue   6/10

Yellow   4/10

(g)   The goodwill in the partnership is to be valued at £45,000 on 31 March 20X9. No separate account for goodwill is to be maintained in the books of the partnership. Any adjusting entries in respect of goodwill are to be made in the capital accounts of the partners.

(h)   The partners have had the assets of the partnership valued at 31 March 20X9. The book value of the assets at that date and the valuation are as follows:

	Book value £	Valuation £
Land and buildings	139,000	164,000
Debtors	18,000	13,000

The valuations are to remain in the books of the new partnership.

(i)   Any amounts to the credit of Red on the date of her retirement should be transferred to a loan account.

Required:

(a)   Prepare the partners' capital accounts as at 31 March 20X9 showing the adjustments that need to be made on the retirement of Red from the partnership.   **(6 marks)**

(b)   Prepare an appropriation account for the partnership for the year ended 31 March 20X9.   **(6 marks)**

(c)   Prepare the partners' current accounts for the year ended 31 March 20X9.
                                                                                                   (6 marks)

(d)   Show the balance on Red's loan account as at 31 March 20X9.   **(2 marks)**
                                                                               (Total: 20 marks)

For suggested answers, see the 'Answers' section at the end of the book.

Chapter 17

MERGERS AND DISSOLUTIONS OF PARTNERSHIPS

This chapter completes your studies of partnerships by looking at the merger of two sole traders and the dissolution of a partnership. It covers syllabus area 2(a).

CONTENTS

1   Drafting a partnership balance sheet after a merger of two sole trader businesses

2   Dissolution of a partnership

LEARNING OUTCOMES

At the end of this chapter you should be able to:

- draft the partnership balance sheet after a merger of two sole traders

- account for the dissolution of a partnership.

1   DRAFTING A PARTNERSHIP BALANCE SHEET AFTER A MERGER OF TWO SOLE TRADER BUSINESSES

1.1   INTRODUCTION

Definition   A **merger of two sole trader businesses** will involve the joining of the two traders and their business assets (and sometimes liabilities) to form a partnership.

The merger of two sole traders presents similar problems to the admission of a partner.

1.2   PROCEDURE

Step 1   Each trader will record the capital profit or loss accruing to him at the date of the merger. Values will be placed on the tangible net assets and goodwill of each trader's business and these values can be incorporated into the trader's books by use of a revaluation account. The entries will be similar to the revaluation of assets on a partnership change. The balancing figure in the revaluation account will be transferred to the trader's capital account.

Step 2 Any assets not being taken over by the partnership are removed from the trader's books by transferring the book value of the asset to the debit of the trader's capital account.

Step 3 The separate books can now be merged at the agreed values. The partnership assets will be the sum of the assets of the two sole traders and each person's capital account will be their opening balance of capital in the partnership.

If goodwill is not to appear as an asset in the balance sheet, the combined amount needs to be written off against each partner's capital account in new profit sharing ratio.

Example

A agrees to amalgamate with C to form X and Co.

The balance sheets of the two businesses at the date of the merger were as follows:

	A £	C £
Fixed assets:		
Freehold property	10,000	
Plant and machinery	4,000	7,000
Motor vehicle	3,000	
	17,000	7,000
Current assets:		
Stock	4,000	3,000
Debtors	2,000	1,000
Cash at bank	2,000	4,000
	25,000	15,000
Loan from F	2,000	
Current liabilities:		
Trade creditors	5,000	6,000
Capital accounts:		
A	18,000	
C		9,000
	25,000	15,000

X & Co was to take over all the assets and liabilities of the two businesses except:

(a) F's loan, for which A agreed to take over responsibility

(b) A was to take over the car.

The following were the agreed values placed on the assets of the old businesses:

	A £	C £
Goodwill	9,000	3,000
Freehold property	14,000	–
Plant and machinery	3,000	6,000
Stock	4,000	2,000
Debtors	2,000	1,000

Trade creditors were taken over at their book value.

Profit sharing in the new firm is 3:1 between A and C.

Goodwill was not to appear in the new firm's balance sheet.

You are required:

(a)   to prepare the balance sheet of X & Co immediately following the amalgamation

(b)   to prepare the closing entries in the books of A and C to record the revaluation and the entries in their capital accounts.

Solution

(a)   **X & Co – Balance sheet after merger**

	£	£
Fixed assets:		
Freehold property		14,000
Plant and machinery (3,000 + 6,000)		9,000
		23,000
Current assets:		
Stock (4,000 + 2,000)	6,000	
Debtors (2,000 + 1,000)	3,000	
Cash (2,000 + 4,000)	6,000	
	15,000	
Current liabilities:		
Trade creditors (5,000 + 6,000)	11,000	
		4,000
		27,000
Capital accounts		
A		20,000
C		7,000
		27,000

(b)   **Books of A**

Revaluation account

	£		£
Plant and machinery – loss	1,000	Goodwill – profit	9,000
Capital account	12,000	Freehold property – profit	4,000
	13,000		13,000

A's capital account

	£		£
Motor car	3,000	Balance b/d	18,000
		F's loan	2,000
Balance c/d to new firm	29,000	Profit on revaluation	12,000
	32,000		32,000

Books of C

Revaluation account

	£		£
Plant and machinery – loss	1,000	Goodwill – profit	3,000
Stock – loss	1,000		
Capital account	1,000		
	3,000		3,000

C's capital account

	£		£
Balance c/d	10,000	Balance b/d	9,000
		Profit on revaluation	1,000
	10,000		10,000

Working

Partners' capital accounts

	A £	C £		A £	C £
Goodwill written down			Balance b/d		
3 : 1 × 12,000	9,000	3,000	from old business	29,000	10,000
Balance c/d	20,000	7,000			
	29,000	10,000		29,000	10,000

ACTIVITY 1

Martin and Joe are two sole traders who agree to merge their businesses and form a partnership. They draw up an agreement which states that their profit-sharing ratio is to be Martin 2: Joe 1, and that their fixed capital will be £15,000 in total, with each partner contributing amounts in their profit-sharing ratio. Any capital in excess of this will be transferred to a current account.

Relevant amounts at the date of the merger are:

	Martin £	Joe £
Balance on capital account	10,000	8,000
Revaluation surplus (including goodwill)	10,000	9,000

The revaluations are to remain in the books of the new partnership.

You are required to write up the capital accounts of each partner immediately before and after the merger.

For a suggested answer, see the 'Answers' section at the end of the book.

1.3 SUMMARY

Use a stepwise approach to a merger of two sole traders as follows.

(1)   Credit the capital account of each sole trader with any profit on revaluation and goodwill (debit if there is an overall loss).

(2)   Debit the capital account of each sole trader with the book value of any assets taken over by a trader.

(3)   Merge the assets of each business and transfer the balances on the capital accounts to the capital accounts of the partnership.

2 DISSOLUTION OF A PARTNERSHIP

2.1 INTRODUCTION

Definition   When a partnership is **dissolved** it is brought to an end.

Possible reasons for dissolution include:

(a)   death or retirement of a partner

(b)   disagreement among the partners

(c)   continuing trading losses

(d)   the completion of the purpose for which the partnership was formed.

Whatever the reason, the accounting treatment is the same.

2.2 OBJECTIVE OF DISSOLUTION

The objective of a dissolution is to dispose of the partnership assets, pay off the liabilities and distribute the balance to the partners according to their entitlements.

The amount each partner receives is the balance on his or her capital account plus his or her share of the profit arising on the disposal of the assets (or minus any share of loss). If the final result is that a partner's account is in deficit, he or she has to pay the money in to allow the other partners to draw out their full entitlement. (There are special rules to deal with the situation arising if a partner with a deficit is insolvent and unable to pay money in, but these rules are not in your syllabus.)

2.3 THE REALISATION ACCOUNT

The first bookkeeping step in dealing with a dissolution to open a **realisation account**, sometimes called a **dissolution account**. All the asset balances except cash in hand and cash at bank are transferred in to the debit of the realisation account. The proceeds of sale of these assets will be credited to the realisation account, the balance on which will then be the profit or loss on the dissolution, subject to some minor items.

The assets could be sold separately or as a single going concern unit. In either case the proceeds are credited to the realisation account.

2.4 DEALING WITH LIABILITIES

The liabilities of the partnership have to be paid – credit cash and debit the liability accounts.

It may be that liabilities are paid off for a little more or less than the book amounts perhaps because of cash discounts or negotiated settlements. Any such difference is debited or credited to the realisation account as representing the loss or profit arising on the final settlement of the liabilities.

2.5 EXPENSES OF DISSOLUTION

The expenses of dissolution are simply debited to the realisation account when paid.

2.6 ASSETS TAKEN OVER BY THE PARTNERS

It may be that partners agree to takeover certain partnership assets at dissolution. To record this, we simply credit realisation account (to which the asset has been transferred as explained in paragraph 2.4) and debit the capital account of the partner concerned.

2.7 PARTNERS' ACCOUNTS

Partners may have both capital accounts and current accounts. The distinction between them ceases to have any meaning on dissolution and current account balances should be transferred to the capital accounts.

2.8 SALE OF BUSINESS AS A GOING CONCERN – GOODWILL

If the business is sold as a going concern, this means that a single sum is received for all or most of the assets. The value of unrecorded goodwill may be an element in the total consideration, but there is no need to record this specially. The total consideration is credited to the realisation account (debit cash) and the value attributed to the goodwill merely adds to the profit on the sale and is thus automatically credited to the partners in their profit-sharing ratios.

2.9 SALE OF BUSINESS AS A GOING CONCERN – LIABILITIES TAKEN OVER

A purchaser of the business may agree to take over all or some of the partnership's liabilities. The easiest way to deal with this is to credit the liabilities taken over to the realisation account, so that the profit or loss arising on the sale in the realisation account is the difference between the consideration and the **net** assets taken over.

2.10 THE FINAL SETTLEMENT WITH THE PARTNERS

When all the entries described above have been recorded, there will remain only the partners' capital accounts and the cash at bank. It only remains to draw cheques to pay the partners the balances due to them. Any partner with a debit balance on his or her capital account will pay in cash to clear the balance.

It could happen that the dissolution is spread over a long period so that payments on account are made to the partners as the sale of the assets proceeds. This so-called 'piecemeal' dissolution is **not** examinable.

2.11 COMPREHENSIVE EXAMPLE

Here is a comprehensive example covering nearly all the procedures described above. Attempt it for yourself, referring back to the explanations above if you need help. Then study the answer which follows it.

A, B and C share profits 4 : 3 : 3. They agreed to dissolve their partnership at the end of the financial year, when the balance sheet appeared as follows:

	£	£
Fixed assets, at cost less depreciation:		
Freehold		40,000
Plant and machinery		15,000
Motor vehicles (three cars)		16,000
		71,000
Current assets:		
Stock	50,000	
Debtors	25,000	
Cash	15,000	
	90,000	
Current liabilities	21,000	
		69,000
Loan account – D		(20,000)
		120,000

Partners' accounts:	A	B	C	
	£	£	£	
Capital	40,000	30,000	20,000	90,000
Current	15,000	10,000	5,000	30,000
	55,000	40,000	25,000	120,000

The following are sold for cash:

	£
Freehold, for	80,000
Plant and machinery, for	13,000
Stock, for	43,000
	136,000

The creditors are settled for £20,000.

C takes over the debtors at an agreed value of £22,000.

A takes over D's loan at its book value.

A, B and C take over the cars at the following valuations:

A	£6,000
B	£8,000
C	£4,000

Realisation expenses are £2,000.

You are required to prepare the ledger accounts to show the closing of the partnership records.

2.12 SOLUTION

Numbers in brackets refer to sequence of entries

Realisation account

Book value of assets	£	£	Sale or disposal proceeds:	£
Realisation expenses			(i) Cash – sold	
To partners – profit on realisation in PSR			(ii) Partners' accounts – assets taken over	
(1) Freehold account		40,000	(2) Cash – sale proceeds	136,000
(1) Plant and machinery			(4) Discount received on	
Account		15,000	Creditors	1,000
(1) Motor vehicles			Partners' accounts –	
account		16,000	assets taken over:	
(1) Stock account		50,000	(5) C debtors	22,000
(1) Debtors account		25,000	(5) A motor car	6,000
(7) Cash – realisation			(5) B motor car	8,000
expenses		2,000	(5) C motor car	4,000
Partners' accounts				
profit on realisation:				
A 40%	11,600			
B 30%	8,700			
C 30%	8,700			
		29,000		
		177,000		177,000

Partners' accounts

	A £	B £	C £		A £	B £	C £
(5) Debtors taken over			22,000	Balances b/d: Capital			
(5) Motor cars taken over	6,000	8,000	4,000	accounts	40,000	30,000	20,000
				Current accounts	15,000	10,000	5,000
(8) Cash to settle	80,600	40,700	7,700		55,000	40,000	25,000
				(6) D's loan account	20,000		
				Realisation account – Profit	11,600	8,700	8,700
	86,600	48,700	33,700		86,600	48,700	33,700

Creditors' account

	£		£
(3) Cash	20,000	Balance b/d	21,000
(4) Realisation account – discount received on settlement	1,000		
	21,000		21,000

D's loan account

	£		£
(6) A's partner account	20,000	Balance b/d	20,000

Cash account

	£	£		£	£
Balance b/d		15,000	(3) Creditors		20,000
			(7) Realisation expenses		2,000
Sale proceeds to realisation account:			Partners' accounts to settle:		
(2) Freehold	80,000		(8) A	80,600	
(2) Plant and machinery	13,000		(8) B	40,700	
(2) Stock	43,000		(8) C	7,700	
		136,000			129,000
		151,000			151,000

2.13 DEBIT BALANCES

After the accounting entries in respect of realisation of the partnership assets on dissolution have been put through, some partners may have debit balances on their capital accounts. These partners owe the partnership the amount of the debit balance. They will have to pay this money into the partnership.

2.14 THE RULE IN GARNER v MURRAY

When a partner has a net debit balance on his capital account after the realisation of the partnership assets, the rule in Garner v Murray will sometimes be applied. Under the rule in Garner v Murray, the debit balance is transferred to the other parties in the ratios of their last agreed capital balances.

Example

A, B and C are dissolving their partnership. After realising all the partnership assets, the balances on the partners' capital accounts were as follows:

A   £10,000

B   £(3,000)

C   £15,000

Although the partners shared profits and losses equally, their last agreed capital account balances were:

A   £20,000

B   £10,000

C   £40,000

The debit balance on B's capital account is allocated as follows:

A   3,000 × 20/60   =   £1,000

C   3,000 × 40/60   =   £2,000

The practical effect of this is that A and C bear B's loss. Many partnership agreements specifically exclude the rule in Garner v Murray.

2.15 SUMMARY

Use a stepwise approach to a dissolution, as follows:

(1)   Transfer the current account balance of each partner to the capital account.

(2)   Open up a realisation account and transfer in all the assets and liabilities of the partnership:

Dr Realisation account with the value

Cr Asset account of the assets

Dr Liability account with the value

   Cr Realisation account of the liabilities

(3)   Deal with any assets taken over by a partner

   Dr Capital account

   Cr Realisation account

(4)   Deal with the cash received on sale of the assets and cash paid to settle liabilities and realisation expenses:

   Dr Cash account with the sale proceeds

   Cr Realisation account of the assets

   Dr Realisation account with the amounts paid to

   Cr Cash account settle liabilities and expenses of dissolution

(5)   Share the balance on the realisation account amongst the partners in their profit-sharing ratio.

(6)   Settle the balances on the capital accounts with cash.

KEY TERMS

Merger – when two sole traders form a partnership. A merger of two sole traders to form a partnership is accounted for by adding together the assets and liabilities that they bring in to the partnership and bringing down the balances on their individual capital accounts in the new partnership capital account.

Dissolution – marks the end of a partnership. A dissolution is effectively the process of paying the partners what is due to them on their capital and current accounts with the cash or assets of the partnership.

SELF TEST QUESTIONS

Paragraph

1	Do the assets of the sole traders who merge to form a partnership have to be revalued?	1.2
2	Give four reasons why a partnership might dissolve.	2.1
3	What is the name of the account which is used to record the transactions associated with a dissolution?	2.3
4	What is the double entry which records the taking of an asset of the partnership by a partner on dissolution?	2.6
5	How are the partners' capital and current accounts dealt with in a dissolution?	2.7
6	What is meant by 'sale of the business as a going concern'?	2.8

EXAM-STYLE QUESTION

SMART AND SWIFT

Smart and Swift were in partnership as hotel proprietors sharing profits and losses: Smart three-fifths, Swift two-fifths. No interest was charged on drawings or credited on capital.

The following was a summary of their trial balances as at 31 December 20X8:

Debits	£	£	Credits	£	£
Debtors		600	Bank overdraft		4,590
Fittings and fixtures		1,800	Loan – Smart at 6%		3,000
Foodstuffs – stock			Partners' capital acc:		
at 31 Dec 20X7		420	Smart	3,000	
Foodstuffs purchased		2,600	Swift	500	
Freehold premises		6,000			3,500
General expenses		810	Sundry creditors		210
Partners' drawings:			Takings		5,100
Smart	520				
Swift	750				
		1,270			
Motor vehicle		700			
Wages		2,200			
		16,400			16,400

For the purpose of accounts as on 31 December 20X8 the stock of foodstuffs was valued at £300, and £200 was to be written off the book value of the motor vehicle and £100 off fittings and fixtures. A provision of £60 was required for accrued general expenses and Smart was to be credited with a year's interest on his loan account.

The partnership was dissolved on 31 December 20X8, it being agreed that:

(a)　Smart should take over the stock of foodstuffs for £250 and part of the fittings and fixtures for £600

(b)　Swift should take over the motor vehicle for £400

(c)　interest on Smart's loan should cease as on 31 December 20X8.

During January 20X9:

(a)　the freehold premises were sold, realising a net amount of £6,800

(b)　£480 was collected from debtors (the balance proving irrecoverable)

(c)　the net proceeds from an auction of the balance of fittings and fixtures were received amounting to £1,400. It was agreed that the few unsold items should be taken over partly by Smart for £40 and the rest by Swift for £20

(d)　creditors were paid in full together with incidental realisation and dissolution expenses of £120

(e)　all amounts receivable or payable by Smart and Swift were settled.

You are required:

(a)   to prepare the profit and loss account for the year ended 31 December 20X8 excluding any profit or loss arising on dissolution

(b)   to prepare the realisation account

(c)   to prepare the cash account for January 20X9

(d)   to prepare partners' capital accounts (in columnar form) showing the final settlement on dissolution.

(20 marks)

For a suggested answer, see the 'Answers' section at the end of the book.

Chapter 18

INCOMPLETE RECORDS

In real life, and in questions, the accounting records may be incomplete. This may be because the records have been lost or destroyed, or because full records were not kept in the first place. There are many different techniques utilised in the preparation of accounts from incomplete records. In an exam question you will have to select the most appropriate ones for the information given to you. Most of the examples in this chapter are based on the accounts of a sole trader, but exactly the same techniques are used to prepare the accounts of partnerships and limited companies with incomplete records. This chapter covers syllabus area 2(a).

CONTENTS

1 Calculation of profit from information about the balance sheet only

2 Preparation of final accounts from limited records

3 Using ratios and percentages

LEARNING OUTCOMES

At the end of this chapter you should be able to:

• derive missing figures from incomplete records.

1 CALCULATION OF PROFIT FROM INFORMATION ABOUT THE BALANCE SHEET ONLY

1.1 DISTINCTION BETWEEN INCOMPLETE AND LIMITED ACCOUNTING RECORDS

Definition   **Limited accounting records** are records kept by a business of certain transactions but additional information is required to prepare financial statements.

Definition   **Incomplete accounting records** are records which the business has not fully completed or where no records at all have been kept of transactions.

Many businesses fall into each of the above categories. Many businesses keep limited accounting information such as daily records of cash received, invoices paid (i.e. some form of purchase day book) and wages paid. They leave it to the accountant who prepares the annual financial statements to make sense of the information and to ask for other information at that time.

With limited accounting records, the accountant thus has (generally) sufficient information to prepare the accounts but no ledger accounts have been prepared. We will look at the procedures used to prepare financial statements in this situation later in the chapter.

A business that has kept very little information on its daily transactions is providing the accountant with the task of preparing financial statements from incomplete data. In this section we will see how limited the data can be and yet still it is possible to prepare financial statements. However these financial statements are more prone to error because of the incomplete records.

In practice, the term incomplete records is used to cover both situations.

1.2 CALCULATION OF THE NET ASSET POSITION AND THE PROFIT FOR A BUSINESS WHICH HAS INCOMPLETE ACCOUNTING RECORDS

The most basic incomplete records situation of all is where one is required to calculate net profit, given details only of capital at the beginning and end of the year and of drawings.

Example

The capital position of a business is as follows:

	31 December	
	20X6	20X7
	£	£
Motor vehicle:		
Cost	2,000	2,000
Depreciation	(800)	(1,200)
	1,200	800
Stock	2,040	2,960
Debtors	865	1,072
Bank	1,017	1,964
Cash	351	86
	5,473	6,882
Creditors	1,706	1,905
	3,767	4,977

Drawings for the year have been estimated at £3,000. An estimate of net profit for the year is required.

Solution

From the basic balance sheet equation capital equals assets less liabilities. Hence the opening and closing capital account balances are £3,767 and £4,977 respectively. Net profit may be calculated by completing his capital account.

Capital account

20X7		£	20X7		£
	Drawings	3,000	1 Jan	Balance b/d	3,767
31 Dec	Balance c/d	4,977		Net profit (bal fig)	4,210
		7,977			7,977
			20X8		
			1 Jan	Balance b/d	4,977

Note that the net profit figure is very much an estimate and depends on the reliability of the drawings and the opening and closing net asset positions.

It also assumes that no new capital has been introduced by the owners during the year.

Alternative solution

An alternative method of calculation is:

	£
Net assets this year end	4,977
Net assets last year end	3,767
Increase in net assets	1,210
Less: Capital introduced by owners	–
Add: Drawings	3,000
Profit for the year	4,210

The alternative method emphasises that profit represents an increase in the net assets of the business unless it is withdrawn by the owners.

Conclusion Profit for the year = Increase in net assets – Capital introduced + Drawings.

ACTIVITY 1

On 1 January 20X5 B Freen commenced business. At that date he purchased a shop premises for £14,000 and paid £2,000 for interior fittings. He also paid £4,000 into the business bank account. On 31 December 20X6 he realised the need for a profit figure for the two years he had been in business, but his records were completely inadequate. At this date the assets he possessed in addition to the premises and fittings were:

	£
Stock	6,000
Debtors	1,040
Motor lorry purchased 30 June 20X6 for	8,000
Cash at bank	2,500

He owed £1,400 to trade creditors and had borrowed £10,000 from a friend. Interest accrued but unpaid on the loan amounted to £200. Freen estimated that he was withdrawing £300 a month from the business.

Required:

Compute the net profit for the two years valuing the fixed assets at cost less depreciation (on a straight line basis): on premises at 2% p.a. and on fittings at 5% p.a. and on the motor lorry at 20% p.a.

For a suggested answer, see the 'Answers' section at the end of the book.

1.3 SUMMARY

A business that has information about assets owned at the year end, but no information on income and expenditure items can not prepare a detailed profit and loss account. The profit for the year can be found by:

- preparing a summarised balance sheet: profit will be the balancing figure

- using the accounting equation:

    Profit for the year = Increase in net assets – Capital introduced + Drawings.

2 PREPARATION OF FINAL ACCOUNTS FROM LIMITED RECORDS

2.1 CASH AND BANK TRANSACTIONS

In the first example above no details were given of transactions taking place during the year. If basic information regarding receipts and payments is provided, it is possible to build up to a balance sheet and profit and loss account, although some important assumptions may well need to be made.

2.2 BASIC PROCEDURE FOR LIMITED RECORDS

The procedure suggested below is a full procedure suitable for a wide range of limited records questions and may be set out in basic steps. We will see later how some of these steps can be cut back on for examination purposes.

Step 1   Set aside a sheet for the trading and profit and loss account and a sheet for the balance sheet. Some information can be inserted straight into the final accounts.

Step 2   Prepare the opening balance sheet from information on assets and liabilities.

Conclusion   The opening capital account balance can be calculated as a balancing figure (Capital = Assets less Liabilities).

Step 3   Insert the opening balances in T-accounts. For example:

Balance	Account
Cash at bank	Cash at bank (bank)
Cash in hand	Cash in hand (cash)
Debtors	Sales ledger control account
Creditors	Purchases ledger control account
Accrued expenses	Separate account for each expense category
Prepayments	Separate account for each expense category

Step 4   Information is almost certain to be given as regards cash and bank transactions. Accordingly the cash and bank accounts can be prepared, making use of double entry principles and completing the entries by debiting and crediting whichever accounts are appropriate.

Notes:

(a)   Cash withdrawn is cash taken out of the bank (Cr bank) and into cash in hand (Dr cash).

(b)   Cash banked operates in the opposite direction – it is a reduction of cash (Cr cash) and an increase in money at bank (Dr bank).

Depending on the degree of incompleteness, cash is likely to contain one or two missing items of information. This aspect of the problem will be receiving more attention later.

Step 5   Insert into the accounts the closing balances provided in the question in respect of debtors, creditors, accrued expenses and prepayments. In simple questions the respective transfers to profit and loss may be calculated as balancing items.

Sales ledger control account

	£		£
Opening debtors b/d	X	Cash	X
Sales (bal fig)	X	Closing debtors c/d	X
	X		X

Purchases ledger control account

	£		£
Cash	X	Opening trade creditors b/d	X
Bank	X	Purchases (bal fig)	X
Closing trade creditors c/d	X		
	X		X

Rates account (assuming paid in advance)

	£		£
Opening prepayment b/d	X	Profit and loss (bal fig)	X
Bank	X	Closing prepayment c/d	X
	X		X

Step 6   Carry out any further adjustments as required, such as dealing with doubtful debts and depreciation.

Example

A business has a cash float of £50 and the following expenses are paid out of the till before cash is banked:

	£
Purchases	20
Wages	100
Expenses	80

The bank statement shows that the takings banked in the period were £4,000.

Write up the cash account and find the value of cash sales.

Solution

Cash

	£		£
Balance b/d	50	Purchases	20
Cash takings (sales) (bal fig)	4,200	Wages	100
		Expenses	80
		Bankings	4,000
		Balance c/d	50
	4,250		4,250

ACTIVITY 2

The following information relates to a business's transactions for a month:

	£
Opening cash	100
Closing cash	50
Opening debtors	460
Closing debtors	420
Cash expenses	750
Bankings	4,220
Cash drawings	1,200
Cash sales	2,500
Credit sales	3,700
Irrecoverable debts written off	50
Discounts allowed	70

Write up the cash account and sales ledger control account to identify cash received from debtors.

For a suggested answer, see the 'Answers' section at the end of the book.

2.3 COMPREHENSIVE EXAMPLE

Yatton does not keep proper books of account. You ascertain that his bank payments and receipts during the year to 31 December 20X8 were as follows:

Bank account

	£		£
Balance 1 Jan 20X8	800	Cash withdrawn	200
Cheques for sales	2,500	Purchases	2,500
Cash banked	3,000	Expenses	800
		Drawings	1,300
		Delivery van	
		(bought 1 Oct 20X8)	1,000
		Balance 31 Dec 20X8	500
	6,300		6,300

From a cash notebook you ascertain that:

	£
Cash in hand 1 January 20X8	70
Cash takings	5,200
Purchases paid in cash	400
Expenses paid in cash	500
Cash in hand 31 December 20X8	30
Drawings by proprietor in cash	Unknown

You discover that assets and liabilities were as follows:

	1 Jan 20X8	31 Dec 20X8
	£	£
Debtors	300	450
Trade creditors	800	900
Expense creditors	100	150
Stock on hand	1,400	1,700

Yatton says that he has no hope of receiving an amount of £100 due from one customer and that an allowance for 10% of debtors would be prudent. Depreciation on the van is to be provided at the rate of 20% per annum.

You are required to prepare a trading and profit and loss account for the year to 31 December 20X8 and a balance sheet at that date.

2.4 SOLUTION TO COMPREHENSIVE EXAMPLE

Step 1 The sheets set aside for the final accounts can be inserted with main headings and certain information such as opening and closing stock can be inserted.

Step 2 The preparation of the opening balance sheet is usually achieved by drawing up a statement of opening capital using information given in the question about the opening balances. A careful scrutiny of the question reveals:

Workings

(W1) **Statement of opening capital**

	Dr	Cr
	£	£
Bank	800	
Cash	70	
Debtors	300	
Trade creditors		800
Expense creditors		100
Stock	1,400	
	2,570	900
	900	
	1,670	

Thus debits (assets) exceeds credits (liabilities) by £1,670.
Accordingly Yatton's business has net assets of £1,670, represented on the balance sheet by his opening capital account.

Step 3   Insert the opening balances into T-accounts if construction of the accounts is required. Leave plenty of space between the ledger accounts.

Thus a ledger account for Bank is not required as the question has already provided this. Accounts for stock and capital are not required as the information can be inserted immediately into the final accounts.

(W2)   **Cash**

	£		£
Balance b/d	70		

(W3)   **Sales ledger control account**

	£		£
Balance b/d	300		

(W4)   **Purchases ledger control account**

	£		£
		Balance b/d	800

(W5)   **Creditors – expenses**

	£		£
		Balance b/d	100

Step 4   Prepare the cash account, and post the cash and bank entries to the other accounts.

(W2)   **Cash**

	£		£
Balance b/d	70	Bank	3,000
Bank	200	Purchases ledger control account	400
Sales ledger control account	5,200	Expenses	500
		Drawings (bal fig)	1,540
		Balance c/d	30
	5,470		5,470

(W3)   **Sales ledger control account**

	£		£
Balance b/d	300	Bank	2,500
		Cash	5,200

(W4)   **Purchases ledger control account**

	£		£
Bank	2,500	Balance b/d	800
Cash	400		

(W5)   **Creditors – expenses**

	£		£
Bank	800	Balance b/d	100
Cash	500		

(W6) **Drawings**

	£		£
Bank	1,300		
Cash	1,540		

(W7) **Van cost**

	£		£
Bank	1,000		

Two points are worth noting at this stage:

(a) The commentary above is designed to show what happens after each step; there is no question of writing out each account on more than one occasion.

(b) If a question gives full details of the bank account (as this one does), there is no need to write it out again as part of your workings.

Step 5 Insert the closing balances and calculate the transfers to profit and loss.

(W4) **Purchase ledger control account**

	£		£
Bank	2,500	Balance b/d	800
Cash	400	Trading and profit and loss	
Balance c/d	900	(bal fig)	3,000
	3,800		3,800

(W5) **Creditors – expenses**

	£		£
Bank	800	Balance b/d	100
Cash	500	Trading and profit and loss	
Balance c/d	150	(bal fig)	1,350
	1,450		1,450

The sales ledger control account has not yet been closed, as there is an adjustment for irrecoverable debts still to be made.

Step 6 Carry out any further adjustments. These will be familiar, and the principles behind them are unchanged.

Bad debts

(W3) **Sales ledger control account**

	£		£
Balance b/d	300	Bank	2,500
Trading and profit and loss		Cash	5,200
(bal fig)	7,850	Irrecoverable debts	100
		Balance c/d (£450 – £100)	350
	8,150		8,150

(W8)   **Irrecoverable debts**

	£		£
Sales ledger control account	100	Profit and loss	135
Provision for doubtful debts	35		
	135		135

(W9)   **Provision for doubtful debts**

	£		£
Balance c/d (10% × £350)	35	Balance b/d	Nil
		Irrecoverable debts	35
	35		35

Depreciation

(W7)   **Van cost**

	£		£
Bank	1,000	Balance c/d	1,000

(W10)   **Van accumulated depreciation**

	£		£
Balance c/d	50	Profit and loss	50

Charge 20% × 3 months × £1,000 = £50

Drawings

(W6)   **Drawings**

	£		£
Bank	1,300	Capital	2,840
Cash	1,540		
	2,840		2,840

The remaining figures can be inserted into the final accounts.

Yatton
Trading and profit and loss account for year ended 31 December 20X8

	£	£
Sales (W3)		7,850
Cost of sales:		
Opening stock	1,400	
Purchases (W4)	3,000	
	4,400	
Less: Closing stock	1,700	
		2,700
Gross profit		5,150
Expenses (W5)	1,350	
Irrecoverable debts (W8)	135	
Depreciation of van (W10)	50	
		1,535
Net profit		3,615

Yatton
Balance sheet as at 31 December 20X8

	£	£	£
Fixed assets:			
Van at cost			1,000
Depreciation to date (W10)			50
			950
Current assets:			
Stocks		1,700	
Debtors (W3)	350		
Less: Allowance for doubtful debts	35		
		315	
Cash at bank		500	
Cash in hand		30	
		2,545	
Less: Current liabilities:			
Trade creditors	900		
Expense creditors	150		
		1,050	
			1,495
			2,445
Capital account:			
Capital at 1 January 20X8 (W1)			1,670
Add: Profit for year			3,615
			5,285
Less: Drawings in year (W6)			2,840
			2,445

2.5 SUMMARY

A methodical approach is required to assemble the incomplete information into a set of accounts and to find the missing figures on the way.

The steps to achieve this are:

(1)   Draft a proforma balance sheet and profit and loss account – slot in figures as you find them.

(2)   Calculate opening capital using opening net assets.

(3)   Use T-account workings for debtors, creditors and expenses with accruals or prepayments: insert opening balances.

(4)   Use T-account workings for cash and bank: insert cash transactions into the T-accounts from Step 3 when completing the cash and bank accounts.

(5)   Insert closing entries in all T-account workings and calculate the transfers to profit and loss account.

3   USING RATIOS AND PERCENTAGES

3.1   INTRODUCTION

In the example above, drawings was the only unknown in the cash account. What happens if there are **two** unknowns in the cash account – for example, drawings and takings? We can still construct the financial statements provided we are given some additional information.

3.2   GROSS PROFIT PERCENTAGE

Definition   **Gross profit percentage** $= \dfrac{\text{Gross profit}}{\text{Sales}} \times 100$

For instance, if we know that sales total £8,000 and the gross profit percentage is 25%, the following can be deduced:

	£	%
Sales	8,000 (given)	100
Less: Cost of sales	6,000	75
Gross profit	2,000	25 (given)

Example

Assume that we are told that the gross profit percentage is 30% and gross profit £6,000. What are sales and cost of sales?

Solution

	£	%
Sales	20,000	100
Less: Cost of sales	14,000	70
Gross profit	6,000 (given)	30 (given)

The percentages provided may have been calculated by reference to a similar business or from the previous years' results of this business.

3.3 MARGINS AND MARK-UPS

The gross profit percentage in the previous examples is also known as the **profit margin**. The percentage of profit is given by reference to sales.

Alternatively information on the **mark-up** may be given.

Definition **Mark-up percentage** $= \dfrac{\text{Gross profit}}{\text{Cost of sales}} \times 100$

Thus, if we know that cost of sales is £6,000 and the mark-up is one-third, we can set out the following:

	£	Ratio
Sales		
Cost of sales (given)	6,000	3
Gross profit		1

The 'ratio' is an alternative to using percentages. One-third is awkward to work with in percentage terms.

In ratio terms gross profit is one part to three parts costs.

Sales are therefore four parts (1 + 3), so total sales = $\dfrac{4}{3} \times £6,000 = £8,000$.

	£	Ratio
Sales	8,000	4
Cost of sales	6,000	3
Gross profit	2,000	1

Example

The sales of a business are £280,000 and there is a mark up on cost of 40%. What are the figures for cost of sales and gross profit?

Solution

	£	%
Sales	280,000	140
Cost of sales (280,000 × 100/140)	200,000	100
Gross profit (280,000 × 40/140)	80,000	40

3.4 CONVERTING MARGINS TO MARK-UPS AND VICE VERSA

Suppose we have been told that sales are £60,000 and the mark-up is 25%. The information given can be set out:

	£	%
Sales	60,000	
Cost of sales		100
Gross profit		25

Laying out the information as above should show that gross profit and cost of sales can still be worked out. In percentage terms sales are 125% (100 + 25). Profit is therefore $\frac{25}{125} \times £60,000 = £12,000$.

	£	%
Sales	60,000	125
Cost of sales	48,000	100
Gross profit	12,000	25

Conclusion   To convert mark-up to margin (where figures are percentages):

$$\text{Margin} = \frac{\text{Mark - up}}{\text{Mark - up} + 100}$$

To convert margin to mark-up:

$$\text{Mark-up} = \frac{\text{Margin}}{100 - \text{Margin}}$$

Example

Kendal, a sole trader, has provided you with the following information relating to the year ended 31 December 20X5.

(a)   He has not made a note of drawings or of cash received. The following items were paid from takings prior to banking:

Purchases	£760
Sundry expenses	£400

(b)   Kendal has estimated that his gross profit percentage is 20%.

(c)   His summarised bank account was as follows:

Bank

20X5		£	20X5		£
1 Jan	Balance b/d	1,700		Rent	1,000
	Bankings	16,940		Electricity	235
				Purchases	16,140
				Drawings	265
			31 Dec	Balance c/d	1,000
		18,640			18,640

(d)   Assets and liabilities were as follows:

	31 Dec 20X5	31 Dec 20X4
	£	£
Stock	4,800	5,600
Debtors	1,650	2,100
Creditors:		
Goods	1,940	1,640
Electricity	65	-
Cash float	2,400	170

(e)   He started paying rent in 20X5. A year's rent was paid in advance on 1 April 20X5.

You are required to prepare:

(a)   a trading and profit and loss account for the year ended 31 December 20X5

(b)   a balance sheet at that date.

Solution

Step 1	Sheets are reserved for the profit and loss account and balance sheet. In particular the trading account becomes a key working in situations where a margin or mark-up is given. Insert the opening and closing stock figures (if given) and also the margin percentages.
Step 2	Up till now the opening balance sheet has been completed in order to derive the opening capital balance. This working will now be done after the sales and purchases ledger control accounts have been completed as it only helps in finding one figure to go into the final accounts.
	We need to recognise that there may be time pressure in the examination and therefore we should spend our time first on the control accounts.
Step 3	Insert the opening balances in T-accounts.
Step 4	Deal with the information given as regards cash and bank transactions. Note that the bank account is not included in the workings, full details being given in the question.
	In addition, no ledger accounts have been shown for the various expenses. Instead workings have been shown on the face of the profit and loss account e.g. rent.
	There is a rent prepayment of £250 (three months rent). The expense is therefore £750. The derivation of the £750 (1,000 – 250) has been shown in brackets by the narrative on the profit and loss account.
	Where **simple** adjustments are to be made, this method allows the speedier preparation of the solution. Continue to use T-accounts if you need to.
Step 5	Insert the closing balances into the accounts. At this point the figure for purchases can be calculated.
	Having reached this far, a little more thought is now required.
	The position as regards unknowns can be summarised as follows:

Debtors	–	The figures for sales and receipts from debtors are unknown.
Cash	–	The figures for drawings and receipts from debtors are unknown.

This is where the gross profit percentage is utilised as follows:

	£	£	%
Sales		22,500	100
Less: Cost of goods sold:			
Opening stock	5,600 (given)		
Purchases	17,200 (calculation)		
	22,800		
Less: Closing stock	4,800 (given)		
		18,000	80
Gross profit		4,500	20 (given)

The sales figure has now been derived, leaving only one unknown in the debtors account – receipts from debtors, which is calculated as a balancing figure.

The resulting double entry (Dr Cash £22,950, Cr Sales ledger control £22,950) means that there is now only one unknown in the cash account, the drawings figure.

Workings

(W1)

Cash

	£		£
Balance b/d	170	Bank	16,940
Debtors	22,950	Creditors – goods	760
		Creditors – expenses	400
		Drawings (bal fig)	2,620
		Balance c/d	2,400
	23,120		23,120

(W2)

Sales ledger control

	£		£
Balance b/d	2,100	Cash (bal fig)	22,950
Trading and profit and loss	22,500	Balance c/d	1,650
	24,600		24,600

(W3)

Purchases ledger control

	£		£
Bank	16,140	Balance b/d	1,640
Cash	760	Trading and profit and loss	
Balance c/d	1,940	(bal fig)	17,200
	18,840		18,840

(W4)

Drawings

	£		£
Bank	265	Capital	2,885
Cash	2,620		
	2,885		2,885

(W5) **Statement of opening capital**

	Dr £	Cr £
Bank	1,700	
Stock	5,600	
Debtors	2,100	
Creditors – goods		1,640
Cash	170	
	9,570	1,640
	1,640	
	7,930	

(a) **Trading and profit and loss account for the year ended 31 December 20X5**

	£	£	%
Sales		22,500	100
Opening stock	5,600		
Purchases	17,200		
	22,800		
Closing stock	4,800		
Cost of sales		18,000	80
Gross profit		4,500	20
Rent (1,000 – 250)	750		
Electricity (235 + 65)	300		
Sundry	400		
		1,450	
Net profit		3,050	

(b) **Balance sheet as at 31 December 20X5**

	£	£
Current assets:		
Stock		4,800
Debtors		1,650
Prepayment		250
Bank		1,000
Cash		2,400
		10,100
Less: Current liabilities:		
Creditors:		
Goods	1,940	
Expenses	65	
		2,005
		8,095
Capital account:		
Opening capital		7,930
Add: Net profit		3,050
		10,980
Less: Drawings		2,885
		8,095

3.5 VARIATIONS ON THE THEME

No two incomplete records questions are quite the same, although the differences between them are often fairly small. Two examples of possible variations are:

(a)   Suppose that stock were destroyed in a fire and that there was enough information to calculate sales, purchases and opening stock. The gross profit percentage would enable sales to be converted to cost of sales. Closing stock could then be calculated as a balancing figure.

(b)   Suppose that a business always received a rebate from its suppliers amounting to 1% of purchases, and that in the current year the rebate amounted to £172. Clearly this tells us that purchases were £17,200. If cash paid to suppliers was unknown, it could be calculated as a balancing figure.

3.6 SUMMARY

Using mark-ups and gross profit percentages you can reconstruct a trading account and use these figures in your other workings:

Sales – a debit entry in the sales ledger control account (if they are all sales on credit).

Cost of sales can be used to find any of its components: **opening stock, closing stock** or **purchases**. Purchases is a credit entry in the purchase ledger control account.

CONCLUSION

No two incomplete records situations are exactly the same whether this is in practice or in examination questions. For examination questions what is required is a knowledge of the techniques covered in this chapter for reconstructing financial statements from a variety of types of incomplete information together with a thorough grasp and application of double entry bookkeeping.

The six step approach set out in the chapter is a good starting point in most questions although all six steps may not always be required. You should then be aware of the use of the cash and bank accounts, sales and purchases control accounts and any margins, mark-ups or other ratios that are given in the question. A good tip is that if a margin or mark-up is given in the question then it is highly likely that the only way to calculate either sales or purchases will be by applying this percentage to the information in the question.

KEY TERMS

Limited accounting records – records kept by a trader of certain transactions but additional information is required to prepare financial statements.

Incomplete accounting records – records which the trader has not fully completed or where no records at all have been kept of transactions.

Mark-up – gross profit calculated as a percentage of cost of sales.

Margin – gross profit calculated as a percentage of sales.

SELF TEST QUESTIONS

Paragraph

1   How can the profit of a business be measured if opening and closing
    net assets and drawings are known?   1.3

2   What is the sales ledger control account?   2.2

3   What are the six basic steps for the approach to an incomplete
    records question?   2.2

4   How is the gross profit percentage calculated?   3.2

5   How is a mark-up percentage calculated?   3.3

6   How is a cost mark-up converted to a profit margin?   3.4

7   If stock were destroyed in a fire but sales, purchases and opening
    stock could be calculated, how would the figure for stock destroyed be
    estimated?   3.5

PRACTICE QUESTION

B LETITSLIDE

B Letitslide is in business but does not keep proper books of account. In order to
prepare his trading and profit and loss account for the year ended 31 December 20X5
you are given the following information:

	20X5 1 Jan £	20X5 31 Dec £
Stock on hand	1,310	1,623
Debtors	268	412
Creditors for goods	712	914
Creditors for expenses	116	103

In addition, you are able to prepare the following summary of his cash and bank
transactions for the year:

Cash account

	£		£
Balance 1 Jan	62	Payments into bank	3,050
Shop takings	4,317	Purchases	316
Cheques cashed	200	Expenses	584
		Drawings	600
		Balance 31 Dec	29
	4,579		4,579

Bank account

	£		£
Balance 1 Jan	840	Cash withdrawn	200
Cheques from customers	1,416	Purchases	2,715
Cash paid in	3,050	Expenses	519
		Drawings	400
		Delivery van	
		(purchased 1 Sep)	900
		Balance 31 Dec	572
	5,306		5,306

In addition, Mr Letitslide says that he had taken goods for personal consumption and estimates those goods cost £100.

In considering the debtors, Mr Letitslide suggests that there is no hope of receiving an amount of £30 from one customer. There are other doubtful debts and a provision is to be made of 5% of the debtors after writing off the irrecoverable debt of £30.

Required:

Allowing depreciation on the delivery van of 20% per annum, prepare the accounts as requested and a balance sheet as at 31 December 20X5.

(25 marks)

EXAM-STYLE QUESTION 1

CYGNUS

Cygnus is a sole trader selling antiques from a rented shop. He has not kept proper accounting records for the year ended 31 January 20X1, in spite of his accountant's advice after the preparation of his accounts for the year ended 31 January 20X0.

His assets and liabilities at 31 January 20X0 and 31 January 20X1 were as follows:

	Reference to notes	31 January		
		20X0		20X1
		£	£	£
Assets				
Shop equipment				
Cost		14,800		
Less Depreciation	2	6,900	7,900	To be calculated
Stock			146,400	128,700
Trade debtors			14,400	15,700
Rent in advance	3		1,000	To be calculated
Cash at bank			–	4,850
Cash in hand			800	900
Liabilities				
Loan – Draco	4		24,000	12,000
Trade creditors			12,100	14,200
Accrued expenses	5		2,300	To be calculated
Bank overdraft			2,600	See summary below

The following summary shows bank receipts and payments by Cygnus.

Receipts	Notes	£	Cash book summary	Notes	£ Payments
Sales revenue banked		131,600	Opening balance		2,600
Proceeds of sale of shop equipment	2	300	Payments for purchases	3	81,400
			Rent paid		8,250
			Purchase of shop equipment	2	1,800
			Sundry expenses	5	18,600
			Interest on loan	4	2,400
			Repayment of loan	4	12,000
			Closing balance		4,850
		131,900			131,900

Before banking the shop takings, Cygnus took various amounts as drawings.

Notes:

(1)　Cygnus fixes his selling prices by doubling the cost of all items purchased.

(2)　During the year, Cygnus sold for £300 equipment that had cost £800, and had a written down value at 1 February 20X0 of £200. He purchased further equipment on 1 August 20X0 for £1,800.

Depreciation is charged at 10% per year on the straight-line basis, with no depreciation in the year of sale and proportionate depreciation in the year of purchase.

(3)　Rent is payable quarterly in advance on 1 January, 1 April, 1 July and 1 October each year. On 1 July 20X0, the annual rent was increased from £6,000 to £9,000.

(4)　The loan from Draco carries interest at 10% per year payable annually on 31 December. On 31 December 20X0, Cygnus repaid £12,000 of the loan. The balance is repayable on 31 December 20X4.

(5)　The accrued expenses at 31 January 20X0 consist of the £200 interest accrued on Draco's loan (see Note 4) and sundry expenses of £2,100. At 31 January 20X1, accruals for sundry expenses amounted to £3,300.

Required:

Prepare for Cygnus a trading and profit and loss account for the year ended 31 January 20X1 and a balance sheet as at that date.　　**(25 marks)**

EXAM-STYLE QUESTION 2

AMY AND BARBARA

Amy and Barbara are in partnership together. They have just completed their second year of trading and have asked for your help in preparing their final accounts for the year ended 31 December 20X6.

The partners have not been able to keep proper accounting records, but they are able to provide you with the following information.

At 1 January 20X6 the business had the following balances:

	Dr £	Cr £
Vehicles at cost	48,000	
Equipment at cost	90,000	
Provisions for depreciation		
Vehicles		12,000
Equipment		18,000
Stock	37,500	
Trade debtors	120,000	
Prepayments		
Advertising	3,000	
Insurance	6,000	
Cash at bank	15,000	
Trade creditors		22,500
Accruals		
Heating and lighting		4,500
Rent and rates		1,500
Capital accounts: Amy		120,000
Barbara		75,000
Current accounts: Amy		34,500
Barbara		31,500
	319,500	319,500

The business also made payments during the year for the following:

	£
Carriage inwards	6,750
Vehicle running expenses	20,250
Insurance	7,500
Heating and lighting	10,500
Telephone	5,250
Advertising	3,375
Rent and rates	22,500
Office supplies	1,875
Suppliers	300,000
	378,000

Additional information

(i)   Stock as at 31 December 20X6 was valued at £55,500.

(ii)   Receipts from customers were £600,000 and there was £82,500 outstanding from customers at 31 December 20X6.

(iii)   Settlement discounts of £7,500 were given to customers.

(iv)   The business owed £15,000 to suppliers as at 31 December 20X6.

(v)   Insurance of £1,500 was paid in advance at 31 December 20X6.

(vi)   During the year irrecoverable debts of £22,500 were written off.

(vii) Invoices totaling £3,375 relating to heating and lighting were unpaid at 31 December 20X6.

(viii) Depreciation on vehicles is to be provided at 25% of their written down value.

(ix)   Depreciation on equipment is to be provided at 20% on its original cost.

(x)   Interest on capital account balances is to be allowed at 10%.

(xi)   Cash drawings during the year were: Amy £90,000; Barbara £45,000.

(xii)   Interest on drawings is to be charged as follows: Amy £3,000; Barbara £1,500.

(xiii) Amy and Barbara have an agreement to share the profits in the ratio 2:1.

Required:

Prepare the following statements for the partnership:

(a)   the trading, profit and loss and appropriation account for the year ended 31
        December 20X6   **(23 marks)**

(b)   the partners' current accounts for the year ended 31 December 20X6 **(5 marks)**

(c)   the balance sheet as at 31 December 20X6.   **(12 marks)**

(You are advised to show any necessary supporting workings.)   **(Total: 40 marks)**

For suggested answers, see the 'Answers' section at the end of the book.

ANSWERS TO ACTIVITIES AND END-OF-CHAPTER QUESTIONS

CHAPTER 1

ACTIVITY 1

State the accounting concept(s) being applied in each of these situations:

(1)	Plant and machinery has a net book value of £24m, but it would only fetch £15m if it were to be sold.	Going concern. The accounts are prepared on the basis that the company will continue in business. The break-up value of plant and machinery is not relevant.
(2)	The plant and machinery is being depreciated over five years.	Accruals concept. The cost of a machine is apportioned to the periods expected to benefit from its use.
(3)	Stock is valued at £23m, even though it will probably sell for £35m.	Two concepts are being applied here: • The historic cost concept requires these assets to be recorded at the £23m cost incurred in acquiring them. • The prudence concept states that the £12m expected profit should not be recognised until it has been realised.
(4)	John Ltd has just bought the trade and assets of a Sally, rival unincorporated business. John has changed Sally's accounting policies, bringing them into line with the rest of the business.	This is the consistency concept. Similar items should be treated in a similar manner throughout the company.

EXAM-STYLE QUESTION

DEFINITIONS

(a) **Accruals**

The accruals concept is that revenue and expenses are recognised in the profit and loss account as they are earned or incurred, not as the money from the revenue income is received or as the payments for the expenses are paid. It also includes the matching concept that accrued costs should be set against related accrued revenues in arriving at the profit or loss for a period.

Example: Rent due but not yet paid is recognised as an expense of the period to which it relates and is therefore set against revenue for the same period, as an accrued expense. Similarly, rent paid in advance for a period falling in a future accounting period is treated as a prepayment (a short-term asset in the balance sheet) and will not be set as an expense against profit until the future period to which the expense relates.

(b)   **Consistency**

Accounting treatment of like items within each accounting period and from one period to the next should be the same, unless either a change is required by legislation or a new accounting standard, or unless circumstances change.

Example: Depreciation rates should remain the same from period to period unless there is clear evidence that changed circumstances require them to change.

(c)   **Prudence**

In preparing financial statements, the traditional view of prudence requires that provision should be made for all known liabilities, including those based on estimates because exact information is not available. Prudence also requires that revenue and profits should not be included in the profit and loss account until their realisation is reasonably certain. A more recent definition of prudence is a degree of caution in preparing financial information under conditions of uncertainty, so that income and assets are not overstated and expenses and liabilities are not understated.

Example: An allowance for doubtful debts should be created out of profits whenever the realisation of all trade debts in full is uncertain, and any increase in this allowance will be set against profits of the current period in which the increase is made. The effect of applying the prudence concept is to recognise losses in the financial statements now, even though it has not yet happened and might never happen.

CHAPTER 2

ACTIVITY 1

The following legal structures would be suitable:

Piano restorer

This should be undertaken as a sole trader. This is because:

- the initial capital investment is low and the level of working capital should also be low

- if things do not work out as planned, Charlie will be able to cease trading without incurring too many financial penalties.

Therefore, there are few benefits from operating as a limited company. The legal formalities and expenses of incorporation would not be worthwhile.

Piano manufacturer

This should be undertaken as a limited liability company.

This is because:

- the initial capital investment is high, and he will also be committing himself to a £36,000 lease

- the working capital tied up in construction working taking four staff for one month will also be high

- if things go wrong, Charlie will still have financial obligations to his landlord and staff. Also there is the possibility of legal action from his staff if any of them were to be injured in the factory.

Therefore, the costs of incorporation will be worth the peace of mind brought by limited liability.

EXAM-STYLE QUESTION

LIMITED COMPANIES COMPARISONS

(a) Trading as a limited company rather than a sole trader

Main advantages

(i) Liability of shareholders is limited to the amount invested by each of them, should the company run into trading difficulties.

(ii) Ownership is usually shared between a number of people, possibly a large number of people.

(iii) Transfer of ownership is easy, through the sale of shares.

(iv) Additional capital can be raised virtually at any time, by using more shares should the company framework allow.

(v) Potentially, tax advantages.

Main disadvantages

(i) Companies are governed by the requirements of the Companies Act in respect of presentation and auditing of accounts within deadlines and under specified formats.

(ii) Costs are involved in formation.

(iii) Greater reporting and recording requirements inevitably lead to greater running costs.

(iv) No longer accountable to themselves only but are now accountable to the owners (shareholders).

(b) Main types of share capital and their characteristics

There are two main types of share capital

(i) **Ordinary share capital**

These are the most common type of share issued by limited companies. They are known as equity shares and as such carry voting rights within the company, to the holder of the shares. Shareholders are the owners of the company, receiving a dividend from profits based on the shares held, should profits be sufficient to declare a dividend. The dividend is not a fixed amount but is proposed by the directors at Annual General Meeting and voted on by the ordinary shareholders.

(ii) **Preference share capital**

Unlike ordinary shares, preference shares are normally quoted at a fixed rate of dividend, such as 7% £1 preference shares. The preference shareholder, as the title suggests, is paid a dividend at the fixed rate, before ordinary shareholders. Usually, preference shares are cumulative which means if profits are not sufficient to allow a dividend to be paid in one financial year then that dividend is carried forward until such times as it can be paid. However, usually the preference share does not carry any voting rights.

Should the company suffer liquidation, however, they would again take preference over the return of their investment if the Articles of Association provide for this, which is usually the case.

CHAPTER 4

ACTIVITY 1

Straight plc: Profit and loss account year ending 31 March 20X6

		£000
Turnover		28,297
Cost of sales (W1)		(18,412)
Gross profit		9,885
Distribution costs		(2,020)
Administrative expenses		(635)
Operating profit		7,230
Interest received and similar items	Note 1	(104)
Profit on ordinary activities after taxation		7,126
Taxation	Note 2	(1,868)
Profit for the financial year		5,258

Note 1 – Interest received and similar items

	£000
Investment income	246
Debenture interest expense	(300)
Bank interest expense	(50)
	(104)

Note 2 – Taxation

	£000
Corporation tax charge for the year	1,924
(Over) Under provision in previous years	(56)
	1,868

Note 3 – Dividends

		£000
Interim dividend paid of	20 pence per share	800
Final dividend proposed of	60 pence per share	2,400

Straight plc: Balance sheet as at 31 March 20X6

		£000	£000
Fixed assets			
Investments			2,885
Tangible fixed assets	Note 4		11,357
			14,242
Current assets			
Stocks		1,263	
Debtors	Note 5	3,122	
Cash		110	
		4,495	
Creditors: Amounts due within 1 year	Note 6	(5,381)	

	£000	£000
Net current assets (liabilities)		(886)
Total assets less current liabilities		13,356
Creditors: Amounts due after one year		(3,000)
Net assets		10,356
Capital and reserves		
Called up share capital		2,000
Share premium		300
P&L Reserve (3,598 + 5,258 – 800)		8,056
Total shareholders' funds		10,356

Notes to the accounts

Note 4 – Tangible fixed assets

	£000
Cost or valuation	15,753
Depreciation	(4,396)
Net Book Value	11,357

Note 5 – Debtors

	£000
Trade debtors	2,967
Prepayments	132
Other debtors	23
	3,122

Note 6 – Creditors: amounts falling due within one year

	£000
Bank overdrafts	1,978
Trade creditors	756
Accruals (300 + 423)	723
Corporation Tax	1,924
	5,381

(*Tutorial note:* The final dividend had been proposed but not declared at the year-end and therefore it is not accrued in the financial statements but only disclosed in the notes.)

(W1) **Cost of sales**

	£000
Opening stock	3,206
Purchases	8,162
Manufacturing wages	7,333
Other manufacturing costs	974
Less closing stock	(1,263)
	18,412

EXAM-STYLE QUESTION 1

FLOYD LTD

Profit and loss account for year ended 31 March 20X5

	£
Sales	998,600
Cost of sales (W1)	830,740
Gross profit	167,860
Administrative expenses (W1)	100,741
Debenture interest (9% × 75,000)	6,750
Profit before taxation	60,369
Corporation tax	31,200
Profit for the financial year	29,169

Balance sheet as at 31 March 20X5

	Cost £	Depn £	£
Fixed assets:			
Tangible assets – plant (W3)	307,400	115,340	192,060
Current assets:			
Stock		61,070	
Debtors	52,030		
Less: Allowance	2,601		
		49,429	
Cash at bank		41,118	
Cash in hand		126	
		151,743	
Creditors: Amounts falling due within one year:			
Creditors		38,274	
Current taxation		31,200	
Debenture interest accrued		6,750	
		76,224	
Net current assets			75,519
Total assets less current liabilities			267,579
Creditors: Amounts falling due after more than one year:			
9% debentures 20X9			75,000
			192,579
Capital and reserves:			
Called up share capital: 25p ordinary shares			100,000
Share premium account			20,000
Profit and loss account (W4)			72,579
			192,579

KAPLAN PUBLISHING

Workings

(W1)

	Cost of sales £	Administrative expenses £
Per question	800,000	100,000
Bad debts (W2)		741
Depreciation (W3)	30,740	
	830,740	100,741

(W2)   **Allowance for doubtful debts account**

	£		£
Profit and loss account:		Balance b/d	1,860
Balance c/d 5% × 52,030	2,601	Administrative costs	741
	2,601		2,601

(W3)   **Accumulated depreciation account**

	£		£
		Balance b/d	84,600
		Profit and loss account:	
		Cost of sales	
Balance c/d	115,340	10% × 307,400	30,740
	115,340		115,340

(W4)   Profit and loss account

	£
Profit and loss account b/d	45,910
Profit for the financial year	29,169
Dividends paid	(2,500)
	72,579

EXAM-STYLE QUESTION 2

MOORFOOT

Moorfoot Limited
Profit and loss account for the year ended 30 June 20X1

	£000
Sales revenue (13,600 + 7)	13,607
Cost of sales (W1)	(7,988)
Gross profit	5,619
Distribution costs (W1)	(1,948)
Administrative expenses (W1)	(2,156)
Operating profit	1,515
Interest payable (10% × 1,000)	(100)
Profit for the financial year	1,415

Moorfoot Limited
Balance sheet as at 30 June 20X1

	£000	£000	£000
Fixed assets			
Tangible assets (W2)			
Land			1,510
Buildings			7,114
Warehouse and office equipment			1,240
Motor vehicles			640
			10,504
Current assets			
Stock		1,660	
Trade debtors (810 + 7 – 30 allowance for doubtful debts – 6 irrecoverable debts)		781	
Prepayments		130	
Cash		140	
		2,711	
Creditors, amounts falling due within one year			
Trade creditors (820 + 18)	838*		
Accruals	360*		
		1,198	
			1,513
Total assets less current liabilities			12,017
Creditors, amounts falling due after more than one year			
Debenture loan			(1,000)
			11,017
Capital and reserves			
Called up share capital			1,200
Share premium account			2,470
Profit and loss account (6,772 + 1,415 – 480 –360)			7,347
			11,017

*Alternatively these items may be shown as:

Trade creditors	820
Accruals (360 + 18)	378

Workings

(W1) **Profit and loss account headings**

	Cost of sales £000	Distribution costs £000	Administrative expenses £000
Purchases (8,100 + 18)	8,118		
Stock 1 July 20X0	1,530		
Distribution costs (1,460 + 120 – 60)		1,520	
Administrative expenses (1,590 + 190 – 70)			1,710
Irrecoverable debts written off			6
Increase in allowance for doubtful debts (30 – 18)			12
Depreciation			
Buildings 2% × 8,300		83	83
Equipment 15% × 1800		135	135
Vehicles 25% × 1,680		210	210
Stock 30 June 20X1	(1,660)		
	7,988	1,948	2,156

(W2) **Tangible assets**

	Land £000	Buildings £000	Warehouse and office equipment £000	Motor vehicles £000
Per trial balance				
Cost	1,510	8,300	1,800	1,680
Accumulated depreciation b/f	–	(1,020)	(290)	(620)
Depreciation for year	–	(166)	(270)	(420)
Net book value at year end	1,510	7,114	1,240	640

CHAPTER 5

ACTIVITY 1

(a) **Share capital: 25 pence ordinary shares**

	Number	£		Number	£
			Brought forward	900,000	225,000
			New issue for cash	500,000	125,000
Carried down	1,400,000	350,000			
	1,400,000	350,000		1,400,000	350,000

Share premium

	£		£
		Brought forward	75,000
		New issue for cash	175,000
Carried down	250,000		
	250,000		250,000

	Price £	Proceeds £
Nominal value	0.25	125,000
Share premium	0.35	175,000
Issue price	0.60	300,000

500,000 shares were issued.

(b)　　　　　　　　**Bradawl Ltd – Balance sheet extracts**

		£
Net assets	£456,789 + £300,000 proceeds	756,789
Capital and reserves		
Called up share capital	1,400,000 ordinary shares of 25 pence each	350,000
Share premium account		250,000
P&L reserve		156,789
		756,789

ACTIVITY 2

(a)　　　　　　　　　　　**Share capital**

	£		£
		Balance b/d (200,000 × 50p)	100,000
		Profit and loss account	
Balance c/d	125,000	(50,000 × 50p)	25,000
	125,000		125,000

Profit and loss

	£		£
Share capital	25,000	Balance b/d	230,000
Balance c/d	205,000		
	230,000		230,000

(b)　　　　　　　　　　　　**Bank**

	£		£
Share capital	25,000		
Share premium	15,000		

Share capital

	£		£
Balance c/d	125,000	Balance b/d	100,000
		Bank	25,000
	125,000		125,000

Share premium

	£		£
Balance c/d	15,000	Bank	15,000

ACTIVITY 3

(a)   **Profit and loss account for the year ended 31 December 20X8**

	£	£
Operating profit		180,000
Finance cost (60,000 × 8%)		(4,800)
Profit before taxation		175,200
Corporation tax		70,000
Profit for the financial year		105,200

(b)   **Balance sheet (extracts) as at 31 December 20X8**

	£
Creditors: amounts falling due within one year	
Corporation tax	70,000
Accrued preference dividend	2,400
	72,400
Creditors: amounts falling due after more than one year	
– £1 8% preference shares	60,000
Capital and reserves	
Called up share capital	
– 50p ordinary shares	75,000
Share premium account	25,000
Plant replacement reserve	50,000
Profit and loss account	172,200
	322,200

Statement of reserves

	Profit and loss	Plant replacement	Share premium
	£	£	£
Balance at 1 January 20X8	90,000	30,000	25,000
Profit for the year	105,200		
Dividends paid	(3,000)		
Transfer	(20,000)	20,000	
Balance at 31 December 20X8	172,200	50,000	25,000

ACTIVITY 4

Profit and loss account

	£000
Profit on ordinary activities before tax	200
Tax (Note 1)	54
Profit for the year	146

Note 1 – Tax charge

	£000
Corporation tax on current year profits at X%	56
Less: over provision in previous year	(2)
	54

Note 2 – Dividends

	£000
Interim dividend paid	5
Final dividend proposed	17
	22

ACTIVITY 5

Dither Ltd: Profit and loss account of 20X2

	£000
Profit before tax	1,036
Taxation Note 1	(364)
Profit after tax	672

Note 1 – Tax charge

	£000
Corporation tax charge on the profits for the year at XX %	353
Under (over) provision for tax in previous years	25
Deferred tax charge (credit)	(14)
	364

Dither Ltd: Balance sheet for 20X2

	£000	£000
Fixed assets		1,369
Current assets	923	
Creditors due within one year *Note 2*	(594)	
Net current assets		329
		1,698
Creditors due after one year: Long-term loan		(200)
Provision for deferred tax *Note 3*		(33)
		1,465
Share capital and reserves		
Ordinary shares		100
Retained profits (693 + 672)		1,365
		1,465

Note 2 – Creditors due within one year

	£000
Sundry	241
Corporation tax	353
	594

Note 3 – Provision for deferred tax

	£000
Opening provision	47
Charge (credit) for the year	(14)
Closing provision	33

PRACTICE QUESTION

X LTD 20X6

Extract from profit and loss account for the year ended 31 December 20X6

	£	£
Taxation		
UK corporation tax at X%	60,000	
Deferred taxation	20,000	
		80,000

Extract from balance sheet as at 31 December 20X6

	£
Creditors: amounts falling due within one year	
Corporation tax	60,000
Provisions for liabilities	
Deferred taxation *Note 1*	70,000

Notes to the accounts

(1)   Deferred taxation provision

	£
Balance brought forward	50,000
Transfer from profit and loss account	20,000
Balance carried forward	70,000

EXAM-STYLE QUESTION

RESERVES

Tutorial note: In practice this type of question would appear as an 'add on' to a longer question about limited company accounts.

(a)   (i)   Reserves are balances in a company's balance sheet forming part of the equity interest and representing surpluses or gains, whether realised or not.

(ii)   **Share premium account**

The surplus arising when shares are issued at a price in excess of their par value.

Revaluation reserve

The unrealised gain when the amount at which fixed assets are carried is increased above cost.

(Other reserves could be described.)

(b)   A **bonus issue** is the conversion of reserves into share capital, with new shares being issued to existing members in proportion to their shareholdings, without any consideration being given by the shareholders.

A **rights issue** is also an issue of new shares to existing members in proportion to their shareholdings, but with payment being made by the shareholders for the shares allotted to them.

The fundamental difference between them is that a rights issue raises funds for the company whereas a bonus issue does not.

CHAPTER 6

ACTIVITY 1

	Cost	Life	Charge	
	£m		£m	
Land	45.0	90 years	0.5	*over the remaining life of the lease*
Main building	80.0	50 years	1.6	*over its useful life (until obsolete)*
Frontage	15.0	10 years	1.5	*over its useful life*
Total	140.0		3.6	

ACTIVITY 2

Straight line method

Annual depreciation charge $\dfrac{£(4,200-200)}{4}$ = £1,000 pa

Reducing balance method

	£
Cost	1,000
Year 1 (£1,000 × 50%)	(500)
NBV	500
Year 2 (£500 × 50%)	(250)
NBV	250
Year 3 (£250 × 50%)	(125)
NBV	125
Year 4 (£125 × 50%)	(63)
Final NBV	62

One particular feature of the reducing balance method is that the net book value never equals zero.

ACTIVITY 3

	Usage	Depreciation charge
		£
Year 1	12,000 hours	$\dfrac{12,000}{60,000}$ × £1,800 = 360
Year 2	9,000 hours	$\dfrac{9,000}{60,000}$ × £1,800 = 270

One advantage of this method is that the original cost of the asset is allocated over accounting periods according to usage of assets. The depreciation charge becomes a function of output or usage rather than of time. Where there is variable use of the asset over time, it can be argued that this method satisfies the matching concept more satisfactorily than the earlier methods.

ACTIVITY 4

The sum of the digits over five years is 15: (5 + 4 + 3 + 2 + 1 = 15)

The annual charges will be as follows:

Year	Cost	Weighting	Charge
1	£72,000	5/15	£24,000
2	£72,000	4/15	£19,200
3	£72,000	3/15	£14,400
4	£72,000	2/15	£9,600
5	£72,000	1/15	£4,800

ACTIVITY 5

(a)   Prepare the T-accounts to record the disposal of this asset.

Fixed asset at cost account   (B/S)

		£			£
Balance b/d		39,000	Disposal a/c	a	39,000
		39,000			39,000

Fixed asset: Provision for depreciation   (B/S)

		£			£
Disposal a/c	b	21,000	Balance b/d	W1	21,000
		21,000			21,000

Cash at bank account   (B/S)

		£		£
Proceeds of disposal	c	12,300		

Disposal of fixed assets account

		£			£
Asset at cost	a	39,000	Provision for deprecation	b	21,000
			Proceeds	c	12,300
		39,000			33,300
			Loss on disposal		5,700
		39,000			39,000

(W1) **Opening depreciation**

The annual charge was (£39,000 cost – £4,000 residual value) / 5 years = £7,000 per annum.

Depreciation will have been charged in 20X1, X2 and X3. This totals £21,000.

(b)   Draft the journal to record this transaction.

Account	Dr	Cr
Fixed asset disposal	39,000	
Machine at cost		39,000
Fixed asset disposal		21,000
Machine: provision for depreciation	21,000	
Cash at bank	12,300	
Fixed asset disposal		12,300
Fixed asset disposal		5,700
P&L: Loss on disposal	5,700	

ACTIVITY 6

Fixed assets at cost: Elevators

		£				£
Balance b/d 20X9		45,000	Disposal a/c	**a**		45,000
Cost of fixed asset: Part-exchange	**c**	20,000				
Cost of fixed asset: Cash		79,000	Balance c/d			99,000
		144,000				144,000
Balance b/d 20Y0		99,000				

Provision for depreciation on fixed assets: Elevators

		£				£
Disposal a/c	**b**	12,000	Balance b/d 20X9	*W1*		12,000
			Charge for the year	*W2*		3,000
Balance c/d		3,000				
		15,000				15,000
			Balance b/d 20Y0			3,000

Disposal of fixed assets account   (P&L)

		£				£
Elevator at cost	**a**	45,000	Provision for deprecation	**b**		12,000
			Proceeds: Part-exchange	**c**		20,000
		45,000				32,000
Profit on disposal			Loss on disposal			13,000
		45,000				45,000

(W1) Opening depreciation

The annual charge was (£45,000 cost – £5,000 residual value) / 20 years = £2,000 per annum.

Depreciation will have been charged in 20X3, X4, X5, X6, X7, X8. This totals £12,000.

(W2) Depreciation charge for 20X9

The annual charge is (£99,000 cost – £9,000 residual value) / 30 years = £3,000 per annum.

ACTIVITY 7

Buildings at cost / valuation

	£		£
Opening	300,000		
Revaluation reserve	420,000		
		c/d	720,000
	720,000		720,000
b/d	720,000		

Depreciation on buildings

	£			£
		Opening	*(£300,000 × 10/50)*	60,000
Revaluation reserve	60,000			
	60,000			60,000

Revaluation reserve

	£		£
		Buildings at cost	420,000
		Accumulated depreciation	60,000
c/d	480,000		
	480,000		480,000
		b/d	480,000

The future depreciation charge will be:

$$\frac{\text{Revalued amount less residual value}}{\text{Remaining useful life of the asset}} = \frac{£720,000}{(50 \text{ years} - 10 \text{ years})} = £18,000 \text{ per annum}$$

ACTIVITY 8

Charlie plc – Extracts from the balance sheet – Goodwill

			20X1 £000	20X2 £000
Opening balance			–	2,880
Acquisitions		(a)	3,000	–
Amortisation	P&L	(b)	(120)	(120)
Impairment	P&L		–	–
Closing balance	B/S		2,880	2,760

Dude's business is old fashioned and well established, and so a 25-year amortisation period is considered to be appropriate. Regular impairment reviews take place to ensure that the carrying value is not in excess of the recoverable amount of the goodwill.

(a)   Calculation of the cost and amortisation   £

Fair value of the consideration	9,000,000
Less: Fair value of the net assets acquired	(6,000,000)
Goodwill at cost	3,000,000

(b)   Annual amortisation charge over 25 years   120,000

EXAM-STYLE QUESTION

ARBALEST

(a)   **Movements on reserves**

	Share premium £000	Revaluation reserve £000	Retained earnings £000	Total £000
At 30 September 20X6	400		4,060	4,460
Rights issue	1,000			1,000
Bonus issue	(1,400)		(600)	(2,000)
Revaluation of assets		500		500
Retained profit for year			370	370
At 30 September 20X7	nil	500	3,830	4,330

Workings

(W1)   Share premium increases on the rights issue by 2 million shares × 50 pence per share.

(W2)   The bonus issue is of 4 million shares with a nominal value of £2,000,000. The share premium will be used up entirely, leaving £600,000 to be transferred from the profit and loss reserve (retained earnings).

(b)   **Movements on fixed assets**

			Cost	
	Land £000	Buildings £000	Plant and machinery £000	Total £000
At 30 September 20X6	2,000	1,500	2,800	6,300
Additions	600	2,400	1,600	4,600
Disposals			(1,000)	(1,000)
Revaluation	500			500
At 30 September 20X7	3,100	3,900	3,400	10,400
Depreciation				
At 30 September 20X6	nil	450	1,000	1,450
Charge for year	nil	46	220	266
Disposals			(800)	(800)
At 30 September 20X7	nil	496	420	916
Net book value 30 September 20X7	3,100	3,404	2,980	9,484

Calculation of depreciation charges

	£000
Buildings:	
2% of 1,500,000	30
2% of 2,400,000 × 4/12	16
	46
Plant and machinery:	
10% of (2,800,000 – 1,000,000)	180
10% of 1,600,000 × 3/12	40
	220

CHAPTER 7

ACTIVITY 1

Range	Cost	NRV	Balance sheet value
	£	£	£
Alpha	480	510	480
Beta	220	200	200
Gamma	170	220	170
Delta	150	200	150
Epsilon	600	450	450
			1,450

The stock will be valued at the lower of cost and net realisable value, which is £1,450.

EXAM-STYLE QUESTION

SAMPI

(a)   **Value of stock using FIFO**

	Opening stock units	Deliveries from factory 8 March units	22 March units
	4,000	3,800	6,000
Sales			
12 March sales	(4,000)	(1,000)	
	–	2,800	
18 March sales		(2,000)	
		800	
24 March		(800)	(2,200)
		–	3,800
28 March			(2,000)
			1,800

The closing stock is therefore:

	£
1,800 at £18	32,400

(b) **Value of stock using weighted average cost basis**

	Number of units	Weighted average cost £	Total value of closing stock £
Opening stock	4,000	13.00	52,000
8 March	3,800	15.00	57,000
Balance	7,800	13.974	109,000
12 March	(5,000)	13.974	(69,870)
	2,800	13.974	39,130
18 March	(2,000)	13.974	(27,948)
	800	13.974	11,182
22 March	6,000	18.00	108,000
	6,800	17.527	119,182
24 March	(3,000)	17.527	(52,581)
	3,800	17.527	66,601
28 March	(2,000)	17.527	(35,054)
	1,800	17.527	31,547

Note: There are some rounding differences in these calculations, because average costs are taken to just 3 decimal places.

Summary:

		£
Stock value:	FIFO	32,400
	Weighted average cost	31,547

CHAPTER 8

ACTIVITY 1

The first two items are potential liabilities. For each of the items, ask two questions:

(i) Is there a present obligation as the result of a past event?

(ii) Is a transfer of economic benefits in settlement probable?

A provision is recognised if the answer to both questions is yes.

(a) Present obligation? – Yes. The past event is the sale of the product, which gives rise to a constructive obligation (see the definition above).

Transfer of benefits probable? – Yes.

Conclusion – Recognise a provision.

(b) Present obligation? – This is uncertain, but there is a possible obligation.

Transfer of benefits probable? – No, because the chances of losing the case are only fifty fifty (probable means more likely than not).

Conclusion – Do not recognise a provision. This is a contingent liability and should be disclosed.

(c) This is a contingent asset. It cannot be recognised, because the likelihood of the gain is only probable, not virtually certain. However, it should be disclosed.

ACTIVITY 2

(a) (1) The loss of the building will not be adjusted for because it does not affect the facts as at the year-end. However, it must be disclosed because it would be misleading to hide such a loss from the shareholders.

(2) This net realisable value provision relates to the value of stock at the year end. Stocks will be reduced in value by £14,000.

(3) The £64,000 outstanding at the year-end must be adjusted for. The later invoices, totalling £171,000, will be disclosed as material non-adjusting items.

(4) The repayment of the loan is a non-adjusting event. However, it will require disclosure as it is the reversal of a window dressing transaction

Overall, Kamoso has got an uncertain future and the going concern concept must be called into doubt. This might require redrafting the accounts on break-up basis.

(b) The draft and revised balance sheets of Kamoso Ltd are as follows:

Kamoso Ltd Balance sheet as at 31 December 20X5

	Draft				Revised	
	£000	£000			£000	£000
Fixed assets		1,126				1,126
Current assets						
Stocks	238		(2)	14 Cr	224	
Trade debtors	436		(3)	64 Cr	372	
Cash	400				400	
	1,074				996	
Current liabilities						
Sundry	700				700	
	700				700	
Net current (liabilities) assets		374				296
Capital employed		1,500				1,422
Ten year loan		(500)				(500)
Net assets		1,000				922

EXAM-STYLE QUESTION

GERMAINE LTD

(a) (i) For an adjustment to be required to the financial statements the event must be material, and either provide additional evidence of conditions existing at the balance sheet date or cast doubt on the application of the going concern concept to the whole or a material part of the entity.

(ii) (1) A possible obligation that arises from past events and whose existence will be confirmed only by the occurrence of one or more uncertain future events not wholly within the entity's control; or

(2) A contingent liability is a present obligation that arises from past events but is not recognised because:

• it is not probable that a transfer of economic benefits will be required to settle the obligation; or

- the amount of the obligation cannot be measured with sufficient reliability.

Note: This definition is given in FRS 12. Your own answer, of course, can give a definition in your own words, but check that you have covered all the necessary points.

(iii) The following table summarises the accounting treatment required by FRS 12 for material contingencies:

Degree of probability	Contingent loss	Contingent gain
Probable	Recognise in financial statements	Disclose by note in financial statements
Possible	Disclose by note in financial statements	No disclosure
Remote	No disclosure	No disclosure

(iv) The date the financial statements are approved by the board of directors.

(b) (i) A provision of £30,000 is required for the legal costs which will be incurred in any case, because this is an action relating to a condition which existed at the balance sheet date.

As the outcome of the case is 70%, this will be categorised as 'possible' rather than 'probable'. The damages and costs to be incurred if the case is lost would be required by FRS 12 to be disclosed by note.

Journal entry:

	£	£
Profit and loss account	30,000	
Provision for legal costs		30,000

Provision for legal costs in relation to action brought by customer.

Disclosure note

A customer has brought an action against the company claiming damages for alleged supply of faulty components. Your company will vigorously defend the action and expects to succeed. If the customer's action is successful, damages and costs could amount to £180,000. A provision of £30,000 has been made to cover costs which will be incurred whether the action is successful or not.

(ii) This is an event requiring adjustment and the allowance for doubtful debts should be reduced by £84,000 in the financial statements.

	£	£
Provision for doubtful debts	84,000	
Profit and loss account		84,000

Reduction in provision for doubtful debts following payment after the balance sheet date.

CHAPTER 9

ACTIVITY 1

(a) **Phibbs plc – Statement of total recognised gains and losses for the year ended 31 December 20X9**

	20X9	20X8
	£m	£m
Profit for the financial year	38	28
Unrealised surplus on revaluation of property	2	1
Total recognised gains and losses relating to the year	40	29

(b) **Reconciliation of movements in shareholders' funds for the year ended 31 December 20X9**

	20X9	20X8
	£m	£m
Profit for the financial year	38	28
Dividends	(18)	(15)
	20	13
Other recognised gains and losses relating to the year (net)	2	1
New share capital subscribed	12	4
Net addition to shareholders' funds	34	18
Opening shareholders' funds	222	204
Closing shareholders' funds	256	222

(c) **Note of historical cost profits and losses for the year ended 31 December 20X9**

	20X9	20X8
	£m	£m
Reported profit before taxation	50	35
Difference between a historical cost depreciation charge and the actual depreciation charge for the year calculated on the revalued amount	3	2
	53	37
Historical cost profit for the year retained after taxation and dividends	23	15

EXAM-STYLE QUESTION

LEONARDO LTD

(a)

Leonardo Ltd

Profit and loss account for the year ended 30 September 20X8

	£000
Turnover	6,840
Cost of sales (working)	(3,988)
Gross profit	2,852
Distribution costs (880 + 50 + 400)	(1,330)
Administrative expenses	(590)
Cost of fundamental reorganisation	(560)
Profit on sale of property	1,200
Operating profit	1,572
Interest payable	(300)
Profit on ordinary activities before taxation	1,272
Tax on profit on ordinary activities	(300)
Profit for the financial year	972

Note: Operating profit is calculated after charging an exceptionally large irrecoverable debt of £400,000 which has been written off.

Tutorial note: Credit should also be given if the irrecoverable and doubtful debt adjustments are made within administrative expenses. The cost of the fundamental reorganisation and the profit on the sale of property are both sufficiently significant to be disclosed as separate items on the face of the profit and loss account.

Working: Calculation of cost of sales

	£000
Opening stock	1,200
Purchases	3,670
	4,870
Less: Closing stock (950 – 68)	882
	3,988

(b)   Additional statements or notes

   (i)   **Statement of total recognised gains and losses**

   This statement contains:

   –   profit for the financial year

   –   unrealised losses or gains on revaluation of assets

   –   prior year adjustments.

   (ii)   **Reconciliation of movements in shareholders' funds**

   This statement contains:

   –   opening and closing shareholders' funds

   –   profit for the financial year

   –   dividends paid for the year

   –   new share capital issued

   –   goodwill written off.

(iii) **Note of historical cost profits and losses**

This note shows what the profit or loss would have been if the profit and loss account had been prepared on a strict historical cost basis.

It contains:

– reported profit before taxation

– adjustment to gains on assets sold in the period to include revaluation gains of previous years

– adjustment to depreciation for the difference between the actual depreciation charge on revalued assets and what depreciation would have been if calculated on historical cost.

CHAPTER 10

ACTIVITY 1

		£
Operating profit		436,000
Add back depreciation		153,000
Less profit on disposal of fixed assets		(47,000)
		542,000
Decrease in stocks	*(64 – 78)*	14,000
Increase in debtors	*(83 – 59)*	(24,000)
Increase in creditors	*(157 – 102)*	55,000
Net cash inflow from operating activities		587,000

ACTIVITY 2

	£
Investment income received	24,000
Interest paid	(42,000)
Preference dividends paid	(53,000)
	(71,000)

Income received	£
Opening debtor	12,000
Add: Investment income	19,000
Less: Closing debtor	(7,000)
Cash received	24,000

Interest paid	£	Dividends paid	£
Opening accrual	19,000	Opening creditor	35,000
Add: Interest charge	55,000	Add: Charge	40,000
Less: Closing accrual	(32,000)	Less: Closing creditor	(22,000)
Cash paid	42,000	Cash paid	53,000

ACTIVITY 3

		£
Opening provision	from the balance sheet	163,000
Add: Tax charge	from the P&L account	135,000
Less: Closing provision	from the balance sheet	(148,000)
Cash paid		150,000

ACTIVITY 4

(a)

Westminster Ltd	£
Cost of disposals	143,000
Less: depreciation	(57,000)
NBV of disposals	86,000
Add: Profit on disposal	66,000
Proceeds of disposal	152,000

(b)

Hammersmith Ltd	£
Cost of disposals	199,000
Less: depreciation	(78,000)
NBV of disposals	121,000
Less: Loss on disposal	(64,000)
Proceeds of disposal	57,000

ACTIVITY 5

		£
Proceeds from share issues	(W1)	180
Payments to redeem loans	(W2)	(365)
		(185)

(W1) Proceeds of share issues

	This year £	Last year £
Ordinary share capital	200	80
Share premium	100	40
	300	120
Increase (proceeds of issue)	180	

(W2) Repayment of loans

	Current	+	Deferred	£
Opening loans	190	+	350	540
Closing loans	55	+	120	175
Decrease	An outflow of cash			365

ACTIVITY 6

	£
Operating profit	187,000
Less: Interest charge	(52,000)
Less: Tax charge	(35,000)
Profit after tax	100,000

The dividend is deducted from post tax profits, and so in this example it is not added back to the profit after tax.

ACTIVITY 7

(1) Calculate the proceeds of disposal.

NBV of £253,000 less Loss of £67,000 = Proceeds of £186,000

(2) Calculate the revaluation gain for the year.

This is the £130,000 increase in the revaluation reserve.

(3) Schedule out the movement in the net book value of fixed assets.

(4) Calculate the depreciation charge as a balancing figure.

Fixed assets at Net book value		£
Opening balance at NBV		900,000
Add: Additions at cost		224,000
Add: Revaluation		130,000
Less: Disposals at NBV		(253,000)
Less: Depreciation	balancing figure	(201,000)
Closing balance at NBV		800,000

(5) Prepare the capital expenditure section of LSTM's cash flow statement.

	£
Proceeds from the disposal of fixed assets	186,000
Payments to acquire fixed assets	(224,000)
	(38,000)

EXAM-STYLE QUESTION 1

CHARLTON LTD

Reconciliation of operating profit to net cash inflow from operating activities

	£
Operating profit (17,215 + 900)	18,115
Depreciation charge	2,363
Profit on sale of fixed asset (W1)	(419)
Increase in stocks (30,918 – 27,200)	(3,718)
Increase in debtors (18,363 – 15,132)	(3,231)
Increase in creditors (10,416 – 3,621)	6,795
Net cash inflow from operating activities	19,905

Cash flow statement for the year ended 31 December 20X6

	£	£
Net cash inflow from operating activities		19,905
Returns on investments and servicing of finance		
Interest paid (given in P&L a/c)	(900)	
Net cash outflow from servicing of finance		(900)
Tax paid (W2)		(5,200)
Capital expenditure		
Payments to acquire tangible fixed assets (W1)	(10,911)	
Receipts from sales of tangible fixed assets		
(given in question)	1,614	
Net cash outflow from capital expenditure		(9,297)
		4,508
Equity dividends paid		(8,400)
Net cash outflow before financing		(3,892)
Financing		
Issue of shares (10,000 + 2,000)	12,000	
Redemption of debentures	(10,000)	
Net cash inflow from financing		2,000
Decrease in cash		(1,892)

Note: Analysis of changes in net debt

	At 1 Jan 20X6	Cash flows	At 31 Dec 20X6
	£	£	£
Cash at bank	4,016	(1,892)	2,124
Debt due within 1 year	(10,000)	10,000	–
	(5,984)	8,108	2,124

Workings

(W1)

Fixed assets – NBV

	£		£
Balance b/d	40,406	Fixed assets disposal	1,195
Bank (bal fig)	10,911	Depreciation (profit and loss)	2,363
		Balance c/d	47,759
	51,317		51,317

Tutorial note: The above account summarises the balances and transactions relating to fixed assets during the year. It was necessary to combine fixed asset cost and fixed asset depreciation in one account because only the net book values were given. The account is required in order to derive the expenditure on fixed assets for the year.

Fixed assets disposal

	£		£
Fixed assets – NBV	1,195	Bank	1,614
Profit on sale (profit and loss)	419		
	1,614		1,614

(W2)

Taxation

	£		£
Bank (bal fig)	5,200	Balance b/d	5,200
Balance c/d	6,000	Profit and loss	6,000
	11,200		11,200

Tutorial note: The taxation paid in the year has been last year's charge. Often there will be a change from last year's estimate and thus a ledger account will derive the correct figure paid.

EXAM-STYLE QUESTION 2

BOGDANOVITCH PLC

Cash flow statement for the year ended 31 December 20X9
Reconciliation of operating profit to net cash inflow from operating activities

	£
Operating profit	1,381
Depreciation charges (W3)	448
Increase in stocks	(660)
Increase in debtors	(323)
Increase in creditors	4
	850

Cash flow statement

	£	£
Net cash inflow from operating activities		850
Taxation (W4)		(255)
Capital expenditure		
Payments to acquire tangible fixed assets (312 + 366) (W2)	(678)	
Receipts from sales of tangible fixed assets (203 + 95)	298	(380)
		215
Equity dividends paid		(300)
		(85)
Financing		
Issue of shares	400	
		400
Increase in cash		315

Workings

(W1)

Plant and machinery (NBV)

	£		£
Balance b/d	2,086	P + M – disposal	184
Bank – purchase	312	Depreciation (bal fig)	111
		Balance c/d	2,103
	2,398		2,398

Plant and machinery – disposal

	£		£
P + M (NBV)	184	Bank – proceeds	203
Depreciation – gain on disposal	19		
	203		203

(W2)

Fixtures and fittings (NBV)

	£		£
Balance b/d	1,381	F & F – disposal	100
Bank – purchase (bal fig)	366	Depreciation	351
		Balance c/d	1,296
	1,747		1,747

Fixtures and fittings – disposal

	£		£
F + F – NBV	100	Bank – proceeds	95
		Depreciation – loss on disposal	5
	100		100

(W3)

Depreciation (profit and loss)

	£		£
P + M – NBV	111	P + M – disposal	19
F + F – disposal	5		
F + F – NBV	351	Profit and loss account	448
	467		467

(W4)

Taxation

	£		£
Bank – tax paid (bal fig)	255	Balance b/d	257
Balance c/d	312	Profit and loss account	310
	567		567

EXAM-STYLE QUESTION 3

WEASEL PLC

Tutorial note: You are not given the operating profit for the year, so you have to calculate it. Since operating profit is profit before interest and taxation, you can calculate it by taking the increase in retained profit in the year, and then add back dividends on the profits, the taxation charge and the interest charge for the year. Note also that, since there have been disposals of plant and machinery, you need to calculate a profit or loss on disposal.

Weasel plc Cash flow statement for the year ended 31 August 20X9

	£000	£000
Cash flow from operating activities (see below)		2,660
Returns on investments and servicing of finance		
Interest paid (10% of 1,500)		(150)
Taxation (400 opening creditors + 500 annual charge		
– 500 closing creditors)		(400)
Capital expenditure		
Purchase of tangible fixed assets	(2,500)	
Proceeds of sale of tangible fixed assets	250	(2,250)
Equity dividends paid		(500)
Cash outflow before financing		(640)
Financing		
Issue of ordinary share capital (2,200 + 2,540)		
– (2,000 + 2,340)	400	
Issue of debentures	500	
		900
Increase in cash in the period (£100 increase in cash in bank + £160 reduction in overdraft)		260

Reconciliation of operating profit to operating cash flow

	£000
Operating profit (W1)	1,710
Depreciation	1,200
Profit on sale of plant (W2)	(50)
Increase in stock (1,400 – 1,200)	(200)
Decrease in debtors (1,400 – 1,500)	100
Decrease in creditors (700 – 800)	(100)
Net cash inflow from operating activities	2,660

Workings

(W1) Calculation of operating profit

	£000
Profit and loss reserve at end of year	2,960
Profit and loss reserve at start of year	2,400
Retained profit for the year	560
Dividends for the year	500
Taxation charge for the year	500
Interest charge for the year (10% of 1,500)	150
Operating profit before interest and taxation	1,710

(W2) **Profit on sale of plant**

	£000
Net book value of assets disposed of (1,000 – 800)	200
Proceeds of sale	250
Profit on sale	50

CHAPTER 11

ACTIVITY 1

$$\text{EPS} = \frac{6,688,000 - 200,000}{10,000,000} \text{ (preference dividends)}$$

$$= 66.88 \text{ pence}$$

ACTIVITY 2

(a)

Profitability:

		20X5	20X6
(1)	Net profit margin		
	$\dfrac{\text{Net profit before tax}}{\text{Sales}}$	$\dfrac{21,500}{202,900} \times 100$	$\dfrac{37,500}{490,700} \times 100$
		= 10.6%	= 7.6%
(2)	Return on capital employed:		
	$\dfrac{\text{Net profit before taxation}}{\text{Net assets employed}}$	$\dfrac{21,500}{119,200} \times 100$	$\dfrac{37,500}{326,600} \times 100$
		= 18.0%	= 11.5%

Liquidity:

		20X5	20X6
(3)	Current ratio:		
	$\dfrac{\text{Current assets}}{\text{Current liabilities}}$	$\dfrac{66,500}{52,300}$	$\dfrac{152,500}{85,900}$
		= 1.3	= 1.8
(4)	Quick ratio:		
	$\dfrac{\text{Current assets - Stock}}{\text{Current liabilities}}$	$\dfrac{35,500}{52,300}$	$\dfrac{57,200}{85,900}$
		= 0.7	= 0.7

Financial stability:

		20X5	20X6
(5)	Gearing:		
	$\dfrac{\text{Long - term debt}}{\text{Net assets employed}}$	Nil	$\dfrac{100,500}{326,600} \times 100$
			= 30.6%
(6)	$\dfrac{\text{Liabilities}}{\text{Shareholders' funds}}$	$\dfrac{52,300}{119,200}$	$\dfrac{185,900}{226,600}$
		= 0.4	= 0.8

(b)   **Comment**

Tutorial note: Comments need not be long. It is better that they are short and to the point. It is a good idea to state whether each ratio is showing a better or worse position compared to last year.

Profitability

Profitability in relation to sales and capital employed has fallen. However, the fall has occurred in a period of sales increasing two and a half times and capital increasing due to the issue of loan stock.

It will take time to invest the additional capital efficiently.

The decline in the profitability compared to sales may also be a short-term problem. For example overheads are not being kept under control in the period of rapid expansion. Alternatively the sales volume may have been achieved by cutting gross profit margins.

Liquidity

The current ratio has increased to give a comfortable level of cover for short-term creditors. Most of the increase, however, is derived from higher stocks. The quick ratio is constant.

Whether these two ratios are good or bad depends on what is normal/efficient in the type of business that Nantred is in.

Financial stability

There has been a major injection of long-term finance during the year, producing a gearing ratio of 30%. The business is thus in a riskier position than last year but the expansion of the business may be necessary to protect the existing business (by becoming larger it may be better able to protect itself).

The liabilities to shareholders' funds show a similar position as the gearing (and for the same reasons).

PRACTICE QUESTION

ELECTRICAL ENGINEERING

Tutorial note:

Fairly straightforward ratio analysis question. Ensure calculations are shown clearly and note that ROOE is based only on capital and reserves, while ROCE includes long-term creditors.

For part (b) comment on the liquidity position of the company, the declining profitability and effect of gearing and interest payable.

		20X1	*20X0*
(a)	Current ratio	30,500: 24,000 = 1.3:1	28,500: 20,000 = 1.4:1
	Quick ratio	16,500: 24,000 = .7:1	15,500: 20,000 = .8:1

Stock turnover in days

$$\frac{14,000}{42,000} \times 365 = 122 \text{ days}$$

$$\frac{13,000}{34,000} \times 365 = 140 \text{ days}$$

Debtors turnover in days

$$\frac{16,000}{60,000} \times 365 \text{ days} = 97 \text{ days}$$

$$\frac{15,000}{50,000} \times 365 = 110 \text{ days}$$

Creditors turnover in days	$\dfrac{24,000}{42,000+15,500}$	$\dfrac{20,000}{34,000+13,000}$
(assume operating expenses incurred on credit terms)		
	$\times 365 = 152$ days	$\times 365 = 155$ days
Gross profit %	$\dfrac{18,000}{60,000}\times100 = 30\%$	
		$\dfrac{16,000}{50,000}\times100 = 32\%$
Net profit % (before tax)	$\dfrac{300}{60,000}\times100 = 0.5\%$	
		$\dfrac{1,700}{50,000}\times100 = 3.4\%$
Interest cover	$\dfrac{2,500}{2,200} = 1.1$ times	$\dfrac{3,000}{1,300} = 2.3$ times
Dividend cover	$\dfrac{(50)}{600} = (0.8)$ times	$\dfrac{1,100}{600} = 1.8$ times
	(No cover)	
ROOE (before taxation)	$\dfrac{300}{13,000}\times100 = 2.3\%$	
		$\dfrac{1,700}{14,000}\times100 = 12.1\%$
ROCE	$\dfrac{2,500}{13,000+6,000}\times100 = 13.2\%$	
		$\dfrac{3,000}{14,000+5,500}\times100 = 15.4\%$
Gearing	$\dfrac{6,000}{13,000+6,000}\times100 = 31.6\%$	
		$\dfrac{5,500}{14,000+5,500} = 28.2\%$

(b)   There has been a decline in the liquidity position of the business. The 'weak' position in 20X0 where quick assets (debtors and bank) do not cover the immediate liabilities has deteriorated even further in 20X1. If this trend were to continue the going concern ability of the business would probably be in question. In addition the cover provided by profits over interest payable has more than halved; this would be considered a poor indicator by the interest bearing creditors. Such creditors may question the decision to declare the same level of dividend for 20X1 as for 20X0, even though the business made an after tax loss.

The business's profitability shows only a small 2% drop at the gross profit level but because of the significant levels of operating expenses and interest payable the net profit percentage in 20X1 is only one seventh of its 20X0 level. Clearly improvements are required if the business is to continue to report positive profit after tax figures.

Finally, management has increased the level of fixed assets; with such poor trading results they should be asked if such expansion was necessary and when the benefits from the use of such resources can be expected to accrue.

EXAM-STYLE QUESTION

HAWK

(a)

Year ended 31 March

		20X1	20X2
(i)	Gross profit as percentage of sales		
	600/1,800 × 100	33.3%	
	700/2,500 × 100		28.0%
(ii)	Operating profit as percentage of sales revenue		
	240/1,800 × 100	13.3%	
	250/2,500 × 100		10.0%
(iii)	Return on capital employed		
	190/1,568 × 100	12.1%	
	200/2,122 × 100		9.4%
	Valid alternative calculations also acceptable		
(iv)	Current ratio		
	700 : 518	1.35:1	
	1,230 : 860		1.43:1
(v)	Quick ratio		
	500 : 518	0.96:1	
	870 : 860		1.01:1
(vi)	Stock turnover (days)		
	200/1,200 × 365	60.8 days	
	360/1,800 × 365		73.0 days
(vii)	Trade debtors – sales (days)		
	400/1,440 × 365	101.4 days	
	750/2,000 × 365		136.9 days
(viii)	Trade creditors – purchases (days)		
	210/1,220 × 365	62.8 days	
	380/1,960 × 365		70.8 days

(b) **Comments on ratios**

(i) Gross profit percentage on sales has declined from 33.3% to 28.0%, a substantial drop. This could possibly be due to a decision to lower prices in order to increase sales revenue, which has risen by 38.9%. A drop in the gross profit percentage might be an indicator of possible error or fraud if another explanation such as a lowering of prices cannot be found.

(ii) Net profit to sales is down from 13.3% to 10%, which is also a large drop, but not as large as the drop in the gross profit percentage. A large rise in distribution costs as a percentage of sales helps to explain this poor result.

(iii) Return on capital employed has declined from 12.1% to 9.4%. This is a reflection of the decline in profitability as shown by ratio (ii) above.

(iv) & (v) The two ratios measuring liquidity have changed little between the two periods, suggesting that the liquidity position is satisfactory at both dates.

(vi) The stock turnover ratio has increased because the stock level has risen faster than the increases in cost of sales and sales. The higher stock could be a reflection of slowing demand for the company's goods towards the end of the period and/or slackness in the company's stock control procedures.

(vii) The debtors days have increased considerably from 101.4 days, a high level, to the even higher level of 136.9 days. The increase suggests slackness in the company's credit control procedures.

(viii) There has been a relatively small increase in the number of days' purchases in trade creditors. The increase is perhaps caused by pressure on the company's liquid resources as a result of the increased stock and trade debtors.

CHAPTER 12

PRACTICE QUESTION

IDENTIFYING SUBSIDIARIES

(a) **Welsh Ltd**

- Even though Polyglot owns 99.99% of the share capital of Welsh by value, it does not own any of the ordinary shares which carry the votes.

- Without the votes, Polyglot is unable to appoint any of the directors.

- Without appointing the directors, Polyglot is unable to control any of the operating policies of Welsh.

- Without control, Welsh is not a subsidiary of Polyglot.

(b) **Gaelic Ltd**

- Even though Polyglot only owns 0.0000249% of the share capital of Gaelic by value, it owns 2/3 of the ordinary shares which carry the votes.

- With 2/3 of the votes, Polyglot is able to appoint all of the directors.

- By appointing the directors Polyglot is able to control the operating policies of Gaelic.

- With control, Gaelic is a subsidiary of Polyglot.

(c) **English Ltd**

- Although Polyglot only owns 45% of the Ordinary shares of English, the remaining shares are spread between 44 other shareholders, with each shareholder only owning 125 shares.

- Therefore, at least 40 of the remaining 45 shareholders would have to turn up and vote against Polyglot in order to defeat any of Polyglot's nominations for the board of directors.

- Therefore it is extremely unlikely that Polyglot will not be able to control the board and the operating policies of English.

- Polyglot controls English because of Dominant Influence, and it is therefore a subsidiary.

- If all of the other 44 shareholders were to act in concert, then Polyglot would not be able to control English, and it would not be a subsidiary.

(d)   **Scotch Ltd**

- Polyglot's voting influence is minimal (0.01%), and it could never win any vote on any subject by itself.

- However, Scotch cannot buy, make or sell anything without the involvement of Polyglot.

- Therefore, it could be said that Polyglot exerts a dominant influence over Scotch, and that they are managed on a unified basis.

- Therefore Scotch is a subsidiary of Polyglot.

CHAPTER 13

ACTIVITY 1

(1)   **Goodwill at cost**

		£000	£000	
(i)	Fair value of the consideration		369	
(ii)	Fair value of the net assets acquired			
	Ordinary shares	80		
	Share premium	40		
	Revenue reserves at acquisition	189		
			309	
	Goodwill at cost		60	Recognise as a fixed asset.

(2)   **Goodwill: Amortisation and NBV**

	£000	
Goodwill at cost	60	
Six years' amortisation at £6,000 pa	(36)	Deduct from group reserves. See below.
Net book value	24	Recognise as a fixed asset.

(3)   **Group reserves**

		£000	£000
(i)	The parent's own reserves at the balance sheet date		158
(ii)	Less: cumulative amortisation of goodwill *(See above)*		(36)
(iii)	The subsidiary's own reserves at the balance sheet date	783	
	Less the subsidiary's reserves at acquisition	(189)	
	Subsidiary's post acquisition reserves		594
(iv)	Total group reserves		716

(4)   **The George Group balance sheet at 31 December 20X7**

		£000
Goodwill at NBV	*As above*	24
Tangible fixed assets	*(22 + 425)*	447
Net current assets	*(17 + 478)*	495
Net assets		966
Ordinary share capital (£1 shares)	*Parent only*	200
Share premium account	*Parent only*	50
Revenue reserves	*As above*	716
		966

ACTIVITY 2

(1)   Ownership interest. Henry owns 24,000 £1 ordinary shares out of a total of 30,000.
This is an 80% interest. Because this is more than 50% then Henry will be able to
appoint Arthur's Board of Directors and control the company. This makes Arthur a
subsidiary of Henry. There is also a 20% minority interest.

(2)   Goodwill at cost

		£000	£000	
(i)	Fair value of the consideration		352	
(ii)	Fair value of the net assets acquired			
	Ordinary shares	30		
	Share premium	20		
	Revenue reserves at acquisition	220		
		270		
	Group share @ 80%		(216)	
	Goodwill at cost		136	Recognise as a fixed asset.

(3)   Goodwill: Amortisation and NBV

	£000	
Goodwill at cost	136	
Seven years amortisation at £17,000 pa	(119)	Deduct from group reserves.
Net book value	17	Recognise as a fixed asset.

(4)   The minority interest in the balance sheet

The minority own 20% of Arthur's net assets of £645,000. Therefore the minority
interest is £129,000.

(5)   Group reserves

		£000	£000
(i)	The parent's own reserves at the balance sheet date		368
(ii)	Less: cumulative amortisation of goodwill *(See above)*		(119)
(iii)	The subsidiary's own reserves at the balance sheet date	595	
	Less the subsidiary's reserves at acquisition	(220)	
	Subsidiary's post acquisition reserves	375	
	Group share @ 80%		300
(iv)	Total group reserves		549

(6) **The Henry Group balance sheet at 31 December 20X7**

		£000
Goodwill at NBV	*(3) above*	17
Tangible fixed assets	*(54 + 246)*	300
Net current assets	*(101 + 399)*	500
Net assets		817
Ordinary share capital (£1 shares)	*Parent only*	90
Share premium account	*Parent only*	49
Revenue reserves	*(5) above*	549
Group shareholders' funds		688
Minority Interests	*(4) above*	129
		817

The net assets under the control of the Henry Group total £817,000. Of this, £688,000 is owned by the Parent Company shareholders, and £129,000 is owned by minority interests.

ACTIVITY 3

The £80,000 Provision for Unrealised Profits will have the following effects on the group balance sheet:

- reduce Group stocks by £80,000

- reduce the subsidiary's reserves by £80,000 when calculating the Group Reserves

- reduce the subsidiary's net assets by £80,000 when calculating the Minority Interests.

The consolidation schedule will look as follows:

	Planet	Star	Adjustments	Group	
	£000	£000		£000	£000
Tangible fixed assets	384	130			514
Investment in Star	210	–	*Cancelled*		–
Current assets					
Stocks	468	235	*£80 Cr PUP*	623	
Sundry	579	654		1,233	
				1,856	
Current liabilities	841	419		1,260	
Net current assets					596
Net assets					1,110
£1 ordinary shares	10	50	*Parent only*		10
Revenue reserves	790	550	*(W1) below*		944
Group shareholders' funds					954
Minority interests			*(W2) below*		156
					1,110

(W1) Group reserves

	£000	£000
The parent's own reserves at the balance sheet date		790
The subsidiary's own reserves at the balance sheet date	550	
Less the subsidiary's reserves at acquisition	(250)	
Less provision for unrealised profits	(80)	
Subsidiary's post acquisition reserves	220	
The Group's 70% share		154
Total group reserves		944

(W2) Minority interests

	£000
The subsidiary's net assets from its own balance sheet	600
Less: Provision for unrealised profits	(80)
The revised net assets	520
The Minority's 30% share of these net assets	156

ACTIVITY 4

(1) 30% gross profit margin: £62,660 $\times$ 30% = £18,798

(2) 30% mark-up on cost $\dfrac{30\%}{130\%} \times$ £62,660 = £14,460

ACTIVITY 5

Step 1 Calculate the unrealised profit.

$\dfrac{25}{125} \times$ £8,000 = £1,600

Note: The denominator in the fraction. The £8,000 is at **selling** price to S Ltd i.e. 100 + 25.

Step 2 Put through the consolidation adjustment.

Consolidated stock must be reduced (credited) by £1,600, the minority interest will be reduced by its share of this (10% $\times$ 1,600), £160, and the remaining 90%, £1,440, will be borne by the group as a reduction in revenue reserves.

This may be achieved by means of a consolidation adjustment put through prior to drawing up the balance sheet.

			£	£
Dr	Consolidated revenue reserves			
	90% $\times$ 1,600		1,440	
Dr	Minority interests			
	10% $\times$ 1,600		160	
	Cr	Consolidated stock		1,600

If the sale of the goods had been from P Ltd to S Ltd then the profit would have been made in the books of P Ltd and there would be no minority interest effect.

The consolidation adjustment would simply be:

		£	£
Dr	Consolidated revenue reserves	1,600	
Cr	Consolidated stock		1,600

Profits made by members of a group on transactions with other group members are quite properly recognised in the accounts of the individual companies concerned. But in terms of the group as a whole, such profits are **unrealised** and must be eliminated from the consolidated accounts as a consolidation adjustment. If the profit is made by the subsidiary then there will be an adjustment to the minority interest.

ACTIVITY 6

Step 1   Shareholdings in S Ltd

	%
Group (32,000/40,000)	80
Minority	20
	100

Step 2   Adjustments

Unrealised profit on stock

$$5,000 \times \frac{25}{125} = £1,000$$

S Ltd sold the goods and made the profit, therefore the consolidation adjustment is:

		£	£
Dr	Consolidated P&L reserve	800	
Dr	Minority interest	200	
Cr	Consolidated stock		1,000

The unrealised profit adjustment is only made for stock remaining in the balance sheet at the year end. Stock not remaining in the balance sheet has been sold outside the group and therefore the profit has been realised.

Step 3   Goodwill

	£	£
Cost of investment		75,000
Less: Share of net assets of S Ltd at the acquisition date		
Share capital	40,000	
Profit and loss account	50,000	
	90,000	
Group share	× 80%	
		72,000
Goodwill – amortise to reserves over 3 years		3,000

Note: This calculation is unaffected by the provision for unrealised profit as the net assets of S Ltd at the date of acquisition are sold.

Step 4   Reserves

Consolidated profit and loss account

	£
P Ltd:	120,000
S Ltd: 80% [(60,000 – 1,000)* – 50,000]	7,200
Less: Goodwill written off	(1,000)
	126,200

Step 5   Minority interest

Net assets of S Ltd at the balance sheet date

	£
Share capital	40,000
Profit and loss account (60,000 – 1,000)*	59,000
	99,000
Minority share	× 20%
	19,800

* The revised reserves figure from Step 2, as reduced by the provision for unrealised profit.

Step 6   P Ltd

Consolidated balance sheet at 31 December 20X4

	£
Goodwill (3 – 1)	2,000
Stock (12 + 5 – 1)	16,000
Other net assets (83 + 95)	178,000
	196,000
Called up share capital	50,000
Profit and loss account	126,200
Minority interest	19,800
	196,000

The consolidation adjustment for any unrealised profit on stock sold between group companies has two/three effects on the consolidation procedure:

- the consolidated stock must be reduced by the amount of the provision

- the consolidated reserves must be reduced by the provision – if the profit was made by S Ltd this will affect S's post acquisition profits

- if the profit was made by S Ltd there will also be an adjustment to the minority interest in the consolidated balance sheet.

ACTIVITY 7

Shareholdings in S Ltd

	Ordinary shares %	Preference shares %
Group	70	40
Minority	30	60
	100	100

Goodwill

	£	£
Cost of investment (90 + 22)		112,000
Less: Share of net assets of S Ltd at the acquisition date		
Ordinary share capital	100,000	
Profit and loss account	10,000	
	110,000	
Group share	× 70%	
		(77,000)
Preference share capital	50,000	
Group share	× 40%	
		(20,000)
		15,000

Reserves – consolidated profit and loss account

	£
P:	150,000
S: 70% (30,000 – 10,000)	14,000
Less: Goodwill written off (15,000/5)	(3,000)
	161,000

Minority interests

	£	£
Net assets of S Ltd		
Attributable to ordinary shareholdings		
Ordinary share capital	100,000	
Profit and loss account	30,000	
Minority share	130,000	
	× 30%	
		39,000

The existence of preference share capital in a subsidiary does not affect the holding company's control of the subsidiary. However, it will have an effect on most of the consolidation workings.

ACTIVITY 8

Step 1   Adjust the value of Y Ltd's net assets as at 30 September 20X4 to fair value.

	£
Net assets per question	350,000
Revaluation of property	20,000
Write-off of stock	(4,000)
	366,000

Step 2   Calculate goodwill.

	£
Fair value of consideration	320,000
Net assets acquired 80% × £366,000	292,800
	27,200

Step 3   Calculate minority interest.

MI share of fair value of net assets (20% × £366,000) = £73,200

ACTIVITY 9

Revision Group: Consolidated balance sheet as at 31 March 2007

	Rev. £	Home. £	Adjustments	Group £
Fixed assets				
Intangible fixed assets			*(W1)*	14,625
Tangible fixed assets	*230,000*	*189,000*		419,000
Investment in Homework	*145,000*	*0*		–
				433,625
Current assets				
Stocks	*45,000*	*12,000*	*(W2) 5,625 Cr, 1,200 Cr*	50,175
Trade and other debtors	*87,000*	*154,000*		241,000
Inter company	*12,000*	*0*	*3,000 Cr(CiT), 9,000 Cr* *contra*	–
Cash	*3,000*	*15,000*	*3,000 Dr (Cash in Transit)*	21,000
				312,175
Creditors				
Trade and other creditors	*73,000*	*15,000*		88,000
Inter company	*0*	*9,000*	*9,000 Dr contra*	–
				88,000
Net current assets				224,175
Net assets				£657,800
Capital & reserves				
Called up share capital				100,000
Group reserves			*(W3)*	430,159
				530,159
Minority interests			*(W4)*	127,641
				£657,800

Workings

(W1) Goodwill

	£	£
Fair value of consideration		145,000
Less: FV of identifiable NA acquired:		
Shares	10,000	
Reserves at date of acquisition	170,000	
Net assets at date of acquisition	180,000	
Group share	25/40	112,500
Goodwill at cost		32,500
Cumulative amortisation to date (99/180)	Reserves	17,875
Book value in the balance sheet	B/S	14,625

(W2) Stocks

From Home. (sub) to Revision (parent)	%	£	From Revision (parent) to Home. (sub)	%	£
Sales Price	160	15,000	Sales Price	100	2,000
Profit	60	5,625	Profit	60	1,200
Cost to group	100	9,375	Cost to group	40	800

Deduct £5,625 from subsidiary's reserves. Deduct £1,200 from parent's reserves.

(W3) Group reserves

	£	£
Parent's reserves		349,000
Less:		
PuP		(1,200)
Goodwill amortised		(17,875)
Group share of subsidiary's post acquisition reserves		
Reserves in the Balance Sheet	336,000	
Less: provision for unrealised profit	(5,625)	
Less pre acquisition reserves	(170,000)	
Post acquisition reserves	160,375	
Group share	25 / 40	100,234
		430,159

(W4) Minority interest

	£
Subsidiary's net assets	346,000
Less provision for unrealised profits	(5,625)
	340,375
Minority share	15 / 40
Minority Interest	£127,641

PRACTICE QUESTION

HANSON LTD

Hanson Ltd and its subsidiary
Group balance sheet as at 31 December 20X8

		£	£
Fixed assets	– intangible		5,450
	– tangible		650,450
			655,900
Current assets			
Stock (W5)		212,990	
Debtors		125,430	
Cash at bank		36,450	
		374,870	
Creditors: amounts falling due within one year		144,550	
Net current assets			230,320
Total assets less current liabilities			886,220
Creditors: Amounts falling due after more than one year (60,000 – 15,000)			(45,000)
			841,220
Capital and reserves			
Called up share capital			350,000
Profit and loss account (W3)			433,045
			783,045
Minority interests (W4)			58,175
			841,220

Workings

(W1) Shareholdings in Pickford Ltd

	Ordinary	Preference
	%	%
Group	75	25
Minority	25	75
	100	100

(W2) **Goodwill**

	£	£
Cost of investment		109,150
Less: Share of net assets at acquisition		
Ordinary share capital	100,000	
Profit and loss account	11,000	
	111,000	
	× 75%	
		(83,250)
Preference share capital	60,000	
	× 25%	
		(15,000)
Goodwill		10,900
Amount amortised to date $(^5/_{10} \times 10,900)$		5,450
Amount remaining in the balance sheet		5,450

(W3) **Consolidated reserves**

	£
Hanson Ltd:	348,420
Less: Provision for unrealised profit on stock	
(25/125 × 1/4 × 24,000)	(1,200)
Pickford Ltd: 75% (132,700 − 11,000)	91,275
Less: amortised	(5,450)
	433,045

(W4) **Minority interest**

Net assets of Pickford Ltd

	£	£
Ordinary share capital	100,000	
Profit and loss account	132,700	
	232,700	
	× 25%	
		58,175

(W5) **Consolidated stock**

	£
Hanson Ltd	143,070
Provision for unrealised profit	(1,200)
Pickford Ltd	71,120
	212,990

EXAM-STYLE QUESTION

SHOPAN

(a)

**Consolidated balance sheet
as at 30 September 20X9**

		£000	£000
Fixed assets			
Intangible assets (W3)			222
Tangible assets (W2)			8,306
			8,528
Current assets			
Stocks	(1,901 + 865)	2,766	
Debtors	(1,555 + 547)	2,102	
Cash	(184 + 104)	288	
		5,156	
Creditors: amounts falling due within 1 year			
Trade creditors	(1,516 + 457)	1,973	
Tax	(431 + 188)	619	
		2,592	
Net current assets			2,564
Creditors: amounts falling due after more than 1 year		(3,270)	
			7,822
Capital and reserves			
Share capital			2,000
Share premium			950
Profit & loss account			4,246
			7,196
Minority interest (W3)			626
			7,822

Workings

(W1) **Holding in Hower Ltd**

Shopan Ltd	= 375,000 ÷ 500,000
	= 75%
Minority interest	= 125,000 ÷ 500,000
	= 25%

(W2) **Revaluation Reserve**

	Dr	Cr
	£	£
Fixed assets	400,000	
Revaluation reserve		400,000

Fixed assets now £(6,273 + 400)k + £1,633k = £8,306,000

(W3) **Goodwill**

	£000	£000
Cost of investment		2,100
Less: net assets acquired:		
Share capital	500	
Share premium	120	
Revaluation reserve	400	
Profit and loss account	1,484	
	2,504	
Group share (75%)		(1,878)
Goodwill arising on consolidation		222

(W4) **Minority interests**

	£000	£000
Net assets at balance sheet date:		
Share capital	500	
Share premium	120	
Revaluation reserve	400	
Profit and loss account	1,484	
	2,504	
MI share (25%)		626

(b) A company is a parent undertaking of a subsidiary undertaking if *any* of the following apply (FRS 2):

- It holds a majority of voting rights in the subsidiary undertaking (SU).

- It is a member of the SU and has the right to appoint or remove directors holding a majority of voting rights at meetings of the board on all or nearly all matters.

- It has the right to exert dominant influence over the SU.

- It has the power to exercise dominant influence over the SU; or
    - it and the SU are managed on a unified basis.

- A parent undertaking is also treated as the parent undertaking of the SU of its subsidiary undertakings.

CHAPTER 14

ACTIVITY 1

Step 1   The master schedule is drafted first, with a column for each company and a 'consolidated' column. The group structure is then summarised at the head of each column. There is also a column for consolidation adjustments. It is not required in this activity but will be later in the chapter.

T is the parent company; W is a 75% owned subsidiary and has been for the entire year.

Step 2   In any example with intra-group dividends, begin by reconciling the amounts receivable by the entire company with the amounts payable by the subsidiaries. This may reveal errors or omissions in accounting for the dividends and, if so, they should be corrected before beginning the consolidation.

Under no circumstances whatever do dividends of subsidiaries ever appear in the consolidated profit and loss account. The dividend income in the holding company's books cancels with the dividend paid/proposed in the subsidiary's books. Any remaining amount of the subsidiary's dividend is automatically included in the minority interest line.

Step 3 For items from 'turnover' to 'net profit after tax' (from ordinary activities), we enter:

For parent company — the full amount

For subsidiary owned throughout the year — the full amount

Step 4 The figure of £33,698 net profit on ordinary activities after tax completes one section of the consolidated profit and loss account, and it represents the total profit from ordinary activities that the directors have obtained by using the assets that they control.

However, not all of this will accrue to the shareholders of T Ltd and the amount that accrues to the minority shareholders in the subsidiaries will be deducted.

In this case, because the companies have only ordinary shares, it is easy to calculate the minority share. It is simply the minority shareholders' fraction of the ordinary shares, multiplied by the last figure, net profit after tax, in the column for the relevant subsidiary.

The resulting sub-total is the amount of profit from ordinary activities that accrues to the parent company shareholders.

Step 5 After minority interest there is a dividend adjustment which does not appear in the consolidated figures. This simply cancels the dividend receivable by T Ltd against the dividend payable by W Ltd.

Step 6 Group reserves brought forward consists of:

(i) all the parent company's profit

(ii) the group share of the subsidiaries' post-acquisition profits

(iii) less goodwill amortised up to the beginning of the current accounting period.

The goodwill has not been deducted from the reserves of any particular company in the group as it represents an adjustment purely taking effect in the consolidation working papers.

Step 7 Once the master schedule has been filled in, the actual consolidated profit and loss account can be written out, using the figures from the 'consolidated' column. The account should follow the statutory formats. Minority interests are required to be shown immediately after profit on ordinary activities after taxation.

Consolidation schedule

Group details	T Ltd	W Ltd 75% 12 months	Cons Adjs.	Consolidated
	£	£	£	£
Turnover	216,300	24,400		240,700
Cost of sales	(136,269)	(15,372)		(151,641)
Distribution costs	(21,630)	(2,440)		(24,070)
Investment income (W1)	–	–		–
Taxation	(28,119)	(3,172)		(31,291)
Net profit after taxation	30,282	3,416		33,698
Minority interest	–	(854) (W2)		(854)
Dividends – Internal (W1)	1,464	(1,464)		
Profit before dividend	31,746			
Dividend	(20,000)			(20,000)
Transfers to reserves	11,746	1,098		12,844
Brought forward	36,728	1,464 (W3)		
Less: Goodwill written off			(6,657) (W4)	31,535
Carried forward	48,474	2,562	(6,657)	44,379

Workings

(W1) Reconciliation of intra-group dividends

	£
Per T, received	1,464
Should agree with: W, paid £1,952 × 75%	1,464

This is an amount due/received from a group company therefore it will not appear in the consolidated profit and loss account.

(W2) 25% × £3,416 = £854

(W3) 75% × £(7,076 – 5,124) = £1,464

(W4) Goodwill on acquisition

	W Ltd £
Share capital	50,000
Reserves at acquisition	5,124
Net assets at acquisition	55,124
Group share	75%
	41,343
Cost of investment	48,000
Goodwill arising	**6,657**

T Ltd and its subsidiary

Consolidated profit and loss account for the year ended 31 March 20X7

	£
Turnover	240,700
Cost of sales	(151,641)
Gross profit	89,059
Distribution costs	(24,070)
Profit on ordinary activities before taxation	64,989
Tax on profit on ordinary activities	(31,291)
Profit on ordinary activities after taxation	33,698
Minority interest	(854)
Net profit after taxation attributable to shareholders of T Ltd	32,844

Statement of reserves

	£
At 31 March 20X6	31,535
Profit for the year	32,844
Dividends paid	(20,000)
At 31 March 20X7	44,379

For a basic consolidated profit and loss account the full amounts for the subsidiary are brought in from turnover down to profit after tax (provided that it has been owned all year). At that point the minority share of the subsidiary's profit after tax is deducted on the minority interest line.

ACTIVITY 2

Consolidation schedule

	Plate £000	Saucer £000	Adjustments	Group £000
Turnover	999	750	323 Dr	1,426
Cost of sales	(427)	(260)	323 Cr, 48 Dr	(412)
Gross profit				1,014
Operating expenses	(252)	(140)		(392)
Dividend from Saucer	120	-	Cancelled	-
Profit before tax				622
Taxation	(130)	(62)		(192)
Profit after tax				430
Minority interests			(W3)	(96)
Group shareholders' profit				334
Dividends	(150)	(200)	Parent only	(150)
Opening reserves			(W4)	656
Closing reserves			(W4)	840

(1)   Eliminate the inter company trade

    Debit   Turnover   £323,000

    Credit   Cost of sales   £323,000

(2)   Increase cost of sales by the closing provision for unrealised profit

    Debit   Cost of sales   £48,000

    (The credit entry reduces the value of stocks in the balance sheet.)

(3)   Minority interests will be affected by their share of the provision for unrealised profit.

	£000
Subsidiary's profit after tax	288
Less: Closing provision for unrealised profit	(48)
Revised profit after tax	240
Minority's 40% share	96

(4)   Group reserve

	Closing		Opening	
	£000	£000	£000	£000
The parent's own reserves		666		506
The subsidiary's own reserves	400		312	
Less: provision for unrealised profit	(48)		-	
Less the subsidiary's reserves at acquisition	(62)		(62)	
Subsidiary's post acquisition reserves	290		250	
Group share @ 60%		174		150
Total group reserves		840		656

PRACTICE QUESTION

E LTD AND F LTD

Step 1   **Dealing with inter-company trading**

- Eliminate from sales **all** inter-company sales at the selling price. Therefore deduct £625.

- Eliminate inter-company sales, £625, from cost of sales.

- Compute unrealised profit in goods not sold i.e. the same calculation as for the consolidated balance sheet.

  Closing stock re goods sold from F to E

  60% × £625 = £375

  Unrealised profit

  $\dfrac{25}{125}$ × £375 = £75

  Add this unrealised profit to cost of sales.

- The reduction in cost of sales is **the net figure** (£625 − £75) = £550.

  Thus if there are no unrealised profits, cost of sales is reduced by the same amount as sales.

  The figures shown/computed above can now be transferred to the consolidation schedule.

Step 2   **Calculation of minority interests**

	£
Minority interest:	
Profit after tax of F Ltd	665
Less: Unrealised profit on intra group sale	(75)
	590

Minority interest 40% × 590 = £236

Step 3   **Group reserves brought forward**

	£
E	797
F: 60% × £(3,955 – 980)	1,785
	2,582

Master schedule

Group details	E Ltd	F Ltd 60% 12 months	Adjustments	Consolidated
	£	£	£	£
Turnover	6,956	3,290	(625)	9,621
Cost of sales	(3,108)	(1,470)	550	(4,028)
Gross profit	3,848	1,820	(75)	5,593
Administrative expenses	(1,184)	(560)	-	(1,744)
Taxation	(1,258)	(595)	-	(1,853)
Profit after taxation	1,406	665	(75)	1,996

Step 4   **E Ltd and its subsidiary**

	£
Turnover	9,621
Cost of sales	4,028
Gross profit	5,593
Administrative expenses	1,744
Profit on ordinary activities before taxation	3,849
Tax on profit on ordinary activities	1,853
Profit on ordinary activities after taxation	1,996
Minority interest	236
Profit attributable to shareholders in E Ltd	1,760

Statement of reserves

	£
As at 31 July 20X6	2,582
Profit for the year	1,760
Dividends	(800)
As at 31 July 20X7	3,542

When an intra-group sale is made by the subsidiary company then any unrealised profit arising is made by the subsidiary. When this is eliminated on consolidation this will also affect the minority interest calculation.

EXAM-STYLE QUESTION

JESSOP AND GRIFFIN

(a) **Consolidated profit and loss account for the year ended 31 December 20X4**

	£000
Turnover (1,200 + 300 – 200)	1,300
Cost of sales (780 + 216 – 200 + 20) (W4)	(816)
Gross profit	484
Distribution costs	(108)
Administrative expenses (72 + 24 + 1) (W1)	(97)
Operating profit	279
Investment income (17 – 80% × 15)	5
Profit on ordinary activities before taxation	284
Tax on profit on ordinary activities	(96)
Profit on ordinary activities after taxation	188
Minority interest (20% × 30)	(6)
Group profit for the year	182

(b) **Consolidated balance sheet as at 31 December 20X4**

	£000	£000
Fixed assets		
Intangible assets: Goodwill (W1)		2
Tangible		510
		512
Current assets		
Stock (216 + 54 – 20)	250	
Debtors (174 + 66)	240	
Bank	110	
	600	
Creditors: Amounts falling due within one year		
Creditors (60 + 39)	99	
Corporation tax	96	
Proposed dividends	96	
	195	
Net current assets		405
		917
Capital and reserves		
Share capital		600
Profit and loss account (W2)		280
		880
Minority interests (W3)		37
		917

Workings

(W1) Intangible assets: goodwill

	£000	£000
Cost of investment		120
Net assets acquired:		
Share capital	120	
Profit and loss account	25	
	145	
Group share (80%)		(116)
Goodwill		4
Amortisation $(2 \times 4 \div 1)$		(2)
		2
Annual charge to P&L		1

(W2) Profit and loss account

	£000	£000
Jessop Ltd		270
Griffin Ltd at balance sheet date	65	
Griffin Ltd at acquisition	(25)	
	40	
Group share (80%)		32
Unrealised profit on inter-group sales (W4)		(20)
Amortisation of goodwill $(2 \times 4 \div 1)$		(2)
		280

(W3) Minority interest

	£000
Net assets at balance sheet date	185
MI share (20%)	37

(W4) Unrealised profit

Closing stocks (balance sheet) and cost of sales (P&L) are both reduced by £20,000 $(200,000 - 120,000 \times 25\%)$.

CHAPTER 15

ACTIVITY 1

Current accounts

		Tor £	Hill £			Tor £	Hill £
20X4				*20X4*			
	Drawings	2,000	1,500		Share of profit	6,000	3,000
31 Dec	Balance c/d	4,000	1,500				
		6,000	3,000			6,000	3,000
20X5				*20X5*			
31 Dec	Drawings	2,500	1,500	1 Jan	Balance b/d	4,000	1,500
	Balance c/d	9,500	4,000		Share of profit	8,000	4,000
		12,000	5,500			12,000	5,500
20X6				*20X6*			
				1 Jan	Balance b/d	9,500	4,000

ACTIVITY 2

Allocation of net profit of £3,680

	Flame £	Smoke £	Total £
Interest on capital	480	320	800
Salaries	6,000	8,000	14,000
Balance of loss £3,680 – £14,800			
= (£11,120) to be shared in ratio 3 : 2	(6,672)	(4,448)	(11,120)
Totals	(192)	3,872	3,680

The double entry in this case would be:

Debit	Credit	With
Profit and loss appropriation account	Smoke's current account	£3,872
Flame's current account	Profit and loss appropriation account	£192

The relevant part of the profit and loss account would show:

	£	£
Net profit		3,680
Allocated to:		
Smoke	3,872	
Flame	(192)	
		3,680

EXAM-STYLE QUESTION

OWEN AND GRIFFITHS

(a)   **Trial balance as at 31 December**

	Dr £	Cr £
Capital account:		
Owen		9,000
Griffiths		10,000
10% loan account:		
Griffiths		5,000
Williams		6,000
Current account balance on 1 January:		
Owen		1,000
Griffiths		2,000
Drawings:	6,500	
Owen	5,500	
Griffiths		
Sales		113,100
Sales returns	3,000	
Closing stock	17,000	
Cost of goods sold	70,000	
Sales ledger control account	30,000	
Purchase ledger control account		25,000
Operating expenses	26,100	
Fixed assets at cost	37,000	
Provision for depreciation		18,000
Bank overdraft		3,000
Suspense (bal fig)		3,000
	195,100	195,100

Tutorial note: The question requires a trial balance to be drawn up before any adjustments are made. Many candidates attempted to make adjustments before the extraction of the trial balance but this was not what was required.

The information in the question refers to 'closing stock' and 'cost of goods sold'. Both of these imply that the year-end adjustments for stock have already been made.

(b)   *Tutorial note:* There is no set format per part (b). The key thing to remember is that parts (b) and (c) of the question are the normal parts of an accounts preparation from a trial balance question.

Adjustments to trial balance

Ref to question				Dr £	Cr £
(i)	(a)		Sales returns	100	
			Sales ledger control		100
	(b)		Purchase ledger control	200	
			Sales ledger control		200
	(c)		Sales ledger control	1,800	
			Sales		1,800
(ii)			Disposal	5,000	
			Fixed asset cost		5,000
			Accumulated depreciation	5,000	
			Disposal		5,000
			Suspense	1,000	
			Disposal		1,000

Tutorial note: The last entry arises as the transaction was originally inserted into the books as a one-sided transaction (Dr Bank). The missing credit entry must therefore make up part of the £3,000 suspense account balance.

Ref				Dr	Cr
(iii)			Expenses	500	
			Drawings – Griffiths		500
			Drawings – Owen	1,000	
			Cost of goods sold		1,000
(iv)			Interest expense	1,100	
			Interest accrual		1,100

(c)

Profit and loss account for the year

	£	£
Sales (113,100 + 1,800)		114,900
Less: Returns (3,000 + 100)		3,100
		111,800
Cost of sales (70,000 – 1,000)		(69,000)
Gross profit		42,800
Operating expenses (26,100 – 1,000 + 500)	25,600	
Loan interest	1,100	
		(26,700)
Net profit for year		16,100
Appropriations:		
Interest		
Owen	900	
Griffiths	1,000	
		(1,900)
		(5,000)
Salary – Owen		9,200
Balance of profit:		
Owen	4,600	
Griffiths	4,600	
		(9,200)

Balance sheet as at 31 December

	£	£	£
Fixed assets:			
Cost (37,000 – 5,000)		32,000	
Depreciation (18,000 – 5,000)		13,000	
			19,000
Current assets:			
Stock		17,000	
Debtors (30,000 – 100 – 200 + 1,800)		31,500	
		48,500	
Current liabilities:			
Creditors (25,000 – 200)	24,800		
Interest	1,100		
Bank overdraft	3,000		
Suspense account	2,000		
	30,900		
Net current assets			17,600
			36,600
Loans			(11,000)
			25,600

	Capital £	Current £	Total £
Owen (see working)	9,000	4,000	13,000
Griffiths (see working)	10,000	2,600	12,600
	19,000	6,600	25,600

Working

Current accounts

	Owen £	Griffiths £		Owen £	Griffiths £
Drawings	6,500	5,500	Balance b/d	1,000	2,000
Adjustment to drawings	1,000		Adjustment to drawings		500
			Interest on capital	900	1,000
			Salary	5,000	
Balance c/d	4,000	2,600	Profit	4,600	4,600
	11,500	8,100		11,500	8,100

CHAPTER 16

ACTIVITY 1

4 months to 30 April 20X8

	£	£
Gross profit (3/18)		15,000
Less: Selling and distribution expenses (3/18)	2,000	
Administration expenses (4/12)	1,000	
		3,000
		12,000
Share of profits: Harry (2/3)		8,000
Barry (1/3)		4,000
		12,000

8 months to 31 December 20X8

	£	£
Gross profit (15/18)		75,000
Less: Selling and distribution expenses (15/18)	10,000	
Administrative expenses (8/12)	2,000	
		12,000
		63,000
Share of profits: Harry (2/4)		31,500
Barry (1/4)		15,750
Gary (1/4)		15,750
		63,000

Each partner's share of profit for the year will be:

			£
Harry	(8,000 + 31,500)		39,500
Barry	(4,000 + 15,750)		19,750
Gary			15,750
			75,000

ACTIVITY 2

Revaluation account

	£		£
Debtors	1,000	Plant and Machinery	5,000
Stock	1,000	Property	17,000
Profit on revaluation			
Blagden	12,000		
MacDonald	8,000		
	20,000		
	22,000		22,000

ACTIVITY 3

Faldo, Woosnam and Newcomer
Balance sheet as at 1 July 20X6

	£
Goodwill	280,000
Other net assets (45,000 + 90,000)	135,000
	415,000

Partners' accounts	Capital	Current	Total
	£	£	£
Faldo	230,000	8,	238,000
Woosnam	82,000	5,	87,000
Newcomer	90,000		90,000
	402,000	13,	415,000

Workings

Goodwill

	£		£
Valuation to capital accounts	280,000		

Capital accounts

	Faldo	Woosnam	Newcomer		Faldo	Woosnam	Newcomer
	£	£	£		£	£	£
Balance c/d	230,000	82,000	90,000	Balance b/d	20,000	12,000	
				Goodwill 3 : 1	210,000	70,000	
				Cash			90,000
	230,000	82,000	90,000		230,000	82,000	90,000

ACTIVITY 4

Capital accounts

	Ratner	Hogg	Friar		Ratner	Hogg	Friar
	£	£	£		£	£	£
				Balance b/d	12,500	8,600	
				Cash			10,000
Balance c/d	22,500	18,600	10,000	Goodwill	10,000	10,000	
	22,500	18,600	10,000		22,500	18,600	10,000
				Balance b/d	22,500	18,600	10,000

Goodwill account

	£		£
Capital Ratner	10,000		
Hogg	10,000	Balance c/d	20,000
	20,000		20,000

EXAM-STYLE QUESTION 1

AL, BERT AND HALL

(a) and (b)

Capital accounts

		Al £	Bert £	Hall £			Al £	Bert £	Hall £
					30 June	Balances b/d	12,000	15,000	
						Cash			20,000
						Goodwill written up (0.5 × (18,000))	9,000	9,000	
1 July	Balance c/d	21,000	24,000	20,000					
		21,000	24,000	20,000			21,000	24,000	20,000
	Goodwill written down (⅓ × 18,000)	6,000	6,000	6,000	1 July	balance b/d	21,000	24,000	20,000
	Balances c/d	15,000	18,000	14,000					
		21,000	24,000	20,000			21,000	24,000	20,000

(c) Goodwill is the difference between the value of a business as a whole and the value of the tangible and other identifiable intangible assets less liabilities.

It is thus a balancing item rather than an item which can be objectively valued in its own right.

Adjustments are required when a new partner joins a business as the new partner is entitled to a share in the future growth of all the partnership assets. His entitlement arises either because he makes a payment to enter the partnership or the other partners consider he will enhance the future profitability of the firm.

His entitlement, is, however, to a share in future growth not past growth. Thus goodwill which has been built up by the existing partners needs to be credited to them.

EXAM-STYLE QUESTION 2

RED, BLUE AND YELLOW

(a)   **Partners' capital accounts**

	Red £	Blue £	Yellow £		Red £	Blue £	Yellow £
Goodwill	–	27,000	18,000	Balance b/d 1.4.X8	14,000	13,000	11,000
(6:4)				Cash		20,000	
Loan account				Revaluation (L&B) (W)	8,000	6,000	6,000
(bal fig)	42,930			Goodwill	18,000	13,500	13,500
Balance c/d 31.3.X9		25,500	12,500	(4:3:3)			
				Current a/c	2,930		
	42,930	52,500	30,500		42,930	52,500	30,500

Working: Revaluation account

	£		£
Receivables	5,000	Land and buildings	25,000
Profit on revaluation:			
Red 4/10	8,000		
Blue 3/10	6,000		
Yellow 3/10	6,000		
	25,000		25,000

(b)   **Red, Blue and Yellow: Appropriation account for the year ended 31 March 20X9**

	£	£
Net profit		53,060
Less partners' salaries		
Red	9,000	
Blue	8,000	
Yellow	6,500	
		23,500
Less interest on capital		
Red (14,000 × 12%)	1,680	
Blue (13,000 × 12%)	1,560	
Yellow (11,000 × 12%)	1,320	
		4,560
Net profit available for appropriation		25,000
Balance of profits shared		
Red 4/10	10,000	
Blue 3/10	7,500	
Yellow 3/10	7,500	
		25,000

(c)   **Partners' current accounts**

	Red £	*Blue* £	*Yellow* £		*Red* £	*Blue* £	*Yellow* £
Drawings	19,000	15,000	14,500	Balance b/d 1.4.X8	1,250	1,080	935
				Interest on capital	1,680	1,560	1,320
Capital a/c	2,930						
Balance c/d 31.3.X9	-	3,140	1,755	Salaries	9,000	8,000	6,500
				Profit	10,000	7,500	7,500
	21,930	18,140	16,255		21,930	18,140	16,255

(d)   **Red: Loan account**

Balance c/f 31.3.X9	42,930	Capital a/c	42,930
	42,930	Current a/c	
			42,930

CHAPTER 17

ACTIVITY 1

Capital accounts – sole traders*

	Martin £	*Joe* £		*Martin* £	*Joe* £
Transfer to partnership	20,000	17,000	Balance b/d	10,000	8,000
			Revaluation	10,000	9,000
	20,000	17,000		20,000	17,000

Capital accounts – partnership

	Martin £	*Joe* £		*Martin* £	*Joe* £
Current account	10,000	12,000	Balance b/d from old		
Balance c/d	10,000	5,000	Business	20,000	17,000
	20,000	17,000		20,000	17,000
			Balance b/d	10,000	5,000

*   These are obviously accounts in separate businesses but here they have been shown together for ease.

EXAM-STYLE QUESTION

SMART AND SWIFT

(a)

Profit and loss account for the year ended 31 December 20X8

	£	£	£
Hotel receipts			5,100
Catering and hotel expenses:			
Foodstuffs (stocks adjusted)	2,720		
Wages	2,200		
General expenses	870		
		5,790	
Depreciation:			
Motor vehicle	200		
Fittings	100		
	300		
Loan interest	180		
		480	6,270
Net loss for the year			1,170
Allocated:			
Smart (three-fifths)			702
Swift (two-fifths)			468
			1,170

(b)

Realisation account

	£	£		£	£
Sundry assets:			Assets taken over:		
Debtors		600	Smart:		
Fittings and fixtures		1,700	Stock of foodstuffs	250	
Stocks of foodstuffs		300	Fittings and fixtures		
Freehold premises		6,000	(part)	600	
Motor vehicle		500	Sundry items	40	
Dissolution expenses		120			890
Profit on realisation:			Swift:		
Smart (three-fifths)	462		Motor vehicle	400	
Swift (two-fifths)	308		Sundry items	20	
		770			420
			Assets realised:		
			Freehold		6,800
			Debtors		480
			Fittings and fixtures		1,400
		9,990			9,990

(c)

Cash account for January 20X9

	£		£
Proceeds of:		Balance b/d	4,590
Freehold	6,800	Dissolution, etc expenses	120
Debtors	480	Sundry creditors £(210 + 60)	270
Fittings and fixtures	1,400	Loan – Smart	3,000
Cash paid in by Swift	830	Cash withdrawn by Smart	1,530
	9,510		9,510

(d)

Capital accounts

	Smart	Swift		Smart	Swift
	£	£		£	£
Drawings	520	750	Balances b/d	3,000	5
Net loss for 19X8	702	468	Loan interest	180	
Assets taken over	890	420	Profit on realisation	462	3
Cash withdrawn	1,530		Cash paid in		8
	3,642	1,638		3,642	1,6

CHAPTER 18

ACTIVITY 1

	1 Jan 20X5	31 Dec 20X6	
	Assets	Liabilities	Assets
Statement of affairs at:			
	£	£	£
Shop premises	14,000		14,000
Shop depreciation 2% × £14,000 × 2 years			(560)
Fittings	2,000		2,000
Fittings depreciation 5% × £2,000 × 2 years			(200)
Cash	4,000		2,500
Stock			6,000
Debtors			1,040
Motor lorry			8,000
Motor lorry depreciation 20% × £8,000 × 6 months			(800)
Trade creditors		1,400	
Loan		10,000	
Accrued interest		200	
		11,600	31,980
			(11,600)
Capital	20,000		20,380

Capital account

	£		£
Drawings 24 × £300	7,200	Opening capital	20,000
Closing capital	20,380	Net profit (bal fig)	7,580
	27,580		27,580

ACTIVITY 2

Cash

	£		£
Balance b/d	100	Expenses	750
Sales	2,500	Bank (bankings)	4,220
Cash from debtors – sales control		Drawings	1,200
(bal fig)	3,620	Balance c/d	50
	6,220		6,220

Sales control

	£		£
Balance b/d	460	Irrecoverable debt	50
Sales	3,700	Discounts allowed	70
		Cash received	3,620
		Balance c/d	420
	4,160		4,160

PRACTICE QUESTION

B LETITSLIDE

**Trading and profit and loss account for
year ended 31 December 20X5**

	£	£
Credit sales (W2)		1,560
Cash sales (W2)		4,317
		5,877
Opening stock	1,310	
Add: Purchases (W3)	3,133	
	4,443	
Less: Closing stock	1,623	
		2,820
		3,057
Gross profit		
Expenses (W4)	1,090	
Irrecoverable debts (W6)	49	
Depreciation (W7)	60	
		1,199
Net profit		1,858

Balance sheet as at 31 December 20X5

Fixed asset:

Delivery van, at cost			900
Less: Depreciation (W7)			60
			840

Current assets:

Stock		1,623	
Debtors	382		
Less: Allowance for doubtful debts (W6)	19		
Cash at bank		363	
Cash in hand		572	
		29	
		2,587	
Less: Current liabilities:			
Trade creditors	914		
Accruals	103		
		1,017	
			1,570
			2,410

Capital account:

At 1 Jan 20X5 (W1)		1,652
Add: Profit for year		1,858
		3,510
Less: Drawings (W5)		1,100
		2,410

Note: As the cash account and bank account have already been summarised it is only necessary to post the other side of the cash and bank entries to the relevant accounts. Some information may be inserted immediately into the final accounts, so leave a page for each of the final accounts. Information can then be inserted as soon as it is available. For example, opening and closing stock can be put straight to the final accounts.

Workings

(W1) **Opening statement of affairs**

	£
Stock	1,310
Debtors	268
Cash	62
Bank	840
	2,480
Less: Creditors (£712 + 116)	828
Capital at 1 Jan 20X5	1,652

Note: There is no need to complete this working before proceeding to post the transactions for the year. It is better to add the items as and when you find them in the question.

(W2)

Sales ledger control

	£		£
Debtors b/d	268	Cheques for sales	1,416
Sales for year (bal fig)	5,877	Irrecoverable debt written off	30
		Cash takings	4,317
		Debtors c/d	382
	6,145		6,145
Balance b/d	382		

Note: The sales control account has been used to find total sales. An alternative approach would be to post the 'shop takings' straight to the trading account as cash sales and the balancing figure in the sales control account would then be £1,560, i.e. the credit sales.

(W3)

Purchases control

	£		£
Cash	316	Creditors b/d	712
Bank	2,715	Drawings	100
Balance c/d	914	Purchases	3,133
	3,945		3,945
		Balance b/d	914

(W4)

Expenses

	£		£
Cash	584	Creditors b/d	116
Bank	519	Profit and loss account	1,090
Balance c/d	103		
	1,206		1,206
		Balance b/d	103

(W5) **Drawings**

	£
Purchases	100
Cash account	600
Bank account	400
	1,100

(W6)

Irrecoverable debts account

	£		£
Irrecoverable debt	30	Profit and loss account	49
Sales control account			
Allowance for doubtful			
debts account 5% × 382	19		
	49		49

Note: As there is no opening allowance for doubtful debts, there is no need to show that account. The £19 can be inserted into the balance sheet.

(W7) **Depreciation**

20% × 900 × 4/12 = £60.

EXAM-STYLE QUESTION 1

CYGNUS

Tutorial note: Exam questions will almost certainly feature a partnership, rather than a sole trader. However, the technique of preparing accounts from incomplete records is exactly the same for all types of organisation. This question is exam standard.

Capital as at 1 February 20X0

		£	£
Assets			
	Shop equipment		7,900
	Stock		146,400
	Trade debtors		14,400
	Rent in advance		1,000
	Cash in hand		800
			170,500
Less:	Liabilities		
	Loan – Draco	24,000	
	Trade creditors	12,100	
	Accrued expenses	2,300	
	Bank overdraft	2,600	41,000
Opening capital			129,500

Trading and profit and loss account for the year ended 31 January 20X1

	Reference to workings	£	£
Sales revenue	2		202,400
Less: Cost of sales			
Opening stock		146,400	
Purchases	1	83,500	
		229,900	
Less: Closing stock		128,700	
			101,200
Gross profit			101,200
Less: Expenses	3		
Rent (8,250 + 1,000 – 1,500)		7,750	
Sundry expenses (18,600 – 2,100 + 3,300)	4	19,800	
Depreciation		1,490	
Profit on sale of equipment (300 – 200)	5	(100)	
Interest on loan (2,400 – 200 + 100)		2,300	
Net profit			31,240
			69,960

Balance sheet as at 31 January 20X1

	£	£
Fixed assets		
Cost (W4)	15,800	
Accumulated depreciation (6,900 – 600 + 1,490) (W4)	7,790	
		8,010
Current assets		
Stock	128,700	
Trade debtors	15,700	
Prepayment: rent in advance (W3)	1,500	
Cash at bank	4,850	
Cash in hand	900	
	151,650	
Current liabilities		
Trade creditors	14,200	
Accrued expenses (3,300 + 100)	3,400	
	17,600	
Net current assets		134,050
Total assets less current liabilities		142,060
Long-term creditors		
Loan – Draco		(12,000)
		130,060
Capital		
As at 1 February 20X0 (see above)		129,500
Profit for year to date		69,960
		199,460
Less: Drawings (W6)		69,400
As at 31 January 20X1		130,060

Workings

(W1) **Calculation of purchases**

Purchases total account

	£		£
Cash paid for purchases	81,400	Opening balance	12,100
Closing balance	14,200	Purchases	83,500
		(balancing figure)	
	95,600		95,600

(W2) **Calculation of sales revenue**

Sales prices are fixed by doubling cost – sales revenue is therefore double the cost of sales = £101,200 × 2 = £202,400.

(W3) **Calculation of rent expense**

Rent went up in July 20X0 from £500 each month to £750 each month. The prepayment at the year end is for two months of rent (February and March). At 31 January 20X1 the prepayment is therefore 2 × £750 = £1,500. The rent expense for the year is £8,250 rent paid + £1,000 opening prepayment – £1,500 closing prepayment = £7,750.

(W4) Fixed assets and depreciation

	Cost	Accumulated depreciation
	£	£
As at 1 February 20X0	14,800	6,900
Less: Items sold	(800)	(600)
	14,000	6,300
Additions	1,800	
	15,800	
Depreciation for year		
£14,000 at 10%		1,400
£1,800 at 10% for six months		90
As at 31 January 20X1	15,800	7,790

(W5) Interest

Accrued interest at the year end = 1 month of interest = 1/12 × 10% × £12,000 = £100. Interest expense for the year = Interest paid £2,400 – opening accrual £200 + closing accrual £100 = £2,300.

(W6) Calculation of drawings

A figure for cash from customers is needed to establish how much cash has been taken in drawings.

Sales total account

	£		£
Opening balance	14,400	Cash for sales (balancing figure)	201,100
Sales (W2)	202,400	Closing balance	15,700
	216,800		216,800

Cash summary

	£		£
Opening balance	800	Banked	131,600
Cash from customers (see above)	201,100	Drawings (balancing figure)	69,400
		Closing balance	900
	201,900		201,900

EXAM-STYLE QUESTION 2

AMY AND BARBARA

(a)   **Trading and profit and loss account for the year ended 31 December 20X6**

	£	£
Sales (W1)		592,500
Opening stock	37,500	
Purchases (W2)	292,500	
Carriage inwards	6,750	
	336,750	
Closing stock	(55,500)	
		(281,250)
Gross profit		311,250
Less: Expenses		
Vehicle running expenses	20,250	
Insurance (6,000 + 7,500 – 1,500)	12,000	
Heating and lighting (4,500 – 10,500 + 3,375)	9,375	
Telephone	5,250	
Advertising (3,000 + 3,375)	6,375	
Rent and rates (22,500 – 1,500)	21,000	
Office supplies	1,875	
Irrecoverable debts	22,500	
Discounts allowed	7,500	
Depreciation:		
Vehicles (48,000 – 12,000 × 25%)	9,000	
Equipment (90,000 × 20%)	18,000	
		(133,125)
Net profit		178,125

Appropriation account

	Total £	Amy £	Barbara £
Net profit for the year	178,125		
Interest on capital (10%)	(19,500)	12,000	7,500
Interest on drawings	4,500	(3,000)	(1,500)
Profit appropriation (2:1)	163,125	108,750	54,375
	–	117,750	60,375

(b)   **Partners' current accounts**

	Amy £	Barbara £		Amy £	Barbara £
Drawings	90,000	45,000	Balance b/d	34,500	31,500
Interest on drawings	3,000	1,500	Interest on capital	12,000	7,500
Balance c/d	62,250	46,875	Profit	108,750	54,375
	155,250	93,375		155,250	93,375

(c)   **Balance sheet at 31 December 20X6**

	Cost £	Accumulated depreciation £	Net book value £
Non-current assets:			
Vehicles (W3)	48,000	21,000	27,000
Equipment (W3)	90,000	36,000	54,000
	138,000	57,000	81,000
Current assets:			
Stock		55,500	
Trade debtors		82,500	
Prepayments		1,500	
Cash at bank (W4)		102,000	
		241,500	
Current liabilities:			
Trade creditors		15,000	
Accruals		3,375	
		18,375	
Net current assets			223,125
			304,125
Partners' capital accounts:			
Amy		120,000	
Barbara		75,000	
			195,000
Partners' current accounts:			
Amy		62,250	
Barbara		46,875	
			109,125
			304,125

Workings

(W1)   **Trade debtors**

	£		£
Balance b/d	120,000	Cash received	600,000
Sales (bal fig)	592,500	Irrecoverable debts	22,500
		Discounts allowed	7,500
		Balance c/d	82,500
	712,500		712,500

(W2)   **Trade creditors**

	£		£
Cash paid	300,000	Balance b/d	22,500
Balance c/d	15,000	Purchases (bal fig)	292,500
	315,000		315,000

(W3)   **Fixed assets**

	Vehicles £	*Equipment* £	*Total* £
Cost	48,000	90,000	138,000
Accumulated depreciation			
At 1 January 20X6	12,000	18,000	30,000
Charge for year	9,000	18,000	27,000
At 31 December 20X6	21,000	36,000	57,000
Net book value	27,000	54,000	81,000

(W4)   **Cash at bank**

	£		£
Balance b/d	15,000	Payments	378,000
Receipts	600,000	Drawings:	
		Amy	90,000
		Barbara	45,000
		Balance c/d	102,000
	615,000		615,000

INDEX